Autonomous Decision Systems, Consumer Behavior, and the Future of Branding in the Age of Intelligence

Markus Rach
https://orcid.org/0009-0000-0480-8734
Canadian University of Dubai, UAE

IGI Global
Scientific Publishing
Publishing Tomorrow's Research Today

VP of Publishing Ethics & Research Integrity Melissa Wagner
Director of Acquisitions Mikaela Felty
Director of Book Development Jocelynn Hessler
Production Manager Mike Brehm
Cover Design Jose Rosado

Published in the United States of America by
IGI Global Scientific Publishing
701 East Chocolate Avenue
Hershey, PA, 17033, USA
Tel: 717-533-8845 | Fax: 717-533-7115
Website: https://www.igi-global.com E-mail: cust@igi-global.com

Library of Congress Cataloging-in-Publication Data

LCCN: 2026019599 (CIP Data Pending)
ISBN13: 979-8-3373-9589-0
Isbn13Softcover: 979-8-3373-9590-6
EISBN13: 979-8-3373-9591-3
British Cataloguing in Publication Data
A Cataloguing in Publication record for this book is available from the British Library.

Table of Contents

Detailed Table of Contents

Autonomous AI agents, including recommendation engines and large language models, increasingly mediate the consumer–brand relationship, delegating exposure, accuracy, and choice to algorithms. This displaces the direct human agency presumed by traditional brand equity theory, so consumer-based brand-equity models lose explanatory power when machines represent, rank, and select brands on a consumer's behalf. Existing frameworks do not capture how a brand gains or loses standing within algorithmic decision processes. Through an integrative literature review, this chapter recasts brand equity from a consumer-held stock into an outcome requiring active, capability-driven maintenance, linking established brand-measurement (awareness, preference, loyalty, financial brand value) to AI-mediated choice. The model proposes that AI adoption drives three dynamic brand capabilities, AI-brand sensing, seizing, and reconfiguring, working through grounding in third-party evidence to build Agentic Brand Equity. The contribution is a testable causal model and measurement logic.

Brand management works on memory. Advertising secures a share of scarce human attention, converts it into memory structures, and those structures are retrieved when a category need arises, long before the transaction. Recommender systems, conversational assistants and agentic checkout remove the purchase from the set of things attention is spent on, so the memory is never queried at the moment of choice and the constraint becomes inclusion in a set a machine assembles. This chapter separates the attention economy into scarcity, allocation and conversion claims and

critically addresses the ethical concerns relating to over-personalization, emotion tracking, data privacy, manipulation, and exploitation, emphasizing the need for standard ethical governance frameworks. The chapter concludes with future research directions for future empirical studies.

Personalization has always been an important aspect of business and with the popularization of e-commerce as well as with the advances in technology; personalization has become vital to achieve customer interest, engagement, satisfaction and loyalty, positively impacting the sales. Recommendation systems act as a key component of the entire personalization cycle by reducing the information overload and recommending items as per the interest of the customer and helping the customer in decision making. Recommendation systems have been evolved from rule-based to Artificial Intelligence (AI)- and Machine Learning (ML)-based systems. The introduction of Generative AI has taken personalization to the next level. However, excessive use of AI may lead to homogeneity in recommendation leading to bias in decision making and affecting diversity of recommendations. AI-based recommendation systems need to strike a right balance in personalization and consumer behavior in order to achieve more realistic and sustainable personalization goals.

This chapter examines how machine learning algorithms increasingly shape consumer decision-making within AI-mediated marketplaces. Focusing on the tension between algorithmically reinforced habit loops and the declining space for serendipitous discovery, the chapter integrates insights from behavioral science, marketing theory, and artificial intelligence. It explores how recommendation engines, predictive analytics, and personalized digital ecosystems optimize engagement by reinforcing existing consumer behaviors, potentially limiting exposure to new brands and alternative choices. Building upon marketing science concepts such as mental availability, brand salience, and consumer memory structures, the chapter analyzes how algorithmic personalization influences brand growth, consumer autonomy, and switching behavior. Through cross-regional examples and theoretical analysis, it

paradigms. Three channel interaction dynamics, four formal propositions, seven managerial principles, and seven future research priorities are presented.

Preface

AN UNOCCUPIED TERRITORY

Brand management is predicated on an assumption that is so widely accepted that it is rarely articulated. Advertising captures attention, which then consolidates into memory, and memory is subsequently queried when a category need arises. Awareness tracking, salience measurement, brand equity scoring, and the consumer survey itself all draw their conclusions from the same source: the human mind. For as long as every purchase navigated this path, these instruments achieved their intended objectives.

However, a growing proportion of purchases no longer do. A segment of the purchasing process has been transferred to a machine, creating a gap in the established scholarly literature and presenting a novel challenge for marketers and brand managers. This volume seeks to address this deficiency.

The premise under transformation is the foundation of modern branding. Aaker (1991) defined brand equity as a set of assets and liabilities attached to a name and symbol, and subsequently proposed a set of measures intended to hold across products and markets (Aaker, 1996). Keller (1993) defined customer-based brand equity as the differential effect of brand knowledge on a consumer's response, observable only by exposing a consumer to the brand and recording the result. Romaniuk and Sharp (2004) operationalized salience as cued retrieval, which presupposes a mind capable of retrieving. These are distinct constructs that share a common premise: the pivotal event takes place within the confines of a human mind.

This premise has gained its standing over decades of research and applied brand management. Bronnenberg et al. (2012) exploited consumer migration as a natural experiment and found brand preferences formed in one market still detectable fifty years after relocation, accounting for roughly 40% of the geographic variation in market share. Madden et al. (2006) reported portfolios of strong brands outperforming the market while carrying lower risk. Datta et al. (2017) matched four survey dimensions of brand equity against scanner sales and found relevance, esteem and knowledge tracking realized purchases, while energized differentiation ran counter to them. Consumer perceptions of a brand are enduring, and their effects are recoverable in both the share price and the transaction record.

Brand equity is therefore a quantifiable asset and losing access to the cognitive processes that sustain it carries consequences a firm can measure on its balance sheet.

The primary change lies not in the underlying concept but in the location of decision-making, which has been in a state of transformation for a quarter of a century. Search engines came first, then recommender systems, then conversational assistants. Each of these technologies has progressively absorbed a portion of the work that a buyer once performed independently. De Bellis and Johar (2020) distinguished systems that recommend from systems that assume the purchase. André et al. (2018) identified the exchange on which such systems operate: they reduce the cost of choosing while diminishing the consumer's sense of authorship over the choice. Bilgihan et al. (2026) draw the same boundary in contemporary terms, between systems that advise and systems that transact. The second class completely removes the consumer from the moment of selection.

The immediate consequence for a brand is becoming evident. A recommender that presents three options has effectively completed the majority of the consideration set formation process. An assistant that names a single product has completed it outright. Once a consumer delegates a repeat purchase, the brand competes for position within a ranking function rather than relying solely on human memory.

The consumer has not withdrawn and has not stopped deciding. The decision has shifted upstream, from the selection stage to the mandate stage. Consequently, a mandate is issued less frequently and in less brand-specific terms compared to a purchase. Brand managers have dedicated decades to mastering the moment of choice, only to discover that this pivotal moment has been rescheduled, without their consent, and with the risk of being ignored or excluded altogether.

THE STATE OF THE FIELD

The transfer of decision-making from human to machine began well before headline-dominating generative models. Häubl and Trifts (2000) demonstrated that an interactive decision aid reduced search effort and improved choice quality simultaneously. Sénécal and Nantel (2004) found consumers who consulted a recommendation selecting it approximately twice as often as those who did not, with the recommender system carrying greater weight than a human expert. Shi and Zhang (2014) followed households across repeated purchases and observed reliance consolidating into habit. Blut et al. (2023) confirmed the pattern meta-analytically across 122 samples. Subsequently, streaming services and short-video platforms completed the conditioning on a large scale. What initially served as a counterbalance to the paradox of choice evolved into the widely accepted condition of algorithmically curated content. Whether that conditioning has displaced discovery is an empirical question rather than a rhetorical one, and Vij (Chapter 6) puts it to a survey of 412 respondents across India, the UAE, the United States, the United Kingdom and Singapore.

Brand research trails this transformation. Banker and Khetani (2019) found consumers following algorithmic recommendations even where the recommendation was demonstrably inferior to what they would have selected unaided. What is novel is not the transfer itself, but the consumer's awareness of making it, coupled with the fact that the system that takes over the workload can now be prompted to return precise brand recommendations.

Machine mediation compresses the choice set. Dellaert et al. (2020) proposed that voice assistants induce local rather than global optimization, because sequential presentation precludes comparison across alternatives. Mari et al. (2026) demonstrated that consumers accept that compression: fewer alternatives evaluated raised both satisfaction and the intention to delegate further control. Bollen et al. (2010) had identified the same pattern within recommender systems, and Gomez-Uribe and Hunt (2016) describe the commercial response, a business predicated on ranking a catalog no consumer could browse. Kaur and Singh (Chapter 5) weigh what that compression costs in variety, and find the answer depends on whether one counts within a consumer's own purchases or across consumers.

Consumers are not deprived of choice but rather relieved of it, and the underlying reason predates the technology. Iyengar and Lepper (2000) showed that a larger assortment can suppress choosing altogether, although the effect proved unstable and the meta-analysis of Scheibehenne et al. (2010) placed the average near zero. Chernev et al. (2015) resolved the dispute by specifying the conditions: overload is reliable where the set is complex, the task difficult, preferences uncertain, and the consumer is minimizing effort rather than optimizing outcome. Digital assortments typically fulfill the first three requirements, while a delegated purchase inherently satisfies the fourth.

Choice curation was never presented to consumers as a loss of control. Instead, it was presented as a gain in convenience.

However, that gain has limits, and those limits are becoming specifiable. Ahmad Husairi and Rossi (2024) found that restricting perceived choice and decision autonomy reduces adoption even where product complexity should make assistance welcome. Song and Lin (2024) established trust as the mediator between perceived machine intelligence and the decision to delegate. Frank and Otterbring (2024) supply a mechanism with a boundary condition attached: high autonomy depresses adoption through a felt loss of power, an aversion that attenuates under scarcity, when the preferred option is visibly depleting. Sukumar and Jain (Chapter 4) locate a different limit, showing that emotion tracking itself provokes resistance once consumers become aware of it.

Acceptance is also unstable within a single consumer. Puntoni et al. (2021) demonstrated that an identical capability is experienced as assistance in one encounter and as intrusion in the next.

Category and identity mark those limits as well. Wien and Peluso (2021) found human recommenders more effective than algorithmic ones for hedonic products and indistinguishable for utilitarian ones. Leung et al. (2018) showed that consumers who identify strongly with a social category resist automation that prevents them from claiming the outcome as their own. Xie et al. (2022) contributed neural evidence of greater cognitive conflict when an algorithm recommends an experience product rather than a search product, and Jin and Zhang (2025) found machine recommendations judged more competent for material than for experiential products. Rix et al. (2025) found consumers discounting a digital product they believe an algorithm produced. The line between instrumental and expressive decisions runs through several of the chapters that follow.

These findings are sufficiently consistent to support a proposition. Delegation is accepted when the decision is instrumental and withheld when it is expressive. Few consumers delegate the choice of a wedding ring. Most will delegate dishwasher tablets, and most will do so without hesitation.

EQUITY IS REROUTED RATHER THAN ERASED

Brand equity has not been eliminated. It has been rerouted. Chang and Park (2024) found brand awareness moderating a recommender's influence on consideration set adoption, closing the gap at low and medium awareness but not at high. Halbauer et al. (2022) report a sharper result: in voice shopping, a high-equity brand presented first produces a choice distribution peaking at that product, whereas a low-equity brand presented first produces a bimodal distribution. Buttenberg (Chapter 1) develops the firm-side implication, asking which capabilities a brand requires once an agent governs discovery.

Brand equity now serves as a prerequisite for algorithmic advantage rather than a substitute for it. This reformulation is one of the most significant propositions in the volume, because it turns a defensive question about preserving brand equity into an empirical one about how equity interacts with retrieval.

The transfer is not costless. McLean et al. (2021) found voice-based brand engagement raising usage intention without raising purchase intention. Klaus and Zaichkowsky (2022) locate the sharpest challenge to conventional branding in low-involvement categories, where the decision is outsourced to a system entirely. Rohden and Espartel (2024) quantified what the consumer forfeits, in reduced perceived control, increased choice uncertainty and lower satisfaction. What consumers value in a recommender remains barely measured, with Cho and Taylor (2025) being among the few to have investigated it. James, Elangovan, Ganesh and Dheepa (Chapter 7) carry the cost question into quick commerce, where the interface is rebuilt continuously and switching is cheap.

A SECOND AUDIENCE FOR PERSUASION

Huang and Rust (2021) set out how marketers deploy artificial intelligence across research, strategy and action. With brand management assuming a human recipient, the reciprocal question arises. What does marketing become when the buyer is a machine?

Persuasion now addresses two audiences at once: a human mind and an algorithmic evaluator. The two respond to different signals, and optimizing for one does not necessarily optimize for the other. The proposition that brand communication has acquired a non-human audience with its own response function has, so far as the corpus described below indicates, not been examined in the peer-reviewed literature.

It might be supposed that the machine is the more rational of the two buyers. The available evidence suggests otherwise. Cherep et al. (2025) subjected a set of models to a multi-attribute choice task under canonical nudges and found them considerably more susceptible than the people whose choices they approximate. Neither chain-of-thought prompting nor few-shot prompting on human data resolved the sensitivity. Allouah et al. (2026) found agents concentrating demand on a small number of modal products and redistributing market shares whenever the underlying model is updated.

Visibility within these systems is stratified and unstable. Jack et al. (2026) audited 533 brands across approximately 37,000 runs and found category leaders appearing in nearly every relevant retrieval while securing only 25% to 41% of the recommendation slots they reached, while roughly half of the brands in the two lowest prominence tiers never surfaced in any run. Schulte et al. (2026) issued identical prompts on consecutive days and found the cited sources overlapping by only 34% to 42%.

Machine visibility is therefore a probability distribution rather than a rank, and a single measurement of it conveys little to a brand manager. That observation carries a methodological implication the field has yet to absorb: monitoring must be repeated and distributional, or it is not monitoring at all. Jose and Mathews (Chapter 9), and Nausalya (Chapter 10), arrive independently at a dual-channel account of salience that gives this instability a place in brand theory.

There is an upside for brand managers: machine visibility can be influenced. Aggarwal et al. (2024) show that adding citations, statistics and quotations to a page raises its visibility in generated responses by as much as 40%, with lower-ranked sources gaining while top-ranked sources lose. Prominence determines the tier from which a brand is retrieved. Optimization alters its position within the retrieved set. Nausalya (Chapter 10) calls for an algorithmic brand salience scale to measure precisely this.

Two consequences arise, both of which disrupt established practices. Visibility is influenced by both effort and accumulated equity, which provides challengers with a form of leverage they have not possessed in a generation. Furthermore, a brand may be prominent in one week's observations and absent in the next without any alteration in the brand itself.

Brand management, therefore, addresses a second audience: more susceptible than the first, less stable, and more responsive to optimization. Its memory is constructed from written accounts of a brand rather than from consumer experiences. It undergoes revisions whenever a model is updated and cannot be surveyed, contacted or observed. Mathew, Sleilati and Vishnoi (Chapter 8) pinpoint the limiting case: in fully agentic commerce no human hears the sonic logo at the moment of choice.

WHAT THE LITERATURE HAS NOT YET DONE

A claim that a literature is thin should itself be subjected to test, so the premise of this volume was verified before any chapter was commissioned. A corpus of 339 articles on brands and machine-mediated consumer decision making, published between 2015 and 2026, was drawn from OpenAlex, screened at source level, and analyzed through co-citation, bibliographic coupling and term co-occurrence, with sensitivity checks across 16 screening specifications. Nearly three in ten records carry no reference list in OpenAlex, so every citation test reported here is a lower bound. A zero indicates undetected rather than absent.

Output grew from 5 articles in 2015 to 109 in 2025. What the field has not acquired at the same rate is a shared foundation of comparable vintage. At a six-citation threshold, the intellectual base on which these articles jointly draw contains nothing published after 2020 and has a median year of 2003, and a third of the corpus is uncited. Brand theory and technology acceptance models developed for an earlier generation of systems are being applied to a setting they were not designed to describe.

Three deficiencies are more consequential than any of the counts.

The first concerns delegation. Depending on specification, delegation vocabulary appears in 1 to 6 of the 339 articles. Of 112 articles combining delegation terminology with brand, 61 are located in computer science and 6 in business and management, and only 2 enter the analytic corpus. The literature is organized around recommendation, a system that proposes and a consumer who disposes, while brand research has barely begun on delegation, a system that acts under a mandate the consumer has transferred. The distinction is not terminological. It separates influencing a choice from holding the authority to make it. The relevant work is being conducted in an adjacent discipline and is not being read across. Balaskas (2026) maps the movement and concludes that delegation turns less on maximizing autonomy than on coupling capability with consent, oversight and recourse.

The second concerns measurement. Not one article in the corpus engages with category entry points, or with mental and physical availability. That tradition's founding journal statement was not detected once across 11,164 reference instances. The most widely applied practitioner account of how brands grow leaves no detectable trace in the journal literature on machine-mediated choice. Its central statements appear in books, which OpenAlex indexes poorly, so the test speaks to journals alone. Even allowing for that limitation, whether advertising continues to build mental availability when an agent performs the selection is an open question supported by too few direct studies to sustain a synthesis.

The third constrains every claim about the scale of this transition. There is no credible published estimate of the share of consumer transactions that is machine-mediated. Practitioner figures circulate freely, but none is supported by a stated method. A field cannot calibrate its urgency without that quantity, and it does not possess it.

The vocabulary results reported here were re-tested against Scopus on 16 September 2026, using the same term families on a parallel corpus of 648 articles retrieved under equivalent restrictions. The recommendation share, the near absence of delegation terminology and the null result for the applied availability constructs all replicate, the last on a more generous field that also searches author keywords and index terms.

A research field whose output has increased by a factor of twenty while its shared intellectual base has not moved past 2003 is not a field in a state of maturation. It is a subject that has drawn attention without yet being developed. The distinction between these two states is crucial, as it determines the scope and potential of an edited volume at this moment.

WHO THIS VOLUME IS FOR

Researchers in marketing and consumer behavior will encounter open problems rather than closed ones, along with constructs specific enough to carry new studies and sustain scholarly argument. Doctoral students will find unoccupied territory and an agenda that converts directly into research designs. Scholars in information systems and human-computer interaction will encounter familiar problems, such as recommender design and trust in automation, but from the brand's perspective rather than the system's. Practitioners will recognize provisional yet applicable frameworks for a circumstance they already face, in which their brands are presented, described or suggested to customers by systems they neither own nor control.

HOW THIS VOLUME RESPONDS

The ten chapters are grouped in three sections.

Section 1. Foundations of Brand Theory in the Agentic Age. The opening section rebuilds the conceptual base by asking what brand equity denotes when a capable intermediary stands between the firm and the buyer. Buttenberg (Chapter 1) extends dynamic capabilities to agentic conditions, and her hypothetical case of a brand performing well on every digital indicator yet nearly invisible in agent responses makes the measurement problem concrete. Rach (Chapter 2) asks whether machine-mediated choice terminates the attention economy as brand management's organizing premise, then specifies the conditions under which a purchase becomes delegable and what accumulates across delegated episodes. Katsota and Duarte (Chapter 3) distinguish story doing from co-creation, experiential marketing and customer engagement, converting a concept introduced in the research literature into a defined persuasion mechanism in which consumers act out brand meaning rather than merely interpret it.

Section 2. Consumer Decision Making, Emotion and Choice. The second section turns to the person, since mediation is granted rather than imposed. Sukumar and Jain (Chapter 4) treat emotional response as an input to conative brand outcomes rather than as a residual. Kaur and Singh (Chapter 5) address the tension between personalization and homogenization, drawing on the recommender systems literature from its origins through deep learning architectures. Vij (Chapter 6) sets habit against serendipity using a survey of 412 respondents across five countries, a substantial base for a question the field has posed more often than it has tested. James, Elangovan, Ganesh and Dheepa (Chapter 7) separate platform intelligence perception from perceived personalization and algorithmic trust in quick commerce, and identify the commercial tension between sponsored placement and platform credibility.

Section 3. Brand Assets, Salience and Machine Visibility. The third section addresses measurement practice directly. Mathew, Sleilati and Vishnoi (Chapter 8) propose a sonic distinctiveness hierarchy for voice interfaces and state the limiting case: in fully agentic commerce no human hears anything at the moment of choice, so sonic equity operates only through preferences formed beforehand. Jose and Mathews (Chapter 9) develop dual-channel brand salience in curated markets and advance six propositions, most of which name a construct, an expected relationship, an indicator and a method. Nausalya (Chapter 10) approaches the same construct from a different direction and identifies amplification, compensation and conflict dynamics, the conflict case being one in which hyper-personalization raises individual conversion while eroding the shared associations on which brand meaning depends.

That convergence merits a note. Two authors, working from different perspectives and unable to cite one another, arrived at the same dual-channel structure. Independent arrival of this kind is weak evidence in isolation and strong evidence in combination with the divergences between the two accounts, which the conclusion treats as a testable difference rather than an inconsistency.

WHAT THIS VOLUME CONTRIBUTES

Contributors disagree in this volume, and the disagreements have been purposefully and carefully preserved: on whether machine mediation weakens brand equity or relocates it, and on whether emotional response survives a synthetic interlocutor. A field at this stage of formation is better served by well-specified disagreement than by premature consensus.

Therefore, this volume does not offer a settled account of a mature subject. It specifies a transition still under way, with sufficient precision that the specification can be tested and, where mistaken, corrected. That is the contribution an edited volume can make early in the development of a field, and it is precisely the contribution this volume attempts.

A century of brand theory has addressed how a brand comes to mind. Almost none has addressed how a brand is retrieved by a system that does not have one. If the chapters that follow provoke the studies, thoughts and ambitions required to close that gap, the volume will have earned its place.

A companion volume, *Trust, Transparency, and Governance in AI-Mediated Branding*, takes up what becomes of accountability once the machine is the party choosing. The two were created together and are best read in sequence, although each stands on its own.

A note on reading. The chapters are arranged so that the sections build on one another, but each was written to be read independently.

Markus Rach
Canadian University of Dubai, UAE

REFERENCES

Aaker, D. A. (1991). *Managing brand equity: Capitalizing on the value of a brand name*. The Free Press.

Aaker, D. A. (1996). Measuring brand equity across products and markets. *California Management Review, 38*(3), 102–120. DOI: 10.2307/41165845

Aggarwal, P., Murahari, V., Rajpurohit, T., Kalyan, A., Narasimhan, K., & Deshpande, A. (2024). GEO: Generative engine optimization. In *Proceedings of the 30th ACM SIGKDD Conference on Knowledge Discovery and Data Mining* (pp. 5–16). Association for Computing Machinery. DOI: 10.1145/3637528.3671900

Ahmad Husairi, M., & Rossi, P. (2024). Delegation of purchasing tasks to AI: The role of perceived choice and decision autonomy. *Decision Support Systems, 179*, 114166. DOI: 10.1016/j.dss.2023.114166

Allouah, A., Besbes, O., Figueroa, J. D., Kanoria, Y., & Kumar, A. (2026). What is your AI agent buying? Evaluation, biases, model dependence, and emerging implications of agentic e-commerce. In *Proceedings of the ACM Web Conference 2026* (pp. 8697–8700). Association for Computing Machinery. DOI: 10.1145/3774904.3792943

André, Q., Carmon, Z., Wertenbroch, K., Crum, A., Frank, D., Goldstein, W., Huber, J., van Boven, L., Weber, B., & Yang, H. (2018). Consumer choice and autonomy in the age of artificial intelligence and big data. *Customer Needs and Solutions, 5*(1–2), 28–37. DOI: 10.1007/s40547-017-0085-8

Balaskas, S. (2026). From recommendations to delegation: A systematic review mapping agentic AI in e-commerce and its consumer effects. *Information (Basel), 17*(3), 222. DOI: 10.3390/info17030222

Banker, S., & Khetani, S. (2019). Algorithm overdependence: How the use of algorithmic recommendation systems can increase risks to consumer well-being. *Journal of Public Policy & Marketing, 38*(4), 500–515. DOI: 10.1177/0743915619858057

Bilgihan, A., Ostinelli, M., Lorenz, M., & Zhang, Y. (2026). The AI agent in the room: Rethinking consumer decision-making in the age of autonomous AI. *Psychology and Marketing, 43*(10), 2509–2516. DOI: 10.1002/mar.70165

Blut, M., Ghiassaleh, A., & Wang, C. (2023). Testing the performance of online recommendation agents: A meta-analysis. *Journal of Retailing, 99*(3), 440–459. DOI: 10.1016/j.jretai.2023.08.001

Bollen, D., Knijnenburg, B. P., Willemsen, M. C., & Graus, M. (2010). Understanding choice overload in recommender systems. In *Proceedings of the Fourth ACM Conference on Recommender Systems* (pp. 63–70). Association for Computing Machinery. DOI: 10.1145/1864708.1864724

Bronnenberg, B. J., Dubé, J.-P. H., & Gentzkow, M. (2012). The evolution of brand preferences: Evidence from consumer migration. *The American Economic Review*, *102*(6), 2472–2508. DOI: 10.1257/aer.102.6.2472

Chang, W., & Park, J. (2024). A comparative study on the effect of ChatGPT recommendation and AI recommender systems on the formation of a consideration set. *Journal of Retailing and Consumer Services*, *78*, 103743. DOI: 10.1016/j.jretconser.2024.103743

Cherep, M., Maes, P., & Singh, N. (2025). LLM agents are hypersensitive to nudges (arXiv:2505.11584). arXiv. https://doi.org//arXiv.2505.11584DOI: 10.48550

Chernev, A., Böckenholt, U., & Goodman, J. (2015). Choice overload: A conceptual review and meta-analysis. *Journal of Consumer Psychology*, *25*(2), 333–358. DOI: 10.1016/j.jcps.2014.08.002

Cho, M., & Taylor, C. R. (2025). Keeping it fresh: What attributes of AI recommender systems do consumers value? *Journal of Research in Interactive Marketing*, •••, 1–18. DOI: 10.1108/JRIM-06-2025-0312

Datta, H., Ailawadi, K. L., & van Heerde, H. J. (2017). How well does consumer-based brand equity align with sales-based brand equity and marketing-mix response? *Journal of Marketing*, *81*(3), 1–20. DOI: 10.1509/jm.15.0340

de Bellis, E., & Johar, G. V. (2020). Autonomous shopping systems: Identifying and overcoming barriers to consumer adoption. *Journal of Retailing*, *96*(1), 74–87. DOI: 10.1016/j.jretai.2019.12.004

Dellaert, B. G. C., Shu, S. B., Arentze, T. A., Baker, T., Diehl, K., Donkers, B., Fast, N. J., Häubl, G., Johnson, H., Karmarkar, U., Oppewal, H., Schmitt, B. H., Schroeder, J., Spiller, S. A., & Steffel, M. (2020). Consumer decisions with artificially intelligent voice assistants. *Marketing Letters*, *31*(4), 335–347. DOI: 10.1007/s11002-020-09537-5

Frank, D.-A., & Otterbring, T. (2024). Autonomy, power and the special case of scarcity: Consumer adoption of highly autonomous artificial intelligence. *British Journal of Management*, *35*(4), 1700–1723. DOI: 10.1111/1467-8551.12780

Gomez-Uribe, C. A., & Hunt, N. (2016). The Netflix recommender system: Algorithms, business value, and innovation. *ACM Transactions on Management Information Systems*, *6*(4), 1–19. DOI: 10.1145/2843948

Halbauer, I., Jacob, S., & Klarmann, M. (2022). Brand presentation order in voice shopping: Understanding the effects of sequential product presentation. *Journal of Retailing*, *98*(4), 759–778. DOI: 10.1016/j.jretai.2022.06.002

Häubl, G., & Trifts, V. (2000). Consumer decision making in online shopping environments: The effects of interactive decision aids. *Marketing Science*, *19*(1), 4–21. DOI: 10.1287/mksc.19.1.4.15178

Huang, M.-H., & Rust, R. T. (2021). A strategic framework for artificial intelligence in marketing. *Journal of the Academy of Marketing Science*, *49*(1), 30–50. DOI: 10.1007/s11747-020-00749-9

Iyengar, S. S., & Lepper, M. R. (2000). When choice is demotivating: Can one desire too much of a good thing? *Journal of Personality and Social Psychology*, *79*(6), 995–1006. DOI: 10.1037/0022-3514.79.6.995

Jack, W., Lehman, N., Maloney, K., & Xu, S. (2026). Prominence-stratified failure modes in retrieval-augmented commercial recommendation: A 37,000-run audit (arXiv:2605.27439). arXiv. https://doi.org//arXiv.2605.27439DOI: 10.48550

Jin, F., & Zhang, X. (2025). Artificial intelligence or human: When and why consumers prefer AI recommendations. *Information Technology & People*, *38*(1), 279–303. DOI: 10.1108/ITP-01-2023-0022

Keller, K. L. (1993). Conceptualizing, measuring, and managing customer-based brand equity. *Journal of Marketing*, *57*(1), 1–22. DOI: 10.1177/002224299305700101

Klaus, P., & Zaichkowsky, J. L. (2022). The convenience of shopping via voice AI: Introducing AIDM. *Journal of Retailing and Consumer Services*, *65*, 102490. DOI: 10.1016/j.jretconser.2021.102490

Leung, E., Paolacci, G., & Puntoni, S. (2018). Man versus machine: Resisting automation in identity-based consumer behavior. *JMR, Journal of Marketing Research*, *55*(6), 818–831. DOI: 10.1177/0022243718818423

Madden, T. J., Fehle, F., & Fournier, S. (2006). Brands matter: An empirical demonstration of the creation of shareholder value through branding. *Journal of the Academy of Marketing Science*, *34*(2), 224–235. DOI: 10.1177/0092070305283356

Mari, A., Mandelli, A., & Algesheimer, R. (2026). AI-assisted shopping on voice assistants: The efficiency-autonomy consumer decision trade-off. *Journal of Interactive Marketing*, *61*(3), 327–344. DOI: 10.1177/10949968251400616

McLean, G., Osei-Frimpong, K., & Barhorst, J. B. (2021). Alexa, do voice assistants influence consumer brand engagement? Examining the role of AI powered voice assistants in influencing consumer brand engagement. *Journal of Business Research*, *124*, 312–328. DOI: 10.1016/j.jbusres.2020.11.045

Puntoni, S., Reczek, R. W., Giesler, M., & Botti, S. (2021). Consumers and artificial intelligence: An experiential perspective. *Journal of Marketing*, *85*(1), 131–151. DOI: 10.1177/0022242920953847

Rix, J., Berger, B., Hess, T., & Rzepka, C. (2025). The algorithm discount: Explaining consumers' valuation of human- versus algorithm-created digital products. *Journal of Management Information Systems*, *42*(2), 633–668. DOI: 10.1080/07421222.2025.2487308

Rohden, S. F., & Espartel, L. B. (2024). Consumer reactions to technology in retail: Choice uncertainty and reduced perceived control in decisions assisted by recommendation agents. *Electronic Commerce Research*, *24*(2), 901–923. DOI: 10.1007/s10660-024-09808-7

Romaniuk, J., & Sharp, B. (2004). Conceptualizing and measuring brand salience. *Marketing Theory*, *4*(4), 327–342. DOI: 10.1177/1470593104047643

Scheibehenne, B., Greifeneder, R., & Todd, P. M. (2010). Can there ever be too many options? A meta-analytic review of choice overload. *The Journal of Consumer Research*, *37*(3), 409–425. DOI: 10.1086/651235

Schulte, J., Bleeker, M., & Kaufmann, P. (2026). Don't measure once: Measuring visibility in AI search (GEO) (arXiv:2604.07585). arXiv. https://doi.org//arXiv.2604.07585DOI: 10.48550

Sénécal, S., & Nantel, J. (2004). The influence of online product recommendations on consumers' online choices. *Journal of Retailing*, *80*(2), 159–169. DOI: 10.1016/j.jretai.2004.04.001

Shi, S. W., & Zhang, J. (2014). Usage experience with decision aids and evolution of online purchase behavior. *Marketing Science*, *33*(6), 871–882. DOI: 10.1287/mksc.2014.0872

Song, J., & Lin, H. (2024). Exploring the effect of artificial intelligence intellect on consumer decision delegation: The role of trust, task objectivity, and anthropomorphism. *Journal of Consumer Behaviour*, *23*(2), 727–747. DOI: 10.1002/cb.2234

Wien, A. H., & Peluso, A. M. (2021). Influence of human versus AI recommenders: The roles of product type and cognitive processes. *Journal of Business Research*, *137*, 13–27. DOI: 10.1016/j.jbusres.2021.08.016

Xie, Z., Yu, Y., Zhang, J., & Chen, M. (2022). The searching artificial intelligence: Consumers show less aversion to algorithm-recommended search product. *Psychology and Marketing*, *39*(10), 1902–1919. DOI: 10.1002/mar.21706

Acknowledgment

The contributors to this volume submitted their work to a rigorous, multi-stage review process that demanded a great deal from everybody. Each author responded to the challenge with patience and seriousness. An edited collection on a moving subject relies on authors who are willing not just to revise but to keep fine-tuning work that is still in progress. The chapters that follow went through this very process, and the insights and knowledge they carry were earned through it.

The reviewers who made that process possible have my sincere gratitude. Each chapter was read by colleagues who generously gave their time without compensation. Their comments elevated the standard of the volume and pushed all authors, including myself, to a better outcome.

Further, I am grateful to the editorial and production team at IGI Global Scientific Publishing for the publishing opportunity and their guidance throughout the proposal, call, review, and production phases. A field moving this quickly required a production schedule to match, and IGI made that possible.

Finally, and most importantly, I thank my family: my wife, Jeanette Rach, and our children, Sophie-Lisanne Rach and Maximilian Rach. Editorial work is paid for in evenings and weekends that belong to others, and they absorbed that cost without complaint. This book exists because they made room for it.

Section 1
Foundations of Brand Theory in the Agentic Age

Brand theory was initially developed with the assumption of a human buyer. This section reconstructs those foundational principles for markets where an intelligent intermediary facilitates the interaction between a firm and a consumer. Three key questions guide the argument: what capabilities a firm requires when agents govern the discovery process, what happens to brand management when attention ceases to be the scarce resource, and how enacted brand experiences persuade when consumers act out brand meaning rather than merely interpret it.

Chapter 1
Dynamic Capabilities for Brand Equity in the Agentic Age:
Sensing, Seizing, and Reconfiguring for Agentic Brand Performance

Katharina Buttenberg
http://orcid.org/0000-0003-1742-0020
Independent Researcher, Munich, Germany

ABSTRACT

Autonomous AI agents, including recommendation engines and large language models, increasingly mediate the consumer–brand relationship, delegating exposure, accuracy, and choice to algorithms. This displaces the direct human agency presumed by traditional brand equity theory, so consumer-based brand-equity models lose explanatory power when machines represent, rank, and select brands on a consumer's behalf. Existing frameworks do not capture how a brand gains or loses standing within algorithmic decision processes. Through an integrative literature review, this chapter recasts brand equity from a consumer-held stock into an outcome requiring active, capability-driven maintenance, linking established brand-measurement (awareness, preference, loyalty, financial brand value) to AI-mediated choice. The model proposes that AI adoption drives three dynamic brand capabilities, AI-brand sensing, seizing, and reconfiguring, working through grounding in third-party evidence to build Agentic Brand Equity. The contribution is a testable causal model and measurement logic.

DOI: 10.4018/979-8-3373-9589-0.ch001

INTRODUCTION

As AI agents increasingly intermediate consumer choice, they delegate brand exposure, evaluation, and selection to algorithms, displacing the direct human agency that traditional brand-equity theory presumes. Especially in e-commerce, an AI tool may already have narrowed the selection before a consumer reaches a brand's interface (Schumacher et al., 2026), hence reducing the awareness gained through advertising. Kenny and Pogrebna (2026) argue that LLM interactions are overtaking conventional search, and deeper AI integrations push the agent into an even more central, proactive role. On current evidence, AI is becoming a primary interface for discovery, comparison, and recommendation, progressively mediating and sometimes managing the brand relationship between companies and consumers, with machines acting on consumers' behalf (Acar & Schweidel, 2026). Cherep et al. (2026) demonstrate this directly: AI agents acting as shoppers shift their selections substantially and predictably in response to option attributes and cues, often more sharply than human decision-makers. This can advantage familiar brands, which are actively requested, and unfamiliar ones, which may be surfaced by automated recommendations (Hardcastle et al., 2025). Managerially oriented work has begun to name this imperative: Cui and van Esch (2025) describe the capacity to be accurately discovered, interpreted, and executed by AI agents as "algorithmic fidelity", yet without specifying a measurable outcome construct or the capability mechanism through which firms attain it.

How brands create and capture value has long been studied under the concept of brand equity, yet its measurement has never been settled. Early approaches treated it as a financial asset before a consumer-based tradition located brand value in the consumer's mind (Rovedder de Oliveira et al., 2023). Subsequent reviews document competing models without consensus and call for measurement to be rethought as digital transformation, and recently AI, reshape brand relationships (France et al., 2025; Gutiérrez Gutiérrez et al., 2024), while the field still lacks measurement standardization and AI-specific constructs (Al-Habsi et al., 2025). Measurement has thus not kept pace with a setting in which a machine, rather than a consumer, is increasingly the proximate decision-maker.

This unresolved measurement problem points to a parallel shift in where brand value is generated. If algorithmic intermediaries condition exposure and selection, the firm's ability to generate equity depends increasingly on its marketing capabilities to adapt to that environment. The dynamic capabilities perspective is well suited to this question, with its attention to sensing opportunities, seizing them, and reconfiguring the resource base under environmental change (Teece et al., 1997; Teece, 2007). Recent work connects AI adoption to this mechanism, showing enterprise AI use builds firm capability through digital adaptiveness and market perception, although such adaptation depends on antecedents including compatibility, top-management support, resource availability, and strategic alignment (Gao et al., 2025; Horani et al., 2025).

The following research brings these threads together, contributing a testable causal model that links AI adoption, the dynamic capabilities of marketing, and brand equity outcomes as a basis for subsequent qualitative and quantitative validation.

BACKGROUND

To build this model, two established streams of research, brand equity and dynamic capabilities, are analyzed alongside a third construct for AI adoption, extending brand equity beyond its consumer-centric foundations.

Brand Equity Literature & Research

A foundational definition of brand equity is the value a brand adds to a product or service beyond functional attributes, making consumers pay more for the branded good than for an otherwise identical item (Farquhar, 1989). The concept gained attention in the late 1980s, shifting focus from short-term sales toward long-term brand profitability as an intangible asset. Aaker (1991) defined brand equity as a set of assets organized around four dimensions: brand loyalty, brand awareness, perceived quality, and brand associations, later operationalized through survey instructions for managers (Aaker, 1996). Keller (1993) developed consumer-based brand equity (CBBE) in parallel, defined as the differential effect of brand knowledge on consumer response to brand marketing. In his associative-network model, brand knowledge consists of brand awareness, including recognition and recall, and brand image, including associations that differ in favorability, strength, and uniqueness. Together, these theories established brand equity as a multidimensional, consumer-side psychological construct.

The literature distinguishes five models. Besides CBBE, finance-based brand equity (FBBE) examines the additional economic value a brand contributes to future revenue or cash flow (Simon & Sullivan, 1993). Sales-based brand equity (SBBE) defines brand equity as the sales or market-share premium attributable to the brand (Kamakura & Russell, 1993; Keller, 1998). Employee-based brand equity (EBBE) extends the concept internally and defines it as the effect of brand knowledge on employees' evaluation of their work environment, including brand commitment, brand citizenship behavior, satisfaction, intention to stay, and positive employee word of mouth (King & Grace, 2009; Piehler et al., 2016; Poulis & Wisker, 2016). Lastly, digital brand equity (DBE) redefines brand equity for the phygital (physical and digital) environment, where brand value is shaped through online touchpoints (France et al., 2025).

These conceptualizations overlap and largely complement one another. EBBE has also been linked to stronger firm performance, shown by the connection between top-quartile employee cultures and significantly higher stock-market returns (Dewar, 2018).

Despite this, disagreement across approaches remains. Gutiérrez Gutiérrez et al. (2024) found that no model enables a comprehensive evaluation and that instruments remain insufficiently verified. Parris and Guzman (2022) found no agreement on definition or measurement, warning against applying pre-Internet definitions to modern concepts. Rovedder de Oliveira et al. (2023) noted that CBBE and FBBE are too often treated separately, proposing a brand-equity chain integrating consumer and firm perspectives.

Brand equity measurement has followed two routes: Keller's (1993) indirect approach, measuring brand-knowledge components, and a direct approach, measuring the effect of that knowledge on consumer response to the marketing mix. Yoo and Donthu (2001) validated a multidimensional CBBE scale cross-culturally but could not fully separate awareness from associations. France et al. (2025) proposed three practitioner-derived online constructs: share of search, digital brand awareness, and digital brand sentiment, while cautioning that such indicators are often descriptive rather than predictive and should be combined with human dimensions such as awareness, emotion, and opinion. The digital environment shifted brand power toward user-generated content and electronic word of mouth, prompting Keller to call for further research on brand value in this context. This reflects a broader reconfiguration of brand authority in a hyperconnected environment, where brands move from single to shared ownership and meaning is co-created across a wider set of stakeholders rather than dictated by firms (Swaminathan et al., 2020). Across all conceptualizations, value ultimately accrues through human cognition, perception, and behavior, whether from consumers, investors, or employees; the digital lens relocates human judgment to online touchpoints rather than changing this.

A more recent stream examines brand equity under AI, but remains fragmented, reporting inconsistent definitions of "AI," a predominance of cross-sectional designs limiting causal inference, and a lack of standardized AI-specific brand equity constructs and metrics (Al-Habsi et al., 2025; Dong, 2025). This gap is addressed through a new construct, Agentic Brand Equity (ABE), in brief, the differential standing a brand holds within the representation and recommendation logic of autonomous AI systems, assessed relative to competitors and defined in full in the Findings section. This assumption is increasingly challenged as autonomous AI agents mediate how brands are discovered, compared, and selected, taking over evaluative work traditionally assigned to people (e.g., Schumacher et al., 2026). A brand may hold strong consumer-based equity while remaining invisible, misrepresented, or uncompetitive within the algorithmic systems shaping consideration sets, a gap neither traditional nor digital frameworks resolve.

Dynamic Capabilities Literature & Research

The dynamic capabilities perspective emerged in response to a limitation of Resource-Based Theory: possessing valuable resources alone does not explain how firms sustain advantage in rapidly changing environments. Dynamic capabilities occupy a distinct position among organizational capabilities because they do not directly produce marketable goods or services, but instead build, integrate, and reconfigure the operational capabilities that do (e.g., Helfat & Winter, 2011). Teece (2007) defined dynamic capabilities as the abilities to sense and seize opportunities and, when necessary, reconfigure a firm's assets. This definition became the foundation for most later research (Schulze & Brusoni, 2022). These capabilities improve the speed and efficiency of a firm's response to environmental turbulence (Fainshmidt et al., 2016). More recently, this logic has been extended beyond individual firms to digital ecosystems (Volz et al., 2025). Wilden et al. (2013) developed a second-order index of Teece's three capacities, drawing sensing items from a scanning scale (Danneels, 2008), seizing items from Jantunen's (2005) knowledge-utilization scale, and reconfiguring items from a Community Innovation Surveys-based scale, using confirmatory tetrad analysis to justify a reflective-formative specification. Their index achieved high composite reliability but only borderline average variance extracted, illustrating both the feasibility and fragility of measuring dynamic capabilities.

The richness of the concept contrasts with the difficulty of measuring it, meaning early research remained largely conceptual. Two limitations recur consistently. First, dynamic capabilities are context-dependent and, as Winter (2003) argued, no general-purpose capabilities exist. Scholars recommend concentrating on a few specific, theoretically justified dimensions rather than the abstract construct, while Schilke et al. (2018) demonstrate that capturing dynamic capabilities fully within a single study is nearly impossible. Second, they are often confused with their outcomes and environmental conditions, which may be better treated as separate dependent and contextual variables (Schilke & Helfat, 2025).

Eisenhardt and Martin (2000) provide a balancing perspective, arguing that dynamic capabilities are not vague constructs but specific, identifiable, and replicable organizational routines. Framed as strategic routines, they can be studied as measurable processes such as product development and resource allocation.

Most marketing capabilities are dynamic because they involve strategic decisions based on market knowledge, anticipation of future trends, and organizational responses to these opportunities (e.g., Day, 2011). Wilden and Gudergan (2015) support this view empirically, showing that frequent use of sensing and reconfiguring strengthens operational marketing capabilities, while environmental turbulence moderates the relationship. Cross-functional capabilities such as brand management and customer relationship management can be classified as dynamic when they support sensing opportunities and reorganizing resources.

Recent extensions adapt the theory to artificial intelligence, where AI strengthens each of the three capacities. Gao et al. (2025) connect AI-enabled digital adaptability to Teece's framework by linking perceptual capacity to sensing, social capacity to seizing, and production capacity to reconfiguring, with market perception mediating the relationship between AI adoption and innovation capability. As autonomous AI agents mediate interactions between consumers and brands, the author argues that brand equity is no longer purely a consumer-side psychological stock but a phenomenon requiring active, capability-driven maintenance. Three domain-specific dynamic capabilities are proposed: AI-Brand Sensing, AI-Brand Seizing, and AI-Brand Reconfiguring, through which firms detect, position, and restructure their brands within algorithmic environments.

AI Adoption Literature & Research

Until recently, AI was mainly discussed within information technology literature. However, with the rise of large language models (LLMs), recommendation engines in digital marketing, and increasing consumer adoption of AI in decision-making processes, more scholars began examining why individuals and organizations adopt new technologies. Models originally developed for functional technologies do not transfer cleanly to AI and cannot fully explain the complexity of AI-related decision-making (Gursoy et al., 2019). AI adoption requires extended or newly integrated frameworks.

A growing body of evidence suggests that adoption and value have become decoupled, representing a major extension of the adoption discussion. McKinsey & Company (2025) reports that although AI use has become nearly universal across organizations, only a small minority of employees experience significant value from it, while more advanced agentic systems remain at an early stage of implementation. Roughly one quarter of organizations have scaled at least one agentic system, usually within only one or two business functions. Established adoption models explain whether firms adopt AI, but not whether they successfully reconfigure themselves to benefit from it. Future measurements must also account for the depth of AI assimilation.

One stream of research examines AI adoption at the individual level, especially from the perspective of managers deciding whether to use AI in organizational decision-making. Cao et al. (2021) argue that managerial attitudes are shaped not only by the perceived benefits of AI but also by its recognized risks, described as the technology's dark side. Drawing on the net valence approach (Breward et al., 2017), they combine the Unified Theory of Acceptance and Use of Technology with Technology Threat Avoidance Theory (Liang & Xue, 2009) to develop the Integrated AI Acceptance-Avoidance Model, which simultaneously considers benefits and concerns.

A second stream approaches adoption at the organizational level. Horani et al. (2025) apply the Technology-Organization-Environment framework together with Diffusion of Innovation theory, identifying relative advantage, top management support, cost-effectiveness, competitive pressure, vendor support, compatibility, AI strategic alignment, and resource availability as drivers of adoption intention. Complexity and government regulation function as barriers, while market uncertainty shows no significant effect. Together, these two streams establish AI adoption as a phenomenon shaped by both individual perceptions and organizational conditions.

The dominant method for measuring AI adoption is the survey-based study analyzed through structural equation modeling, reflecting the methodological tradition of technology-acceptance research. Three limitations follow. First, established acceptance models were not designed specifically for AI (e.g., Cao et al., 2021). Second, most studies measure behavioral intention rather than actual adoption or sustained use. Third, reliance on self-reported managerial perceptions introduces familiar risks of single-source and common-method bias. These limitations are directly relevant to the present research because they indicate that adoption, when measured only as intention or the presence of tools, is an incomplete indicator of whether AI genuinely reshapes firm operations.

The literature review reveals a consistent gap across all three research streams. Brand equity, dynamic capabilities, and AI adoption all lack consensus measurement and remain grounded in assumptions of human agency that autonomous AI agents increasingly disrupt. From this synthesis emerge the study's core constructs: Agentic Brand Equity, Dynamic Brand Capabilities, and AI adoption. Having established this theoretical foundation, the next step is to develop a research approach through which these constructs can be operationalized and empirically tested within an AI-mediated brand environment.

RESEARCH APPROACH AND METHODOLOGY

The research approach develops a proposed model and a set of research propositions to be tested qualitatively and quantitatively in later research stages; this chapter's contribution is therefore primarily conceptual. The aim is to review and compare established constructs within the brand-equity literature, relate them to dynamic capabilities, and adapt them to AI-mediated interactions between firms and consumers. An integrative review is the appropriate method because the relevant fields remain emerging and fragmented, and the objective is to synthesize and reconceptualize existing work rather than aggregate comparable effect sizes, as would be required in a systematic review or meta-analysis (Snyder, 2019; Torraco, 2005). Consistent with this approach, the review is purposive rather than exhaustive: sources were selected for their theoretical relevance to the three streams under synthesis, and the corpus is intended to represent foundational and current debates rather than provide a complete census of the field. To ensure transparency and traceability, the literature was collected through a structured four-stage search and selection process.

First, structured searches were conducted in Google Scholar using Boolean keyword strings combining the core construct domains. A representative string was ("AI agent" OR "algorithmic choice" OR "autonomous recommendation") AND ("brand equity" OR "brand asset" OR "marketing capability"). Google Scholar was selected for its broad cross-disciplinary coverage, which suits a synthesis spanning marketing, strategy, and information-systems research, and because it is suitable for emerging fields where relevant work remains dispersed across venues rather than consolidated within a single indexed database. The platform has known limitations, including unstable result counts, inconsistent Boolean and wildcard support, and the inclusion of non-peer-reviewed material. These limitations were mitigated through the inclusion and exclusion criteria outlined below and through backward and forward citation tracing of seminal works to ensure foundational literature was captured.

Second, the search was time-bounded to prioritize the rapidly evolving evidence base. Literature on AI, agentic systems, and algorithmic choice was restricted to the 2015–2026 period, while foundational brand-equity and dynamic-capabilities theory was drawn from earlier seminal work because these constructs necessarily predate the period of interest. The corpus therefore deliberately combines contemporary empirical research with established theoretical anchors.

Third, transparent inclusion and exclusion criteria were applied across five source categories: peer-reviewed journal articles and top-tier conference papers (e.g., AOM, AMA, ACM, NeurIPS, ICLR); seminal monographs defining foundational constructs (e.g., Aaker, 1991; Keller, 1998); methodological references; a limited number of practitioner and consultancy sources (e.g., McKinsey & Company; Harvard Business Review) documenting agentic-commerce developments not yet reflected in peer-reviewed research; and a small number of recent preprints retained when they reported directly relevant findings unavailable elsewhere. All non-peer-reviewed sources are identified as such in the text and treated as supplementary rather than confirmatory; blog posts and technical documentation were excluded. Application of these criteria yielded a final corpus of 62 sources: 48 peer-reviewed journal articles and conference papers, five seminal monographs, three methodological references, five practitioner and consultancy sources, and one preprint. Four additional sources, foundational brand-equity and methodological citations, were introduced for grounding and added after the systematic search.

Fourth, data were extracted by cross-tabulating how selected studies operationalize human versus machine decision parameters. The resulting corpus was analyzed through thematic synthesis (Snyder, 2019) to identify and categorize emerging structural dimensions of agentic choice. Because the procedure relies on a single search engine rather than multiple indexed databases, a supplementary verification search was conducted in a second database (Elsevier ScienceDirect) using five construct-pairing strings, returning 341 records. Title and abstract screening confirmed retrieval of corpus items meeting the criteria and identified two recent managerially oriented conceptual papers (Cui & van Esch, 2025; van Esch & Cui, 2026), now cited, but no peer-reviewed study proposing a measurement construct or causal model for brand equity under agentic mediation. Large language model tools were used to refine search strings and support the initial organization of sources, while all records, citations, and inclusion decisions were verified by the author against the original sources.

To address psychometric limitations common in survey-based technology-adoption research, the planned empirical phase will incorporate the procedural guidelines proposed by Podsakoff et al. (2003) to reduce common method variance. Because reliance on single-source managerial responses can artificially inflate observed behavioral relationships, the study will separate measurement of the predictor variable (AI adoption) from the criterion variables (capabilities and equity outcomes) both temporally and psychologically and will collect multi-informant data pairs within each surveyed organization.

The review then proceeded through three analytical steps. First, constructs were compared across the different brand-equity streams in terms of definitions, sub-dimensions, and measurement approaches. Second, the dynamic-capabilities and technology-adoption literatures were evaluated to extract the dimensions of sensing, seizing, and reconfiguring. Third, the adjusted constructs were integrated into a proposed causal framework prepared for qualitative validation and subsequent quantitative structural equation modeling.

FINDINGS

The central argument is that once AI agents enter the choice process, brand equity is no longer purely a consumer-side psychological stock. It also requires a technical capability that ensures products and brands remain legible and that their benefits and value propositions are understandable to LLMs. Firms must establish organizational capabilities that secure favorable brand outcomes, including whether and how prominently the brand is retrieved by the system, how positively the system expresses sentiment toward it, how strongly it is endorsed, how it is framed against competitors, and how consistently and accurately it is represented to consumers.

The model further conceptualizes brand equity as the result of a causal chain. AI adoption, captured through the extent of AI usage, breadth of applications, implementation stage, and perceived value of adoption, and moderated by managerial behavioral intention, is theorized as the upstream resource. Adoption alone, however, does not protect a brand. Its branding value is realized only when firms develop dynamic brand capabilities: the ability to sense how agents represent the brand, seize opportunities to position it favorably within ranking and recommendation logics, and reconfigure brand assets to become machine-readable. These capabilities function as the mechanism that converts AI adoption into Agentic Brand Equity (ABE), defined in full in the following subsection and measured through Salience, Favorability, and Accuracy, with Stability as a second-order property.

The contribution is twofold. Theoretically, the study introduces Agentic Brand Equity as a novel and empirically auditable outcome construct and positions dynamic brand capabilities as the mechanism linking firm-level AI adoption to brand value, connecting three research streams that have largely evolved separately. Practically, it reframes the managerial task, a claim developed further in the Conclusion. The objective is to establish a plausible and testable causal model that can be validated through qualitative and quantitative research in subsequent stages.

Agentic Brand Equity Definition

Agentic Brand Equity (ABE) is defined as the differential standing a brand holds within the representation and recommendation logic of autonomous AI systems. It refers to the degree to which they retrieve, represent, evaluate, substantiate, and surface a brand more reliably and favorably than an unbranded or competing equivalent, assessed relative to a competitor set. ABE does not replace established conceptions of brand equity but redistributes them along an agent-mediated chain.

The consumer-based tradition provides the facets describing what the system retrieves and expresses, namely Salience and Favorability. The digital tradition, which relocated brand value to online touchpoints and metrics such as share of search and digital sentiment, directly precedes these same facets in machine-mediated form. The agent becomes the latest and most influential digital touchpoint. The sales-based tradition reappears downstream as selection, meaning whether the agent actually recommends or transacts the brand. The finance-based tradition reemerges as the financial value generated when agents control the funnel. The employee-based tradition internalizes human inputs rather than functioning as a downstream evaluation dimension: employee and customer testimonies become upstream grounding data shaping the model's recommendation pathways. Two additional facets without direct consumer-based equivalents complete the construct: Accuracy and Stability, both arising from the agent itself as a fallible and stochastic intermediary. As summarized in Table 1, historical paradigms diverge from the proposed agentic framework across four structural attributes.

To illustrate the variance that ABE captures and existing frameworks do not, consider a hypothetical mid-size German skincare brand with strong digital brand equity by every established indicator: review sentiment averaging 4.6 of 5 across major retail platforms, above-category social engagement, and first-page organic visibility for its core category terms. Under the digital tradition, this brand is healthy. A standardized prompt battery run against this profile would plausibly return a very different picture. Across ten category-level queries (e.g., "recommend a sensitive-skin moisturizer under €30") posed to three widely used assistants, the brand appears in only one response, an appearance rate of 0.1, and never enters the top three of any ranked recommendation, while two better-documented competitors appear in eight and six responses respectively. Where the brand does surface, one system misstates a core attribute, describing a fragrance-free formulation as containing fragrance, a rendering that would be penalized on the Accuracy facet, and hedges its account for lack of corroborating third-party evidence. Every conventional digital indicator is green, yet the brand holds near-zero standing within the systems assembling consumer consideration sets. Digital brand equity cannot register this deficit because its metrics measure human-facing touchpoints, whereas the deficit resides in the agent's representation and recommendation logic. This is precisely the differential standing ABE is constructed to measure. The illustration is hypothetical. Each element corresponds to a documented behavior of current systems: weak retrieval of sparsely documented entities (Mallen et al., 2023), contestable visibility rankings (Aggarwal et al., 2024), and confidently rendered factual errors (Huang et al., 2025).

Salience represents the agentic translation of brand awareness as defined by Keller (1993), which consumer-based equity conceptualizes as the retrievability of the brand node from consumer memory through recall and recognition. In an agent-mediated category query, the equivalent issue becomes whether, and how prominently, the system retrieves the brand when generating a response. Salience is proposed to be measured through inclusion in search results and ranking position within relevant queries, functioning as the agentic equivalent of top-of-mind awareness. Aggarwal et al. (2024) demonstrate that this standing is real, consequential, and contestable, showing that the structure and wording of brand content can substantially increase visibility within generative-engine responses. Kumar and Lakkaraju (2024) extend this by showing that carefully crafted product-page text can significantly increase the probability of becoming a model's top recommendation.

Later work reframes awareness as mental availability, meaning the brand's propensity to come to mind across category entry points triggering buyer consideration (Romaniuk & Sharp, 2016; Sharp, 2010). Salience functions as the agentic counterpart: the agent's category query becomes the machine-mediated entry point, while appearance rate and ordinal rank act as analogs of mental market share. Unlike mindshare-based awareness, this standing is inherently relative and zero-sum: within a ranked response of finite length, one brand's gain in position is necessarily another's loss. Salience can be operationalized through measures such as appearance frequency across a standardized prompt battery and ordinal ranking relative to a defined competitor set. A commercial measurement market is already forming around these quantities: "share-of-model" visibility tracking and managerial audit instruments (e.g., Cui & van Esch, 2025) now quantify brand standing within AI assistants.

Favorability represents the agentic translation of two closely related consumer-based constructs: the favorability of brand associations and perceived quality (Yoo & Donthu, 2001). The critical distinction lies in where it is measured. Favorability is derived from the system's own representation of the brand rather than from the consumer reviews underlying that representation because, under agentic mediation, it is the system's rendering, not the original evidence, that reaches the consumer. The two may diverge significantly. Since AI systems do not possess emotions toward brands, Favorability does not measure affect. Instead, it measures whether the system's account of the brand is positive or negative, which attributes it emphasizes, and how it positions the brand relative to competitors. Consumer ratings and employee opinions remain important, but their function changes: they become informational material the system processes rather than direct indicators of brand standing. The system's assessment changes systematically depending on framing and attribution structures (Germani & Spitale, 2025). Two factors shape an LLM's assessment of a brand. The first is the availability and quality of brand-related information accessible to the system. A well-represented brand provides stronger informational grounding than a minimally represented one. The second factor is the system itself, since identical source material may be framed differently across models or prompts. Expressing brands more or less favorably is a known and controllable property of these systems rather than a fixed reflection of their underlying sources (Kumar & Lakkaraju, 2024; Zhuo et al., 2024).

Accuracy has no direct equivalent in existing brand-equity frameworks. Earlier conceptualizations treat the relevant judgment as a human perception, so the represented brand cannot meaningfully be evaluated as true or false because, in consumer-based terms, perception itself constitutes reality (Keller, 1993). An autonomous intermediary disrupts this assumption, because AI systems can generate false propositions and present them with apparent authority. Brand equity theory therefore requires a dimension none of the established forms needed: the factual correctness of brand representation against a verifiable ground truth.

Huang et al. (2025) identify entity-error hallucination as a major failure mode, showing that models perform more reliably on high-frequency knowledge while struggling with long-tail entities. Tian et al. (2023) extend this from factual recall to calibration, showing that frontier models produce poorly calibrated confidence judgments. Accuracy is operationalized as a hallucination-penalized accuracy score benchmarked against a ground-truth brand fact sheet and supplemented by a positioning-fit measure capturing brand misframing.

Stability is not an independent facet but a property of the other three dimensions: the extent to which Salience, Favorability, and Accuracy remain consistent across platforms, prompt formulations, and repeated executions. Emerging preprint evidence suggests that equivalent inputs can produce contradictory outputs (Kumar & Mishra, 2025), while prompt sensitivity varies substantially across models and datasets, with no system demonstrating complete invariance (Zhuo et al., 2024). Stability can be operationalized as the dispersion of first-order facet scores, for example the coefficient of variation of Salience, Favorability, and Accuracy across repeated runs, paraphrased prompts, and platforms. High Stability reflects a consistent representation; low Stability one that fluctuates with context.

Table 1. Brand Equity Model Comparison

Attribute	CBBE	FBBE	SBBE	EBBE	DBE	ABE
Core definition	Differential effect of brand knowledge on consumer response to marketing	Additional economic value a brand contributes to future earnings or cash flow	Sales or market-share premium attributable to the brand	Effect of brand knowledge on employees' evaluation of their work environment	Brand equity reconceptualized for the phygital environment	Differential standing within autonomous AI systems' representation and recommendation logic, relative to a competitor set
Locus of value	In the consumer's mind	In the firm and capital markets	In market outcomes	Inside the organization	At online and phygital touchpoints	In the AI system's representation logic
Key dimensions / indicators	Awareness, perceived quality, associations, loyalty	Brand-attributable cash flow, price premium, stock return	Brand-driven sales volume, market share, revenue premium	Brand commitment, citizenship behavior, satisfaction, intention to stay, employee WOM	Share of search, digital brand awareness, digital brand sentiment	First order Salience, Favorability, Accuracy; second order Stability

continued on following page

Table 1. Continued

Attribute	CBBE	FBBE	SBBE	EBBE	DBE	ABE
Typical measurement approach	Consumer surveys and validated scales	Financial modeling via Tobin's Q and decomposition of intangible assets	Brand intercept in choice / market-share models; incremental sales estimation	Employee surveys linked to firm performance	Digital and SEO analytics, social listening, sentiment analysis	Standardized prompt battery across platforms, scored against a competitor set; audit of LLM and recommender outputs
Key limitation	Awareness and associations not cleanly separable; culture-bound validity; no monetary estimate	Ignores consumer perceptions; aggregate and lagged; limited diagnostic insight	Lacks consumer-perception and marketing-mix elements; limited diagnostic ability	Internal focus; evidence largely cross-sectional	Indicators often descriptive rather than predictive	New construct without a validated scale; not yet grounded in evidence
Representative sources	Aaker (1991, 1996); Keller (1993); Yoo & Donthu (2001)	Simon & Sullivan (1993)	Kamakura & Russell (1993); Keller (1998)	King & Grace (2009); Piehler et al. (2016); Poulis & Wisker (2016)	France et al. (2025)	Keller (1993); Yoo & Donthu (2001); Aggarwal et al. (2024); Zhuo et al. (2024); Huang et al. (2025); Kumar & Mishra (2025)

Brand Outcomes as Downstream Measurement

Three indicators capture downstream brand-equity performance.

Selection represents the immediate conversion of Agentic Brand Equity into choice. It examines whether the agent recommends, shortlists, or purchases the brand instead of a competitor. It reflects the sales and market-share premium associated with traditional brand equity, now realized through agentic choice rather than human deliberation. As the first observable consequence of a brand's standing, Selection is also the most directly testable outcome today, since agentic choice shifts predictably in response to option attributes and persuasive cues (Cherep et al., 2026). In future model testing, Selection can be operationalized through win rate and basket-inclusion rate relative to a competitor set, measured across a standardized prompt battery.

Financial performance represents the firm-level value generated by the brand, now reached through agentic mediation rather than human evaluation alone. It is the agentic counterpart of finance-based brand equity: the economic value a brand contributes to future earnings and cash flow. As agents mediate discovery, comparison, and transaction, both the price premium a brand can sustain and the demand it retains become dependent on agent-mediated selection. Financial performance can be operationalized through agent-attributable revenue or market share, the price premium maintained under agentic comparison, and brand-attributable cash-flow effects.

Traditional brand performance preserves the human outcomes of the brand within the agentic chain rather than replacing them, specifically awareness, preference, and loyalty. These dimensions persist because a core principle of the brand-equity literature remains valid: value ultimately accrues through human cognition, while digital transformation merely relocated human judgment to online touchpoints rather than eliminating it (France et al., 2025). Under agentic mediation, consumers step back from direct evaluation but not from their relationship with the brand, so these outcomes persist while increasingly being shaped by ABE, since agents now determine which brands consumers encounter. Loyalty reenters the framework at this stage. It does not operate as a representational facet, because agents reassess each query independently rather than forming habitual preferences, but remains a downstream human outcome of brand standing, one that strong ABE can reinforce and weak ABE can gradually erode. A partial exception arises in subscription and auto-replenishment flows, where consumers can encode preferred brands or exclusions directly into the agent's decision rules, re-internalizing loyalty into the representational layer as a machine-readable parameter (Schumacher et al., 2026), an encoding requirement taken up below under AI-Brand Reconfiguring.

Specifying the Agentic Capability Constructs

For the evaluation of Dynamic Brand Capabilities, the author closely follows Wilden et al. (2013), who developed the three capabilities based on Teece's framework and argued that they form the higher-order construct rather than merely reflect it. The same logic applies here: the dimensions need not move together, yet each remains essential. None transfers unchanged into the agentic environment, so each is re-specified below together with Grounding, the evidence base through which the capabilities influence Agentic Brand Equity.

This adaptation is a re-specification rather than a relabeling of the general marketing triad, and the two triads differ on all three anchors. In Wilden et al.'s (2013) operationalization, sensing scans markets and sector practices; seizing acts on customer demand by investing in solutions; and reconfiguring renews internal management methods and business processes. The object of AI-Brand Sensing, by contrast, is not a market of human actors but a machine intermediary's representation of the brand, an artifact that can be audited but not surveyed. AI-Brand

Seizing operates not on customer demand but on the external evidence base from which systems construct that representation, through routines with no equivalent among the general seizing items. AI-Brand Reconfiguring restructures brand assets for machine legibility rather than renewing internal processes for human execution. Whether the three constructs are also empirically distinct remains an open question, addressed through the discriminant-validity strategy outlined below.

AI-Brand Sensing refers to the firm's ability to monitor and interpret how AI systems retrieve, describe, recommend, or misrepresent the brand. Firms must now observe the model's own outputs, which frequently misrepresent brands (Acar & Schweidel, 2026). Sensing establishes whether the brand is surfaced and, if so, how accurately, thereby influencing Salience and Favorability.

AI-Brand Seizing refers to the firm's ability to position the brand effectively within the information environments on which AI systems rely. The central task becomes less about persuading consumers directly and more about supplying AI systems with accurate, strategically advantageous brand information. This environment remains contestable because the information associated with an option can alter what the model ultimately recommends (Kumar & Lakkaraju, 2024). Controlled-setting evidence suggests that market acceptance may increasingly run through acceptance by the agent itself (Cherep et al., 2026; Kumar & Lakkaraju, 2024), although market-wide displacement of human evaluation remains to be demonstrated. Seizing primarily influences Salience and Accuracy.

AI-Brand Reconfiguring refers to the firm's ability to restructure brand assets, touchpoints, and governance processes so that the brand remains legible when decision-making is delegated to agents. In agentic commerce, loyalty must effectively be encoded to survive agent-mediated decisions (Schumacher et al., 2026). Reconfiguring supports Favorability and Stability. In practice, this may involve restructuring product data, attribute taxonomies, and loyalty conditions into machine-readable formats or redesigning content-governance routines so that the evidence AI systems rely upon remains consistent and current. Distinctive brand assets follow the same logic: colors, logos, and characters are human recognition cues (Romaniuk & Sharp, 2016), whose machine equivalent is structured brand identifiers such as names, attribute taxonomies, and entity markers that let systems recognize and correctly attribute brands.

Because newly proposed dynamic capabilities can easily overlap with existing capability and brand constructs, establishing the discriminant validity of AI-Brand Sensing, Seizing, and Reconfiguring relative to established measures is an explicit objective of both the planned qualitative phase and the subsequent quantitative validation. This requires testing the three capabilities against established dynamic-capability scales, such as those proposed by Wilden et al. (2013), to confirm that they load onto distinct factors rather than remeasure existing constructs. In particular, these constructs must be differentiated from firm-level AI capability as conceptualized within the resource-based tradition (Mikalef & Gupta, 2021), since that framework measures general organizational AI capability rather than the brand-specific and agent-directed capacities proposed here.

Grounding represents the convergence point of the three capabilities. AI systems do not directly perceive brands but construct representations from third-party evidence, so the capabilities operate only through this informational base. Sensing interprets the evidence, Seizing supplies it, and Reconfiguring maintains its consistency over time. Grounding refers to the breadth, quality, recency, and citation frequency of the evidence available to the system. Brands supported by consistent and credible evidence are retrieved more confidently and represented more favorably. Weakly documented brands are hedged, omitted, or inaccurately inferred because models perform significantly worse on low-frequency and sparsely documented entities (Mallen et al., 2023) and may filter them out before consumers or agents encounter them (Schumacher et al., 2026). Grounding influences Salience, Favorability, Accuracy, and Stability, and is specified within the model as a mediator between Dynamic Brand Capabilities and Agentic Brand Equity, a relationship tested in subsequent research propositions.

For practitioners, the three capabilities translate into assignable work: an agentic visibility audit, owned by the brand or insights function, operationalizes AI-Brand Sensing by benchmarking a standardized prompt battery against a defined competitor set; a grounding program, typically run by SEO and content teams, operationalizes AI-Brand Seizing through structured product data and corroborating third-party evidence; and machine-legibility governance, necessarily cross-functional, operationalizes AI-Brand Reconfiguring by keeping brand assets consistent and citable. Assigning ownership matters because this work currently falls between brand, SEO, and data teams without a clear owner.

Dynamic managerial capabilities provide the microfoundation for the entire process. Adner and Helfat (2003) define them as the capabilities managers use to build, integrate, and reconfigure organizational resources, grounded in managerial human capital, social capital, and cognition. Cognition is particularly important here because recognizing AI systems as genuine intermediaries is itself a cognitive act. Dynamic managerial capabilities operate upstream of both AI adoption and Dynamic Brand Capabilities. The intention to adopt AI (Cao et al., 2021) represents the visible expression of managerial cognition. Transforming sensing, seizing, and reconfiguring into brand-relevant action depends on managerial human and social capital. AI adoption provides the resource, dynamic managerial capabilities determine whether it is recognized and strategically directed, and Dynamic Brand Capabilities convert it into standing within algorithmic decision-making systems.

Firm-Level AI Adoption as the Upstream Resource

Conceptualizing firm-level artificial intelligence (AI) adoption requires moving beyond a binary record of whether a firm has procured the technology, because acquisition and real assimilation regularly diverge. A firm may use AI widely but shallowly, or embed it deeply in one area while leaving the rest untouched. AI adoption is therefore treated as a multidimensional construct whose facets need not move together (Helfat & Peteraf, 2003): how extensively AI is deployed, how deeply it is assimilated, and how autonomously it operates.

Scale of deployment is the extent of AI use across the firm: how often and how much AI is used, and across how many business functions. It captures the breadth of a firm's exposure to AI, regardless of how deeply that use is rooted.

Depth of assimilation is how far AI has moved from early experimentation toward routine use embedded in core rather than peripheral processes (Dey & Ghose, 2025). It is the firm's qualitative position in the assimilation lifecycle, distinct from scale, since an application can be widespread yet experimental.

Autonomy of operation is how far AI acts and decides without human control. It carries particular weight here because handing judgment to autonomous agents is precisely what reshapes how brands are discovered, evaluated, and chosen (Acar & Schweidel, 2026; Schumacher et al., 2026). This facet sits at the automation–augmentation paradox, in which firms balance delegating decisions to AI against using it to extend managerial judgment (Raisch & Krakowski, 2021).

It is the configuration across the three facets, not any one alone, that matters. This is why firms with similar headline adoption can differ sharply in their readiness to defend brand equity once choice is delegated to autonomous agents. Two related constructs are left open at this stage. Managerial intention to adopt AI (Cao et al., 2021) plausibly acts as an antecedent that drives a firm across the three facets, while the benefits a firm gains from adoption act as a downstream outcome. Rather than fixing their position in advance, the model holds both open for the qualitative phase, where interviews with branding and AI practitioners establish whether intention and realized value are best read as antecedents, components, or consequences of adoption.

PROPOSED MODEL FOR FURTHER RESEARCH

The model in Figure 1 sets out a single causal chain. AI adoption sits at the start as the upstream resource, profiled across the scale of deployment, depth of assimilation, and autonomy of operation. Its value only appears once the firm builds dynamic brand capabilities, namely AI-brand sensing, seizing, and reconfiguring. These capabilities do not reach agentic brand equity directly but work through Grounding, the body of third-party evidence an AI system draws on when it represents the brand: Sensing reads that evidence base, seizing feeds it, and reconfiguring keeps it stable. The strength of that evidence is what then shapes how the brand is surfaced and judged through Salience, Favorability, Accuracy, and, secondarily, Stability.

Agentic brand equity, in turn, produces brand outcomes in an agent-mediated market. Running above the whole process are dynamic managerial capabilities, the microfoundation that decides whether AI is recognized as consequential and steered into capability-building rather than left as idle technology. The deliberate absence of a direct arrow from adoption to equity carries the core claim of the model: adoption alone does not protect a brand.

Figure 1. Proposed model for testing

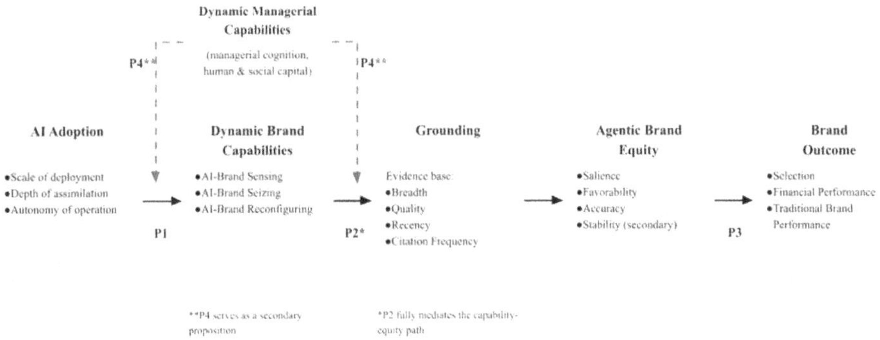

Source: Author

The four propositions displayed in the model require testing in further research:

- **P1:** AI adoption drives the development of dynamic brand capabilities. The more extensively, deeply, and autonomously a firm uses AI, the greater its need and raw material for building them.
- **P2:** Dynamic brand capabilities raise agentic brand equity through Grounding. Grounding is expected to fully mediate this path: because AI systems construct brand representations from retrievable third-party evidence rather than perceiving brands directly, capabilities improve Salience, Favorability, Accuracy, and, secondarily, Stability only insofar as they strengthen the evidence the system relies on.
- **P3:** Agentic brand equity drives brand outcomes, including selection, financial performance, and traditional brand performance. A brand that is well represented inside AI systems is more likely to be chosen and to hold its commercial standing.

- **P4:** Dynamic managerial capabilities condition the chain. They moderate the path from AI adoption to dynamic brand capabilities (P1), shaping whether adoption is recognized and directed into capability-building, and, secondarily, the path from those capabilities to Grounding (P2).

FUTURE RESEARCH DIRECTIONS

A conceptual model was developed through an integrative review, which carries the central limitation that the proposed relationships are theoretically argued rather than empirically tested. The next step is a qualitative phase based on expert interviews, grounding and refining the proposed constructs, particularly the Dynamic Brand Capabilities, and strengthening the case for the distinctiveness of Agentic Brand Equity. This phase is planned as semi-structured interviews with senior brand and marketing decision-makers, such as CMOs and brand leads, with an indicative sample of 20 to 30 informants. This addresses the measurement gap identified in the review, since established consumer-based scales were not designed for environments in which a machine is the immediate decision-maker. Following the qualitative phase, a quantitative phase would test the model through structural equation modeling, for which partial least squares estimation is anticipated given the formative higher-order specification of the capability construct and the theory-developing stage of the research. The target sample comprises multi-informant data pairs from an indicative minimum of 200 consumer-facing firms with active AI deployments, with covariance-based estimation reserved for subsequent confirmatory replication. Future research should also examine systemic prompt fluctuations across platforms to establish cross-market variance metrics that turn the conceptual foundations of Stability into operational benchmarks.

A second limitation concerns the evidentiary status of part of the source base. Because agent-mediated commerce is recent and rapidly evolving, the peer-reviewed literature does not yet fully capture it, so the synthesis relies on a deliberately mixed corpus. Claims regarding the current behavior of agentic systems and the state of the market rely additionally on a limited number of practitioner and consultancy sources and recent preprints, identified as such throughout the text and treated as supplementary rather than confirmatory. While this evidence base is sufficient to motivate the framework and its propositions, it is not sufficient to validate them empirically.

Several empirical regularities referenced in the framework, particularly the manipulability of brand Salience within agentic recommendation systems and the predictability of agentic Selection across varying option attributes, currently depend on early-stage or not yet peer-reviewed findings. Establishing these relationships through replicable evidence is a central objective of the phases that follow, and the propositions advanced here should be interpreted in that context.

Beyond validation, several directions warrant investigation. First, the evidence that agent representations can be deliberately manipulated (Aggarwal et al., 2024; Kumar & Lakkaraju, 2024) implies an adversarial dimension: competitors may distort a rival brand's representation, making defensive monitoring a natural extension of the Accuracy facet. Second, the same manipulability raises a boundary condition: if consumers come to regard agents as gameable rather than neutral, trust in the mediation channel may erode, weakening the link between ABE and Selection. Third, optimizing for agent visibility sits in tension with emerging consumer-protection and transparency expectations, so the regulatory treatment of grounding practices deserves scrutiny. Relatedly, van Esch and Cui (2026) identify an internal counterpart: "agentic brand drift," whereby a firm's own AI-orchestrated operations gradually erode its intended identity, suggesting that inward- and outward-facing agentic brand governance warrant joint investigation. Fourth, because agentic-commerce adoption and consumers' comfort with delegation vary across markets and cultures (Schumacher et al., 2026), the strength of the proposed relationships is likely to be market-contingent, inviting cross-market comparative designs. Finally, the zero-sum character of Salience implies competitive representational dynamics, suggesting market-level and game-theoretic extensions of the firm-level lens adopted here.

CONCLUSION

This chapter set out to address a gap within the existing brand-equity literature. Across all established conceptualizations, whether consumer-based, financial, sales-based, employee-based, or digital, brand value ultimately depends on human cognition, perception, and behavior. This assumption weakens once autonomous AI agents mediate how brands are discovered, compared, and selected, since a brand may retain strong consumer-based equity while remaining invisible or misrepresented within the algorithmic systems shaping consideration sets. Through an integrative review of brand equity, dynamic capabilities, and AI adoption, the chapter identified this common reliance on human agency, together with the persistent lack of consensus measurement, and used that gap to develop an integrated and testable model.

These constructs are linked through a single causal logic in which AI adoption provides the resource, managerial capabilities determine whether the resource is strategically acted upon, and dynamic brand capabilities transform it into Agentic Brand Equity. As argued above, the model deliberately contains no direct path from AI adoption to brand equity. The resulting contribution is twofold. Theoretically, the chapter introduces Agentic Brand Equity as a novel and empirically auditable outcome construct while positioning dynamic brand capabilities as the mechanism connecting firm-level AI adoption to brand value. Practically, it reframes the managerial challenge: investment in AI generates brand advantage only when firms build the capabilities required to act on it, so that adoption yields resilient brand performance rather than declining standing within agentic environments.

The model is presented as a plausible and testable causal framework rather than a verified empirical result. Its contribution lies in specifying how brands gain or lose standing once autonomous AI agents, rather than consumers, become the immediate decision-makers and in providing a corresponding measurement logic for this environment. The chapter thus establishes a foundation for the qualitative and quantitative validation phases that constitute its next steps. Building this standing also carries governance obligations: optimizing a brand's representation within agentic systems must remain compatible with transparency and consumer-protection expectations.

AI USAGE DISCLOSURE & CONFLICT OF INTEREST STATEMENT

Claude (Anthropic) was used solely for grammar, spelling, and readability improvements and for the editors' quality-check prompt. ChatGPT (OpenAI) was used solely to transform presentation slides into a printable graphic. No AI tools were used to create, generate, or contribute to the scholarly content of this chapter.

This research received no specific grant from any funding agency in the public, commercial, or not-for-profit sectors.

REFERENCES

Aaker, D. A. (1991). *Managing brand equity: Capitalizing on the value of a brand name*. Free Press.

Aaker, D. A. (1996). *Building strong brands*. Free Press.

Acar, O. A., & Schweidel, D. A. (2026, March–April). Preparing your brand for agentic AI. *Harvard Business Review*. https://hbr.org/2026/03/preparing-your-brand-for-agentic-ai

Adner, R., & Helfat, C. E. (2003). Corporate effects and dynamic managerial capabilities. *Strategic Management Journal, 24*(10), 1011–1025. DOI: 10.1002/smj.331

Aggarwal, P., Murahari, V., Rajpurohit, T., Kalyan, A., Narasimhan, K., & Deshpande, A. (2024). GEO: Generative engine optimization. In *Proceedings of the 30th ACM SIGKDD Conference on Knowledge Discovery and Data Mining* (pp. 5–16). Association for Computing Machinery. DOI: 10.1145/3637528.3671900

Al-Habsi, Z. S., Mohamed, H. R., & Methuku, H. (2025). AI-driven brand equity: A systematic review of consumer perceptions, engagement, and loyalty in the age of intelligent branding. *TPM. Testing, Psychometrics, Methodology in Applied Psychology, 32*(S7). https://tpmap.org/submission/index.php/tpm/article/view/1984

Breward, M., Hassanein, K., & Head, M. (2017). Understanding consumers' attitudes toward controversial information technologies: A contextualization approach. *Information Systems Research, 28*(4), 760–774. DOI: 10.1287/isre.2017.0706

Cao, G., Duan, Y., Edwards, J. S., & Dwivedi, Y. K. (2021). Understanding managers' attitudes and behavioral intentions towards using artificial intelligence for organizational decision-making. *Technovation, 106*, 102312. Advance online publication. DOI: 10.1016/j.technovation.2021.102312

Cherep, M., Ma, C., Xu, A., Shaked, M., Maes, P., & Singh, N. (2026). *A framework for studying AI agent behavior: Evidence from consumer choice experiments* [Preprint]. arXiv. /arXiv.2509.25609DOI: 10.48550

Cui, Y. G., & van Esch, P. (2025). The end of search as we know it: Only those chosen by AI agents will survive in the delegate economy. *Business Horizons*. Advance online publication. DOI: 10.1016/j.bushor.2025.11.006

Danneels, E. (2008). Organizational antecedents of second-order competences. *Strategic Management Journal, 29*(5), 519–543. DOI: 10.1002/smj.684

Day, G. S. (2011). Closing the marketing capabilities gap. *Journal of Marketing, 75*(4), 183–195. DOI: 10.1509/jmkg.75.4.183

Dewar, C. (2018). *Culture: 4 keys to why it matters*. McKinsey & Company. https://www.mckinsey.com/capabilities/people-and-organizational-performance/our-insights/the-organization-blog/culture-4-keys-to-why-it-matters

Dey, D., & Ghose, D. (2025). Integrating AI adoption frameworks with digital maturity models: Strategic pathways in a rapidly evolving technological landscape. *Journal of Contemporary Business Research, 1*(2), 156–170. Advance online publication. DOI: 10.1177/3049513X251387463

Dong, Y. (2025). Implementation of artificial intelligence for brand equity. *Cogent Business & Management, 12*(1), 2471538. Advance online publication. DOI: 10.1080/23311975.2025.2471538

Eisenhardt, K. M., & Martin, J. A. (2000). Dynamic capabilities: What are they? *Strategic Management Journal, 21*(10–11), 1105–1121. DOI: 10.1002/1097-0266(200010/11)21:10/11<1105::AID-SMJ133>3.0.CO;2-E

Fainshmidt, S., Pezeshkan, A., Frazier, M. L., Nair, A., & Markowski, E. (2016). Dynamic capabilities and organizational performance: A meta-analytic evaluation and extension. *Journal of Management Studies, 53*(8), 1348–1380. DOI: 10.1111/joms.12213

Farquhar, P. H. (1989). Managing brand equity. *Marketing Research, 1*(3), 24–33.

France, S. L., Davcik, N. S., & Kazandjian, B. J. (2025). Digital brand equity: The concept, antecedents, measurement, and future development. *Journal of Business Research, 192*, 115273. Advance online publication. DOI: 10.1016/j.jbusres.2025.115273

Gao, Y., Liu, S., & Yang, L. (2025). Artificial intelligence and innovation capability: A dynamic capabilities perspective. *International Review of Economics & Finance, 98*, 103923. Advance online publication. DOI: 10.1016/j.iref.2025.103923

Germani, F., & Spitale, G. (2025). Source framing triggers systematic bias in large language models. *Science Advances, 11*(45), eadz2924. Advance online publication. DOI: 10.1126/sciadv.adz2924 PMID: 41202130

Gursoy, D., Chi, O. H., Lu, L., & Nunkoo, R. (2019). Consumers acceptance of artificially intelligent (AI) device use in service delivery. *International Journal of Information Management, 49*, 157–169. DOI: 10.1016/j.ijinfomgt.2019.03.008

Gutiérrez Gutiérrez, M. M., Perona Páez, J. J., & Gutiérrez Bonilla, F. (2024). Models of brand equity: A systematic and critical review. *Cogent Business & Management*, *11*(1), 2433168. Advance online publication. DOI: 10.1080/23311975.2024.2433168

Hardcastle, K., Vorster, L., & Brown, D. M. (2025). Understanding customer responses to AI-driven personalized journeys: Impacts on the customer experience. *Journal of Advertising*, *54*(2), 176–195. DOI: 10.1080/00913367.2025.2460985

Helfat, C. E., & Peteraf, M. A. (2003). The dynamic resource-based view: Capability lifecycles. *Strategic Management Journal*, *24*(10), 997–1010. DOI: 10.1002/smj.332

Helfat, C. E., & Winter, S. G. (2011). Untangling dynamic and operational capabilities: Strategy for the (n)ever-changing world. *Strategic Management Journal*, *32*(11), 1243–1250. DOI: 10.1002/smj.955

Horani, O. M., Al-Adwan, A. S., Yaseen, H., Hmoud, H., Al-Rahmi, W. M., & Alkhalifah, A. (2025). The critical determinants impacting artificial intelligence adoption at the organizational level. *Information Development*, *41*(3), 1055–1079. DOI: 10.1177/02666669231166889

Huang, L., Yu, W., Ma, W., Zhong, W., Feng, Z., Wang, H., Chen, Q., Peng, W., Feng, X., Qin, B., & Liu, T. (2025). A survey on hallucination in large language models: Principles, taxonomy, challenges, and open questions. *ACM Transactions on Information Systems*, *43*(2), 42. Advance online publication. DOI: 10.1145/3703155

Jantunen, A. (2005). Knowledge-processing capabilities and innovative performance: An empirical study. *European Journal of Innovation Management*, *8*(3), 336–349. DOI: 10.1108/14601060510610199

Kamakura, W. A., & Russell, G. J. (1993). Measuring brand value with scanner data. *International Journal of Research in Marketing*, *10*(1), 9–22. DOI: 10.1016/0167-8116(93)90030-3

Keller, K. L. (1993). Conceptualizing, measuring, and managing customer-based brand equity. *Journal of Marketing*, *57*(1), 1–22. DOI: 10.1177/002224299305700101

Keller, K. L. (1998). *Strategic brand management: Building, measuring, and managing brand equity*. Prentice Hall.

Kenny, G., & Pogrebna, G. (2026, March). LLMs are overtaking search: Here's how to adjust your online presence. *Harvard Business Review*. https://hbr.org/2026/03/llms-are-overtaking-search-heres-how-to-adjust-your-online-presence

King, C., & Grace, D. (2009). Employee based brand equity: A third perspective. *Services Marketing Quarterly*, *30*(2), 122–147. DOI: 10.1080/15332960802619082

Kumar, A., & Lakkaraju, H. (2024). *Manipulating large language models to increase product visibility* [Preprint]. arXiv. /arXiv.2404.07981DOI: 10.48550

Kumar, P., & Mishra, S. (2025). Robustness in large language models: A survey of mitigation strategies and evaluation metrics. *Transactions on Machine Learning Research.* https://openreview.net/forum?id=Bchvaaod6g

Liang, H., & Xue, Y. (2009). Avoidance of information technology threats: A theoretical perspective. *Management Information Systems Quarterly, 33*(1), 71–90. DOI: 10.2307/20650279

Mallen, A., Asai, A., Zhong, V., Das, R., Khashabi, D., & Hajishirzi, H. (2023). When not to trust language models: Investigating effectiveness of parametric and non-parametric memories. In *Proceedings of the 61st Annual Meeting of the Association for Computational Linguistics (*Volume 1*: Long Papers)* (pp. 9802–9822). Association for Computational Linguistics. DOI: 10.18653/v1/2023.acl-long.546

McKinsey & Company. (2025). *The state of AI: How organizations are rewiring to capture value.* McKinsey & Company. https://www.mckinsey.com/capabilities/quantumblack/our-insights/the-state-of-ai

Mikalef, P., & Gupta, M. (2021). Artificial intelligence capability: Conceptualization, measurement calibration, and empirical study on its impact on organizational creativity and firm performance. *Information & Management, 58*(3), 103434. Advance online publication. DOI: 10.1016/j.im.2021.103434

Parris, D. L., & Guzman, F. (2022). Evolving brand boundaries and expectations: Looking back on brand equity, brand loyalty, and brand image research to move forward. *Journal of Product and Brand Management, 31*(2), 191–234. DOI: 10.1108/JPBM-06-2021-3528

Piehler, R., King, C., Burmann, C., & Xiong, L. (2016). The importance of employee brand understanding, brand identification, and brand commitment in realizing brand citizenship behaviour. *European Journal of Marketing, 50*(9/10), 1575–1601. DOI: 10.1108/EJM-11-2014-0725

Podsakoff, P. M., MacKenzie, S. B., Lee, J. Y., & Podsakoff, N. P. (2003). Common method biases in behavioral research: A critical review of the literature and recommended remedies. *The Journal of Applied Psychology, 88*(5), 879–903. DOI: 10.1037/0021-9010.88.5.879 PMID: 14516251

Poulis, A., & Wisker, Z. (2016). Modeling employee-based brand equity (EBBE) and perceived environmental uncertainty (PEU) on a firm's performance. *Journal of Product and Brand Management, 25*(5), 490–503. DOI: 10.1108/JPBM-04-2015-0852

Raisch, S., & Krakowski, S. (2021). Artificial intelligence and management: The automation–augmentation paradox. *Academy of Management Review*, *46*(1), 192–210. DOI: 10.5465/amr.2018.0072

Romaniuk, J., & Sharp, B. (2016). *How brands grow: Part 2: Including emerging markets, services, durables, B2B and luxury brands*. Oxford University Press.

Rovedder de Oliveira, M. O., Heldt, R., Silveira, C. S., & Luce, F. B. (2023). Brand equity chain and brand equity measurement approaches. *Marketing Intelligence & Planning*, *41*(4), 442–456. DOI: 10.1108/MIP-06-2022-0222

Schilke, O., & Helfat, C. E. (2025). Unlocking dynamic capabilities: Pathways for empirical research. *Journal of Management Scientific Reports*. Advance online publication. DOI: 10.1177/27550311251318724

Schilke, O., Hu, S., & Helfat, C. E. (2018). Quo vadis, dynamic capabilities? A content-analytic review of the current state of knowledge and recommendations for future research. *The Academy of Management Annals*, *12*(1), 390–439. DOI: 10.5465/annals.2016.0014

Schulze, A., & Brusoni, S. (2022). How dynamic capabilities change ordinary capabilities: Reconnecting attention control and problem-solving. *Strategic Management Journal*, *43*(12), 2447–2477. DOI: 10.1002/smj.3413

Schumacher, K., Keutel, M., Kluge, P., Giebel, K., & Wendler, T. (2026, March). *Europe's agentic commerce moment: Decision influence is here; execution is coming*. McKinsey & Company. https://www.mckinsey.com/capabilities/quantumblack/our-insights/europes-agentic-commerce-moment-decision-influence-is-here-execution-is-coming

Sharp, B. (2010). *How brands grow: What marketers don't know*. Oxford University Press.

Simon, C. J., & Sullivan, M. W. (1993). The measurement and determinants of brand equity: A financial approach. *Marketing Science*, *12*(1), 28–52. DOI: 10.1287/mksc.12.1.28

Snyder, H. (2019). Literature review as a research methodology: An overview and guidelines. *Journal of Business Research*, *104*, 333–339. DOI: 10.1016/j.jbusres.2019.07.039

Swaminathan, V., Sorescu, A., Steenkamp, J.-B. E. M., O'Guinn, T. C., & Schmitt, B. (2020). Branding in a hyperconnected world: Refocusing theories and rethinking boundaries. *Journal of Marketing*, *84*(2), 24–46. DOI: 10.1177/0022242919899905

Teece, D. J. (2007). Explicating dynamic capabilities: The nature and microfoundations of (sustainable) enterprise performance. *Strategic Management Journal, 28*(13), 1319–1350. DOI: 10.1002/smj.640

Teece, D. J., Pisano, G., & Shuen, A. (1997). Dynamic capabilities and strategic management. *Strategic Management Journal, 18*(7), 509–533. DOI: 10.1002/(SICI)1097-0266(199708)18:7<509::AID-SMJ882>3.0.CO;2-Z

Tian, K., Mitchell, E., Zhou, A., Sharma, A., Rafailov, R., Yao, H., Finn, C., & Manning, C. D. (2023). Just ask for calibration: Strategies for eliciting calibrated confidence scores from language models fine-tuned with human feedback. In *Proceedings of the 2023 Conference on Empirical Methods in Natural Language Processing* (pp. 5433–5442). Association for Computational Linguistics. DOI: 10.18653/v1/2023.emnlp-main.330

Torraco, R. J. (2005). Writing integrative literature reviews: Guidelines and examples. *Human Resource Development Review, 4*(3), 356–367. DOI: 10.1177/1534484305278283

van Esch, P., & Cui, Y. G. (2026). Agentic brand drift: How AI-orchestrated organizations will lose their identity and how to get it back. *Business Horizons*. Advance online publication. DOI: 10.1016/j.bushor.2026.05.013

Volz, F., Münch, C., Küffner, C., & Hartmann, E. (2025). Digital ecosystems and their impact on organizations—A dynamic capabilities approach. *International Journal of Management Reviews, 27*(3), 398–419. Advance online publication. DOI: 10.1111/ijmr.12396

Wilden, R., & Gudergan, S. P. (2015). The impact of dynamic capabilities on operational marketing and technological capabilities: Investigating the role of environmental turbulence. *Journal of the Academy of Marketing Science, 43*(2), 181–199. DOI: 10.1007/s11747-014-0380-y

Wilden, R., Gudergan, S. P., Nielsen, B. B., & Lings, I. (2013). Dynamic capabilities and performance: Strategy, structure and environment. *Long Range Planning, 46*(1–2), 72–96. DOI: 10.1016/j.lrp.2012.12.001

Winter, S. G. (2003). Understanding dynamic capabilities. *Strategic Management Journal, 24*(10), 991–995. DOI: 10.1002/smj.318

Yoo, B., & Donthu, N. (2001). Developing and validating a multidimensional consumer-based brand equity scale. *Journal of Business Research, 52*(1), 1–14. DOI: 10.1016/S0148-2963(99)00098-3

Zhuo, J., Zhang, S., Fang, X., Duan, H., Lin, D., & Chen, K. (2024). ProSA: Assessing and understanding the prompt sensitivity of LLMs. In *Findings of the Association for Computational Linguistics: EMNLP 2024*. Association for Computational Linguistics. /arXiv.2410.12405DOI: 10.48550

ADDITIONAL READING

Datta, H., Ailawadi, K. L., & van Heerde, H. J. (2017). How well does consumer-based brand equity align with sales-based brand equity and marketing-mix response? *Journal of Marketing*, *81*(3), 1–20. DOI: 10.1509/jm.15.0340

Davenport, T., Guha, A., Grewal, D., & Bressgott, T. (2020). How artificial intelligence will change the future of marketing. *Journal of the Academy of Marketing Science*, *48*(1), 24–42. DOI: 10.1007/s11747-019-00696-0

Dietvorst, B. J., Simmons, J. P., & Massey, C. (2018). Overcoming algorithm aversion: People will use imperfect algorithms if they can (even slightly) modify them. *Management Science*, *64*(3), 1155–1170. DOI: 10.1287/mnsc.2016.2643

Eisenhardt, K. M., & Graebner, M. E. (2007). Theory building from cases: Opportunities and challenges. *Academy of Management Journal*, *50*(1), 25–32. DOI: 10.5465/amj.2007.24160888

Lemon, K. N., & Verhoef, P. C. (2016). Understanding customer experience throughout the customer journey. *Journal of Marketing*, *80*(6), 69–96. DOI: 10.1509/jm.15.0420

Oliver, R. L. (1999). Whence consumer loyalty? *Journal of Marketing*, *63*(4, suppl1), 33–44. DOI: 10.1177/00222429990634s105

Schilke, O. (2014). On the contingent value of dynamic capabilities for competitive advantage: The nonlinear moderating effect of environmental dynamism. *Strategic Management Journal*, *35*(2), 179–203. DOI: 10.1002/smj.2099

Wilden, R., Devinney, T. M., & Dowling, G. R. (2016). The architecture of dynamic capability research: Identifying the building blocks of a configurational approach. *The Academy of Management Annals*, *10*(1), 997–1076. DOI: 10.5465/19416520.2016.1161966

KEY TERMS AND DEFINITIONS

Accuracy: The factual correctness of a brand's representation by an AI system, assessed against a verifiable ground truth and penalized for hallucination.

Agentic Brand Equity (ABE): The differential standing a brand holds within the representation and recommendation logic of autonomous AI systems, assessed relative to a competitor set.

Dynamic Brand Capabilities: The firm's higher-order capacities to sense how AI systems represent the brand, to seize opportunities to position it within ranking and recommendation logics, and to reconfigure brand assets so that the brand remains machine-legible.

Favorability: The valence and framing of an AI system's own account of a brand, read from the system's rendering rather than from the underlying review sentiment.

Grounding: The breadth, quality, recency, and citation frequency of the third-party evidence an AI system draws on to represent a brand; the mediating evidence base through which dynamic brand capabilities reach Agentic Brand Equity.

Salience: The agentic translation of brand awareness, namely whether and how prominently an AI system retrieves a brand when answering a category query, measured by appearance rate and ordinal rank against a competitor set.

Stability: A second-order property capturing the degree to which Salience, Favorability, and Accuracy hold steady across platforms, prompt wordings, and repeated runs.

Chapter 2
When the Machine Chooses:
Brand Management Under Selection Scarcity

Markus Rach
http://orcid.org/0009-0000-0480-8734
Canadian University Dubai, UAE

ABSTRACT

Brand management works on memory. Advertising secures a share of scarce human attention, converts it into memory structures, and those structures are retrieved when a category need arises, long before the transaction. Recommender systems, conversational assistants and agentic checkout remove the purchase from the set of things attention is spent on, so the memory is never queried at the moment of choice and the constraint becomes inclusion in a set a machine assembles. This chapter separates the attention economy into scarcity, allocation and conversion claims and argues that scarcity survives while allocation and conversion may not. It argues that the dispute over whether brands still matter turns on prior brand equity. The Choice Liquidity Architecture specifies when a purchase is delegable, what determines inclusion, and what accumulates across episodes, with five testable propositions.

INTRODUCTION

For half a century, marketing has organized itself around a scarcity. Simon (1971) observed that a wealth of information creates a poverty of attention, and that the problem of an information rich world is therefore the efficient allocation of the attention that information consumes. Goldhaber (1997) carried the observation

DOI: 10.4018/979-8-3373-9589-0.ch002

onto the network, arguing that attention, not information, is the natural currency of an economy in which content is effectively free; Davenport and Beck (2001) translated the idea into management practice. Falkinger (2007, 2008) gave it formal expression, modeling attention as a scarce resource whose allocation determines which signals reach a receiver at all. Brand management inherited the premise and built on it: if attention is scarce, its task is to secure a share of it, to convert that share into memory, and to arrange that memory so the brand comes to mind when a category need arises.

That inheritance is visible in the field's central constructs. Keller (1993) located brand equity in the differential effect of brand knowledge on consumer response, presupposing a mind that holds the knowledge, while Romaniuk and Sharp (2004) refined salience into the quality and quantity of a memory network, which assumes retrieval by a person in a buying situation. The two schools disagree considerably about what brand strength consists of, and the Ehrenberg-Bass tradition challenges the centrality of perceived differentiation directly (Romaniuk et al., 2007), yet they share one assumption: the decisive event happens inside the human mind.

However, a growing share of consumption no longer works that way. Recommender systems compress an assortment into a shortlist, conversational assistants answer with one suggestion rather than a page of results, and agentic systems accept a goal and execute the steps required to satisfy it. Machine initiated checkout reached the market across 2024 and 2025, from Perplexity's shopping assistant (Perplexity AI, 2024) to OpenAI's instant checkout and agentic commerce protocol (OpenAI, 2025), and a system now performs the search, the comparison and increasingly the selection. The scarce resource in the transaction may therefore no longer be the attention of a human; it may be inclusion in a consideration set that a machine assembles.

This chapter examines whether that shift ends the attention economy as the organizing premise of brand management, and what follows if it does, testing how far the current body of knowledge can carry the question before extending it conceptually. The contribution is integrative rather than foundational. It reports no new data but reorganizes constructs that already exist, so that a dispute currently conducted on belief can be settled on evidence.

The chapter's evidence base was assembled through structured searches of the Consensus corpus of more than 220 million indexed peer reviewed records (Consensus, n.d.). Six question level searches were run and are reported here so that the absence they establish can be checked. The first asked whether delegating purchase decisions to artificial intelligence agents weakens the influence of brand equity on consumer choice, the second whether hedonic and utilitarian purchase types moderate willingness to delegate. The third asked whether consumers can instruct agents to exclude specific brands persistently, the fourth whether a need for physical or sensory inspection limits delegation. The fifth asked whether repeated algorithmic recommendation narrows the set of brands considered, and the sixth how algorithmic visibility in generated answers affects brand competition. Retrieved records were screened for peer reviewed status, for a consumer or brand outcome, and for a machine that performs or materially constrains the selection; the searches were run in August 2026 and repeated with the same result. Five of the six returned fewer than five studies answering the question directly, which is the platform's own stated threshold for reporting a consensus, so no consensus was reported for any of them; the sixth returned an answer resting on preprints. This absence of empirical evidence is not a reason to avoid this chapter's central question; to the contrary, it is a reason to state it precisely enough for researchers to answer it.

Furthermore, the question is live enough to have produced a public disagreement between two of the field's most prominent voices (Pauwels, 2026; Sharp, 2026). This chapter argues, in five stages, that their positions are not rivals but descriptions of different parts of the same distribution.

First, this chapter sets out the assumptions of the attention economy and asks which of them machine mediation actually breaks; second, it states the displacement case and the continuity case in their strongest forms. Third, it proposes that the dispute is mis-specified, because attention scarcity is not replaced but relocated, and that the useful reframing is from a scarcity of attention to a scarcity of selection. Fourth, it argues that the practical consequence is not the death of human focused brand work but its migration, from the moment of purchase toward the experience that follows it. Fifth, it proposes the Choice Liquidity Architecture, which specifies the conditions under which each position holds, and states five propositions allowing for rigorous testing.

BACKGROUND

The Three Claims of the Attention Economy

The attention economy began as an observation by Simon (1971), which Goldhaber (1997) named and Davenport and Beck (2001) turned into management practice. It expanded with digital media, and above all with the rise of platforms that sell audience access to advertisers and treat human attention as a currency (O'Reilly et al., 2024). Where content is effectively unlimited and costs almost nothing to produce, the binding constraint is the attention available to receive it, and attention becomes what the market trades (Heitmayer, 2025). Every instrument of brand management assumes it. The claim is repeated more often than it is examined, usually as a synonym for clutter (Patilinet, 2024), and contested at its foundation, because cognitive science does not support treating attention as a single expendable resource (White,

2024). Bruineberg (2026) reconstructs the assumptions behind Simon's passage and observes that the term attention has likely no stable referent. Kübler (2023), interviewing fitness influencers, finds that attention is not uniformly desirable even for those whose income depends on it; he further argues on that basis for a contextual rather than a universal treatment of attention in marketing. Its analytical content is narrower than the usage suggests and worth restating, because the question of whether it survives machine mediation depends on which of its claims is at stake.

The attention economy rests on three propositions. The first is a scarcity claim: human attention is bounded and cannot expand to meet the supply of information (Simon, 1971). The second is an allocation claim (Simon, 1971): bounded attention is rationed competitively, so signals contend for a limited share. Falkinger (2007) later gave this formal expression, while Bruineberg (2026) contests it, arguing that attention is distributed through competition, not assigned by an allocator. The third is a conversion claim, and it is the marketing addition: attention secured can, under some conditions, be encoded into memory structures that later influence choice (Nedungadi, 1990; Wedel & Pieters, 2000). The memory conversion is however neither automatic nor uniform: Wedel and Pieters (2000) found that fixations on pictorial and brand elements build accurate brand memory, while text fixations do not, and Chandon et al. (2009) identified shelf positions that gain attention without gaining evaluation. Simonov et al. (2025), in an eye tracking experiment, observed that attention to an advertisement raises both brand recall and purchase probability, so the conversion claim holds where attention is actually given. Conversion is what makes advertising an investment, and not an expense (Keller, 1993; Romaniuk & Sharp, 2004).

Each of the stated propositions can fail independently. If machines do the browsing, the scarcity claim may survive untouched, because human attention remains as bounded as before; what changes is that less of it is spent on the purchase. The allocation claim may fail in a specific sense, because the contest for a place in the choice set is no longer decided by competing for a person's notice. The conversion claim may fail in the most consequential sense, because a memory structure that is never queried at the moment of choice cannot influence it, however well formed.

Hansen (2024) makes a related argument outside the marketing domain: generative systems monetize through cognitive lock-in rather than through attention capture, thus the attention economy is the wrong unit of analysis for what these systems do. The claim is not that attention ceases to matter, but that it ceases to be the binding constraint.

Which Assumptions Machine Mediation Breaks

Machine mediation breaks these claims through three mechanisms operating at different points in the decision, and the first is compression of the choice set. Interactive decision aids have been known to restructure consideration sets (Häubl & Trifts, 2000); machine mediation extends the effect into voice assisted shopping. Mari et al. (2026), in an online experiment with a custom voice application covering low involvement utilitarian purchases, found that evaluating fewer alternatives is associated with higher decision satisfaction and a greater willingness to cede decision autonomy to the assistant, a finding that persists across private label and national brands, and across price levels. Consumers accept a narrower evaluation as a trade of autonomy for efficiency, and brand type did not alter that willingness. However, the study measures satisfaction and delegation intention rather than consideration set inclusion, thus the implication for inclusion remains inferred rather than tested.

The second is substitution of the decisive cue. Wang et al. (2025) ran an experiment in which generative recommendation reduced selection of licensed character brands by 46 percentage points: scenario congruent items rose to the top of the ranking, and scenario tags supplanted brand salience as the dominant cue. Due to the small sample size, the study's magnitude serves as a direction, not an established effect size; however, the direction matches the price sensitivity mechanism Diehl et al. (2003) identified a quarter century ago. Machine ordered environments re-weight the inputs to choice, and not in favor of the brand.

The third is displacement of the search itself. Cui and van Esch (2025) argue that agent based intermediation compresses choice sets, reshapes market access, and redefines brand visibility, so that firms increasingly compete for algorithmic selection rather than for human search, while Mehmet (2025) frames the same transition as a move from ranked lists of links to synthesized single answers, with consequences for discoverability that the discipline has not yet measured. Sarstedt et al. (2026) go further and propose machine marketing as a subdiscipline, treating artificial intelligence customers as autonomous market participants, and generative engine optimization as the equivalent of search engine optimization. That succession framing is challenged within the applied field, where practitioners dispute whether generative engine optimization names a distinct discipline or just a search engine optimization relabeling (Holland, 2026).

Delegation in Consumer Research

Marketing research has built a substantial body of work on machine assisted choice (André et al., 2018; Dellaert et al., 2020; Häubl & Trifts, 2000; Puntoni et al., 2021). It developed largely without contact with brand theory, and every study in that body sits at low delegation depth, because the consumer still confirms. It also developed apart from the human factors work on levels of automation, which has allocated function between operator and machine for decades, and is used below to bound the delegation depth construct (Parasuraman et al., 2000).

Häubl and Trifts (2000) established the foundational result, showing that interactive decision aids improve decision quality while reducing effort, by restructuring which alternatives a consumer examines at all. Diehl et al. (2003) found that agents which lower the cost of finding quality information can increase price sensitivity, because the same search efficiency that surfaces good options also surfaces cheaper ones; that result is a warning against assuming that better matching favors established brands. André et al. (2018) framed the normative question. They treated delegated choice as a matter of consumer autonomy and welfare rather than of efficiency alone, and asked what it means for preferences to be served by a system that also shapes them.

The more recent strand is closer to the present question. De Bellis and Johar (2020) mapped the barriers to consumer adoption of autonomous shopping systems, distinguishing the technical from the psychological, and locating the decisive obstacles in the latter. Puntoni et al. (2021) argued that consumer facing artificial intelligence should be understood experientially rather than functionally, because what consumers make of these systems depends on how the encounter feels rather than on what the system computes. Dellaert et al. (2020) set out an agenda for voice assistants and consumer decisions that anticipated much of what is now happening, including the restructuring of repeat and replenishment purchasing.

However, what the current research did not do is link to brand theory. Researchers studied decision quality, effort, autonomy, adoption, and experience, whereas brand outcomes have been examined in a few instances only: brand awareness and trust in recommended products (Chang & Park, 2024), brand self connections (Bharti et al., 2026), and loyalty under agentic intermediation (Bilgihan et al., 2025). That work sits outside the delegation literature, and does not engage the memory based constructs of brand equity or salience. The result is two adjacent bodies of work that never met, and a set of questions that fall precisely in the gap between them.

THE DISPUTE OVER MACHINE MEDIATED CHOICE

The Shape of the Dispute

The just mentioned dispute has a peculiar shape: even the field's most prominent voices argue with unusual confidence and unusually little evidence. Sharp (2026), in a post disputing how his position had been reported, argues that little changes, on the grounds that buying is already habitual, that intermediaries are as old as commerce, and that an assistant asked to shop will be expected to honor the brand preferences its owner already carries. Pauwels (2026) holds that the ground itself is moving, pointing in his newsletter to the growing share of machine performed browsing, and to agents optimizing the proxies they were trained on, instead of the preferences of the person they serve.

These two positions are not rhetorical variants: they make different and incompatible predictions, with each having supporting evidence in academic literature. A third position, set out below, accepts the continuity mechanism but predicts concentration rather than stability, so it is not a midpoint between the two.

The Continuity Case

The strongest version of the continuity argument is not that nothing changes, but that delegation inherits preference. On this reading, an agent is a new intermediary among old ones, as per Sharp's (2026) statement; consumers have long delegated purchase decisions to surrogates such as doctors, retail assistants, and mechanics (Solomon, 1986). The continuity case holds that brand preference survived those intermediaries, because the consumer specifies the goal, and the intermediary only serves it. Solomon's own account is less reassuring for the continuity case: the surrogate takes over the evaluation, not the goal; the consumer keeps control of what he wants and loses control of which brand supplies it. That is the distinction the rest of this chapter turns on: an instruction to reorder the usual executes brand memory, but an instruction to find the best option replaces it.

The evidence for this position is factual. Chang and Park (2024) find that brand awareness continues to raise trust in recommended products; artificial intelligence moderates the effect rather than eliminating it. It narrows the brand advantage at low and medium awareness, and leaves it intact at high awareness. That is a precise boundary condition in favor of strong brands, and it runs in the same direction as the double jeopardy regularity, in which larger brands hold both more buyers and slightly more loyal ones (Ehrenberg et al., 1990). Anesbury et al. (2016) observed that online grocery shoppers bought quickly, and largely from the first category page, using the retailers' default display ordering; pre ordered choice environments were therefore already the norm in some categories before generative systems arrived.

A second argument for continuity is that buying in categories where buyers rotate among a small set of acceptable brands, rather than buying one exclusively, is already habitual and already inattentive. Hoyer (1984) observed that shoppers of a common repeat purchase product examined very few packages and spent only seconds in the category. Sharp (2010) defines the regularities: buyers hold small repertoires of brands, most purchases are repeat purchases within them, and the patterns that govern brand performance, double jeopardy among them, are stable across categories, countries, and decades. Therefore, if choice was never deliberative for most purchases, then automating the non deliberation removes nothing, and delegation continues habit instead of breaking it. The asset that mattered before was a memory structure, making the brand the default; that is the asset which determines what the consumer tells the agent to do.

This argument is strong. It predicts that the observable consequences of delegation will be smaller than the rhetoric suggests, and it fits the observation that default ordered choice in online grocery left shopping behavior looking much as it did in store (Anesbury et al., 2016). Whether it survives the transition from arranging options to picking one is the empirical question.

The Displacement Case

The displacement argument does not require the disappearance of brand memory; it requires only that the point at which memory operates ceases to be the point at which the outcome is determined.

Klaus and Zaichkowsky (2020, 2022) argue that consumers using voice assistants outsource low involvement decisions to algorithms, and give correspondingly little attention to the brand comparison that conventional decision models assume. Mo et al. (2026) theorize the same relationship as surrogacy, treating voice assistants as shopping surrogates, rather than as advisers. Rohden et al. (2025) show that consumer response differs according to whether a recommendation is attributed to a voice assistant or to a person, which establishes that the identity of the recommender is itself a variable in the outcome.

The mechanism that makes displacement plausible is not machine perception, but provenance. A generative answer is assembled from a retrieved source set, and Aggarwal et al. (2024) demonstrate that the visibility of a source within such answers can be systematically raised by altering the source's own content: a brand's representation in the channel is therefore mediated by the content of sites it does not own. Betello et al. (2026) show that large language model rankings are systematically sensitive to brand geographic origin, though the direction differs by model. Across three zero shot rankers, one favored European brands, and another North American ones, while a third stayed balanced, and stated user location mattered more than brand origin. Retrieval is therefore not neutral toward brand attributes no marketer selected; if inclusion is determined by a retrieved source set whose composition the brand only partly controls, then investment in memory structures may be necessary, but not sufficient.

Bilgihan et al. (2025) push the argument into the relationship itself, contending that agents restructure the basis of loyalty by inserting a party between the customer and the brand. The durable relationship may then attach to the agent or the platform, rather than to the product.

A recurring error in the applied discussion is to frame the question as one of machine perception, asking whether a system can see a logo, or hear a sonic cue. Contemporary systems are multimodal, combining a language model with visual and audio input (Yin et al., 2024), and the answer is usually yes, so the question is uninformative. The operative determinant is not modality, but provenance.

The reframing changes what is actionable, and what is measurable. Speculation about whether a machine appreciates a distinctive asset is not testable; what determines inclusion in a retrieved source set is testable, because the set can be observed, its composition can be described, and interventions on it can be evaluated. It also relocates responsibility inside the firm: if provenance governs mediated visibility, then the relevant levers sit with functions that have never been treated as brand functions.

The applied benchmarking tradition is therefore measuring the right thing for the wrong channel: assessing distinctive assets against human recognition measures such as fame and uniqueness (Romaniuk, 2018) is exactly correct for the human channel, and silent about the mediated one. Neither direction has been tested.

The Firm Side of Machine Mediation

Machine mediation also happens inside the firm, where it raises a question the consumer side literature neglects: who controls the brand's elements once execution is delegated? Van Esch and Cui (2026) argue that organizations which delegate execution to autonomous systems experience a drift in identity. Brand identity has historically been built from an accumulation of human choices about what to say, what to make, and what to refuse; when those choices are made by systems optimizing measurable objectives, the accumulated result can satisfy every metric while ceasing to express anything in particular. Sarstedt et al. (2026) reach the same ground, from the market side.

The two halves of the transition reinforce one another. A firm optimizing for machine selection produces assets shaped by what machines reward, and those assets constitute the brand's expression in human channels as well, since maintaining two separate creative domains is both complex and costly, and the machine facing one is the domain with the tractable metric. The risk is not that machine oriented brand work displaces human oriented work by decision, but that it displaces it by default, by measurable objectives crowding out unmeasurable ones.

The same logic is visible at the largest platforms, and it is stated openly. Speaking in May 2025, Meta's founder and CEO, Mark Zuckerberg, described an advertising system in which “you come to us, you tell us what your objective is, you connect to your bank account, you don't need any creative” (Thompson, 2025). The advertiser needs no targeting demographic and no measurement beyond reading the results the system returns, a change Zuckerberg called a redefinition of the category. Five days later, he put the operating principle more plainly, saying that advertisers are encouraged not to restrict what the system is allowed to do (Zuckerberg, 2025). Meta, Google, and Amazon together are forecast to account for 62.3% of worldwide digital advertising spend in 2026 (Clark, 2026). This is not a marginal proposition about one firm's product roadmap; it is a glimpse into a likely commercially driven platform future of AI mediated branding and marketing communication.

Two consequences emerge. The first is that the brand cedes control over how, when, and where it appears in exchange for cost efficiency and measured short term return, and the pressure to make that trade is designed rather than incidental. A Meta spokesperson stated that campaigns applying manual controls beyond certain thresholds may be moved to a reduced automation status, and prompted to re-enable automation (Kulp, 2026). The second is that the firm side and the consumer side of machine mediation are the same phenomenon observed from opposing ends: a consumer delegating selection to an agent, and a brand delegating creative to a platform, are doing the same thing; both grant authority to a system that optimizes a stated objective. If brand meaning has historically been made through choices about how, when, and where a brand appears, then delegating those choices moves the site of its making. That step goes beyond what Zuckerberg claims, which concerns how advertising is bought rather than how meaning is made, and it is stated here as an inference.

There is a cultural cost as well; it operates on a different mechanism. McCracken (1986) described advertising as one of the instruments through which meaning moves from a culturally constituted world into consumer goods, and Ritson and Elliott (1999) showed ethnographically that advertising meanings acquire social uses within peer interaction, including ritual use and metaphor; that presupposes an advertisement the group holds in common. Both accounts make shared exposure constitutive, rather than incidental. An advertisement that reaches a million people separately, and an advertisement that reaches a million people commonly, are not the same object, even at identical reach.

Machine mediation accelerates a shift already underway from mass delivery toward individually targeted delivery (Boerman et al., 2017), and agentic commerce extends it further, since an answer assembled for one person is by construction not seen by anyone else. If the cultural function of advertising depends on commonality, then the shift weakens that function regardless of what happens to conversion; in practice, brands become less able to participate in the shared references that make them meaningful beyond their category. Better targeting cannot rebuild that capability, because targeting is the mechanism that erodes it.

A Third Position: Duplication

Reducing the dispute to two names understates it, and the third position is the most consequential of them. On the continuity side, Ritson (2026) makes a stronger claim than Sharp (2026) does: his argument is not that agents leave brands where they were, but that agents amplify incumbency, because a model trained on the open web has learned to trust the brands that appear most often, and most favorably, in the most places. The consequence he draws is uncomfortable for challengers, rather than reassuring for everyone. Search returned a page of links; an agent returns one answer or three. In his phrasing, a brand is either the answer or it is invisible. That is a continuity position about mechanism and a displacement position about consequence, and it predicts concentration, rather than stability.

Nelson-Field (2026), who builds attention measurement instruments, has declined to accept the framing; her position is that attention becomes the training input which keeps automated systems honest. She frames the shift as one from asking "How many impressions did our campaign serve?" to "How many seconds of quality attention did we actually earn?" (Nelson-Field, 2026).

Roach (2024, 2025) proposes that the answer is neither continuity nor displacement, but duplication: on his account artificial intelligence is not only a new toolkit for making brand content, but a whole new audience to make it for. Brands now address two audiences with opposite cognitive properties. Advertising's sales response decays between exposures, which is what the adstock tradition models (Broadbent & Fry, 1995), even though consistent creative can compound across years (System1 Group & IPA, 2025); large language models retain what they were trained on, and reward well structured information, rather than emotional resonance. Roach (2024) also places share of model in the lineage running from share of voice through share of search, which locates the new measure inside an existing tradition, rather than presenting it as a break.

This chapter assumes duplication as the best description of the current transitional period, in which brands address both human and machine audiences at once. Compounding strengthens that case, because it gives the human facing half a mechanism the machine facing half does not have. The architecture developed below specifies when each audience is decisive.

Evidence on the Pace of the Transition

The displacement argument is often asserted without evidence; some is now available, and it is more equivocal than either side allows. Cloudflare, which reports managing traffic for around 20% of the web (Cloudflare, 2025), publishes the ratio of pages crawled by an artificial intelligence platform to visitors that platform refers back. In the first week of August 2025, the ratios were approximately 50,000 to 1 for Anthropic, 887 to 1 for OpenAI, and 118 to 1 for Perplexity. In the news and publications vertical, they were 2,500 to 1, 152 to 1, and 32.7 to 1 respectively (Belson, 2025). On the consumer side, Chapekis and Lieb (2025) found that Google searches producing an artificial intelligence summary yielded a click on a conventional result in 8% of visits, against 15% where no summary appeared; only 1% of visits produced a click on a link inside the summary itself.

Four qualifications rarely travel with these numbers. The first is that the crawl to referral ratios are not a measure of shopping. Cloudflare reports that nearly 80% of this crawling is corpus acquisition for model training rather than mediation of a purchase (Belson, 2025). The second, which the source does not address, is that referral counts may be undercounted where a client sends no referrer header, inflating the apparent asymmetry. The third is that the firm publishing the measurements also sells a product premised on them, having moved to block artificial intelligence crawlers by default and charge for access (Cloudflare, 2025). The fourth is that Google disputed the click study, calling its methodology flawed and its query set unrepresentative of search traffic, though without specifying the flaw (Goodwin, 2025). An independent critique put the sample at roughly 66,000 queries, a very small fraction of Google's monthly volume, with age group margins of error from 7.9 to 13.7 percentage points (Montti, 2025).

Taken together, the data establish that the relationship between publishers and search has changed materially; they do not establish that consumers have delegated purchasing, which is a different claim, and the evidence for it does not exist.

The Case for a Slower Transition

Agentic checkout has not stuck, yet. In March 2026, The Information reported that OpenAI was scaling back plans for purchases completed inside the conversation (Gehan & Muppidi, 2026); the company confirmed that instant checkout was transitioning to merchant applications, where purchases could occur more seamlessly. Trade coverage read the move as evidence that conversational platforms are not displacing applications on the timetable the sector's announcements imply; Shopify's president said only about a dozen Shopify merchants were using the artificial intelligence shopping integrations (Goodwin, 2026). The retreat arrived roughly five months after instant checkout launched, and it concerns the consumer feature rather than the underlying protocol.

The optimization industry around machine visibility is less substantial than its funding suggests. Its foundational citation is a single computer science paper showing that content changes can raise source visibility in generative answers by up to 40% (Aggarwal et al., 2024); that result came from a benchmark against an engine the authors built themselves. On a 200-query subset run against a deployed engine, the same methods gained 22% on one visibility measure and 37% on the other (Aggarwal et al., 2024). The headline figure is, nonetheless, reported as a measured commercial outcome on live systems. Practitioners are among the more skeptical voices. Law (2025) argues that the overlap with search optimization is large enough that treating the two as distinct processes is not useful, and trade coverage records a practitioner estimate that 80% of generative optimization is fundamental search optimization (Guaglione, 2026). Both arguments come from firms with commercial interests in established search optimization, and the position is contested: King argues in the same coverage that generative engines constitute a distinct channel that needs its own treatment, as social media once did (as cited in Guaglione, 2026).

There is a second argument with opposing direction: what matters may not be how many mediated visitors arrive, but what each one is worth. Analytics across 1,277 domains report that visitors arriving from generative systems convert on subscription prompts at roughly three times the rate of search, social, and direct traffic, while remaining under 1% of overall traffic (Rizk, 2025). That figure warrants the caution applied above to Cloudflare and Pew: it is reported on a vendor blog, from the vendor's own analytics product, without independent audit, and a conversion recorded on a subscription prompt is not a purchase.

No peer reviewed study has tested whether mediated traffic converts differently from other traffic, so the direction reported here is a claim awaiting examination rather than a finding, and testing it is a research direction this chapter puts forward.

A bibliometric analysis of 339 peer reviewed articles on brands and artificial intelligence mediated consumer decision making, reported in the preface to this volume (Rach, 2026b), located delegation vocabulary in between one and six articles, depending on specification. Blind manual coding of a stratified sample confirmed a single case and surfaced none that the automated test had missed. The same analysis returned no article using mental availability, physical availability, or category entry points, and, across 11,164 reference instances, no citation of Romaniuk and Sharp (2004), the canonical journal statement of the salience half of that framework. Both results were re-tested against Scopus on 16 September 2026, on a parallel corpus of 648 articles retrieved under equivalent restrictions and searched with the same term families; the near absence of delegation vocabulary and the null result for the availability constructs both replicate, the latter on a field that also searches author keywords and index terms and is therefore more generous than the test it repeats (Rach, 2026b). The six Consensus searches reported in the introduction to this chapter returned the same absence.

Two literatures exist, but do not meet: work on delegation sits in computer science and information systems, brand memory in marketing, and the constructs that would connect them, and the studies that would test the connection, have not been built. Dellaert et al. (2020) set an agenda for exactly this territory six years ago, and André et al. (2018) framed the autonomy question before that. The agenda was not taken up at the pace the technology moved.

FROM ATTENTION SCARCITY TO SELECTION SCARCITY

Asking whether the attention economy is ending treats attention as a single quantity that either binds or does not; the better question is which scarcity binds, and at which point in the decision.

Human attention remains bounded, and nothing about machine mediation expands it; what machine mediation does is remove the purchase decision from the set of things that attention must be spent on. The scarcity does not disappear; the expenditure moves elsewhere. Simon's (1971) claim survives intact, and becomes irrelevant to the transaction at the same time.

What binds at the point of purchase instead is inclusion: a generative answer names a handful of options and a voice interface names one or two, a reduction consumers accept in exchange for efficiency (Dellaert et al., 2020; Mari et al., 2026). The constraint is not how much notice a person can give, but how many slots the system will surface, and on this account properties of the retrieval process decide those slots, not properties of a memory network. This is a scarcity of selection, and its economics differ: attention could, in principle, be purchased at the margin through media weight. A slot in a retrieved source set is not yet purchasable that directly, though platforms are building paid placement into generative surfaces, and an optimization industry already sells indirect access. The difference is the length of the route, not the absence of a market. The reframing also answers the objection raised at the outset; White (2024) and Bruineberg (2026) argue that attention has no stable referent that could be metered, which makes the older framing hard to hold to account. Selection has one. A slot in a retrieved set is discrete and countable, so the objection that weakens the earlier framing supports this one.

The reframing has an immediate analytical benefit, since it converts an unfalsifiable dispute about whether attention still matters into a tractable question about where the binding constraint sits in a given category. The claim is not that the regimes differ by definition, but that regime membership predicts an outcome measured independently of it: in selection limited categories, brand share should track surfacing rate for category prompts more closely than it tracks unaided recall, and the gap between the two should widen with delegation depth. The reframing also predicts heterogeneity rather than a single answer. Where delegation is shallow and the human still selects, attention scarcity binds and the continuity position is correct; where delegation is deep and the system selects, selection scarcity binds and the displacement position is correct.

The two regimes can be distinguished on observable properties: they differ in who performs the final selection, in how wide the choice set is, and therefore how recoverable an omission is, in when brand memory is queried, and in which competitive lever applies. Table 1 summarizes the distinction.

Table 1. Attention scarcity and selection scarcity compared

Property	Attention scarcity regime	Selection scarcity regime
Who selects	The consumer	The system, within granted authority
Binding constraint	Share of a bounded human notice	A slot in a narrow retrieved set
When brand memory is queried	When the consideration set forms, through internal and external search	Earlier, when delegation is configured
Cost of omission	Recoverable; the set is wide	Unrecoverable within the episode; the set is narrow, often a handful of options or fewer
Principal lever	Media weight and distinctiveness	Presence in third party source material
Ownership of the lever	Largely owned by the brand	Only partly owned by the brand
Diagnostic measure	Unaided recall and salience	Surfacing rate for category prompts

One refinement comes from outside marketing: a literature on platform power argues that visibility is not simply a substitute for attention, but a layer inserted above it. O'Reilly et al. (2024) argue that platforms extract what they term algorithmic attention rents because they control the allocation of human attention, not because they have replaced it; attention remains the underlying commodity even where visibility is the proximate contest. Cotter (2019) shows how participants come to treat algorithmic visibility as a rule governed game whose rules they infer and play; Carah (2017) describes brands tuning cultural production to algorithmic decision making rather than to audiences directly.

The implication is that selection scarcity sits on top of attention scarcity rather than replacing it: a slot in a retrieved set is valuable, because a person will eventually read what the system returns. This is why the attention economy is better described as relocating than as ending, and why brands cannot simply abandon one contest for the other.

If selection scarcity binds at the purchase, and attention scarcity continues to bind everywhere else, then brand work does not move from human to machine. It splits. The split is not clean: where the consumer names a brand at configuration, memory still decides and the system executes; where the consumer names a goal, the system decides within the authority granted. Delegation depth is the variable that says which of the two is happening.

The machine facing half concerns inclusion, and its object is the retrieval process: presence and characterization in the third party sources from which answers are assembled, consistent product representation across the listings a system draws on, and attributes that a parser can read. This work has more in common with distribution than with communication and resembles the pursuit of physical availability more than that of mental availability.

The human facing half concerns everything the machine does not decide. Two areas acquire weight. The first is the granting of authority, because delegation is not automatic but granted, withheld, and revised, and the conditions governing it are consumer psychology of an entirely conventional kind. Ahmad Husairi and Rossi (2024) show that perceived choice and decision autonomy govern willingness to hand over control; Mari et al. (2026) show the trade of autonomy against efficiency being made explicitly. A brand that shapes whether and how a consumer delegates has influenced the purchase without competing for a slot.

The second, and the more neglected, is the post purchase experience, whose importance under delegation is not merely that satisfied customers repurchase, but that the mechanism of dissatisfaction changes character. A disappointed customer in an unmediated market switches, and the switch is a decision that must be remade each period, and can be won back by subsequent marketing, whereas a disappointed customer with an agent can instruct that agent, and the instruction persists. Busch (2025) locates the consumer's decision at the earlier moment when the agent is deployed and its parameters, preferences, and permitted suppliers are set. A negative preference expressed once to a system that honors standing instructions is not a lapse in a habit: it is a rule, and it executes without further attention from the person who set it. If standing instructions persist in that way, then under delegation the asymmetry between winning and losing a customer widens, and it widens in favor of losing.

Bilgihan et al. (2025) approach it from the loyalty side. No study was found that examines persistent negative instruction to an agent as a brand outcome.

THE CHOICE LIQUIDITY ARCHITECTURE

The preceding sections set out what the literature can settle and what it cannot: that scarcity survives while allocation and conversion may not, that the dispute plausibly turns on prior equity, and that no body of work connects delegation to brand memory. The framework this chapter presents is built on that ground. It extends choice liquidity (Rach, 2026a), the algorithmically driven reconfiguration of consideration set membership across sequential purchase episodes, from a construct into a three layer architecture, specifying what produces liquidity, what determines inclusion once it is produced, and what accumulates over repeated episodes.

The first layer establishes whether a purchase is delegable at all, and it has two dimensions. The first is delegation depth, the authority a consumer transfers, running from augmentation, where the consumer instructs and confirms, through recommendation and delegated selection to autonomous transaction, where the system chooses and pays within a granted authority. Delegation depth is not perceived decision autonomy, which describes the consumer's felt sense of control rather than the authority actually transferred (Ahmad Husairi & Rossi, 2024), and it is not the levels of automation tradition in human factors, which allocates function between operator and machine across acquisition, analysis, decision, and action (Parasuraman et al., 2000). Marketing has no validated measure of it. Huang and Rust (2021) supply the nearest progression, later arguing that the customer need not be human (Huang & Rust, 2022), but the continuum proposed here is constructed, not inherited.

The second dimension is proxy evaluability, the extent to which a purchase's decisive attributes can be represented in the data a system processes. Proxy evaluability is not involvement, which describes the personal relevance a consumer brings to a category rather than the attribute structure of the purchase (Zaichkowsky, 1985), and it is not the classical separation of search and experience goods (Nelson, 1970), which asks whether an attribute can be assessed before purchase rather than whether a proxy can assess it. It subsumes the utilitarian and hedonic distinction without reducing to it: Longoni and Cian (2022) show that consumers prefer machine recommenders when utilitarian attributes are salient and resist them when hedonic attributes are. Wien and Peluso (2021) find the hedonic half of the same pattern through the different mechanism of mentalizing, showing a human recommender advantage for hedonic but not for utilitarian products. Low proxy evaluability also captures what an agent cannot do because it has no body; Peck and Childers (2003) showed that haptic information matters for products varying on material properties such as texture, hardness, temperature, and weight, and that description only partly substitutes. Lal and Sarvary (1999) formalized the economics: where non digital attributes matter but not overwhelmingly, and shopping is a destination rather than incidental, remote channels can raise prices toward monopoly levels. Consumers stop inspecting, and incumbency hardens into loyalty.

The two dimensions interact rather than combining additively, and the boundary condition is stated in the source literature: Longoni and Cian found that the category effect is eliminated under hybrid human and machine decision making, which is to say that at low delegation depth, proxy evaluability ceases to discriminate. The dependency also runs the other way, since consumers withhold authority in categories whose decisive attributes they believe a system cannot assess. The two dimensions are therefore a conditioning structure rather than orthogonal axes, and purchase situations should migrate along the rising diagonal rather than fill the space. Figure 1 sets out the architecture.

Figure 1. The Choice Liquidity Architecture

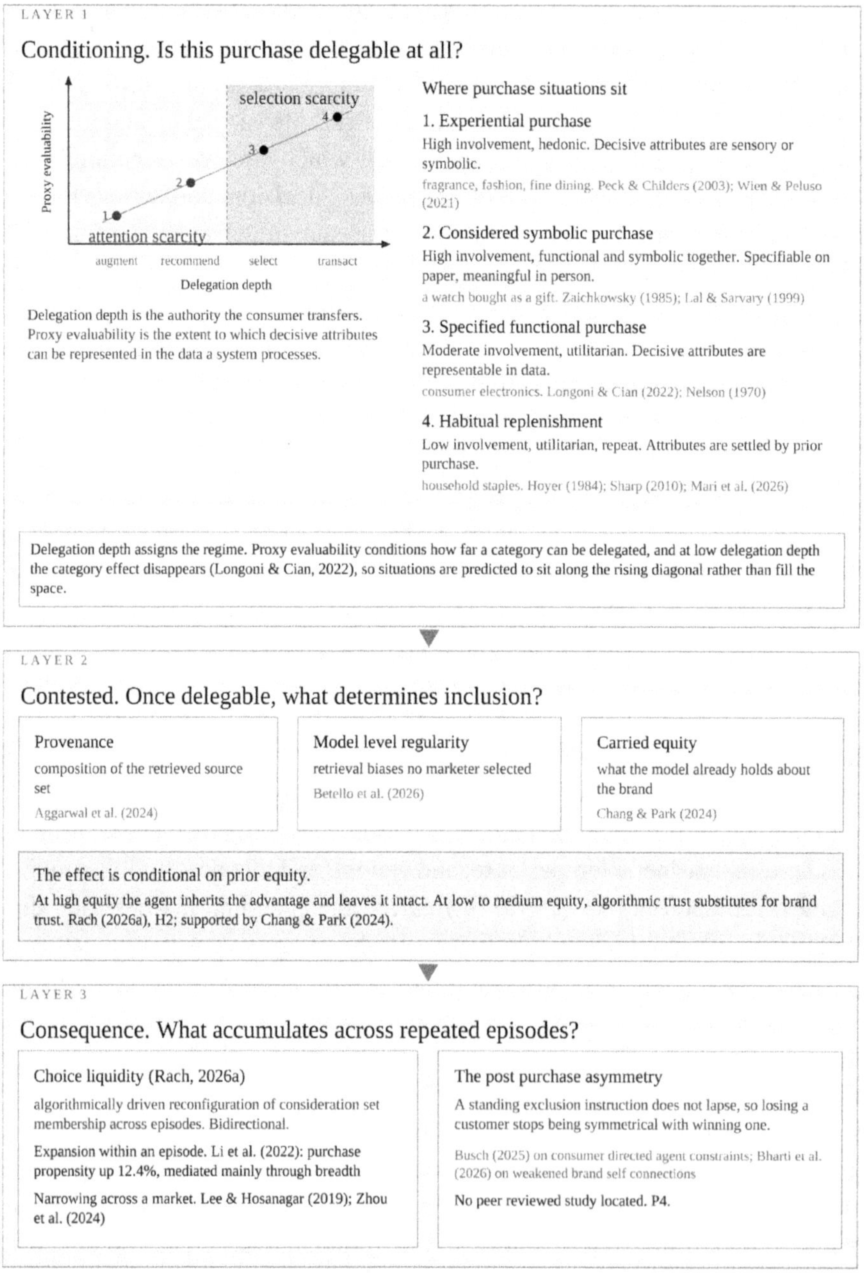

The second layer applies where a purchase is delegable and asks what determines inclusion in the set the system assembles. Three determinants operate. Provenance is the composition of the retrieved source set, which the brand only partly owns (Aggarwal et al., 2024): where proxy evaluability asks whether an attribute can in principle be represented in data, provenance asks whether it has been represented, and by whom. The first is a property of the category, the second of the current corpus, and only the second is manageable. Model level regularity describes retrieval behavior no marketer selected, such as the model specific geographic skew in brand ranking that Betello et al. (2026) document.

The third determinant is carried equity, what the system has already absorbed about the brand, and it resolves the dispute: Chang and Park's (2024) awareness result is the evidence. Read through the architecture, the continuity position describes the high equity case, in which the agent inherits an existing advantage and leaves it intact, whereas the displacement position describes the low and medium equity case, in which algorithmic trust substitutes for brand trust. Chang and Park measured awareness, not equity, so the translation to carried equity is a step this argument takes on its own. The two positions describe different segments of the equity distribution, and Rach (2026a) stated the prediction as a hypothesis.

The third layer describes what accumulates when the process repeats, and this is where choice liquidity operates. It is bidirectional by construction. Within a single episode, personalized recommendation expands the consideration set, and Li et al. (2022) established through causal mediation on a randomized field experiment that this expansion is the mechanism raising purchase propensity by 12.4% and basket value by 1.7%, with breadth mattering far more than depth. Across episodes and across a market, the direction reverses, since Lee and Hosanagar (2019) report from a randomized field experiment that collaborative filters decrease aggregate sales diversity even where individual diversity rises, so that each consumer experiences variety while the market experiences concentration. Zhou et al. (2024) supply the engine, taking as established that recommender predictions bias the ratings consumers subsequently give. They simulate the consequence of feeding those ratings back as training data, and find that less popular and less distinctive items are disproportionately harmed. The echo chamber tendency should be stated precisely: Ge et al. (2020) observed it in click behavior, and found it relatively mitigated in purchase behavior.

The core constructs are measurable. Choice liquidity was specified with three operationalizations: within subject variance in consideration set membership across episodes, the proportion of novel brands introduced per episode, and the Shannon entropy of the brand distribution (Rach, 2026a). Delegation depth can be measured for a category as the share of transactions in which a system performs the final selection, and proxy evaluability as the share of a category's decisive attributes that consumers rate as assessable from a written description alone. Carried equity can be measured as a brand's unprompted surfacing rate across a fixed panel of category entry point prompts, held constant across model versions and disjoint from the prompts used to measure the outcome, so that it is observed before, and separately from, the share it predicts. If a standing exclusion instruction does not lapse, losing a customer stops being symmetrical with winning one. Busch (2025) locates the design requirements consumer law must reach at the moment the agent's parameters are set, and Bharti et al. (2026) find that machine recommendation weakens brand self connections.

Five propositions follow. Table 2 states each with its current evidential status.

Table 2. Propositions of the Choice Liquidity Architecture and their evidential status

Proposition	Statement	Evidential status
P1	In selection limited categories, brand share tracks surfacing rate for category prompts more closely than it tracks unaided recall, and the gap widens with delegation depth	Untested as stated; the component evidence on category moderation is strong
P2	The effect of machine mediation on brand advantage is conditional on prior equity, substituting for brand trust at low and medium equity and leaving it intact at high equity	Partially supported for brand awareness (Chang & Park, 2024); untested at full delegation
P3	The within episode expansion and cross market concentration documented for recommender systems intensify with delegation depth, so categories with transacting agents show greater aggregate concentration than matched categories with recommendation only	The component findings are supported by two randomized field experiments (Lee & Hosanagar, 2019; Li et al., 2022) and one simulation (Zhou et al., 2024); the extension to transacting agents is untested
P4	Dissatisfaction expressed as a standing instruction produces a longer and less recoverable exclusion than dissatisfaction expressed as switching	Untested; no peer reviewed study located
P5	A brand's surfacing rate in a generative channel is predicted more strongly by its presence and characterization in third party sources than by the strength of its owned distinctive assets	Mechanism demonstrated in computer science on a self built engine, with smaller gains on a deployed one (Aggarwal et al., 2024); untested in consumer categories

IMPLICATIONS FOR BRAND MANAGEMENT

This chapter proposes five implications for brand management, the first being diagnostic: a firm should locate its category on the two conditioning dimensions, measured as the share of transactions in which a system performs the final selection, and the share of decisive attributes assessable from a written description alone. The regime determines which of the four that follow apply.

Second, measurement: brand tracking measures human retrieval through awareness, consideration, and preference, so if a material share of category demand routes through an intermediary, those instruments describe a shrinking portion of the outcome. The response is to add a second series, recording what intermediaries surface for category relevant prompts, and to track both, treating divergence between them as a finding rather than as noise. Such a series earns its place, the way mindset metrics did, by adding explanatory power beyond the marketing mix variables already in the model (Srinivasan et al., 2010). It must first demonstrate test retest reliability; the behavior of a given model service can change substantially between versions (Chen et al., 2024), and outputs are sensitive to semantically equivalent changes in prompt formatting (Sclar et al., 2024).

Third, where asset investment is directed: if inclusion in a retrieved set is determined partly by third party sources, then those sources are a distinct object of management from the owned asset portfolio; they are not obviously the responsibility of any existing function. Retailer listings, review aggregators, and editorial coverage sit conventionally with channel management or public relations rather than with brand management. Under machine mediation, they are inputs to brand visibility.

Fourth, creative allocation: if machine oriented optimization crowds out human oriented work by default, rather than by decision, then the allocation between them should be made explicit and defended, rather than allowed to drift. A firm that cannot say what share of its brand investment goes to inclusion, and what share to meaning, is not making the trade-off; it is having it made by whichever objective is easier to measure.

Fifth, the post purchase asymmetry. If negative instruction to an agent persists in a way that ordinary defection does not, then service recovery is worth more than conventional models allow, since customer equity models derive lifetime value from brand switching patterns, which assume a departed customer can still switch back (Rust et al., 2004). Firms in categories with meaningful delegation should test that assumption before relying on it.

FUTURE RESEARCH DIRECTIONS

The five propositions in Table 2 are the primary agenda, since each is stated so that it can be tested or dismissed, and three further questions arise that the framework does not settle. First, provenance: if a brand's representation in a generative channel is predicted less by its own assets than by its presence and characterization in third party sources, then the lever for mediated visibility sits largely outside the owned estate. Aggarwal et al. (2024) demonstrate the mechanism on a self built engine; P5 states the consumer category version.

Second, the applied framework: the most direct contribution available is to test whether these constructs survive translation. Are mental availability and machine retrieval empirically separable? Do category entry points and the prompts consumers address to intermediaries overlap only partially, with the divergence a measurable property of a category, rather than a constant?

Third, cultural consequence. Advertising creates shared meaning through common exposure (McCracken, 1986; Ritson & Elliott, 1999), and machine mediation accelerates the shift from mass to personalized delivery, so the cultural function of advertising may attenuate for reasons unrelated to the purchase mechanism. Whether personalization reduces the shared cultural stock of brand meaning has not been asked in this form.

SCOPE AND LIMITATIONS

Four limitations bound the argument of this chapter.

The first is that the evidence base is thin and unevenly distributed. The strongest empirical results available concern voice assistants and recommender systems, which are mediation but not delegation in the full sense, since the consumer still confirms; the transition at issue, from a system that arranges options to one that selects and transacts, is the transition on which almost no peer reviewed evidence exists.

The second is that several load bearing sources are recent, and some are not yet in final form; advance online publications have not settled into volumes, and proceedings papers in new venues have not accumulated scrutiny.

The third is that the applied dispute, which motivates the chapter, is conducted outside the peer reviewed record. Positions attributed here to individual scholars are drawn from public professional commentary, rather than from published work, and they are cited as evidence of what the applied field believes rather than as findings.

The fourth is that the chapter is written from inside marketing, and inherits its vocabulary. A treatment grounded in information systems or human computer interaction would frame delegation as an allocation of function between human and machine, would draw more fully on the automation and trust literature that this chapter uses only to bound the delegation depth construct, and might arrive at different constructs.

CONCLUSION

The attention economy is not ending, but it is ceasing to be the right unit of analysis for the purchase itself (Hansen, 2024). Human attention remains as scarce as Simon (1971) described it, and no development in machine mediation makes it less so. What is ending, in a growing set of categories, is the assumption that the purchase decision is one of the things that scarce attention is spent on.

That is a narrower claim than the death of the attention economy, and a more useful one, because it identifies what actually changes: when a system performs the selection, the binding constraint at the moment of purchase shifts from a share of notice to a slot in a set, and the determinants of that slot are only partly owned by the brand. Brand work does not thereby move from human to machine. It divides, with the machine facing half concerned with inclusion and resembling distribution more than communication, and the human facing half concerned with the granting of authority beforehand and the experience afterward.

Under delegation, a dissatisfied customer no longer merely switches: a customer with an agent can encode dissatisfaction as a standing instruction, and if standing instructions do not lapse, the exclusion outlasts any single campaign. Marketing has spent a century learning how to be remembered; it has spent very little time on how not to be permanently excluded.

Neither position is established, and neither is settled here; the two describe different regimes. The Choice Liquidity Architecture specifies which regime applies and why, through three questions: is the purchase delegable, what determines inclusion once it is, and what accumulates over repeated episodes.

DECLARATION OF GENERATIVE AI USE

Generative artificial intelligence was used in preparing this chapter and is disclosed here as required. Claude (Anthropic) assisted with language editing to improve readability, with locating candidate literature, and with checking bibliographic details against Crossref and publisher records. Consensus was used to search the peer reviewed record.

All intellectual content is the author's own, including the research question, the argument, the reframing and framework proposed here, the propositions and every conclusion drawn. No generative system is credited as an author, and the author takes full responsibility for the content.

One further disclosure is owed. The author is the editor of this volume, and two of the sources this chapter relies on are his own: a conference paper that supplies the choice liquidity construct and the propositions built on it, and the preface, which reports the bibliometric analysis cited here. Both are identified at each use.

REFERENCES

Aggarwal, P., Murahari, V., Rajpurohit, T., Kalyan, A., Narasimhan, K., & Deshpande, A. (2024). GEO: Generative engine optimization. In *Proceedings of the 30th ACM SIGKDD Conference on Knowledge Discovery and Data Mining* (pp. 5–16). Association for Computing Machinery. DOI: 10.1145/3637528.3671900

Ahmad Husairi, M., & Rossi, P. (2024). Delegation of purchasing tasks to AI: The role of perceived choice and decision autonomy. *Decision Support Systems, 179*, 114166. DOI: 10.1016/j.dss.2023.114166

André, Q., Carmon, Z., Wertenbroch, K., Crum, A., Frank, D., Goldstein, W., Huber, J., van Boven, L., Weber, B., & Yang, H. (2018). Consumer choice and autonomy in the age of artificial intelligence and big data. *Customer Needs and Solutions, 5*(1–2), 28–37. DOI: 10.1007/s40547-017-0085-8

Anesbury, Z., Nenycz-Thiel, M., Dawes, J., & Kennedy, R. (2016). How do shoppers behave online? An observational study of online grocery shopping. *Journal of Consumer Behaviour, 15*(3), 261–270. DOI: 10.1002/cb.1566

Belson, D. (2025, August 28). A deeper look at AI crawlers: Breaking down traffic by purpose and industry. *Cloudflare Blog*. https://blog.cloudflare.com/ai-crawler-traffic-by-purpose-and-industry/

Betello, F., Missault, P., Czinczoll, T., & Beliuha, M. (2026). Your LLM has a passport: Investigating brand origin geographic bias in e-commerce rankings. In *Proceedings of the 2026 ACM Conference on Fairness, Accountability, and Transparency* (pp. 8089–8106). Association for Computing Machinery. DOI: 10.1145/3805689.3806438

Bharti, M., Bharti, M., Wani, T., & Shahid, S. (2026). The FOMO effect: How AI recommendations drive consumer dependence and weaken brand-self connections. *Journal of Consumer Behaviour, 25*(3), 1078–1106. DOI: 10.1002/cb.70117

Bilgihan, A., Ostinelli, M., Zhang, Y., & Lorenz, M. (2025). Artificial intelligence (AI) agents and the future of customer loyalty. *International Journal of Contemporary Hospitality Management, 37*(9), 3240–3262. DOI: 10.1108/IJCHM-03-2025-0373

Boerman, S. C., Kruikemeier, S., & Zuiderveen Borgesius, F. J. (2017). Online behavioral advertising: A literature review and research agenda. *Journal of Advertising, 46*(3), 363–376. DOI: 10.1080/00913367.2017.1339368

Broadbent, S., & Fry, T. (1995). Adstock modelling for the long term. *Journal of the Market Research Society, 37*(4), 1–18. DOI: 10.1177/147078539503700404

Bruineberg, J. (2026). Rethinking the cognitive foundations of the attention economy. *Philosophical Psychology, 39*(6), 2400–2422. DOI: 10.1080/09515089.2025.2502428

Busch, C. (2025). Consumer law for AI agents. *German Law Journal, 26*(7), 1367–1382. DOI: 10.1017/glj.2026.10188

Carah, N. (2017). Algorithmic brands: A decade of brand experiments with mobile and social media. *New Media & Society, 19*(3), 384–400. DOI: 10.1177/1461444815605463

Chandon, P., Hutchinson, J. W., Bradlow, E. T., & Young, S. H. (2009). Does in-store marketing work? Effects of the number and position of shelf facings on brand attention and evaluation at the point of purchase. *Journal of Marketing, 73*(6), 1–17. DOI: 10.1509/jmkg.73.6.1

Chang, W., & Park, J. (2024). A comparative study on the effect of ChatGPT recommendation and AI recommender systems on the formation of a consideration set. *Journal of Retailing and Consumer Services, 78*, 103743. DOI: 10.1016/j.jretconser.2024.103743

Chapekis, A., & Lieb, A. (2025, July 22). *Google users are less likely to click on links when an AI summary appears in the results.* Pew Research Center. https://www.pewresearch.org/short-reads/2025/07/22/google-users-are-less-likely-to-click-on-links-when-an-ai-summary-appears-in-the-results/

Chen, L., Zaharia, M., & Zou, J. (2024). How is ChatGPT's behavior changing over time? *Harvard Data Science Review, 6*(2). Advance online publication. DOI: 10.1162/99608f92.5317da47

Clark, D. (2026, April 13). *Meta to surpass Google in digital ad revenues for first time ever* [Press release]. EMARKETER. https://www.emarketer.com/press-releases/meta-to-surpass-google-in-digital-ad-revenues-for-first-time-ever/

Cloudflare. (2025, July 1). *Cloudflare just changed how AI crawlers scrape the internet-at-large* [Press release]. https://www.cloudflare.com/press/press-releases/2025/cloudflare-just-changed-how-ai-crawlers-scrape-the-internet-at-large/

Consensus. (n.d.). *Consensus research database.* https://help.consensus.app/en/articles/10055108-consensus-research-database

Cotter, K. (2019). Playing the visibility game: How digital influencers and algorithms negotiate influence on Instagram. *New Media & Society, 21*(4), 895–913. DOI: 10.1177/1461444818815684

Cui, Y. G., & van Esch, P. (2025). The end of search as we know it: Only those chosen by AI agents will survive in the delegate economy. *Business Horizons*. Advance online publication. DOI: 10.1016/j.bushor.2025.11.006

Davenport, T. H., & Beck, J. C. (2001). *The attention economy: Understanding the new currency of business*. Harvard Business School Press.

de Bellis, E., & Johar, G. V. (2020). Autonomous shopping systems: Identifying and overcoming barriers to consumer adoption. *Journal of Retailing*, *96*(1), 74–87. DOI: 10.1016/j.jretai.2019.12.004

Dellaert, B. G. C., Shu, S. B., Arentze, T. A., Baker, T., Diehl, K., Donkers, B., Fast, N. J., Häubl, G., Johnson, H., Karmarkar, U. R., Oppewal, H., Schmitt, B. H., Schroeder, J., Spiller, S. A., & Steffel, M. (2020). Consumer decisions with artificially intelligent voice assistants. *Marketing Letters*, *31*(4), 335–347. DOI: 10.1007/s11002-020-09537-5

Diehl, K., Kornish, L. J., & Lynch, J. G.Jr. (2003). Smart agents: When lower search costs for quality information increase price sensitivity. *The Journal of Consumer Research*, *30*(1), 56–71. DOI: 10.1086/374698

Ehrenberg, A. S. C., Goodhardt, G. J., & Barwise, T. P. (1990). Double jeopardy revisited. *Journal of Marketing*, *54*(3), 82–91. DOI: 10.1177/002224299005400307

Falkinger, J. (2007). Attention economies. *Journal of Economic Theory*, *133*(1), 266–294. DOI: 10.1016/j.jet.2005.12.001

Falkinger, J. (2008). Limited attention as a scarce resource in information-rich economies. *Economic Journal (London)*, *118*(532), 1596–1620. DOI: 10.1111/j.1468-0297.2008.02182.x

Ge, Y., Zhao, S., Zhou, H., Pei, C., Sun, F., Ou, W., & Zhang, Y. (2020). Understanding echo chambers in e-commerce recommender systems. In *Proceedings of the 43rd International ACM SIGIR Conference on Research and Development in Information Retrieval* (pp. 2261–2270). Association for Computing Machinery. DOI: 10.1145/3397271.3401431

Gehan, A., & Muppidi, S. (2026, March 5). OpenAI scales back shopping plans for ChatGPT. *The Information*. https://www.theinformation.com/articles/openai-scales-back-shopping-plans-chatgpt

Goldhaber, M. H. (1997). The attention economy and the Net. *First Monday*, *2*(4). Advance online publication. DOI: 10.5210/fm.v2i4.519

Goodwin, D. (2025, July 24). Google's AI Overviews are hurting clicks: Pew study. *Search Engine Land.* https://searchengineland.com/google-ai-overviews-hurting-clicks-study-459434

Goodwin, D. (2026, March 6). OpenAI's big ChatGPT Instant Checkout plan just changed. *Search Engine Land.* https://searchengineland.com/chatgpt-instant-checkout-plan-change-471033

Guaglione, S. (2026, March 10). GEO hype busted: How it differs (and how it doesn't) from SEO. *Digiday.* https://digiday.com/media/geo-hype-busted-experts-call-it-more-seo-than-new-discipline/

Hansen, M. (2024). From attention economy to cognitive lock-ins. *Big Data & Society, 11*(3), 20539517241275878. DOI: 10.1177/20539517241275878

Häubl, G., & Trifts, V. (2000). Consumer decision making in online shopping environments: The effects of interactive decision aids. *Marketing Science, 19*(1), 4–21. DOI: 10.1287/mksc.19.1.4.15178

Heitmayer, M. (2025). The second wave of attention economics: Attention as a universal symbolic currency on social media and beyond. *Interacting with Computers, 37*(1), 18–29. DOI: 10.1093/iwc/iwae035

Holland, A. (2026, June 2). How "it's just SEO" took over the GEO conversation. *Search Engine Land.* https://searchengineland.com/its-just-seo-geo-conversation-479158

Hoyer, W. D. (1984). An examination of consumer decision making for a common repeat purchase product. *The Journal of Consumer Research, 11*(3), 822–829. DOI: 10.1086/209017

Huang, M.-H., & Rust, R. T. (2021). Engaged to a robot? The role of AI in service. *Journal of Service Research, 24*(1), 30–41. DOI: 10.1177/1094670520902266

Huang, M.-H., & Rust, R. T. (2022). AI as customer. *Journal of Service Management, 33*(2), 210–220. DOI: 10.1108/JOSM-11-2021-0425

Keller, K. L. (1993). Conceptualizing, measuring, and managing customer-based brand equity. *Journal of Marketing, 57*(1), 1–22. DOI: 10.1177/002224299305700101

Klaus, P., & Zaichkowsky, J. L. (2020). AI voice bots: A services marketing research agenda. *Journal of Services Marketing, 34*(3), 389–398. DOI: 10.1108/JSM-01-2019-0043

Klaus, P., & Zaichkowsky, J. L. (2022). The convenience of shopping via voice AI: Introducing AIDM. *Journal of Retailing and Consumer Services, 65*, 102490. DOI: 10.1016/j.jretconser.2021.102490

Kübler, K. (2023). Influencers and the attention economy: The meaning and management of attention on Instagram. *Journal of Marketing Management, 39*(11–12), 965–981. DOI: 10.1080/0267257X.2022.2157864

Kulp, P. (2026, April 7). How Meta's AI push is changing ad creation. *Marketing Brew*. https://www.marketingbrew.com/stories/2026/04/07/meta-ai-ad-creation

Lal, R., & Sarvary, M. (1999). When and how is the Internet likely to decrease price competition? *Marketing Science, 18*(4), 485–503. DOI: 10.1287/mksc.18.4.485

Law, R. (2025, April 7). GEO, LLMO, AEO: It's all just SEO. *Ahrefs Blog*. https://ahrefs.com/blog/geo-is-just-seo/

Lee, D., & Hosanagar, K. (2019). How do recommender systems affect sales diversity? A cross-category investigation via randomized field experiment. *Information Systems Research, 30*(1), 239–259. DOI: 10.1287/isre.2018.0800

Li, X., Grahl, J., & Hinz, O. (2022). How do recommender systems lead to consumer purchases? A causal mediation analysis of a field experiment. *Information Systems Research, 33*(2), 620–637. DOI: 10.1287/isre.2021.1074

Longoni, C., & Cian, L. (2022). Artificial intelligence in utilitarian vs. hedonic contexts: The "word-of-machine" effect. *Journal of Marketing, 86*(1), 91–108. DOI: 10.1177/0022242920957347

Mari, A., Mandelli, A., & Algesheimer, R. (2026). AI-assisted shopping on voice assistants: The efficiency-autonomy consumer decision trade-off. *Journal of Interactive Marketing, 61*(3), 327–344. DOI: 10.1177/10949968251400616

McCracken, G. (1986). Culture and consumption: A theoretical account of the structure and movement of the cultural meaning of consumer goods. *The Journal of Consumer Research, 13*(1), 71–84. DOI: 10.1086/209048

Mehmet, M. (2025). From search rankings to synthesised answers: Propositions for consumer behaviour in the age of generative AI search. *Journal of Consumer Behaviour, 24*(6), 2948–2950. DOI: 10.1002/cb.70044

Mo, L., Sands, S., & Leckie, C. (2026). Outsourcing choice: AI voice assistants as shopping surrogates. *Journal of Retailing and Consumer Services, 89*, 104657. DOI: 10.1016/j.jretconser.2025.104657

Montti, R. (2025, July 24). Validity of Pew research on Google AI search results challenged. *Search Engine Journal*. https://www.searchenginejournal.com/validity-of-pew-research-on-google-ai-search-results-challenged/552055/

Nedungadi, P. (1990). Recall and consumer consideration sets: Influencing choice without altering brand evaluations. *The Journal of Consumer Research*, *17*(3), 263–276. DOI: 10.1086/208556

Nelson, P. (1970). Information and consumer behavior. *Journal of Political Economy*, *78*(2), 311–329. DOI: 10.1086/259630

Nelson-Field, K. (2026, March 17). *Why your AI needs a human trainer: The future of attention*. Think with Google. https://business.google.com/uk/think/future-of-marketing/future-of-attention-human-centric-ai-marketing/

O'Reilly, T., Strauss, I., & Mazzucato, M. (2024). Algorithmic attention rents: A theory of digital platform market power. *Data & Policy*, *6*, e6. DOI: 10.1017/dap.2024.1

Open, A. I. (2025, September 29). *Buy it in ChatGPT: Instant Checkout and the Agentic Commerce Protocol*. https://openai.com/index/buy-it-in-chatgpt/

Parasuraman, R., Sheridan, T. B., & Wickens, C. D. (2000). A model for types and levels of human interaction with automation. *IEEE Transactions on Systems, Man, and Cybernetics. Part A, Systems and Humans*, *30*(3), 286–297. DOI: 10.1109/3468.844354

Patilinet, S. (2024, September 19). Attention is advertising's currency, let's agree on its value. *Marketing Week*. https://www.marketingweek.com/attention-currency-marketing-value/

Pauwels, K. (2026, April 12). *Who owns the web when agents browse?* [Post]. LinkedIn. https://www.linkedin.com/pulse/who-owns-web-when-agents-browse-prof-dr-koen-pauwels-qmbre

Peck, J., & Childers, T. L. (2003). To have and to hold: The influence of haptic information on product judgments. *Journal of Marketing*, *67*(2), 35–48. DOI: 10.1509/jmkg.67.2.35.18612

Perplexity, A. I. (2024, November 18). *Shop like a pro: Perplexity's new AI-powered shopping assistant*. https://www.perplexity.ai/hub/blog/shop-like-a-pro

Puntoni, S., Reczek, R. W., Giesler, M., & Botti, S. (2021). Consumers and artificial intelligence: An experiential perspective. *Journal of Marketing*, *85*(1), 131–151. DOI: 10.1177/0022242920953847

Rach, M. (2026a). Algorithmic trust and choice liquidity: A dual-pathway framework for AI-mediated consumer decision architecture. In *Proceedings of the International Conference on Artificial Intelligence Management and Trends* (pp. 85–88). Abu Dhabi School of Management.

Rach, M. (2026b). Preface. In Rach, M. (Ed.), *Autonomous decision systems, consumer behavior, and the future of branding in the age of intelligence*. IGI Global.

Ritson, M. (2026, June 22). Mark Ritson: Claude is my Cannes bartender. My AI agent is favoring established brands. *The Drum*. https://www.thedrum.com/opinion/mark-ritson-ai-agents-are-already-learning-which-brands-to-pick

Ritson, M., & Elliott, R. (1999). The social uses of advertising: An ethnographic study of adolescent advertising audiences. *The Journal of Consumer Research, 26*(3), 260–277. DOI: 10.1086/209562

Rizk, I. (2025, November 6). AI traffic converts at 3x the rate of other channels (study). *Microsoft Clarity Blog*. https://clarity.microsoft.com/blog/ai-traffic-converts-at-3x-the-rate-of-other-channels-study/

Roach, T. (2024, July 11). "Share of model" is the new marketing measure for the AI era. *Marketing Week*. https://www.marketingweek.com/tom-roach-share-of-model-ai-era/

Roach, T. (2025, November 20). Winning hearts, minds and models: Brand building in an AI world. *Tom Roach*. https://thetomroach.com/2025/11/20/winning-hearts-minds-and-models-brand-building-in-an-ai-world/

Rohden, S. F., Espartel, L. B., & Lopes, J. C. (2025). From voice to choice: Understanding the consumer response to voice assistant and human recommendations. *International Journal of Consumer Studies, 49*(6), e70128. DOI: 10.1111/ijcs.70128

Romaniuk, J. (2018). *Building distinctive brand assets*. Oxford University Press.

Romaniuk, J., & Sharp, B. (2004). Conceptualizing and measuring brand salience. *Marketing Theory, 4*(4), 327–342. DOI: 10.1177/1470593104047643

Romaniuk, J., Sharp, B., & Ehrenberg, A. S. C. (2007). Evidence concerning the importance of perceived brand differentiation. *Australasian Marketing Journal, 15*(2), 42–54. DOI: 10.1016/S1441-3582(07)70042-3

Rust, R. T., Lemon, K. N., & Zeithaml, V. A. (2004). Return on marketing: Using customer equity to focus marketing strategy. *Journal of Marketing, 68*(1), 109–127. DOI: 10.1509/jmkg.68.1.109.24030

Sarstedt, M., Adler, S. J., & Imschloss, M. (2026). Machine marketing: Rethinking the customer in the age of generative AI. *Journal of Marketing Analytics*. Advance online publication. DOI: 10.1057/s41270-026-00521-y

Sclar, M., Choi, Y., Tsvetkov, Y., & Suhr, A. (2024). Quantifying language models' sensitivity to spurious features in prompt design [Conference session]. *The Twelfth International Conference on Learning Representations*. DOI: 10.48550/arXiv.2310.11324

Sharp, B. (2010). *How brands grow: What marketers don't know*. Oxford University Press.

Sharp, B. (2026, June 26). *No that's not what I said* [Post]. LinkedIn. https://www.linkedin.com/posts/professorbyronsharp_byron-sharp-appeared-to-go-on-record-this-activity-7476139656070402048-oJWk

Simon, H. A. (1971). Designing organizations for an information-rich world. In Greenberger, M. (Ed.), *Computers, communications, and the public interest* (pp. 37–72). The Johns Hopkins Press.

Simonov, A., Valletti, T., & Veiga, A. (2025). Attention spillovers from news to ads: Evidence from an eye-tracking experiment. *JMR, Journal of Marketing Research*, *62*(2), 294–315. DOI: 10.1177/00222437241256900

Solomon, M. R. (1986). The missing link: Surrogate consumers in the marketing chain. *Journal of Marketing*, *50*(4), 208–218. DOI: 10.1177/002224298605000406

Srinivasan, S., Vanhuele, M., & Pauwels, K. (2010). Mind-set metrics in market response models: An integrative approach. *JMR, Journal of Marketing Research*, *47*(4), 672–684. DOI: 10.1509/jmkr.47.4.672

System1 Group & IPA. (2025). *The magic of compound creativity* [Report]. https://system1group.com/compound-creativity-system1-ipa

Thompson, B. (2025, May 1). An interview with Meta CEO Mark Zuckerberg about AI and the evolution of social media. *Stratechery*. https://stratechery.com/2025/an-interview-with-meta-ceo-mark-zuckerberg-about-ai-and-the-evolution-of-social-media/

van Esch, P., & Cui, Y. G. (2026). Agentic brand drift: How AI-orchestrated organizations will lose their identity and how to get it back. *Business Horizons*. Advance online publication. DOI: 10.1016/j.bushor.2026.05.013

Wang, R., Lu, X., & Wang, X. (2025). Decision agency: How can generative AI reconstruct consumer behavior in trendy toys? In *Proceedings of the 2025 International Conference on Generative Artificial Intelligence for Business* (pp. 375–382). Association for Computing Machinery. DOI: 10.1145/3766918.3766980

Wedel, M., & Pieters, R. (2000). Eye fixations on advertisements and memory for brands: A model and findings. *Marketing Science*, *19*(4), 297–312. DOI: 10.1287/mksc.19.4.297.11794

White, D. J. (2024). Paying attention to attention: Psychological realism and the attention economy. *Synthese*, *203*(2), 43. Advance online publication. DOI: 10.1007/s11229-023-04460-4

Wien, A. H., & Peluso, A. M. (2021). Influence of human versus AI recommenders: The roles of product type and cognitive processes. *Journal of Business Research*, *137*, 13–27. DOI: 10.1016/j.jbusres.2021.08.016

Yin, S., Fu, C., Zhao, S., Li, K., Sun, X., Xu, T., & Chen, E. (2024). A survey on multimodal large language models. *National Science Review*, *11*(12), nwae403. Advance online publication. DOI: 10.1093/nsr/nwae403

Zaichkowsky, J. L. (1985). Measuring the involvement construct. *The Journal of Consumer Research*, *12*(3), 341–352. DOI: 10.1086/208520

Zhou, M., Zhang, J., & Adomavicius, G. (2024). Longitudinal impact of preference biases on recommender systems' performance. *Information Systems Research*, *35*(4), 1634–1656. DOI: 10.1287/isre.2021.0133

Zuckerberg, M. (2025, May 6). *A conversation with Mark Zuckerberg* [Conference session]. Stripe Sessions 2025, San Francisco, CA, United States. https://stripe.com/sessions/2025/a-conversation-with-mark-zuckerberg

KEY TERMS AND DEFINITIONS

Agentic System: A computational system that accepts a goal from a consumer and executes the sequence of steps required to satisfy it, including selection and transaction, within an authority the consumer has granted.

Attention Economy: The framework holding that human attention is the binding scarce resource in an information rich environment, that signals compete for a share of it, and that a secured share can be converted into memory that later influences choice.

Carried Equity: What a generative system has already absorbed about a brand, observable as the brand's unprompted surfacing rate across a fixed panel of category entry point prompts. It is a machine side analogue of brand equity rather than brand equity itself, since a system has no consumer response.

Choice Liquidity: The algorithmically driven reconfiguration of consideration set membership across sequential purchase episodes, treated as a property of the decision environment rather than of any single decision.

Delegation: The transfer of a defined portion of purchasing authority from a consumer to a system, bounded by category, budget or occasion, and revocable by the consumer.

Delegation Depth: The degree of purchasing authority a consumer transfers to a system, running from augmentation, where the consumer instructs and confirms, to autonomous transaction, where the system selects and pays within a granted authority.

Generative Engine Optimization: The practice of altering content so that a brand or source is more likely to be retrieved and cited within an answer synthesized by a generative system.

Mental Availability: The propensity of a brand to be thought of in a buying situation, understood as a function of the number and quality of the memory structures linking it to category entry points.

Proxy Evaluability: The extent to which the attributes decisive for a purchase can be represented in the data a system processes, which is low where judgment depends on sensory inspection or on experiential attributes.

Selection Scarcity: The condition in which the binding constraint at the point of purchase is the number of slots an intermediary will surface, rather than the quantity of human attention available.

Chapter 3

From Narrative to Reality: The Evolution of Immersiveness in Advertising

Aikaterini Katsota
FCH/Universidade Católica Portuguesa, Lisbon, Portugal

Alexandre Duarte
http://orcid.org/0000-0002-2665-864X
ICNOVA - FCSH/Universidade Nova de Lisboa, Lisboa, Portugal

ABSTRACT

This article explores how advertising persuasion changes as brand communication shifts from traditional narrative-driven storytelling to immersive, technology-powered experiences. While narrative transportation has been a key factor in advertising, the rise of extended reality (XR) technology and the metaverse question whether narrative-based models are sufficient for understanding its influence. This chapter presents a conceptual framework that redefines advertising persuasion as an embodied, participatory process. The framework describes a progression from narrative transportation toward "story-doing," where consumers actively bring brand meanings to life, and highlights key mechanisms that shape immersive persuasion, along with boundary conditions such as cognitive load, technological readiness, and ethical design. This conceptual work enhances advertising theory by combining psychological and technological perspectives on immersion, providing managerial insights for developing effective immersion-based advertising strategies.

DOI: 10.4018/979-8-3373-9589-0.ch003

INTRODUCTION

Storytelling has long been recognized as one of the most effective persuasive strategies in advertising, evolving from a creative communication technique into a theoretically grounded branding approach that shapes how consumers make meaning (Duarte & Soeiro, 2025). Narrative advertising helps consumers organize brand-related information through coherent story structures that stimulate emotional engagement, vivid mental imagery, and identification with protagonists. Central to this process is narrative transportation, a psychological state in which individuals become mentally immersed in a story world, temporarily reducing counterarguing and increasing favorable attitudes toward both the narrative and the advertised brand (Green & Brock, 2000; Escalas, 2007; Kang et al., 2020). Consequently, narrative advertising has consistently been linked to stronger brand evaluations, improved memory, and deeper consumer–brand relationships (Lundqvist et al., 2013; Kim et al., 2017).

Recent technological developments, however, challenge the assumption that symbolic narratives primarily drive advertising persuasion. The rapid adoption of Extended Reality (XR) technologies, including Augmented Reality (AR), Virtual Reality (VR), and Mixed Reality (MR) has transformed how consumers experience brand communication by replacing passive observation with active participation. Rather than merely imagining branded experiences, consumers increasingly interact with virtual products, navigate immersive environments, and embody digital identities through avatars (Milgram et al., 1995; Bailenson, 2018; Xi et al., 2023). These developments reposition immersion from a predominantly psychological phenomenon toward an embodied and technologically mediated experience.

This transformation becomes even more significant within the Metaverse, understood not simply as a collection of virtual worlds but as a persistent sociotechnical ecosystem characterized by interoperability, continuous social interaction, and digital ownership (Ball, 2022; Dolata & Schwabe, 2023; Njoku et al., 2023). In these environments, advertising extends beyond message delivery to become part of the lived experience itself. Brands no longer communicate exclusively through predefined narratives but increasingly construct environments in which consumers participate, interact, and co-create value over time (de Regt et al., 2021; Dwivedi et al., 2022).

An equally important driver of this transformation is the growing integration of artificial intelligence (AI) and autonomous decision systems into immersive environments. AI-powered recommender systems increasingly determine which branded experiences consumers encounter, while machine learning algorithms personalize virtual environments, recommend digital products, adapt narrative pathways, and optimize advertising content in real time according to behavioral data. Likewise, generative AI enables brands to create dynamic virtual assets, conversational agents, and personalized interactions that evolve continuously as users engage with immersive environments. As autonomous systems assume greater responsibility for selecting, adapting, and delivering persuasive experiences, advertising becomes not only immersive but also algorithmically responsive, raising new theoretical questions regarding persuasion, agency, transparency, and consumer autonomy.

The concepts of immersion, presence, embodiment, and interactivity therefore distinguish immersive advertising from traditional communication models. Technological immersion refers to the objective characteristics of a mediated environment, including sensory richness, realism, responsiveness, and interactivity, that facilitate the subjective experience of presence, or the psychological sensation of "being there" (Slater & Wilbur, 1997; Cummings & Bailenson, 2015). Presence subsequently enables embodiment, whereby consumers perceive virtual bodies or avatars as extensions of themselves, allowing branded experiences to become directly integrated into identity construction (Bailenson, 2018; Persky & Colloca, 2023). Rather than interpreting brand meaning symbolically, consumers increasingly enact that meaning through interaction, exploration, and social participation.

Despite rapid advances in immersive media, current research remains fragmented. Narrative advertising literature continues to emphasize psychological transportation through storytelling, whereas research on XR technologies and the Metaverse primarily focuses on technological capabilities, platform architectures, and virtual economies (Park & Kim, 2022; Cheng et al., 2022). Meanwhile, emerging work on AI-enabled marketing largely examines personalization algorithms and recommendation systems independently from theories of immersive persuasion. Consequently, there remains no integrated framework explaining how persuasion evolves when narrative storytelling intersects with immersive technologies and AI-driven autonomous decision systems.

To address this gap, this chapter develops a conceptual framework explaining how advertising persuasion evolves from narrative transportation toward immersive, experience-centered engagement. Building upon research in narrative persuasion, consumer psychology, immersive media, metaverse studies, and AI-enabled marketing, the chapter proposes that persuasion increasingly emerges through story-doing, a process whereby consumers actively enact, rather than merely interpret, brand meanings through embodied participation within intelligent, adaptive environments. Unlike co-creation or experiential marketing, which primarily describe collaborative activities or memorable experiences, story-doing refers specifically to a persuasion mechanism in which narrative meaning is continuously constructed through interaction among consumers, immersive technologies, autonomous systems, and branded environments.

Methodologically, this chapter adopts a conceptual synthesis approach, integrating interdisciplinary literature rather than conducting a systematic review. Sources were selected based on three criteria: 1) their theoretical contribution to narrative persuasion and consumer psychology; 2) their relevance to immersive technologies, XR, and metaverse research; and 3) their contribution to emerging scholarship on AI-enabled marketing and autonomous decision systems. By synthesizing these complementary research streams, the chapter develops an integrative framework that identifies the principal mechanisms, moderators, and outcomes of immersive advertising while generating theoretically grounded propositions for future empirical investigation.

The chapter proceeds as follows. First, it reviews literature on narrative advertising and narrative transportation before examining immersion, presence, embodiment, and metaverse environments as evolving foundations of persuasive communication. It then introduces a conceptual framework explaining the transition from storytelling to story-doing and develops a series of formal propositions regarding immersive advertising. Finally, the chapter discusses theoretical and managerial implications, identifies ethical and technological boundary conditions, including AI-driven personalization, and outlines directions for future research.

THEORETICAL FRAMEWORK

Narrative Advertising and Narrative Transportation

Narrative advertising has long been recognized as one of the most effective forms of persuasive communication because it embeds commercial messages within coherent stories rather than presenting isolated product claims (Kumar & Gupta, 2016; Lundqvist et al., 2013). Unlike informational advertising, narrative advertisements encourage consumers to process brand communications holistically by integrating characters, events, and causal relationships into meaningful experiences (Adaval & Wyer, 1998). This narrative structure reduces resistance to persuasion by shifting attention away from explicit commercial intent toward story comprehension and emotional engagement (Escalas, 2007).

The principal mechanism underlying narrative advertising is narrative transportation, defined as the psychological process through which individuals become cognitively, emotionally, and imaginatively absorbed in a story world (Green & Brock, 2000). During transportation, consumers devote attentional resources to following the narrative, reducing counterarguing while increasing acceptance of attitudes, beliefs, and meanings embedded within the story. Numerous studies have demonstrated that transportation positively influences brand attitudes, purchase intentions, emotional attachment, and consumer memory (Brechman & Purvis, 2015; Kang et al., 2020; Kim et al., 2017).

Narrative transportation is strengthened by identification with characters and perceived self-relevance. Consumers mentally simulate the experiences of protagonists, allowing symbolic brand meanings to become incorporated into their own self-concepts (Escalas, 2007). Consequently, advertising narratives function not only as vehicles for information but also as symbolic resources through which consumers negotiate identity, aspirations, and social belonging.

Importantly, narrative persuasion does not operate solely through emotion. Transportation integrates affective, cognitive, and imaginative processing into a unified psychological experience. Rather than evaluating persuasive claims analytically, consumers construct meaning through experiential interpretation, explaining why narrative advertising often produces more enduring persuasion than argument-based approaches (Green, 2021).

Despite its enduring importance, narrative transportation was developed primarily in relation to traditional media environments, including television, cinema, print, and online video. Three assumptions underlie this theoretical perspective.

First, consumers are generally treated as observers who witness narratives rather than influence them. Although identification may be strong, the storyline remains predetermined by advertisers.

Second, immersion is conceptualized principally as a psychological phenomenon, emerging from imagination rather than direct perceptual interaction. Consumers mentally enter fictional worlds without physically engaging with them.

Third, persuasive effects are considered episodic, occurring during discrete advertising exposures that begin and end with the narrative itself.

These assumptions have successfully explained advertising persuasion for several decades. However, they become increasingly restrictive as advertising migrates toward persistent, interactive, and technologically immersive environments in which consumers actively participate in constructing brand experiences rather than merely interpreting them.

From Narrative Transportation to Story-Doing

The evolution of immersive media fundamentally changes the relationship between consumers and brand narratives. Rather than replacing storytelling, immersive technologies transform its persuasive function. Stories continue to provide symbolic coherence and emotional framing, but persuasion increasingly emerges through consumers' actions within branded environments rather than through observation alone.

This transition is captured by the concept of story-doing, originally introduced by de Regt et al. (2021) to describe how virtual reality enables consumers to experience brand narratives through participation. Building upon this foundation, the present chapter conceptualizes story-doing as a distinct persuasion mechanism rather than simply a marketing practice.

Story-doing may be defined as a process through which consumers construct, negotiate, and internalize brand meaning by actively performing narrative roles within immersive environments, where interaction, embodiment, and autonomous technological adaptation jointly shape the persuasive experience. This definition distinguishes story-doing from several related concepts frequently used in marketing literature, such as co-creation, experiential marketing, or consumer engagement.

On one hand, co-creation emphasizes collaborative value creation between firms and consumers but does not necessarily involve narrative enactment or immersive participation. Experiential marketing focuses on designing memorable consumer experiences but does not explain how consumers become active agents within evolving brand narratives. Finally, customer engagement describes psychological and behavioral investment in brands but remains largely outcome-oriented rather than explaining the mechanisms through which persuasive experiences emerge.

On the other hand, story-doing incorporates elements of all three constructs while extending them through embodied participation. Consumers do not simply engage with brands, collaborate in value creation, or consume experiences. They enact narratives through continuous interaction with intelligent environments, virtual identities, and other participants. Consequently, persuasion shifts from symbolic interpretation toward performative meaning construction. Brand meaning is no longer transmitted from advertiser to audience but continuously negotiated through interaction among consumers, branded environments, autonomous systems, and social communities.

This distinction becomes increasingly important within XR and metaverse environments, where artificial intelligence dynamically personalizes content, adapts virtual spaces, and modifies consumer experiences in real time. Rather than presenting identical narratives to every consumer, AI-driven immersive systems generate individualized pathways through branded environments, making persuasion increasingly adaptive, responsive, and participatory. Story-doing, therefore, represents not merely a technological evolution of storytelling but a broader transformation in the logic of advertising persuasion itself.

Immersion, Presence, and Embodiment in XR Environments

Immersion constitutes the defining characteristic of extended reality (XR) environments and represents the principal distinction between immersive advertising and conventional media. Unlike narrative immersion, which arises primarily through imagination and cognitive engagement with a story, technological immersion is determined by the objective properties of the mediated environment, including sensory richness, interactivity, responsiveness, and perceptual realism (Slater &

Wilbur, 1997). These technological affordances create conditions under which consumers experience brand communication not as a symbolic representation but as a lived environment.

Although the terms *immersion*, *presence*, and *embodiment* are frequently used interchangeably in both academic and practitioner literature, they represent distinct yet interdependent constructs. Immersion refers to the technological capacity of a system to deliver rich multisensory experiences, whereas presence describes the psychological consequence of immersion—the subjective sensation of "being there" within a mediated environment (Cummings & Bailenson, 2015). Embodiment extends this process further by allowing users to experience a virtual body or avatar as part of their own physical self (Bailenson, 2018). Understanding these distinctions is essential because each mechanism contributes differently to advertising persuasion.

Technological immersion depends on the degree to which XR systems successfully integrate visual realism, spatial audio, natural interaction, haptic feedback, and real-time responsiveness (Qin & Lei, 2019). As these affordances increase, consumers devote progressively fewer cognitive resources to interpreting the technology itself and more to interacting with the branded environment. Consequently, attention shifts away from the communication medium toward the experience it facilitates, reducing awareness of mediation while strengthening experiential realism.

Presence emerges when consumers psychologically accept the mediated environment as the primary frame of reference during interaction (Slater & Wilbur, 1997). Rather than observing a branded experience from an external perspective, individuals perceive themselves as situated within it. For advertising, this distinction is theoretically significant because persuasive influence no longer depends exclusively on symbolic interpretation or imaginative transportation. Instead, consumers respond directly to experiences that are perceived as psychologically authentic, increasing emotional engagement, memory formation, and perceived brand credibility (Alcañiz et al., 2019).

Closely related to presence is telepresence, which refers to the experience of occupying a remote or virtual location while physically remaining elsewhere (Schloerb, 1995). Although presence emphasizes the subjective sensation of "being there," telepresence highlights the technological capacity to dissolve spatial boundaries through mediated interaction. Within immersive advertising, telepresence enables consumers to explore virtual flagship stores, branded events, digital showrooms, and experiential product demonstrations that would otherwise be inaccessible. Consequently, brand communication becomes less constrained by geographical location and increasingly oriented toward experiential accessibility.

Embodiment represents a further evolution of immersive persuasion. Whereas presence positions consumers inside a virtual environment, embodiment enables them to experience a virtual body as an extension of themselves (Procter, 2020).

Through avatars, consumers can move, manipulate objects, interact socially, and express identities in ways that closely resemble physical-world behavior. This sensorimotor involvement transforms advertising from an observational activity into a participatory experience in which brand meanings are enacted rather than merely interpreted.

From a consumer behavior perspective, avatar embodiment substantially reshapes the relationship between identity and branding. Traditional advertising encourages consumers to imagine themselves using products or identifying with brand symbols (Duarte, 2023). XR environments instead allow consumers to perform those identities directly through customized avatars, virtual possessions, and social interaction (Park & Kim, 2022; Miao et al., 2022). Because these identities are enacted rather than imagined, consumers develop stronger feelings of psychological ownership, self-extension, and emotional attachment toward branded experiences (Belk, 2013).

Recent developments in artificial intelligence further amplify these mechanisms (Leandro & Duarte, 2026). AI systems increasingly personalize immersive environments by dynamically adapting content, recommending products, modifying virtual spaces, and generating individualized interactions according to users' preferences and behavioral histories. Rather than exposing every consumer to identical persuasive experiences, intelligent XR systems continuously optimize environmental stimuli, avatar interactions, and narrative progression in real time. As a result, presence and embodiment become adaptive psychological states that evolve throughout the consumer journey rather than remaining static outcomes of technological immersion alone.

This convergence of immersive technologies and autonomous decision systems represents an important theoretical development. Persuasive experiences are increasingly co-produced by consumers and algorithmic agents that monitor engagement, predict preferences, and modify virtual environments accordingly. AI therefore functions not merely as an enabling technology but as an active participant in immersive persuasion, shaping which experiences consumers encounter, how those experiences unfold, and which brand meanings become most salient. The persuasive process becomes adaptive rather than fixed, shifting advertising from static communication toward intelligent experiential orchestration.

At the same time, greater immersion does not necessarily translate into greater persuasion. Previous research demonstrates that excessively immersive environments may generate cognitive overload, simulator sickness, privacy concerns, or psychological discomfort when technological complexity exceeds users' cognitive resources or technological readiness (Cummings & Bailenson, 2015; Xi et al., 2023). Likewise, highly personalized immersive experiences raise ethical questions regarding transparency, algorithmic manipulation, autonomy, and informed consent. AI systems capable of continuously optimizing persuasive stimuli may increase advertising effectiveness while simultaneously reducing consumers' awareness of commercial influence. These considerations suggest that ethical design and responsible AI governance should be regarded as important boundary conditions rather than secondary implementation issues.

Taken together, immersion, presence, telepresence, and embodiment form a sequential process through which immersive advertising transforms persuasion. Technological immersion creates the conditions for presence; presence facilitates embodiment; embodiment enables identity enactment; and AI-driven personalization continuously adapts these experiences to individual consumers. Consequently, persuasion shifts from interpreting narratives to participating in adaptive brand environments, providing the conceptual bridge between traditional narrative transportation and the story-doing framework developed in the following sections.

The Metaverse as an Advertising Ecosystem

The emergence of the Metaverse represents more than the evolution of immersive technologies; it signifies a fundamental transformation in the architecture of brand communication. Unlike isolated virtual reality applications or augmented reality experiences, the Metaverse consists of persistent, shared, and interoperable virtual environments in which consumers, organizations, digital assets, and increasingly autonomous intelligent agents interact continuously over time (Park & Kim, 2022; Ritterbusch & Teichmann, 2023). Consequently, advertising is no longer confined to discrete campaigns or temporary promotional events but becomes embedded within evolving digital ecosystems that support long-term consumer participation.

A defining characteristic of the Metaverse is persistence. Traditional advertising exposures occur within limited temporal windows, ending when the advertisement or campaign concludes. In contrast, metaverse environments continue to exist independently of individual user sessions, allowing consumers to return repeatedly to branded spaces, maintain virtual possessions, and sustain relationships with both brands and communities. This persistence fundamentally alters the temporal logic of persuasion. Rather than seeking immediate behavioral responses, brands increasingly cultivate ongoing experiential relationships in which meaning develops through repeated interaction and cumulative participation (Ball, 2022).

Equally important is the high degree of interactivity that characterizes immersive virtual environments. Consumers are no longer passive recipients of commercial messages but active participants who explore branded worlds, manipulate virtual objects, collaborate with other users, and influence the evolution of shared experiences. Such interactions shift persuasion from one-way communication toward reciprocal engagement, where consumers actively contribute to the production of brand meaning. As de Regt et al. (2021) argue, immersive environments transform storytelling into story-doing by enabling consumers to enact rather than simply observe brand narratives.

The economic dimension of the Metaverse further reinforces this transformation. Virtual goods, non-fungible digital assets, branded wearables, and customizable avatars increasingly function as symbolic resources through which consumers express identity and social status (Belk, 2013; Mancuso et al., 2023). Unlike conventional promotional merchandise, these digital possessions often remain visible across multiple interactions and communities, allowing brands to become integrated into consumers' ongoing identity performances. The persuasive value of virtual products, therefore, extends beyond ownership to encompass social visibility, self-expression, and community participation.

Artificial intelligence significantly amplifies these dynamics by transforming virtual environments into adaptive advertising systems (Gao et al., 2023). Rather than presenting identical experiences to all users, AI continuously analyzes behavioral data to personalize virtual spaces, recommend branded activities, adapt promotional content, and optimize consumer journeys in real time. Recommendation algorithms determine which branded environments users encounter, generative AI produces personalized digital assets and conversational experiences, and intelligent virtual agents provide context-sensitive assistance that evolves according to individual preferences and previous interactions. Advertising thus becomes increasingly responsive, adaptive, and autonomous.

This development represents an important shift in the role of brands within immersive environments. Traditionally, firms controlled persuasive communication by designing fixed advertising messages that consumers interpreted individually. Within AI-enabled metaverse environments, however, persuasion emerges from ongoing interactions among consumers, intelligent systems, and branded ecosystems. Autonomous agents increasingly influence not only which experiences consumers encounter but also how those experiences unfold, introducing a dynamic and continuously optimized form of persuasive communication.

Several contemporary brand initiatives illustrate this transition. Gucci Town on Roblox transformed a branded space into a persistent social environment where consumers could participate in interactive experiences, customize avatars, and acquire virtual fashion items that functioned as expressions of digital identity (Heo, 2025). Similarly, Nike .SWOOSH extends traditional brand communities into immersive digital ecosystems where consumers can collect, wear, and eventually co-create virtual products, strengthening long-term engagement beyond conventional purchasing behavior (Diki et al., 2025). In gaming environments such as Fortnite, branded activations have demonstrated that consumers often value participation in memorable virtual experiences more than exposure to conventional advertising, highlighting the growing importance of experiential engagement over message repetition (Sidorenko-Bautista et al., 2025). These initiatives suggest that immersive advertising increasingly succeeds by creating environments that consumers willingly inhabit rather than advertisements they simply observe.

Nevertheless, the increasing autonomy of intelligent advertising systems also introduces important ethical and managerial challenges. AI-driven personalization depends upon continuous data collection, behavioral prediction, and algorithmic decision-making, raising concerns regarding privacy, transparency, consumer autonomy, and potential manipulation (Kumar, 2024). The same technologies that enable highly relevant and engaging experiences may also intensify persuasive influence by adapting commercial content beyond consumers' conscious awareness. Furthermore, personalization algorithms risk reinforcing existing preferences, reducing consumer exposure to diverse products or alternative brand experiences through algorithmic filtering. Consequently, responsible immersive advertising requires balancing personalization with transparency, user control, and ethical governance.

From a theoretical perspective, the Metaverse should therefore be understood not merely as another communication channel but as an intelligent advertising ecosystem in which persuasion emerges through the interaction of immersive technologies, autonomous decision systems, digital identities, and persistent social participation. Brands no longer communicate exclusively through narratives; they increasingly design adaptive environments within which narratives evolve continuously through consumer interaction and algorithmic mediation. This perspective provides the conceptual foundation for understanding why persuasion in immersive environments extends beyond narrative transportation toward the process of story-doing.

FROM STORYTELLING TO "STORY-DOING": A CONCEPTUAL FRAMEWORK FOR IMMERSIVE ADVERTISING

Core Idea of the Framework

The preceding discussion suggests that the evolution of immersive technologies requires a reconsideration of how advertising persuasion is conceptualized. Traditional narrative theories explain persuasion primarily through psychological transportation, whereby consumers become cognitively and emotionally immersed in a story world. While this mechanism remains important, immersive advertising environments introduce additional psychological and technological processes that fundamentally alter how persuasive experiences are created.

The framework proposed in this chapter argues that narrative transportation constitutes the entry point into immersive persuasion rather than its ultimate outcome. As consumers enter immersive XR environments, technological immersion generates psychological presence, which subsequently enables embodiment through avatars and virtual identities. These mechanisms transform consumers from passive observers of brand narratives into active participants capable of shaping, negotiating, and performing brand meaning within persistent virtual environments.

The sequential ordering of these mechanisms is theoretically grounded in their distinct functional roles within the immersive persuasion process. Technological immersion represents an environmental condition rather than a psychological response. By increasing sensory richness, responsiveness, and interactivity, it creates the perceptual conditions necessary for consumers to experience presence, or the subjective sensation of "being there." Presence, in turn, provides the psychological basis for embodiment, because consumers are more able to experience an avatar or virtual body as an extension of the self when they first perceive the mediated environment as an experienced reality. Embodiment subsequently enables identity enactment, allowing consumers to move from experiencing the branded environment to actively performing meanings and identities within it, thereby providing the conditions for story-doing.

The framework therefore rejects a parallel-effects account in which technological immersion, presence, embodiment, and identity enactment operate as independent mechanisms exerting simultaneous and additive effects on persuasion. Such an account would overlook the functional dependency between the stages: consumers cannot meaningfully enact an embodied brand identity without first experiencing the virtual environment as sufficiently present, and presence itself depends on the technological affordances that make the environment perceptually and interactively convincing. The proposed sequence should not, however, be interpreted as strictly linear or deterministic; rather, the mechanisms are sequentially ordered while remaining dynamically interactive, particularly because AI-driven personalization can continuously modify the conditions under which subsequent stages unfold. This logic is consistent with the framework's broader proposition that immersive persuasion develops progressively from technological immersion and psychological presence toward embodied participation and, ultimately, story-doing.

Unlike traditional advertising, where persuasive communication largely follows a linear sender–receiver logic, immersive environments distribute persuasive influence across multiple actors. Consumers interact not only with branded content but also with other users, intelligent virtual agents, adaptive algorithms, and persistent digital environments that continuously evolve. Consequently, persuasion becomes an emergent process arising from the interaction between human participation and autonomous technological adaptation.

Within this framework, story-doing represents the central persuasive mechanism through which narrative meaning is enacted rather than interpreted. Story-doing integrates narrative transportation, technological immersion, presence, embodiment, interactivity, and persistence into a dynamic process of experiential meaning construction. Consumers do not simply imagine brand stories; they perform them through repeated interactions with intelligent environments that adapt continuously to their behaviors and preferences.

Artificial intelligence further extends this process by transforming immersive environments into adaptive persuasive systems. Recommendation algorithms personalize branded experiences, generative AI creates dynamic content, and autonomous virtual agents modify interactions according to users' behavioral patterns. Consequently, persuasive communication evolves from static storytelling toward continuously optimized experiential ecosystems in which consumers and intelligent systems jointly shape brand meaning. Figure 1 summarizes the conceptual relationships proposed in this chapter.

Figure 1. Conceptual Model (self-elaboration)

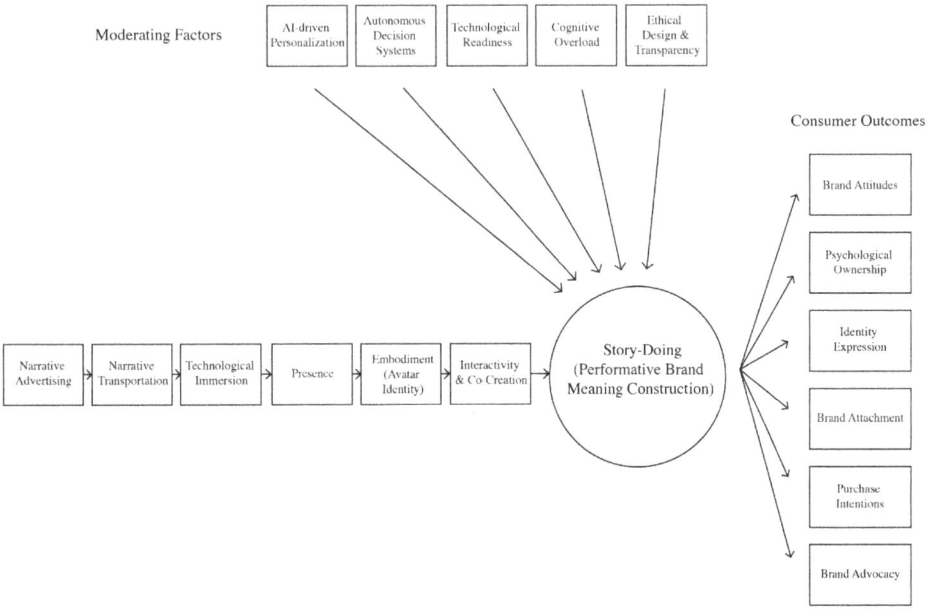

The framework proposes that persuasive effectiveness is influenced not only by sequential psychological mechanisms but also by contextual factors that strengthen or constrain immersive experiences. AI-enabled personalization, ethical design, cognitive load, and consumers' technological readiness moderate the relationships between immersion and persuasion, suggesting that immersive advertising effectiveness depends upon both technological sophistication and responsible implementation.

Conceptual Propositions

Based on the proposed framework, the following propositions are advanced:

Proposition 1 (P1) - Narrative transportation positively influences consumers' willingness to engage with immersive brand environments by facilitating the transition from cognitive immersion to technological immersion.

Narrative transportation continues to function as the psychological gateway into persuasive experiences. Consumers who become emotionally and cognitively involved in brand narratives are more likely to seek deeper interaction within immersive environments, making transportation an antecedent rather than a substitute for XR-based persuasion.

Proposition 2 (P2) - Technological immersion enhances consumers' sense of presence, which in turn strengthens emotional engagement, perceived authenticity, and persuasive effectiveness.

As XR technologies increase sensory realism and responsiveness, consumers experience stronger psychological presence. This heightened sense of "being there" reduces awareness of mediation and allows brand experiences to be processed as personally meaningful rather than symbolically observed.

Proposition 3 (P3) - Avatar embodiment positively influences identity integration, psychological ownership, and brand attachment by enabling consumers to enact rather than merely imagine brand-related identities.

Embodiment transforms advertising from representational communication into performative experience. Through avatars, consumers express identities, acquire virtual possessions, and participate in branded communities, allowing symbolic brand meanings to become integrated into the extended self.

Proposition 4 (P4) - Interactivity, co-creation, and persistent participation jointly facilitate story-doing, which mediates the relationship between immersive experiences and favorable consumer outcomes.

Story-doing represents the central persuasive mechanism of immersive advertising. Rather than passively interpreting brand messages, consumers actively construct brand meaning through repeated interaction within persistent virtual environments. Consequently, story-doing explains how immersive experiences translate into stronger brand relationships, advocacy, and long-term engagement.

Proposition 5 (P5) - The relationships proposed in P1 to P4 are positively moderated by AI-driven personalization and consumers' technological readiness, but negatively moderated by cognitive overload, perceived manipulation, and inadequate ethical transparency.

(P5a) Artificial intelligence enables immersive environments to adapt dynamically to consumers' preferences, increasing relevance and engagement.

(P5b) However, excessive personalization, intrusive data collection, algorithmic opacity, or cognitively demanding experiences may reduce trust, increase resistance, and diminish persuasive effectiveness. Ethical design and transparency, therefore, function as essential boundary conditions for responsible immersive advertising.

DISCUSSION AND IMPLICATIONS

The proposed framework suggests that immersive advertising represents more than the adoption of new communication technologies; it reflects a fundamental transformation in the logic of persuasive communication. Traditional advertising theories have largely conceptualized persuasion as a process of message transmission, in which consumers interpret symbolic meanings embedded within narratives. Although narrative transportation has substantially expanded this perspective by emphasizing psychological immersion and emotional engagement, it nevertheless assumes that consumers remain primarily observers of pre-constructed stories. The framework developed in this chapter argues that immersive environments fundamentally alter this assumption by transforming consumers into active participants in the creation and performance of brand meaning.

From this perspective, the transition from storytelling to story-doing is not simply a technological evolution but a conceptual shift in advertising theory. Storytelling explains how narratives persuade through cognitive and emotional immersion, whereas story-doing explains how persuasion increasingly emerges through embodied participation, social interaction, and continuous engagement within persistent digital environments. Rather than replacing narrative transportation, story-doing extends it by demonstrating that psychological immersion constitutes only the first stage of persuasive experiences that become increasingly enacted through interaction.

The framework also contributes to the growing literature on immersive marketing by integrating concepts that have often been examined independently. Previous studies have explored presence, embodiment, virtual identity, co-creation, or metaverse marketing as separate mechanisms influencing consumer behavior. The present framework proposes that these constructs operate sequentially and interactively. Technological immersion facilitates psychological presence; presence enables embodiment; embodiment encourages identity enactment; and these processes culminate in story-doing, through which consumers actively negotiate and construct brand meaning. This integrated perspective provides a more comprehensive explanation of immersive persuasion than approaches focusing on individual technological affordances in isolation.

A further contribution lies in the incorporation of artificial intelligence and autonomous decision systems as active components of the persuasive process. Existing advertising models generally regard AI as an operational tool for improving targeting, personalization, or customer service. In contrast, the proposed framework positions AI as a theoretical mechanism that continuously shapes immersive experiences through adaptive content generation, intelligent recommendation systems, autonomous virtual agents, and algorithmic optimization. Persuasion, therefore, becomes increasingly dynamic, with commercial experiences evolving in response to consumers' behaviors rather than remaining fixed at the moment of campaign design.

This perspective also extends emerging research on AI-enabled branding by highlighting the reciprocal relationship between consumers and intelligent systems. Consumers no longer interact solely with brand-created environments but increasingly engage with algorithmically mediated ecosystems that continuously learn from behavioral data and modify persuasive stimuli accordingly. Consequently, advertising effectiveness depends not only on creative execution but also on the quality of algorithmic adaptation, personalization strategies, and the transparency of autonomous decision-making processes. The chapter, hence, contributes to the broader discussion of how AI reshapes consumer–brand relationships within digitally mediated environments.

The proposed framework likewise advances understanding of consumer identity in immersive environments. Traditional branding literature has emphasized symbolic consumption, whereby products and brands communicate identity through ownership and social signaling. Immersive environments extend this process by enabling consumers to perform identities directly through avatars, virtual possessions, and social participation. Identity consequently becomes enacted rather than represented, strengthening psychological ownership and reinforcing emotional attachment to brands that facilitate meaningful self-expression. This perspective helps explain why immersive advertising often generates deeper engagement than conventional communication despite containing relatively little explicit persuasive messaging.

At the same time, the framework recognizes that increased immersion does not automatically produce superior persuasive outcomes. AI-driven personalization, continuous behavioral monitoring, and adaptive algorithmic optimization introduce significant ethical considerations concerning transparency, consumer autonomy, privacy, and psychological well-being. The same technologies capable of creating highly relevant and engaging brand experiences may also intensify persuasive influence beyond consumers' conscious awareness. These issues become particularly important in persistent virtual environments where interactions accumulate over extended periods and algorithmic systems continuously refine persuasive strategies. Ethical governance should therefore be regarded as a central theoretical consideration rather than merely a practical implementation issue.

Taken together, the framework positions immersive advertising as an adaptive socio-technical process in which persuasion emerges through the interaction of narrative structures, immersive technologies, embodied participation, and intelligent decision systems. By integrating these perspectives within a single conceptual model, the chapter contributes to advertising theory while providing a foundation for future empirical research examining the effectiveness, boundary conditions, and ethical implications of story-doing in increasingly intelligent immersive environments.

Managerial Implications

The proposed framework offers several implications for organizations seeking to develop immersive advertising strategies within XR environments and the Metaverse.

Design Experiences Rather than Advertisements

Managers should recognize that immersive advertising is not simply a three-dimensional extension of conventional campaigns. Replicating television commercials or static promotional messages within virtual environments is unlikely to exploit the unique affordances of XR technologies. Instead, brands should design experiences that encourage exploration, interaction, and participation, allowing consumers to discover brand meaning through action rather than passive exposure. Creative briefs should, therefore, prioritize experiential objectives, such as exploration, collaboration, or problem-solving, alongside traditional communication objectives, including awareness and recall.

Treat Avatar Design as a Branding Strategy

Avatars should not be viewed merely as graphical representations of users but as vehicles for identity construction. Brands should design digital products, virtual apparel, and interactive environments that enable consumers to express personally meaningful identities. Successful immersive branding increasingly depends on creating opportunities for self-expression rather than maximizing visual logo exposure. Virtual goods should therefore provide symbolic value, social visibility, and opportunities for customization that strengthen consumers' psychological attachment to the brand.

Measure Immersive Performance Beyond Traditional Metrics

Traditional advertising metrics, including impressions, click-through rates, and reach, capture only a limited portion of immersive consumer experiences. Organizations should complement conventional performance indicators with metrics that reflect immersive engagement, including average interaction time within virtual environments; return visitation rates; avatar customization and digital ownership; social interaction frequency; perceived presence and embodiment; psychological ownership; community participation; and long-term customer lifetime value.

These indicators better capture the relationship-building potential of persistent immersive environments.

Evaluate Persistence as a Strategic Investment

Persistent branded environments require considerably greater investment than short-term campaigns. Managers should therefore evaluate persistence according to strategic rather than promotional objectives. Persistent immersive environments are most appropriate when organizations seek to cultivate long-term brand communities, encourage repeated interaction, support digital product ecosystems, strengthen customer loyalty, and facilitate ongoing co-creation. Conversely, organizations pursuing short-term promotional objectives may obtain greater value from temporary XR activations than from maintaining permanent virtual spaces.

Use AI Responsibly

Artificial intelligence offers substantial opportunities for improving immersive advertising through personalization, adaptive storytelling, conversational agents, and predictive recommendation systems. However, excessive personalization or opaque algorithmic decision-making may undermine consumer trust.

Organizations should therefore adopt responsible AI principles. Some recommendations are:

- communicate clearly when AI personalizes experiences;
- allow consumers to control personalization settings;
- minimize unnecessary behavioral data collection;
- audit algorithms for fairness and bias; and
- monitor consumer well-being alongside commercial performance.

Responsible AI governance is likely to become a competitive advantage as immersive advertising becomes increasingly dependent on autonomous decision systems.

Balance Immersion with Consumer Well-Being

Greater immersion is not always desirable. Excessive sensory stimulation, prolonged engagement, or highly persuasive adaptive systems may contribute to cognitive overload, discomfort, or perceptions of manipulation. Managers should therefore optimize immersive experiences according to consumer comfort rather than technological capability alone. Ethical design, including transparency, user autonomy, and meaningful consent, should be regarded as a strategic component of immersive brand management rather than merely a regulatory requirement.

LIMITATIONS

Like all conceptual research, this chapter has several limitations that should be considered when interpreting its contributions.

First, the proposed framework has not yet been subjected to empirical validation. Although the relationships among narrative transportation, presence, embodiment, story-doing, and consumer outcomes are grounded in existing theoretical and empirical literature, the integrated model remains conceptual and requires quantitative and qualitative testing across diverse immersive environments.

Second, the chapter synthesizes research from multiple disciplines, including advertising, consumer psychology, immersive media, information systems, and artificial intelligence. While this interdisciplinary approach strengthens theoretical integration, differences in terminology, methodological traditions, and conceptual assumptions across these fields may influence the interpretation of individual constructs.

Third, immersive advertising technologies continue to evolve rapidly. Advances in generative AI, wearable computing, spatial computing, and autonomous virtual agents may introduce new forms of consumer interaction that extend beyond the scope of the present framework. Consequently, the model should be regarded as a theoretical foundation capable of evolving alongside technological developments rather than as a definitive explanation of immersive persuasion.

FUTURE RESEARCH DIRECTIONS

The proposed framework offers several opportunities for future empirical investigation.

A first priority should be the empirical validation of the conceptual model. Future studies could examine the sequential relationships among narrative transportation, technological immersion, presence, embodiment, story-doing, and consumer outcomes using structural equation modeling, experimental research, or longitudinal designs. Such studies would help determine whether story-doing functions as the mediating mechanism proposed in this chapter and whether the relationships remain stable across different immersive technologies.

Second, future research should investigate how different immersive platforms influence persuasive effectiveness. Virtual reality, augmented reality, mixed reality, gaming platforms, and persistent metaverse environments offer distinct technological affordances that may strengthen or weaken the mechanisms proposed in the framework. Comparative studies across platforms would clarify how technological characteristics interact with consumer behavior.

Third, greater attention should be devoted to the role of artificial intelligence in immersive persuasion. Future research could examine how recommendation algorithms, generative AI, intelligent virtual agents, and autonomous decision systems influence consumer trust, perceived authenticity, psychological ownership, and long-term brand relationships. Understanding how consumers respond to increasingly autonomous persuasive systems represents an important research priority for both marketing scholars and information systems researchers.

Fourth, the ethical dimensions of immersive advertising deserve considerably more attention. Researchers should investigate how algorithmic transparency, privacy concerns, informed consent, perceived manipulation, and psychological well-being influence consumer acceptance of AI-enabled immersive experiences. Particularly, future work should examine the conditions under which personalization enhances consumer value without undermining autonomy or trust.

Fifth, cross-cultural research may provide valuable insights into immersive consumer behavior. Cultural differences in technology acceptance, privacy expectations, identity expression, and avatar usage may influence the effectiveness of story-doing across international markets. Comparative studies could therefore extend the generalizability of the proposed framework.

Finally, future research should explore how emerging technologies—including spatial computing, digital twins, emotionally intelligent conversational agents, and embodied generative AI—reshape immersive advertising over the coming decade. As autonomous systems become increasingly capable of adapting persuasive experiences in real time, understanding the evolving relationship between human agency and algorithmic influence will become one of the central challenges for advertising scholarship.

CONCLUSIONS

The evolution of immersive technologies is fundamentally reshaping the nature of advertising persuasion. While traditional advertising has relied primarily on narrative storytelling to influence consumer attitudes and behaviors, immersive environments increasingly enable consumers to participate directly in the creation and enactment of brand meaning. This chapter has argued that this transformation represents more than a technological innovation; it constitutes a conceptual shift in how persuasive communication should be understood.

Building upon research in narrative transportation, immersive media, consumer psychology, metaverse studies, and AI-enabled marketing, the chapter proposed an integrative framework explaining the transition from storytelling toward story-doing. Within this framework, narrative transportation serves as the psychological entry point to immersive persuasion, while technological immersion, presence, embodiment, interactivity, and persistence progressively transform consumers from passive observers into active participants in branded experiences. Story-doing was introduced as a distinct persuasive mechanism through which consumers construct and internalize brand meaning by performing narrative roles within adaptive virtual environments.

The framework further demonstrates that artificial intelligence and autonomous decision systems are no longer peripheral technologies supporting advertising execution but increasingly constitute integral components of persuasive communication. Recommendation algorithms, intelligent virtual agents, and generative AI continuously personalize immersive experiences, influencing not only which branded environments consumers encounter but also how those environments evolve throughout the interaction. Persuasion, therefore, becomes an adaptive process jointly shaped by consumers and intelligent systems rather than a fixed sequence designed solely by advertisers.

The chapter contributes to advertising theory in three principal ways. First, it extends narrative transportation theory by positioning transportation as the beginning rather than the endpoint of immersive persuasion. Second, it conceptualizes story-doing as a distinct mechanism that integrates narrative engagement, embodiment, co-creation, and identity performance within persistent virtual environments. Third, it incorporates artificial intelligence and autonomous decision systems into a unified conceptual model explaining how immersive advertising evolves in increasingly intelligent digital ecosystems.

From a managerial perspective, the findings suggest that organizations should move beyond adapting traditional advertising formats to immersive technologies. Instead, brands should design persistent, participatory environments that facilitate identity expression, meaningful interaction, and long-term relationship development while simultaneously ensuring ethical governance, algorithmic transparency, and responsible AI implementation. As immersive technologies continue to converge with artificial intelligence, competitive advantage is likely to depend less on technological sophistication alone than on organizations' ability to create adaptive, trustworthy, and consumer-centered experiences.

Ultimately, the transition from storytelling to story-doing reflects the emergence of a new persuasion paradigm in which brand meaning is no longer communicated exclusively through narratives but increasingly co-created through intelligent, immersive, and continuously evolving consumer experiences.

REFERENCES

Adaval, R., & Wyer, R. S.Jr. (1998). The role of narratives in consumer information processing. *Journal of Consumer Psychology, 7*(3), 207–245. DOI: 10.1207/s15327663jcp0703_01

Alcañiz, M., Bigné, E., & Guixeres, J. (2019). Virtual reality in marketing: A framework, review, and research agenda. *Frontiers in Psychology, 10*(JULY), 439498. DOI: 10.3389/fpsyg.2019.01530 PMID: 31333548

Bailenson, J. (2018). *Experience on demand: What virtual reality is, how it works, and what it can do*. W. W. Norton & Company. https://psycnet.apa.org/record/2019-04570-000

Ball, M. (2022). *The metaverse: And how it will revolutionize everything*. Liveright Publishing.

Belk, R. W. (2013). Extended self in a digital world. *The Journal of Consumer Research, 40*(3), 477–500. DOI: 10.1086/671052

Brechman, J. M., & Purvis, S. C. (2015). Narrative, transportation and advertising. *International Journal of Advertising, 34*(2), 366–381. DOI: 10.1080/02650487.2014.994803

Cheng, R., Wu, N., Chen, S., & Han, B. (2022). Will Metaverse be NextG Internet? Vision, hype, and reality. *IEEE Network, 36*(5), 197–204. DOI: 10.1109/MNET.117.2200055

Cummings, J. J., & Bailenson, J. N. (2015). How Immersive Is Enough? A Meta-Analysis of the Effect of Immersive Technology on User Presence. *Media Psychology, 19*(2), 272–309. DOI: 10.1080/15213269.2015.1015740

de Regt, A., Plangger, K., & Barnes, S. J. (2021). Virtual reality marketing and customer advocacy: Transforming experiences from story-telling to story-doing. *Journal of Business Research, 136*, 513–522. DOI: 10.1016/j.jbusres.2021.08.004

Diki, D. W., Egi, E. A. F., & Lubis, M. L. (2025). Nike's Strategy in Cultivating Customer Advocacy: A Case Study on Successful Brand Engagement and Consumer Loyalty. *International Journal of Technological Innovation for Society, 1*(3).

Dolata, M., & Schwabe, G. (2023). What is the Metaverse and who seeks to define it? Mapping the site of social construction. *Journal of Information Technology, 38*(3), 239–266. DOI: 10.1177/02683962231159927

Duarte, A. (2023). The relationship between brands and consumers. In *Dias, P. & Duarte, A. (2023), Social Brand Management in a Post Covid-19 Era* (pp. 3–16). Routledge., DOI: 10.4324/9781003382331-2

Duarte, A., & Soeiro, R. (2025), Destinations, Experiences, and Places: The Role of Storytelling in Tourism Advertising, in Thematic Dossier – Place Branding and Public Diplomacy Special edition on Ibero-American States, *JanusNet,* 15(2), 94-113. https://doi.org/DOI: 10.26619/1647-7251.DT0125.5

Dwivedi, Y. K., Hughes, L., Baabdullah, A. M., Ribeiro-Navarrete, S., Giannakis, M., Al-Debei, M. M., Dennehy, D., Metri, B., Buhalis, D., Cheung, C. M. K., Conboy, K., Doyle, R., Dubey, R., Dutot, V., Felix, R., Goyal, D. P., Gustafsson, A., Hinsch, C., Jebabli, I., & Wamba, S. F. (2022). Metaverse beyond the Hype: Multidisciplinary Perspectives on Emerging Challenges, Opportunities, and Agenda for Research, Practice and Policy. *International Journal of Information Management, 66*, 102542. DOI: 10.1016/j.ijinfomgt.2022.102542

Escalas, J. E. (2007). Self-Referencing and Persuasion: Narrative Transportation versus Analytical Elaboration. *The Journal of Consumer Research, 33*(4), 421–429. DOI: 10.1086/510216

Gao, B., Wang, Y., Xie, H., Hu, Y., & Hu, Y. (2023). Artificial Intelligence in Advertising: Advancements, Challenges, and Ethical Considerations in Targeting, Personalization, Content Creation, and Ad Optimization. *SAGE Open, 13*(4), 21582440231210759. Advance online publication. DOI: 10.1177/21582440231210759

Green, M. C. (2021). Transportation into Narrative Worlds. *Entertainment-Education Behind the Scenes,* 87–101. https://doi.org/DOI: 10.1007/978-3-030-63614-2_6

Green, M. C., & Brock, T. C. (2000). The role of transportation in the persuasiveness of public narratives. *Journal of Personality and Social Psychology, 79*(5), 701–721. DOI: 10.1037/0022-3514.79.5.701 PMID: 11079236

Heo, J. (2025). Marketing Luxury Fashion in the Metaverse: The Case of Gucci Town on Roblox. *Thunderbird International Business Review*. Advance online publication. DOI: 10.1002/tie.70024

Kang, J. A., Hong, S., & Hubbard, G. T. (2020). The role of storytelling in advertising: Consumer emotion, narrative engagement level, and word-of-mouth intention. *Journal of Consumer Behaviour, 19*(1), 47–56. DOI: 10.1002/cb.1793

Kim, E., Ratneshwar, S., & Thorson, E. (2017). Why Narrative Ads Work: An Integrated Process Explanation. *Journal of Advertising, 46*(2), 283–296. DOI: 10.1080/00913367.2016.1268984

Kumar, H. (2024). Virtual worlds, real opportunities: A review of marketing in the metaverse. *Acta Psychologica, 250,* 104517. DOI: 10.1016/j.actpsy.2024.104517 PMID: 39413664

Kumar, V., & Gupta, S. (2016). Conceptualizing the Evolution and Future of Advertising. *Journal of Advertising, 45*(3), 302–317. DOI: 10.1080/00913367.2016.1199335

Leandro, A., & Duarte, A. (2026). An Analysis of Advertising Campaigns Powered by Artificial Intelligence. In Santos, J. D., Botelho Pires, P., & Pratas, J. (Eds.), *Artificial Intelligence Transforming Marketing. Contributions to Management Science.* Springer., DOI: 10.1007/978-3-032-22360-9_9

Lundqvist, A., Liljander, V., Gummerus, J., & Van Riel, A. (2013). The impact of storytelling on the consumer brand experience: The case of a firm-originated story. *Journal of Brand Management, 20*(4), 283–297. DOI: 10.1057/bm.2012.15

Mancuso, I., Messeni Petruzzelli, A., & Panniello, U. (2023). Digital business model innovation in metaverse: How to approach virtual economy opportunities. *Information Processing & Management, 60*(5), 103457. DOI: 10.1016/j.ipm.2023.103457

Miao, F., Kozlenkova, I. V., Wang, H., Xie, T., & Palmatier, R. W. (2022). An emerging theory of avatar marketing. *Journal of Marketing, 86*(1), 67–90. DOI: 10.1177/0022242921996646

Milgram, P., Takemura, H., Utsumi, A., & Kishino, F. (1995). Augmented reality: A class of displays on the reality–virtuality continuum. In Das, H. (Ed.), *Telemanipulator and telepresence technologies* (Vol. 2351, pp. 282–292). SPIE., DOI: 10.1117/12.197321

Njoku, J. N., Nwakanma, C. I., Amaizu, G. C., & Kim, D.-S. (2023). Prospects and challenges of Metaverse application in data-driven intelligent transportation systems. *IET Intelligent Transport Systems, 17*(1), 1–21. DOI: 10.1049/itr2.12252

Park, S.-M., & Kim, Y.-G. (2022). A Metaverse: Taxonomy, components, applications, and open challenges. *IEEE Access : Practical Innovations, Open Solutions, 10,* 4209–4251. DOI: 10.1109/ACCESS.2021.3140175

Persky, S., & Colloca, L. (2023). Medical extended reality trials: Building robust comparators, controls, and sham. *Journal of Medical Internet Research, 25,* e45821. DOI: 10.2196/45821 PMID: 37991836

Procter, L. (2020). I Am/We Are: Exploring the Online Self-Avatar Relationship. *The Journal of Communication Inquiry, 45*(1), 45–64. DOI: 10.1177/0196859920961041

Qin, H., & Lei, J. (2019). The application of virtual reality technology in advertising communication. *Proceedings - 2019 International Conference on Virtual Reality and Intelligent Systems, ICVRIS 2019*, 73–76. https://doi.org/DOI: 10.1109/ICVRIS.2019.00027

Ritterbusch, G. D., & Teichmann, M. R. (2023). Defining the Metaverse: A systematic literature review. *IEEE Access : Practical Innovations, Open Solutions, 11*, 12368–12377. DOI: 10.1109/ACCESS.2023.3241809

Schloerb, D. W. (1995). A Quantitative Measure of Telepresence. *Presence (Cambridge, Mass.)*, *4*(1), 64–80. DOI: 10.1162/pres.1995.4.1.64

Sidorenko-Bautista, P., Castillo-Abdul, B., Herranz-de-la-Casa, J. M., & Abellán-Hernández, M. (2025). Marketing, advertising, and branding in Fortnite: How do brands and companies connect today to audiences through the metaverse? *Cogent Social Sciences*, *11*(1), 2458058. DOI: 10.1080/23311886.2025.2458058

Slater, M., & Wilbur, S. (1997). A framework for immersive virtual environments (FIVE): Speculations on the role of presence in virtual environments. *Presence (Cambridge, Mass.)*, *6*(6), 603–616. DOI: 10.1162/pres.1997.6.6.603

Xi, N., Chen, J., Gama, F., Riar, M., & Hamari, J. (2023). The challenges of entering the metaverse: An experiment on the effect of extended reality on workload. *Information Systems Frontiers*, *25*(2), 659–680. DOI: 10.1007/s10796-022-10244-x PMID: 35194390

KEY TERMS AND DEFINITIONS

Artificial Intelligence (AI): Computational systems capable of analyzing data, learning from user behavior, and autonomously adapting advertising content, recommendations, and interactions to optimize consumer experiences within immersive digital environments.

Autonomous Decision Systems: Intelligent algorithmic systems that independently analyze consumer data and make real-time decisions regarding content personalization, recommendation, and interaction within digital advertising environments, often with limited human intervention.

Avatar Embodiment: The psychological experience through which individuals perceive a virtual avatar as an extension of themselves, enabling identity expression, social interaction, and engagement with brands in immersive environments.

Immersive Advertising: A form of advertising that employs extended reality technologies to create interactive, multisensory experiences in which consumers actively participate in branded environments rather than passively receive promotional messages.

Metaverse: A persistent, shared, and interconnected network of virtual environments where individuals, organizations, digital assets, and intelligent systems interact continuously through immersive technologies and digital identities.

Narrative Transportation: A psychological state in which consumers become cognitively, emotionally, and imaginatively absorbed in a narrative, reducing critical evaluation of persuasive messages while increasing engagement with the story and the brand.

Presence: The subjective sensation of being physically located within a mediated virtual environment, despite remaining in a different physical location. Presence enhances realism and intensifies consumer engagement with immersive experiences.

Psychological Ownership: The feeling that a virtual object, avatar, or branded experience belongs to oneself, even without legal ownership, strengthening emotional attachment, identity expression, and long-term relationships with brands.

Story-Doing: A persuasive mechanism in which consumers construct and internalize brand meaning through active participation, embodiment, and interaction within immersive environments, transforming narratives from observed stories into lived experiences.

Technological Immersion: The objective capacity of an immersive system to provide rich sensory stimulation, interactivity, realism, and responsiveness that support users' psychological experience of presence.

Section 2
Consumer Decision Making, Emotion, and Choice

Mediation is granted by consumers rather than imposed upon them, and the conditions of that grant are established within the individual rather than within the system. This section specifies them. It traces the progression from emotional response to conative brand outcomes, the cost personalization exacts in variety, the displacement of discovery by algorithmic habit, and the fate of loyalty when the storefront itself is continuously reconstructed.

Chapter 4
Emotion AI and Conative Brand Outcomes:
Through the Lens of Affective–Cognitive Mechanisms

Sneha Sukumar
http://orcid.org/0009-0008-1042-5455
Christ University, Bangalore, India

Pooja Jain
http://orcid.org/0000-0003-1523-8460
Christ University, Bangalore, India

ABSTRACT

The chapter explores the role of Emotion AI (EAI) in influencing the psychology of consumer decision-making and conative brand outcomes through the lens of affective-cognitive mechanisms. Grounded in Dual Process Theory, Elaboration Likelihood Model, and Affect as Information Theory, the chapter proposes a conceptual framework explaining how emotional stimuli influence affective-cognitive engagement, resulting in conative brand outcomes and highlights the moderating role of affective trust. Adopting a narrative review approach, the chapter develops theoretically grounded propositions for future empirical studies. The chapter further critically addresses the ethical concerns relating to over-personalization, emotion tracking, data privacy, manipulation, and exploitation, emphasizing the need for standard ethical governance frameworks. The chapter concludes with future research directions for future empirical studies.

DOI: 10.4018/979-8-3373-9589-0.ch004

INTRODUCTION

Background and Context

The dynamic nature of marketing practices adopted by brands is witnessing a new wave of change characterized by the use of emotion AI, enabling brands to engage users emotionally and thereby enhancing consumer experience. Valued at $2,137.5 million in 2024 and expected to reach $13,397.1 million by 2033, at a compound annual growth rate (CAGR) of 22.9% between 2025 and 2033, the global emotion AI market is witnessing a significant period of growth and expansion, as demonstrated in Figure 1.

Emotion Artificial Intelligence (EAI), a subset of affective computing, uses techniques to interpret and respond to human emotions in real-time, enhancing the overall consumer experience. Originally proposed by Rosalind Picard in her seminal book: Affective Computing published by the MIT Press in 1997, establishes affective computing as an interdisciplinary field linking computers, psychology, and human-computer interactions. Machines were developed to capture human emotions through facial expressions, vocal features, and other physiological signals. Meanwhile, EAI techniques focus on the commercial application of these human-computer interactions (Puntoni et al., 2020). The early stage of EAI applications saw the use of unimodal architectures that independently analyzed modalities such as facial expressions, voice analysis, physiological signals, and text-based detection. Over time, due to its limited applications, the field has seen a significant shift from unimodal to multimodal emotion recognition (MER) systems. These systems could capture multiple modalities simultaneously, providing more accurate results (Poria et al., 2017). A diagrammatic representation of the components of EAI is shown in Figure 2. This shift has extended the commercial use of EAI, also known as artificial emotional intelligence, across sectors such as marketing, education, the automotive industry, and healthcare (Monteith et al., 2022; Narimisaei et al., 2024).

Furthermore, the integration of machine learning (ML) and deep neural networks into EAI platforms enables advanced emotion recognition, developing a robust understanding of human emotions (Kapoor & Verma, 2024). In today's consumer-centric marketing experiences, the concept of artificial empathy- the ability of AI systems to interpret and respond to human emotions mimicking human empathy- has brought in the sophistication of the human-AI interactions, shaping what a consumer feels, thinks, and responds (Liu-Thompkins et al., 2022). Notably, EAI platforms have been shown to enhance consumer experience by personalizing advertisements. For instance, back in 2013, Coca-Cola used Affectiva's facial coding technology to interpret consumers' emotional responses during advertising testing before the main campaign launch. This helped Coca-Cola analyze the emotional engagement and potential fixations required before the campaign launch (McClellan, 2013). Such an approach complements traditional marketing strategies, boosting brand engagement.

However, recent studies by Puntoni et al. (2020) and Kirk and Givi (2024) demonstrate that increased personalization raises originality concerns, making users uncomfortable, leading to resistance and distrust. Consequently, EAI platforms need to strategically balance authenticity and emotion tracking to minimize user resistance.

Figure 1. Emotion AI Market Size and Forecast (2021–2033)

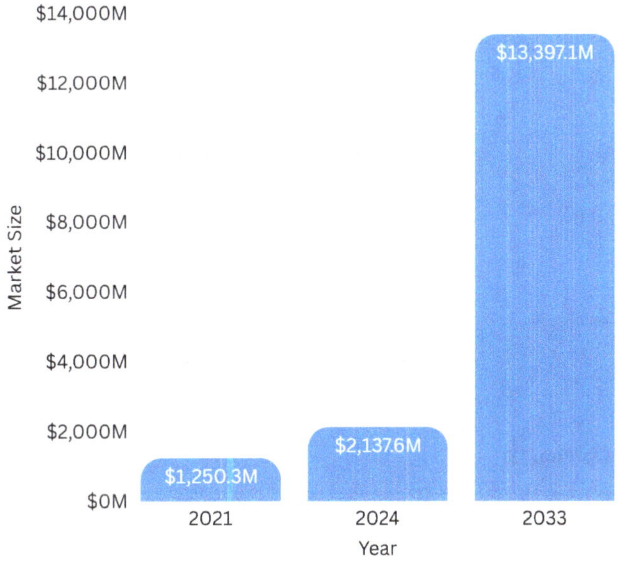

Note: Based on data from Grand View Research (n.d.) https://www.grandviewresearch.com/industry-analysis/emotion-ai-market-report

Figure 2. Components of EAI

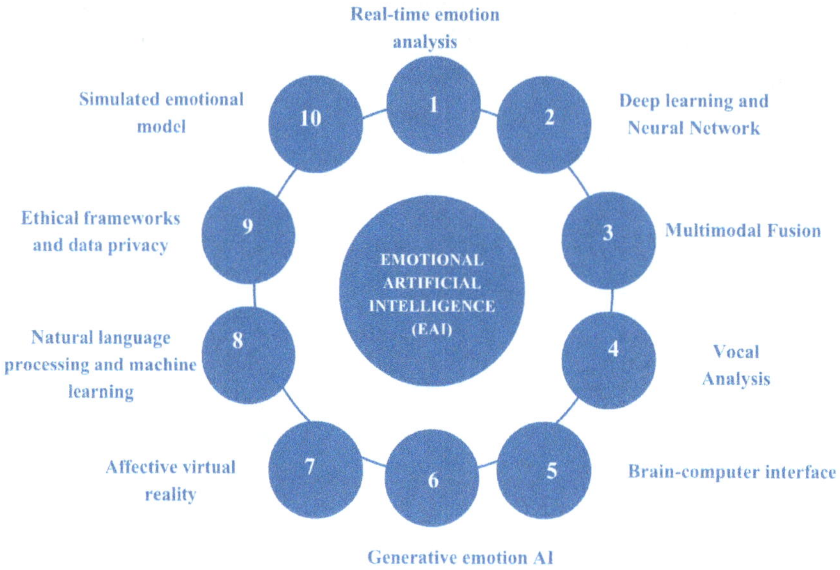

Source: Authors' own work

Problem Statement

Despite the recent accelerated growth of EAI literature, two significant gaps remain. First, a theoretical gap in the lack of studies on understanding the psychological process of consumer decision-making in an EAI environment. Previous studies were primarily outcome-oriented, such as consumer engagement (Bilal et al., 2023), consumer satisfaction (Pan, 2025), brand outcomes and ethical concerns (Fabiano, 2025). The psychological mechanisms of consumer decision-making in an EAI environment remain underexplored (Asutay & Västfjäll, 2024). These findings signify a gap in understanding how emotionally intelligent systems influence human decision-making (Huang & Rust, 2021). Similarly, a study by Puntoni et al. (2020) highlights how artificial intelligence engages consumers emotionally. However, there is insufficient understanding of how affective engagement translates into behavioral outcomes.

Second, highlighting a methodological gap, most existing frameworks treat affective and cognitive dimensions of consumer engagement as two independent constructs. However, consumer engagement operates through the simultaneous working of these constructs. Prior studies have primarily examined the role of affective engagement in an EAI environment, neglecting the interrelatedness of cognitive and affective engagement in these settings (Assunção et al., 2022). Studies addressing the combined affective and cognitive mechanisms of decision-making are under-explored (Cristofaro et al., 2022). The lack of this integrated approach has hindered the holistic growth of EAI. Therefore, studies integrating both affective and cognitive dimensions of consumer decision-making that impact brand outcomes in an EAI environment are to be further explored (Liu-Thompkins et al., 2022; Asutay & Västfjäll, 2024). The chapter addresses these gaps by proposing a novel affective-cognitive framework for future studies. The multidisciplinary nature of EAI, spanning across consumer psychology, computer science, and ethics, provides an emerging platform for brands to use EAI as a strategic marketing tool to influence decision-making (Mohiddin et al., 2026). Prior research primarily drew on the domains of sociology, psychology, computer science, and physiology in isolation. However, with the multidisciplinary nature of recent research, the literature has evolved, to incorporate an interdisciplinary approach (Arya et al., 2021). Therefore, studies are required to explore the affective-cognitive role of EAI stimulus on consumer decision-making.

Research Questions

The chapter addresses the following research questions:

RQ1: How does emotion AI influence brand outcomes within immersive environments?
RQ2: How does emotion AI shape the affective–cognitive mechanism in consumer decision-making?
RQ3: What are the ethical considerations governing the use of emotion AI in brand engagements?

The chapter proceeds as follows. The Methodology section details the narrative review approach. Background and Evolution of Emotion AI traces the development of the field. EAI in Marketing surveys current applications. Theoretical Underpinnings develops the theoretical background, and the Conceptual Framework presents the model and its propositions. Ethical Considerations examines the risks, and the closing sections discuss implications and future research directions.

Chapter Contribution

The chapter makes four novel contributions to the literature on EAI and consumer decision-making. First, it deepens understanding of the psychology of consumer decision-making within an EAI environment, thereby addressing the gaps as discussed in the above sections. Second, the chapter draws on the role of "affect" as an active input to cognitive processing, highlighting the interdependent role of affective-cognitive mechanisms. Third, it develops a novel conceptual framework drawn upon the theories of Elaboration Likelihood Model, Dual Process Theory, and Affect as Information theory. The framework highlights the potential of EAI stimuli to simultaneously engage users at the affective and cognitive levels, with affective trust as a moderator influencing conative brand outcomes. Fourth, the chapter emphasizes the need for mandatory ethical regulations on the use of EAI platforms to ensure transparency and ethical use of user data. However, the chapter has its own limitations. Being a conceptual paper, the chapter paves the way for future empirical studies.

METHODOLOGY

The chapter adopts a narrative review methodology to review existing scholarly literature on the role of EAI in conative brand outcomes and consumer decision-making through the dimensions of affective-cognitive engagement. A narrative review was considered more appropriate than a systematic literature review (Baumeister & Leary, 1997) due to the fragmented, multidisciplinary nature of the literature across disciplines such as marketing, psychology, and computer science. The literature was based on peer-reviewed articles from the Scopus database using the following search terms: "affective computing", "artificial emotion intelligence", "emotion intelligence", "emotion AI", "brand engagement", "consumer decision-making". From the available articles, title and abstract screening was conducted based on relevance to the psychology of consumer decision-making, with a focus on the affective-cognitive dimensions of consumer behavior. Articles focusing exclusively on the technical architecture of EAI, rather than the psychology of consumer behavior were excluded from the study. No time boundary was set for the article selection process, to include prominent and foundational studies spanning across the years. However, limitations of this approach, such as a lack of replicability and the author's selection bias, are acknowledged.

BACKGROUND AND EVOLUTION OF EMOTION AI

Emotion AI, a sub-component of affective computing, as defined by Kapoor & Verma (2024), refers to the ability of an AI system to detect, interpret, and respond to human emotions via multiple modalities such as audio, visual, text, speech, and facial expressions. The multimodal emotion recognition (MER) is a six-step process, starting with (1) data collection from audio, visuals and texts; (2) filtering of collected data such as noise filtering, data mining and feature extraction; (3) multimodal fusion, combining data from multiple modalities into a single comprehensive model; (4) model training; (5) emotion analysis and classification; (6) pattern identification and analysis of the classified emotions. This data is then used for pattern identification, behavior prediction, and a feedback mechanism (Zhu et al., 2024).

The origin of EAI dates back to the early 1990s, when systems were developed on an unimodal emotion recognition system. Single source of data, such as facial expressions, voice and speech patterns were the primary sources of behavioral analysis. However, this unimodal interpretation model had its own disadvantage, primarily the inability to capture multiple emotions simultaneously. This shortcoming was met in the 2000s, as the field saw a shift from individual modal interpretation to simultaneous multimodal interpretation. With the increasing use of EAI systems across sectors such as health, education, psychotherapy, and media, these systems have evolved not only technically but also started interpreting human emotions in a more efficient manner. Figure 3 describes the practical applications of EAI in today's scenario. Notably, the 2010s saw the most evolutionary shift in the field of EAI. Deep learning and machine learning models were integrated into EAI systems (Poria et al., 2017), enabling real-time emotion analysis for more accurate emotion detection. Techniques such as Convolutional Neural Networks (CNNs) and Recurrent Neural Networks (RNNs) in AI platforms enable deeper and efficient interpretation of human emotions (Singh & Srivastava, 2026). Although, technical advancements were at an all-time high, the field witnessed increased ethical concerns with regards to data manipulation, unethical data tracking, and lack of pre-consent from the users, to name a few (S et al., 2026). The current decade is characterized by enhanced real-time sentiment analysis, generative model integration, and a growing need for ethical AI regulation. Table 1 further provides a brief timeline of affective computing from the 1970s to the present stage.

Figure 3. Practical Applications of EAI

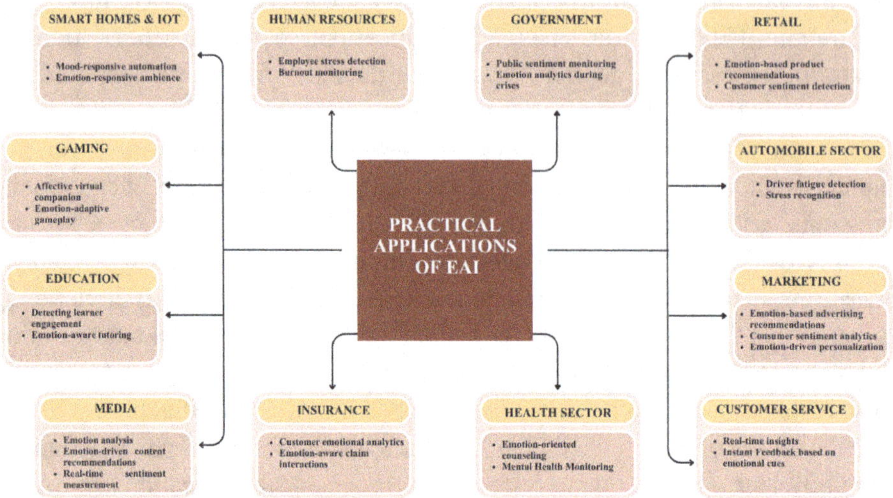

Source: Authors' own work

Table 1. Affective computing: A brief timeline

1970s	Growing recognition of computational emotion recognition and the development of Facial Action Coding System (FACS) to interpret human emotions on system by Dr. Paul Ekman and Dr. Wallace V. Friesen
1980s	A shift toward user-centric computing is evident in the increased Human–computer interaction (HCI). Emotional Intelligence in AI (EAI) started gaining prominence
Early 1990s	The use of emotionally responsive systems began to increase. The interdisciplinary nature of EAI started gaining relevance with speech emotion recognition, laying the foundation for the field
Late 1990s	Affective Computing developed by Rosalind Picard. The foundational theoretical framework was published in the Affective Computing book (1997). Unimodal measuring techniques gain visibility to measure human emotions
Early 2000s	The interdisciplinary nature of the field is further explored by introducing machine learning for real-time emotion detection. A shift is seen from an unimodal to a multimodal recognition system. Tools like automated facial emotion system and bio signals were adapted
Late 2000s	First International Conference on Affective Computing and Intelligent Interaction (ACII) was conducted. Increased use of EEG in neuromarketing, and commercial use of wearable devices were seen for marketing analytics and commercial use
Early 2010s	Large-scale development of real-time emotion detection increases. Rise of social media sentiment analysis along with consumer-behavior prediction model, with focus on neuroscience. Development of EAI in digital advertising is seen.

continued on following page

Table 1. Continued

Late 2010s	Multimodal affective computing techniques are expanding in practical applications across sectors. Major AI companies invest in human-computer interactions
Early 2020s	EAI merged with metaverse platforms for a more personalized environment. The growth of EAI across sectors has led to further study of consumer behavior patterns. Ethical AI regulations widened to regulate the field
Future Phase	Enhanced focus on an emotion-aware metaverse with neuro-adaptive, hyper-personalized immersive marketing. EAI is increasingly being used to promote sustainable and ethical consumption patterns, which is further used for predictive consumer behavior analytics

EAI IN MARKETING

Tools and Techniques

Real-time sentiment analysis and the personalization of advertisements through emotion AI have revolutionized how brands intend to create meaningful relationships with consumers (PadmavathyA & Alamelu, 2025). Artificial emotional intelligence is increasingly used in marketing to understand consumer behavior patterns, determine demand, enhance the shopping experience, and much more. Tools such as Electroencephalogram (EEG), Functional Magnetic Resonance Imaging (fMRI), Support Vector Machines (SVMs), Principal Component Analysis (PCA), and Consumer Sentiment Analysis (CSA) powered by machine learning, natural language processing, and predictive analytics aid in content optimization. These tools analyze individuals' eye movements, gaze duration, sentiments, emotional responses, and brain wave frequencies, measuring real-time consumer responses to the advertisement campaign. Further description of these tools and their applications has been provided in Table 2. ML algorithms and deep neural networks help capture consumer emotions and attention levels, with their respective real-time behavioral outcomes aiding a real-time feedback mechanism. This feedback should be critically evaluated by brands for enhancing future marketing strategies (Chornous et al., 2025). Furthermore, these ML models can interpret a wide range of emotions as they are trained on large datasets for accurate predictions, empowering marketers to build predictive models and eventually strategize their branding techniques for conative brand outcomes (Yadav, 2024), as in the case of Mars Incorporated and Affectiva. The company applied neuromarketing techniques such as facial coding and emotion analytics to predict short-term sales with an accuracy of 75% (iMotions, 2019).

Brands also apply neuromarketing tools such as EEG and eye-tracking to analyze consumer behavior patterns. These techniques effectively capture cognitive and affective consumer engagement, enabling brands to optimize shelf placement, packaging design, and point-of-sale displays. This enhances product visibility, thereby boosting sales. Further, affective computing uses neuroscientific methods to induce affective (emotions) and cognitive (memory recall and attention) triggers that influence consumer decision-making and brand judgment (Alsharif et al., 2025). Affective computing techniques analyze emotional feedback received and aim to deliver personalized advertisements for product refinement and better market outreach (Pervez et al., 2024). Combining such AI-embedded multimodal marketing strategies helps to approach the target audience with a more personalized marketing approach, ensuring better consumer relationship management (Cambria, 2016). This emotionally rich content fosters stronger brand connection through enhanced engagement and trust between brands and consumers (Sallaku et al., 2025). A summary of the use of neuromarketing tools has been provided in the table below.

Table 2. Applications of neuromarketing tools

NEUROMARKETING TOOLS	USAGE	APPLICATIONS
1. EEG DATA ANALYSIS • Convolutional Neural Networks (CNN) • Support Vector Machines (SVM)	• Measures brain activity and provide real-time insights into emotional responses. • Detects emotion patterns and intensity over time.	• Content optimization with a target audience approach • Improve user interface • Brand recall assessment • Product preference evaluation • Impulsive buying behavior assessment
2. fMRI DATA ALGORITHMS • Principal Component Analysis (PCA) • Deep Learning	• Measures blood flow and brain activity • Detects patterns such as brand preference and purchase intention	• Brand positioning analysis • Advertisement effectiveness evaluation • Product packaging assessment • Customer experience evaluation • Celebrity endorsement evaluation • Luxury brand perception analysis
3. EYE TRACKING DATA • K-Means Clustering • CNN	• Measures consumer attention, attention hotspots, and gaze duration	• Visual attention mapping • Consumer preference analysis • Shelf placement optimization • Purchase decision evaluation • Social media /influencer content evaluation • Personalized marketing assessment
4. FACIAL EXPRESSION ANALYSIS • CNN • Multimodal Analysis	• Micro-expressions are analyzed • Integrated with EEG, and physiological measurements, helps in overall emotion analysis	• Advertisement testing • Analyzing brand content reaction • Consumer satisfaction analysis • Product design evaluation • Cognitive load detection

EAI and Brand Outcomes

ML-embedded multimodal emotion recognition systems facilitate stronger consumer-brand relationships and behavioral outcomes (Bai et al., 2025). In their study, Bai et al. (2025) emphasized the role of affective-cognitive integration on an EAI platform in accelerating consumer engagement and eventually influencing purchase intention. Additionally, Pan (2025) demonstrates the role of affective attachment in aiding long-term brand loyalty, while Shao et al. (2025) demonstrate that perceived empathy and affective trust significantly influence consumer intention, positive word of mouth, and purchase intention through affective-cognitive consumer engagement. The high-arousal emotional state induced by EAI reduces the cognitive effort required for brand evaluations, accelerating conative brand outcomes and brand attitude (Zanger et al., 2022).

For example, the cosmetic brand L'Oréal introduced an AI-enabled beauty assistant, ModiFace for personalized skin analysis, product recommendations, product comparisons and virtual try-on. The platform uses personalized information and inputs for product recommendation and allows the consumer to virtually try them on (L'Oréal, 2018). This interactive interface acts as an EAI stimulus, enhancing consumer engagement. While personalized recommendations and virtual try-on characteristics enhance affective engagement, diagnostic information and product analysis enhance cognitive engagement. Such engagement positively impacts brand outcomes such as purchase intention, brand loyalty, word of mouth, and brand recommendation (Chakraborty et al., 2024).

Despite these benefits, EAI has its own demerits that must be acknowledged. First, the emotions or the artificial empathy stimulated by the systems may be under question, as they may be perceived as algorithmically fabricated emotional cues rather than a natural one (Lule et al., 2026). Fabricated emotions are considered manipulated or artificial, reducing the natural impact of the firsthand emotions that are developed. This impacts the credibility and reliability of artificial emotional intelligence systems. Second, stimulation overload causes emotional and cognitive dissonance, leading to distrust of EAI platforms (Liu-Thompkins et al., 2022). Third, Puntoni et al. (2020) and Kirk and Givi (2024) highlight increased personalization through sentiment analysis and emotion tracking can lead to consumer anxiety and resistance. This would reduce consumer engagement and thereby the positive impact on the brand. Therefore, brands must ensure that these cues are properly optimized to meet privacy and ethical standards.

THEORETICAL UNDERPINNINGS

This chapter draws its theoretical foundation based upon three interrelated theories: (1) Dual Process Theory, (2) Elaboration Likelihood Model, and (3) Affect as Information Theory. The study selected these theories based on their relevance to the chapter's objective: understanding the affective-cognitive role of EAI platforms in consumer decision-making. The theories, in integration, provide a strong foundational understanding required to build an empirically strong framework for future studies.

Dual Process Theory (DPT)

Dual Process Theory (DPT), initially proposed by Evans (1984) and later popularized by Kahneman (2011) proposes that individuals process information through two distinct systems. System 1, which is fast, automatic, and affect-driven, resulting in quick decision-making, with less cognitive effort. System 2, on the other hand, is comparatively slow, thoughtful, and more conscious, resulting in more intense decision-making where complex decision-making is involved (Samson & Voyer, 2012). In an EAI environment, the affective element of System 1 acts as an active input that induces cognitive and reflective processing in System 2, resulting in deeper consumer engagement. System 1 stimulation is more prominent in hedonic environments, whereas System 2 is more prominent in complex decision-making environments. Emotion-embedded AI platforms equipped with real-time emotion analysis can monitor and modify emotions to improve cognitive processing, encouraging meaningful consumer engagement (Liu-Thompkins et al., 2022). However, this theory has been criticized by Evans and Stanovich (2013), who argue that the binary approach (System 1 and System 2) toward the psychology of consumer decision-making has limited applications. Neurological studies emphasize the simultaneous or continuous engagement of both affective and cognitive dimensions of consumer decision-making rather than an independent or hierarchical approach, as mentioned in DPT. This could be traced to the unethical use of EAI platforms, as extensive emotions could lead to over-personalization and manipulation of natural responses.

Elaboration Likelihood Model (ELM)

The elaboration likelihood model (ELM), grounded in dual-process theory highlights the concept of user engagement through either the central route (logic-driven analysis) or the peripheral route (emotion-driven analysis). Originally formulated by Petty and Cacioppo (1986), the framework elaborates on the affective-cognitive dimension of consumer behavior. The central route draws upon analytical, logical, and rational processing, whereas the peripheral route draws upon the hedonic and emotional route. Informative content, such as product descriptions, product comparisons, and purchase guidance, engages users at a deeper cognitive level through the central route. In contrast, emotional features such as affective tone, emotional cues, aesthetics, and emotional storytelling engage users on an affective level through the peripheral route (Lai et al., 2025; Bilal et al., 2023). MER systems foster stronger consumer engagement through a combined affective-cognitive model. Marketing strategists can optimize this strategy to strengthen the consumer experience. Critically, however, this framework needs theoretical application in a multimodal environment, where affective and cognitive mechanisms operate simultaneously and independently (Morris et al., 2005), thereby requiring a more integrated approach.

Affect as Information Theory (AIT)

Affect as Information Theory (AIT), originally developed by Schwarz and Clore (1983), significantly explains how affective engagement impacts consumer judgment and decision-making. The theory provides a theoretical background for how emotional responses, such as enjoyment, artificial empathy, and inspiration, form the center of cognitive responses, ultimately down-stream to behavioral outcomes such as purchase intention, word-of-mouth, and willingness to pay. Additionally, as an intrinsic motivator, the "affect" factor helps consumers decide what they like, want, and value the most, aiding cognitive decision-making and, ultimately, user response (Clore & Bar-Anan, 2007; Wakefield, 2006). Consequently, a higher level of affective responses strengthens brand attitude, among users (Zanger et al., 2022; Gary, 2024). The theory thus establishes a strong relationship between affective-cognitive mechanisms impacting decision outputs. The issue of "misattribution effect" which is the feeling of manipulated emotion creation, is often associated in such an environment, jeopardizing transparency and ethical standards.

The integration of these three interrelated frameworks provides a strong theoretical foundation for the conceptual model proposed in the section below.

CONCEPTUAL FRAMEWORK

Drawing on the theoretical framework discussed in the section above, the chapter proposes an affective-cognitive framework that impacts conative brand outcomes in an EAI environment. The framework, as shown in Figure 4, proposes EAI as the stimulus environment, influencing affective and cognitive consumer engagement simultaneously. Affective trust acts as a moderator between consumer engagement and conative brand outcomes.

EAI stimulus is the affective trigger generated by the system. These triggers, through real-time emotion detection, personalized content, artificial empathy, and multimodal emotional cues, stimulate affective responses. "Empathy" factor in EAI stimulus enhances the affective nature of consumer engagement, resulting in enhanced consumer satisfaction and WOM intentions (Rohden & Espartel, 2026).

Consumer Engagement comprises affective, cognitive, and behavioral responses, highlighting a user's emotional, rational, and psychological interaction, respectively. These dimensions cannot be treated as independent dimensions; rather, they are interdependent aspects of consumer behavior. (Brodie et al., 2011).

Affective Engagement (A.E.) refers to the emotional engagement a consumer develops during their interaction with the stimulus. (A.E.) comprises emotional arousal and valence (Zanger et al., 2022). Arousal is the degree of emotional activation or deactivation during a response; valence refers to the degree to which this response is considered positive or negative (Van Berlo et al., 2020).

Cognitive Engagement (C.E.) refers to the rational and analytical dimension of consumer behavior. C.E. influences attention span capacity, memory recall, and evaluation ability (Kahneman, 2011).

Conative Brand Outcomes refers to the final behavioral outcomes resulting in positive brand outcomes such as higher conversion rates, purchase intention, word of mouth, brand advocacy, and brand loyalty. These outcomes determine the consumer-brand relationship and long-term engagement with the brand.

Affective trust – refers to the emotional trust developed during an emotional engagement. Trust developed during such interactions influences conative brand outcomes, such as brand loyalty and brand attitude formation (Rather et al., 2019). It further strengthens emotional consumer engagement and plays a pivotal role in measuring user satisfaction and, ultimately, brand value and long-term brand loyalty (Özdemir et al., 2020).

Figure 4. Conceptual Framework

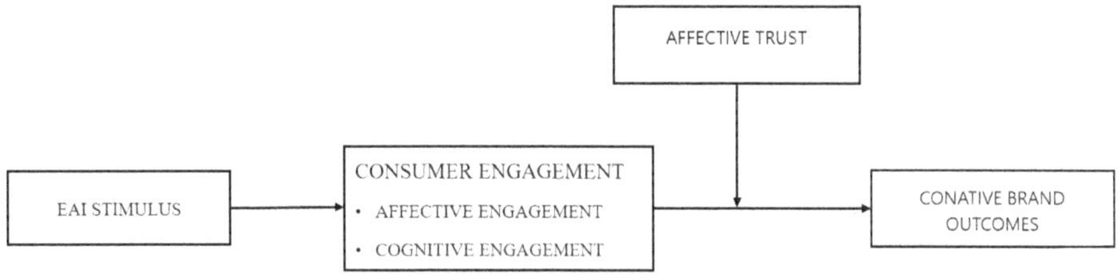

Source: Authors' own work

Framework Propositions

Proposition 1 (P1): EAI stimulus positively influences affective consumer engagement.

Through sentiment analysis and real-time emotion tracking, MER systems enable emotion-embedded AI platforms to analyze human emotions effectively, fostering affective attachment and artificial empathy. Grounded in AIT, affective responses act as active inputs for shaping cognitive processing, shaping brand attitude formation, and the consumer-brand relationship (Bai et al., 2025). Furthermore, Liu-Thompkins et al. (2022) and Lule et al. (2026) studied the role of artificial empathy on consumer experience. Artificial empathy embedded in EAI platforms induces emotional attachment with the brands, facilitating a strong consumer-brand relationship. Such empathy-driven engagements reduce cognitive and affective load on users, thereby accelerating the consumer decision-making process (Liu-Thompkins et al., 2022; Mohiddin et al., 2026). Building on this argument, Lule et al. (2026) further find that artificial empathy embedded in EAI platforms deepens emotional attachment, extending beyond individual transactions to shape perceptions of brand identity. In his study, Pan (2025) demonstrates the role of affective attachment developed by personalized EAI interactions contributing to long-term affective brand loyalty. Therefore, EAI platforms positively induce affective engagement, impacting conative brand outcomes. However, brands must ensure not to over-personalize or continuously track the emotions, as this could lead to tampering with natural responses.

Proposition 2 (P2): EAI stimulus positively influences cognitive consumer engagement.

As highlighted by Hollebeek et al. (2014), affective and cognitive dimensions of consumer behavior operate interdependently rather than independently. EAI platforms, through increased user attention span, memory recall, and decision-making, strongly influence cognitive consumer engagement. Grounded in DPT, the initial affective response via System 1 stimulates logical or analytical responses, which are activated via System 2. Such engagement encourages consumers to be more deeply involved with and evaluative of the brand (Kahneman, 2011). Assunção et al. (2022) validate the role of EAI stimuli in reducing the cognitive load required, thereby improving users' attention span. Furthermore, the Elaboration Likelihood Model also extends on the same note. Bilal et al. (2023) point out that an integrative affective-cognitive model produces stronger behavioral intentions and brand attitude than an individual-dimension model. The advent of ML and deep learning models has been advantageous in this context. The heightened feedback mechanism of such models is beneficial for brands and marketers, as it enhances marketing efficiency and product development (Zhang et al., 2025). However, caution is required to avoid cognitive overload, as it can disrupt natural human processing, leading to negative emotions such as fear and anxiety (Munteanu, 2024). Therefore, EAI platforms positively influence cognitive engagement.

Proposition 3 (P3): Affective trust positively moderates the relationship between affective-cognitive engagement and conative brand outcomes.

In an emotion-embedded AI environment, users often interact based on a hedonic or enjoyment level. For this to convert to behavioral outcomes, trust plays a crucial moderating role. Even from a marketing perspective, in any strong consumer-brand relationship, trust plays a very important foundational mechanism. Such a perception about EAI platforms reduces negative emotions such as fear, anxiety, and uncertainty. A study by Özdemir et al. (2020) demonstrates the role of affective trust in strengthening emotional consumer engagement, in measuring user satisfaction, and, ultimately, brand value and long-term brand loyalty. Affective trust gained through such affective engagement leads to positive behavioral intentions such as consumer-brand relationship, purchase intention, repurchase intention, and brand loyalty (Rather et al., 2019; Shao et al., 2025). The empathy factor strengthens affective trust among the user, serving as a guiding tool for enhanced advertising efficiency. Such an approach strengthens marketing efficiency, accelerates engagement, and improves conversion rates (Yadav, 2024). Furthermore, affective trust enhances consumer-brand relationships by reducing psychological distance from the brand, fostering a strong brand attitude, and thereby strengthening brand advocacy and brand loyalty (Chaudhuri & Holbrook, 2001).

Proposition 4 (P4): Affective-cognitive engagement positively impacts conative brand outcomes.

The combined affective-cognitive model of consumer engagement has a stronger impact on behavioral outcomes than the individual model. Affective trust plays an important role in strengthening such outcomes. Affective engagement fosters an emotional attachment to the brand, while cognitive engagement fosters a rational thought process, collectively strengthening the brand relationship (Samson & Voyer, 2012). The high emotional arousal-valence dimension further reduces the cognitive effort required for brand/product evaluation (Van Berlo et al., 2020). This accelerates the decision-making process. The study by Bilro and Loureiro (2020) further extends the argument for the significance of an integrated affective-cognitive model in an emotion-embedded AI platform on brand outcomes. Generally, in such an environment, brand attachment and brand loyalty is observed. Similarly, Rather et al. (2019) validate the role of affective-cognitive engagement in stronger purchase intention and positive word-of-mouth behavior. Mustikasari et al. (2025) further adds to this argument by emphasizing the role of affective engagement in positively influencing brand attitude, and purchase and repurchase intentions. Therefore, EAI platforms are capable of engaging users affectively and cognitively, positively influencing conative brand outcomes. A preliminary study by Asiabar et al. (2024) has shown an overall increase in consumer engagement and user satisfaction with the use of an EAI platform. Furthermore, affective engagement influences cognitive processing through rational thinking. This affective-cognitive model positively impacts brand commitment, strengthening brand loyalty and advocacy (Sallaku et al., 2025). Reduced cognitive effort needed for evaluation aids in enhanced decision-making and evaluation. Thereby, affective-cognitive mechanisms positively influence conative brand outcomes.

However, the proposed framework is better suited to situations where consumers are not merely driven by the pricing or the functional necessity of the product.

In such scenarios, consumer decision-making is not just restricted to utilitarian attributes of the product/brand. Such a consumer attitude can enhance emotional engagement. EAI interfaces work effectively when there is scope for affective/hedonic engagement. Hence, this framework emphasizes stronger conative outcomes and decision-making when consumers are involved on an affective level rather than just a utilitarian level.

ETHICAL CONSIDERATIONS

One major concern with the use of AI is the issue of ethical responsibility, transparency, and authenticity (Sallaku et al., 2025). Artificial empathy affectively engages consumers, helping brands to personalize advertisements through emotion detection and analysis. Therefore, with the growing ethical concerns, brands need to be mindful of the privacy and ethical issues associated with emotional and data tracking of users. Brands must be cautious about the automatic-emotion capturing mechanism, as the sensitive data collected can be misused for mass surveillance, potentially leading to data manipulation and exploitation. Auto-emotion recognition systems should be used for the rightful capture of data and not for biases or exploitation based on gender, age, sex, or rationality (Narimisaei et al., 2024). Personalized artificial emotional intelligence captures real-time user emotions, helping brands to personalize their advertisements and products according to consumer preferences (PadmavathyA & Alamelu, 2025). The integration of personalized EAI with brands should not be used to exploit or manipulate data and consumers. Data collected should be used for specific, time-bound purposes only, and not for unauthorized purposes (Fabiano, 2025). Storing of biometric data without user consent is unethical and should be restricted. The "Hawthorne" and "watching-eye" effects are possible in an EAI environment, where users, when aware of emotion monitoring, can alter their natural emotional responses. This could lead to user resistance and issues with user autonomy (Schlund & Zitek, 2024). When consumers are conscious of constant emotion tracking for enhanced personalized products, they may question the authenticity of the products, perceiving it as a manipulative approach (Hu & Min, 2023). To avoid this, transparency, consent, and privacy should be given due priority.

Bias is another significant challenge faced in an EAI environment. Human emotions are complex and not uniform. In this context, system and emotional bias is very common. Algorithmic bias in poorly designed systems could bring in emotional disparities, negatively impacting consumer decision-making. Such a bias develops a system bias toward certain stimuli and emotions. Similarly, data set bias, which draws on the data set used to train the AI platform, could result in an inaccurate and biased representation of data. This brings in cultural bias, as the standard data used for training may not be universally applicable (Rhue, 2023). The system would falsely or inappropriately capture emotions based on the standard data set provided before. Thereby, an all-inclusive data set should be used for training purposes to avoid future biases. Gender bias based on gender stereotypes is another common bias seen in empathy-embedded platforms. Men are considered to have more neutral emotions than women, who, in general, have pleasant emotions. This stereotype could result in unfair observations. Consequently, EAI models must provide logical explanations for their findings to minimize bias (S et al., 2026). Information presented through EAI platforms induces cognitive processing, wherein such information acts as an anchor for decision-making. Over-reliance on such information could cause anchoring effects subjective to cognitive bias, hindering natural cognitive processing (Rhue, 2023). These biases reduce the accuracy of EAI platforms, resulting in reduced consumer engagement and conversion rates. Therefore, EAI-enabled marketing platforms should ensure transparency and ethical use of EAI techniques.

In light of these ethical concerns, the need for a comprehensive ethical governance framework in EAI environments is gaining prominence. Developed economies such as the UK and the USA have standard regulatory frameworks, whereas developing countries need to develop an increased focus on such concerns. The ethical-governance gap enhances the risk of data manipulation and exploitation. The fear of emotional risk associated with emotional manipulation and exploitation reduces the affective trust in AI platforms (Babiker et al., 2026). Consequently, a global ethical standard could ensure transparency and consumer protection.

SOLUTIONS AND RECOMMENDATIONS: THEORETICAL AND MANAGERIAL IMPLICATIONS

Theoretical Implications

The book chapter contributes to the growing literature on emotion AI and consumer behavior by providing a deeper understanding of how EAI influences consumer decision-making through the emotive-cognitive mechanism. Grounded in DPT, ELM, and AIT, the chapter advances a deeper understanding of consumer decision-making in an emotion-embedded AI environment. These theories elaborate on how EAI stimulus can simultaneously engage users affectively and cognitively, influencing consumer-brand relationships and consumer decision-making. Such an approach would provide a better understanding of how emotional cues influence decision-making. The chapter adds on to the existing literature by identifying research gaps and suggesting future research directions. The chapter, therefore, calls for more interdisciplinary multimodal models linking emotional and cognitive engagement to behavioral outcomes. The chapter further highlights emerging ethical concerns, such as privacy issues, data manipulation, and data tracking. The need for ethical governance of the use of EAI to protect consumer interests is highlighted in the above sections. The multidisciplinary approach of the chapter, combining, consumer behavior, human-computer interactions, marketing and digital ethics, deepens theoretical understanding of the topic, paving the way for future studies.

Managerial Implications

The transition from affective computing to commercial artificial emotional intelligence has progressed rapidly in recent years (Wang et al., 2022). Marketers are increasingly using EAI to predict consumer behavior patterns and enhance user satisfaction by mimicking human-like empathy stimuli. The chapter focuses on the psychology of consumer decision-making, enabling marketing practitioners to develop products based on the psychology of consumer behavior patterns. Affective and cognitive engagement of consumers helps dive deeper into actual consumer behavior rather than at the surface level. Marketing managers should strategically use EAI techniques such as eye-tracking, facial coding, etc., to pre-test advertising campaigns before campaign launch. This could enhance campaign effectiveness. Brand managers should employ personalized recommendations to build affective trust thereby reducing decision uncertainty and improving purchase intention. Marketers and brand managers can utilize this opportunity to bring in transparency and trust to improve brand relationships. However, prior research has emphasized the negative role of over-personalization of emotional stimuli resulting in inaccurate responses. Therefore, brands should prioritize moderated personalization and build platforms that can detect user resistance and distrust concerns arising out of hyper-personalization. Adding on, regulatory requirements such as consent mechanism, transparency, and ethical use of AI should be perceived by brands as value-enhancing frameworks with the potential to improve platform effectiveness rather than as mere regulatory obligations. This could enhance long-term brand engagement and improve the conversion rates. Taking into consideration the scope of stimuli overload, a well-balanced emotive-cognitive model is required to reduce cognitive overload that leads to impulsive decisions. Furthermore, through multimodal fusion technologies, thereby consumer engagement and behavior patterns can be understood in a more efficient way, improving future marketing strategies. The chapter further highlights the role of EAI as a strategic marketing tool in personalizing brand content to build a deeper consumer-brand relationship. Developing such emotional engagement is mutually beneficial for both the consumer and the brand, as it enhances the consumer-brand relationship, strengthening brand position, and brand loyalty (Dwivedi, 2015).

FUTURE RESEARCH DIRECTIONS

The fast-evolving sector of EAI has seen a substantial wave of change in the past decade. The future of affective computing holds immense potential for further growth. However, the emotion recognition interface needs more robustness and accuracy. The chapter therefore proposes future research directions. The conceptual framework proposed in this chapter needs further empirical testing and validation through less-studied approaches such as experimental studies and longitudinal studies. In addition, studies spanning across disciplines and geographical boundaries are required to establish generalization. Large Language Model and other deep learning models offer a more comprehensive understanding of the EAI environment. Emotion-aware metaverse platforms that use MER applications could create highly accurate and reliable emotion recognition systems for practical applications in sectors such as healthcare, sports, stress reduction, the automobile industry, and individual health tracking. Such an integrated model into a multimodal EAI platform should be studied from a marketing perspective (Al-Saadawi et al., 2024). Furthermore, Lule et al. (2026) emphasizes the need for studies on the role of EAI applications in a metaverse environment. Further studies are needed to explore how artificial empathy can ensure consumer value through enriched affective and social engagement. Further exploration can be conducted on the effect of real-time emotion tracking mechanism on personalized brand advertisements (Lule et al., 2026). The conceptual framework proposed in the chapter can also be empirically tested in such environments. Finally, future studies could potentially develop standardized scales to measure ethical governance within commercial EAI platforms to promote enhanced transparency and responsibility.

CONCLUSION

The use of EAI platforms in marketing has significantly reshaped the marketing environment, enabling a consumer-centric approach. Real-time emotion analysis develops a strong feedback mechanism, thereby influencing future behavioral outcomes. Through the affective-cognitive lens of consumer behavior, the chapter provides a strong understanding of the psychology of consumer decision-making. As the literature on EAI continues to grow, future studies must ensure that transparency and ethical standards are met, to bring in a more holistic approach.

ACKNOWLEDGMENT

This research received no specific grant from any funding agency in the public, commercial, or not-for-profit sectors.

REFERENCES

Al-Saadawi, H. F. T., Das, B., & Das, R. (2024). A systematic review of trimodal affective computing approaches: Text, audio, and visual integration in emotion recognition and sentiment analysis. *Expert Systems with Applications*, *255*, 124852. DOI: 10.1016/j.eswa.2024.124852

Alsharif, A. H., Wang, J., Isa, S. M., Salleh, N. Z. M., Dawas, H. A., & Alsharif, M. H. (2025). The synergy of neuromarketing and artificial intelligence: A comprehensive literature review in the last decade. *Future Business Journal*, *11*(1), 170. DOI: 10.1186/s43093-025-00591-x

Arya, R., Singh, J., & Kumar, A. (2021). A survey of multidisciplinary domains contributing to affective computing. *Computer Science Review*, *40*, 100399. DOI: 10.1016/j.cosrev.2021.100399

Asiabar, M. G., Asiabar, M. G., & Asiabar, A. G. (2024). Analyzing the role of artificial emotional intelligence in personalizing human brand interactions: A mixed-methods approach. *Research Square*. https://doi.org/DOI: 10.21203/rs.3.rs-5037977/v1

Assunção, G., Patrão, B., Castelo-Branco, M., & Menezes, P. (2022). An Overview of Emotion in Artificial Intelligence. *IEEE Transactions on Artificial Intelligence*, *3*(6), 867–886. DOI: 10.1109/TAI.2022.3159614

Asutay, E., & Västfjäll, D. (2024). Affective integration in experience, judgment, and decision-making. *Communications Psychology*, *2*(1), 126. DOI: 10.1038/s44271-024-00178-2 PMID: 39706883

Babiker, A., Basel Almourad, M., AlShakhsi, S., Liebherr, M., & Ali, R. (2026). Do emotions matter in AI? The mediating role of emotional response between perceived risk and trust. *AI & Society*, *41*(6), 5717–5734. Advance online publication. DOI: 10.1007/s00146-026-02929-7

Bai, S., Yang, Y., Yu, D., & Tan, Y. (2025). Unlocking the secrets of user engagement: The role of multimodal information and sentiment signals in AI agent design. *Journal of Research in Interactive Marketing*, •••, 1–19. DOI: 10.1108/JRIM-01-2025-0035

Baumeister, R. F., & Leary, M. R. (1997). Writing narrative literature reviews. *Review of General Psychology, 1*(3), 311–320. DOI: 10.1037/1089-2680.1.3.311

Bilal, M., Zhang, Y., Cai, S., Akram, U., & Halibas, A. (2023). Artificial intelligence is the magic wand making customer-centric a reality! An investigation into the relationship between consumer purchase intention and consumer engagement through affective attachment. *Journal of Retailing and Consumer Services, 77*, 103674. DOI: 10.1016/j.jretconser.2023.103674

Bilro, R., & Loureiro, S. (2020). A consumer engagement systematic review: Synthesis and research agenda. *Spanish Journal of Marketing - ESIC, 24*(3), 283–307. DOI: 10.1108/SJME-01-2020-0021

Brodie, R. J., Hollebeek, L. D., Jurić, B., & Ilić, A. (2011). Customer engagement. *Journal of Service Research, 14*(3), 252–271. DOI: 10.1177/1094670511411703

Cambria, E. (2016). Affective computing and sentiment analysis. *IEEE Intelligent Systems, 31*(2), 102–107. DOI: 10.1109/MIS.2016.31

Chakraborty, D., Polisetty, A., Sowmya, G., Rana, N. P., & Khorana, S. (2024). Unlocking the potential of AI: Enhancing consumer engagement in the beauty and cosmetic product purchases. *Journal ofRetailing and Consumer Services, 79*, 103842. Advance online publication. DOI: 10.1016/j.jretconser.2024.103842

Chaudhuri, A., & Holbrook, M. B. (2001). The chain of effects from brand trust and brand affect to brand performance: The role of brand loyalty. *Journal of Marketing, 65*(2), 81–93. DOI: 10.1509/jmkg.65.2.81.18255

Chornous, G., Dimitrov, R., Fareniuk, Y., Penkova, M., & Nosko, R. (2025). Integration of feeling AI tools to support marketing solutions in e-commerce. *ACCESS Access to Science Business Innovation in Digital Economy, 6*(2), 415–436. DOI: 10.46656/access.2025.6.2(10)

Clore, G. L., & Bar-Anan, Y. (2007). Affect-as-information. In Baumeister, R. F., & Vohs, K. D. (Eds.), *Encyclopedia of social psychology* (pp. 14–16). Sage., DOI: 10.4135/9781412956253

Cristofaro, M., Giardino, P. L., Malizia, A. P., & Mastrogiorgio, A. (2022). Affect and cognition in managerial decision making: A systematic literature review of neuroscience evidence. *Frontiers in Psychology, 13*, 762993. Advance online publication. DOI: 10.3389/fpsyg.2022.762993 PMID: 35356322

Dwivedi, A. (2015). A higher-order model of consumer brand engagement and its impact on loyalty intentions. *Journal of Retailing and Consumer Services, 24*, 100–109. DOI: 10.1016/j.jretconser.2015.02.007

Evans, J. St. B. T. (1984). Heuristic and analytic processes in reasoning. *British Journal of Psychology, 75*(4), 451–468. DOI: 10.1111/j.2044-8295.1984.tb01915.x

Evans, J. St. B. T., & Stanovich, K. E. (2013). Dual-process theories of higher cognition: Advancing the debate. *Perspectives on Psychological Science : A Journal of the Association for Psychological Science, 8*(3), 223–241. DOI: 10.1177/1745691612460685 PMID: 26172965

Fabiano, N. (2025). *Affective computing and emotional data: Challenges and implications in privacy regulations, the AI Act, and ethics in large language models* (arXiv No. 2509.20153). arXiv. https://doi.org//arXiv.2509.20153DOI: 10.48550

Gary, J. (2024). Examining the interplay of information, emotions, and behavior: PLS-ANN analysis. *Frontiers in Communication, 9*, 1411870. Advance online publication. DOI: 10.3389/fcomm.2024.1411870

Grand View Research. (n.d.). Emotion AI market size, share & trends analysis report. https://www.grandviewresearch.com/industry-analysis/emotion-ai-market-report

Hollebeek, L. D., Glynn, M. S., & Brodie, R. J. (2014). Consumer brand engagement in social media: Conceptualization, scale development and validation. *Journal of Interactive Marketing, 28*(2), 149–165. DOI: 10.1016/j.intmar.2013.12.002

Hu, Y., & Min, H. (2023). The dark side of artificial intelligence in service: The "watching-eye" effect and privacy concerns. *International Journal of Hospitality Management, 110*, 103437. DOI: 10.1016/j.ijhm.2023.103437

Huang, M.-H., & Rust, R. T. (2021). A strategic framework for artificial intelligence in marketing. *Journal of the Academy of Marketing Science, 49*(1), 30–50. DOI: 10.1007/s11747-020-00749-9

iMotions. (2019, April 5). MARS - affectiva. Affectiva. https://www.affectiva.com/success-story/mars/

Kahneman, D. (2011). *Thinking, fast and slow*. Farrar, Straus and Giroux.

Kapoor, A., & Verma, V. (2024). Emotion AI: Understanding emotions through artificial intelligence. *International Journal of Engineering Science and Humanities, 1*(1), 223–232. DOI: 10.62904/0vcbvb24

Kirk, C. P., & Givi, J. (2024). The AI-authorship effect: Understanding authenticity, moral disgust, and consumer responses to AI-generated marketing communications. *Journal of Business Research, 186*, 114984. DOI: 10.1016/j.jbusres.2024.114984

L'Oréal. (2018, March 16). *L'Oréal acquires ModiFace, further expanding its worldwide expertise in beauty tech* [Press release]. https://www.loreal-finance.com/eng/news-release/loreal-acquires-modiface-further-expanding-its-worldwide-expertise-beauty-tech

Lai, Q., Jin, Y., Wu, T., & Ying, T. (2025). Rational, emotional or both: Decoding service robot adoption in tourism from elaboration likelihood model perspective. *Journal of Hospitality and Tourism Technology, 16*(5), 966–985. DOI: 10.1108/JHTT-03-2024-0194

Liu-Thompkins, Y., Okazaki, S., & Li, H. (2022). Artificial empathy in marketing interactions: Bridging the human-AI gap in affective and social customer experience. *Journal of the Academy of Marketing Science, 50*(6), 1198–1218. DOI: 10.1007/s11747-022-00892-5

Lule, B., Wuryaningrat, N. F., Walean, R. H., & Mandagi, D. W. (2026). Artificial empathy in marketing: Conceptual mapping, antecedents and consequences. *International Journal of Innovation Science*, •••, 1–24. DOI: 10.1108/IJIS-08-2025-0411

McClellan, S. (2013, January 18). Unilever, Coca-Cola utilize facial analysis to enhance ad tests. *MediaPost*. https://www.mediapost.com/publications/article/191418/unilever-coca-cola-utilize-facial-analysis-to-enh.html

Mohiddin, S. K., Sharmila, S., & Slimani, K. (2026). Navigating the future of Emotion AI: technical barriers, ethical concerns, and sustainable advancements. *In Information systems engineering and management (pp. 207–226).* https://doi.org/ DOI: 10.1007/978-3-032-14778-3_10

Monteith, S., Glenn, T., Geddes, J., Whybrow, P. C., & Bauer, M. (2022). Commercial use of emotion artificial intelligence (AI): Implications for psychiatry. *Current Psychiatry Reports, 24*(3), 203–211. DOI: 10.1007/s11920-022-01330-7 PMID: 35212918

Morris, J. D., Woo, C., & Singh, A. J. (2005). Elaboration likelihood model: A missing intrinsic emotional implication. *Journal of Targeting. Measurement and Analysis for Marketing, 14*(1), 79–98. DOI: 10.1057/palgrave.jt.5740171

Munteanu, T. (2024, July 25). *The role of emotions in consumer decision-making*. https://www.tokinomo.com/blog/role-emotions-consumer-decision-making

Mustikasari, A., Hurriyati, R., Dirgantari, P. D., Sultan, M. A., & Sugiana, N. S. S. (2025). The role of artificial intelligence in brand experience: Shaping consumer behavior and driving repurchase decisions. *International Journal of Advanced Computer Science and Applications, 16*(4). Advance online publication. DOI: 10.14569/IJACSA.2025.0160432

Narimisaei, J., Naeim, M., Imannezhad, S., Samian, P., & Sobhani, M. (2024). Exploring emotional intelligence in artificial intelligence systems: A comprehensive analysis of emotion recognition and response mechanisms. *Annals of Medicine and Surgery (London), 86*(8), 4657–4663. DOI: 10.1097/MS9.0000000000002315 PMID: 39118764

Özdemir, S., Zhang, S., Gupta, S., & Bebek, G. (2020). The effects of trust and peer influence on corporate brand–consumer relationships and consumer loyalty. *Journal of Business Research, 117*, 791–805. DOI: 10.1016/j.jbusres.2020.02.027

Padmavathy, A. M., & Alamelu, R. (2025). Harnessing personalized emotional ai for enhanced consumer engagement in intelligent marketing. *Donglixue Yu Kongzhi Xuebao*, •••, 13–22. DOI: 10.71058/jodac.v9i1002

Pan, X. (2025). A conceptual framework on AI-driven consumer behavior in the age of digital branding. *Frontiers in Business, Economics and Management, 19*(3), 58–64. DOI: 10.54097/3aasrp70

Pervez, F., Shoukat, M., Usama, M., Sandhu, M., Latif, S., & Qadir, J. (2024). Affective computing and the road to an emotionally intelligent metaverse. *IEEE Open Journal of the Computer Society, 5*, 195–214. DOI: 10.1109/OJCS.2024.3389462

Petty, R. E., & Cacioppo, J. T. (1986). The elaboration likelihood model of persuasion. *Advances in Experimental Social Psychology, 19*, 123–205. DOI: 10.1016/S0065-2601(08)60214-2

Picard, R. W. (1997). *Affective Computing*. MIT Press. DOI: 10.7551/mitpress/1140.001.0001

Poria, S., Cambria, E., Bajpai, R., & Hussain, A. (2017). A review of affective computing: From unimodal analysis to multimodal fusion. *Information Fusion, 37*, 98–125. DOI: 10.1016/j.inffus.2017.02.003

Puntoni, S., Reczek, R., Giesler, M., & Botti, S. (2020). Consumers and artificial intelligence: An experiential perspective. *Journal of Marketing, 85*(1), 002224292095384. DOI: 10.1177/0022242920953847

Rather, R. A., Tehseen, S., Itoo, M. H., & Parrey, S. H. (2019). Customer brand identification, affective commitment, customer satisfaction, and brand trust as antecedents of customer behavioral intention of loyalty: An empirical study in the hospitality sector. *Journal of Global Scholars of Marketing Science*, *29*(2), 196–217. DOI: 10.1080/21639159.2019.1577694

Rhue, L. (2023). The anchoring effect, algorithmic fairness, and the limits of information transparency for emotion artificial intelligence. *Information Systems Research*, *35*(3), 1479–1496. DOI: 10.1287/isre.2019.0493

Rohden, S. F., & Espartel, L. B. (2026). Emotional artificial intelligence: The impact of chatbot empathy and emotional tone on consumer satisfaction and word of mouth. *International Journal of Human-Computer Studies*, *210*, 103764. DOI: 10.1016/j.ijhcs.2026.103764

S, S. G., Chandrasekaran, B., & J, O. (2026). Ethics and bias in emotional AI. *Frontiers in Artificial Intelligence*, *9*. https://doi.org/DOI: 10.3389/frai.2026.1768696

Sallaku, K., Macca, L. S., Santoro, G., & Thu Phan, T. (2025). Advertising in the digital era: Can AI evoke emotions like humans? *Business Process Management Journal*, *31*(5), 1785–1811. DOI: 10.1108/BPMJ-07-2024-0637

Samson, A., & Voyer, B. (2012). Two minds, three ways: Dual system and process models in consumer psychology. *AMS Review*, *2*(2-4), 48–71. Advance online publication. DOI: 10.1007/s13162-012-0030-9

Schlund, R., & Zitek, E. M. (2024). Algorithmic versus human surveillance leads to lower perceptions of autonomy and increased resistance. *Communications Psychology*, *2*(1), 53. DOI: 10.1038/s44271-024-00102-8 PMID: 39242768

Schwarz, N., & Clore, G. L. (1983). Mood, misattribution, and judgments of well-being: Informative and directive functions of affective states. *Journal of Personality and Social Psychology*, *45*(3), 513–523. DOI: 10.1037/0022-3514.45.3.513

Shao, C., Kim, Y., & Xu, L. Z. (2025). From ai chatbot to brand support: An exploration of perceived empathy and ethics in shaping trust and word of mouth. *Communication Reports*, *39*(1), 69–81. DOI: 10.1080/08934215.2025.2519253

Singh, B. K., & Srivastava, U. K. (2026). A Systematic Review on the Evolution of Emotional Artificial Intelligence. *IARJSET*, *13*(1). Advance online publication. DOI: 10.17148/IARJSET.2026.13159

Van Berlo, Z. M., Van Reijmersdal, E. A., Smit, E. G., & Van Der Laan, L. N. (2020). Brands in virtual reality games: Affective processes within computer-mediated consumer experiences. *Journal of Business Research, 122*, 458–465. DOI: 10.1016/j.jbusres.2020.09.006

Wakefield, R. L. (2006). Affect as information in the decision to use technology. P*roceedings of the Twelfth Americas Conference on Information Systems (AMCIS), 354.*

Wang, Y., Song, W., Tao, W., Liotta, A., Yang, D., Li, X., Gao, S., Sun, Y., Ge, W., Zhang, W., & Zhang, W. (2022). A systematic review on affective computing: Emotion models, databases, and recent advances. *Information Fusion, 83–84*, 19–52. DOI: 10.1016/j.inffus.2022.03.009

Yadav, T. (2024). AI in Neuromarketing: Understanding Consumer Emotions and Behavior through Machine Learning. *IJFMR - International. Journal of Multidisciplinary Research, 6*(5), 28154. Advance online publication. DOI: 10.36948/ijfmr.2024.v06i05.28154

Zanger, V., Meißner, M., & Rauschnabel, P. A. (2022). Beyond the gimmick: How affective responses drive brand attitudes and intentions in augmented reality marketing. *Psychology and Marketing, 39*(7), 1285–1301. DOI: 10.1002/mar.21641

Zhang, H., Liu, Y., Jiang, M., Chen, J., Wang, M., & Paas, F. (2025). Emotional Artificial Intelligence in Education: A Systematic Review and Meta-Analysis. *Educational Psychology Review, 37*(4), 106. DOI: 10.1007/s10648-025-10086-4

Zhu, X., Guo, C., Feng, H., Huang, Y., Feng, Y., Wang, X., & Wang, R. (2024). A review of key technologies for emotion analysis using multimodal information. *Cognitive Computation, 16*(4), 1504–1530. DOI: 10.1007/s12559-024-10287-z

ADDITIONAL READING

Clore, G. L., Gasper, K., & Garvin, E. (2001). Affect as information. In Forgas, J. P. (Ed.), *Handbook of affect and social cognition* (pp. 121–144). Psychology Press.

Loewenstein, G., & Lerner, J. S. (2003). The role of affect in decision making. In Davidson, R. J., Scherer, K. R., & Goldsmith, H. H. (Eds.), *Handbook of affective sciences* (pp. 619–642). Oxford University Press.

KEY TERMS AND DEFINITIONS

Affective Computing: Is an interdisciplinary field that is built on systems integrated with artificial intelligence capable of interpreting, analyzing and responding to human emotions. The field integrates artificial intelligence, human-computer interaction, psychology of consumer behavior and machine learning to enable emotion-aware technology.

Affective Engagement: Refers to the psychological attachment and emotional bond characterized by enjoyment, empathy and excitement that a consumer develops instantly in response to exposure to an external stimulus.

Affective Trust: The emotional trust a consumer develops during affective engagement with an emotion AI system, which strengthens the link between engagement and conative brand outcomes.

Cognitive Engagement: Refers to the extent of mental absorption and thought processes toward an external stimulus. It reflects rational thinking and thought process involved guiding consumer decision-making.

Conative Brand Outcome: Refers to the degree of consumers' participation and involvement in response to the cognitive and affective engagement resulting in a positive behavior toward the brand.

Consumer Decision-Making: Refers to the process through which individuals analyze the situation, and evaluate the alternatives available based on prior cognitive and affective engagement, shaping judgments and behavioral intentions.

Emotion Artificial Intelligence (EAI): EAI refers to the artificial intelligence technology that interprets, analyzes, and responds to human emotions by decoding facial expressions, voice and speech analysis, physiological signals, and behavioral patterns. In marketing, EAI facilitates empathetic consumer engagement and supports informed consumer decision-making.

Chapter 5

Balancing Personalization and Homogenization in AI-Generated Consumer Recommendations

Jaspreet Kaur
http://orcid.org/0000-0002-7480-9844
Hans Raj Mahila Maha Vidyalaya, Jalandhar, India

Harpreet Singh
http://orcid.org/0000-0001-7202-3912
Hans Raj Mahila Maha Vidyalaya, Jalandhar, India

ABSTRACT

Personalization has always been an important aspect of business and with the popularization of e-commerce as well as with the advances in technology; personalization has become vital to achieve customer interest, engagement, satisfaction and loyalty, positively impacting the sales. Recommendation systems act as a key component of the entire personalization cycle by reducing the information overload and recommending items as per the interest of the customer and helping the customer in decision making. Recommendation systems have been evolved from rule-based to Artificial Intelligence (AI)- and Machine Learning (ML)-based systems. The introduction of Generative AI has taken personalization to the next level. However, excessive use of AI may lead to homogeneity in recommendation leading to bias in decision making and affecting diversity of recommendations. AI-based recommendation systems need to strike a right balance in personalization and consumer behavior in order to achieve more realistic and sustainable personalization goals.

DOI: 10.4018/979-8-3373-9589-0.ch005

INTRODUCTION

Innovative approaches have shortened the product life cycle due to radical technological advancements. New inventions are introduced in the market in a frantic manner to meet the customers' expectations of advancement (Virilio, 1986). The ability to filter and present pertinent content to individuals has become a battleground in the information age we live in today. This strategy has become an essential part of the fiercely competitive world of e-commerce today to thrive by providing an outstanding personalized experience to customers. Now the focus of business organizations has shifted from mass production to mass customization, human-centeredness, and personalization (Sheth et al., 2000); every individual customer is treated as a market (Pine and Gilmore, 2013). Millions of product varieties are sold to a small number of consumers due to advancements in production capabilities and information technology. This mass customization is related to personalization (Kotler, 1989; Westbrook and Williamson, 1993; Pine, 1993; Kay, 1993; Hart, 1995; Tseng and Jiao, 2001; Dollarhide and Anderson, 2020) and with the advancement of information and communication technology social networking, online blogs, and communities have developed, which provide invaluable information about buyers' needs, tastes and wants. In addition, these platforms provide marketers an opportunity to connect with buyers and achieve the goals of customization and personalization (Harzer, 2013). This customization has led to the building up of the learning relationship between business houses and buyers because buyers invest their energy and time to provide information about their needs to the business houses, and due to which a large amount of data and information has been lying with the business houses which could be used by these organizations to give suggestions and recommendations to buyers (Sandrin, 2021).

BACKGROUND

Personalization

Personalization enhances customer engagement and adoption because marketers have access to the personal information of consumers. Business houses recognize the unique needs of every individual and provide them with unique products as per their requirements (Stevenson, 2019). By using a design thinking approach, marketers find out the unfulfilled needs and requirements of buyers and treat these unmet needs and requirements as opportunities for their business houses. Finally, these marketers come up with new and improved products, services, and experiences, etc., for buyers to fulfill their unmet needs and create value (Abraham et al., 2017).

Personalization has therefore evolved as a key component to achieve customer engagement and satisfaction, ultimately leading to sales. Personalized product recommendations are becoming more important as consumers' reliance on digital platforms for purchases grows and e-commerce businesses become more competitive (Guan et al., 2019). In a cutthroat digital world, these suggestions are not only helpful for boosting sales but are also becoming more and more necessary for drawing in and keeping customers' interest and loyalty. In fact, personalized customer experience has become the new normal today in terms of customer expectations, rather than being a luxury (Wasilewski et al., 2025). The importance of personalization can be sensed from survey reports published by leading consulting organizations such as McKinsey & Company, which revealed that 71% of customers anticipated individualized interactions from businesses, and 76% were irritated when these weren't provided (Arora et al., 2021). Personalized recommendations are a great way to improve business performance because they increase client lifetime value, sales, and conversion rates. E-commerce platforms can increase sales volumes, boost customer investment, and better control strategies by providing customers with products that suit their needs and interests. The purchase process becomes more efficient as a result of fewer barriers (El Alam and Bitar, 2024). As per the findings of McKinsey & Company, it was shown that personalized marketing can boost sales by 5 to 15%, lower client acquisition expenses by up to 50%, and boost marketing return on investment by 10 to 30%. Additionally, it has been demonstrated that personalization enhances performance and yields better customer results. Personalization accounts for 40% more revenue for businesses with greater growth rates than for those with slower growth rates (McKinsey & Company, 2023). With the introduction of the first customized direct marketing letters in the 19th century, personalization-a fundamental component of contemporary marketing-has a long history. In e-commerce, its use grew during the first decade of the twenty-first century (Chandra et al., 2022). Companies have been attempting to meet customer needs through personalization for a while now, leveraging analytics and data to create more relevant customer experiences (Stein et al., 2025). Recommendation systems play a vital role in achieving personalization. This system helps buyers in decision-making (Rashid et al., 2002) and recommends to customers the items that are bought by others and reduces information overload (Schafer, Konstan and Riedl, 1999).

Recommender Systems

The contemporary recommender system was introduced in the 1990s. Information retrieval is a task of search engines, and the information filtering concept initiated the system of recommendations, and the comparison of the concept of information retrieval and information filtering was conducted by Belkin and Croft in the year 1992. In the year 1992 only, Tapestry recommender system was proposed by Goldberg et al., 1992, which is based on collaborative filtering, and this collaborative filtering was based on human evaluation. GroupLens, the News Recommender Service, was started by the researchers at the University of Minnesota and the Massachusetts Institute of Technology (Resnick et al., 1994). Ringo System has been providing recommendations about music and video (Shardanand & Maes, 1995). With a due course of time, the e-commerce industry has realized the importance of recommender systems, with NetPerception emerging as the first business user of recommender system in the year 1996 (Riedl, 2013; Dong et al., 2022). Schafer et al. (1999) highlighted the usage of recommender system by major E-Commerce operators like Best Buy, Amazon, and JCPenney, and all these recommender systems have been based on collaborative filtering until 2005. Major research was conducted from 2006 to 2009 on Matrix factorization models due to the Netflix prize (Koren, 2008; Koren, 2009). Due to rapid progress in recommender system, the ACM conference series (an annual event) on Recommender Systems (RecSys) was launched in 2007 (Konstan and ACM conference on Recommender systems, 2007), and in the year 2007 a model of logistic regression which has been devised by Richardson et al. (2007), which reduced the error of recommender systems by 30%. Factorization machines (FMs) were proposed by Rendle (2010) in the year 2010, while Juan et al. (2016) developed Field Aware Factorization Machines inspired by Factorization Machines. Therefore, in the early days of e-commerce (known as the pre-AI era), personalization was dominated by various rule-based recommendation systems, including decision trees and association rule mining (Kim et al., 2002; Lim et al., 2011), which further evolved to include semantics- and topology-based knowledge graphs to provide more relevant and accurate suggestions (Wasilewski et al., 2025).

Figure 1. A comparison of AI-Based and Rule-Based Recommendation Systems (Al-Hasan et al., 2024; Ho, 2024).

Feature	AI-Based System	Rule-Based System
Personalization	High	Low
Scalability	Excellent	Poor
Adaptability	Dynamic	Static
Data Handling	Complex & Unstructured	Simple & Structured
Accuracy	High (learns from data)	Moderate to Low
Maintenance	Low (automated learning)	High (manual rule updates)
Real-Time Recommendations	Yes	Limited

However, the variety and complexity of information the e-commerce ecosystem currently generates, has led to the evolution of Artificial Intelligence (AI)-based recommendation systems. AI and Machine Learning (ML) systems have the ability to automatically learn from data and progressively improve their functioning without explicit programming. It comprises a variety of techniques and algorithms intended to predict or make decisions based on patterns and conclusions derived from the underlying data (Figure 1). Neural network based recommender system has been developed for academic and industrial purposes since 2016 like Wide and Deep model (Cheng et al., 2016) and Deep FM (Guo et al., 2018). These recommender models have improved the performance of apps. For recommending videos to view on YouTube, DNN (Covington et al., 2016) and correct-SFX (Yi et al., 2019) have been developed. DIN (Deep Interest Network) (Zhou et al., 2018) and DIEN (Deep Interest Evolution Network) (Zhou et al., 2019) models have been developed, followed by DCN (Deep and Cross Network) (Wang et al., 2017) and DCN V2 (Wang et al., 2021).

Brands and AI

Brands have been using AI tools to examine and evaluate customers' data to achieve hyper-personalization and scaled-individualization. AI tools (ChatGPT, Midjourney, DALL-E) have been supporting brands by creating advertisements and personalized messages for customers to engage with the brands. AI tools have been designing logos, captions, taglines, and storylines for the brands (Hue and Hung, 2025). Organizations such as Amazon, Netflix, Myntra, Flipkart, Ajio, Spotify, Starbucks, etc., use different types of AI based recommender systems to suggest items or products to buyers that align with their needs, requirements, and tastes. For example, Amazon has been a pioneer in adopting collaborative-filtering recommendation systems based on the principle of "customers who bought X also bought Y" approach in the early 2000s (Stratoflow, 2025a; Marketing with Dave, 2026). This system analyzes the browsing history, past purchases, and co-purchase patterns to create a personalized experience for each visitor. Industry sources widely report that this system generates approximately one third of Amazon's total sales. The figure originates in trade commentary rather than in any disclosure by the company, and it should be read as an estimate (VWO, n.d.; Rebuy Engine, n.d.; Argoid, 2023). Amazon's strategy demonstrates that recommendation-driven personalization can become a structural revenue driver rather than a peripheral feature. However, it also signals dependency of a firm on continuous data collection while raising longer-term questions about algorithmic transparency and customer trust (Marketing with Dave, 2026). On the other hand, Netflix achieves personalization by using a retention mechanism to uniquely present and recommend titles. These unique visual presentations include artwork selection, the labeling of recommendation rows (e.g., "Because You Watched..."), etc. It was reported that around 80 percent of the hours viewed on Netflix originate from its recommendation system rather than from active search by the subscriber (Gomez-Uribe and Hunt, 2016). It has been estimated that Netflix's recommendation system helped the company to save over a billion dollars a year through reduced subscriber churn (Gomez-Uribe and Hunt, 2016). The Netflix case illustrates how personalization can function as a retention mechanism in subscription-based business models. In addition, this strategy suggests that personalization can be used to make upstream content-investment decisions, thereby extending its role beyond marketing into strategic resource allocation (Stratoflow, 2025b). In another strategy, Starbucks uses its "Deep Brew" AI platform to combine transactional data from its Rewards loyalty program with contextual signals including weather, time of day, and location to generate individualized product and offer recommendations delivered through its mobile application (Klover.ai, 2025; AI Plus Info, 2026). Starbucks therefore blends personalization with its loyalty-program architecture through the targeted analytics capabilities of the "Deep Brew" system to simultaneously achieve marketing objectives and operational objectives such as demand forecasting, staffing, inventory, etc. (AI Plus Info, 2026). Using such strategies involving AI, brands have been able to achieve higher levels of customer satisfaction and loyalty (Katrandjiev, Naydenov and Dinev, 2025). However, there is a requirement for a human check on AI-generated content (Katrandjiev, Naydenov and Dinev, 2025).

Personalization, Recommendation System and Consumer Behavior

By providing customers with products that suit their needs and interests, e-commerce platforms can increase their sales volumes while also improving customer engagement and control strategies. The personalized strategy and recommendation system help to make the purchasing process less complicated and more efficient. According to Lambrecht and Tucker (2019), personalized product suggestions make use of sophisticated algorithms to evaluate consumer data, predict preferences, and tailor the purchasing experience for every individual user. Personalized product recommendations are a direct link between the consumer's buying experience and AI's analytical capabilities. These technologies offer a more engaging and satisfying shopping experience by using a vast amount of data to forecast and influence consumer preferences. This could lead to higher conversion rates and greater customer loyalty (El Alam and Bitar, 2024). The retail sector has been significantly impacted by the adoption of this personalized strategy, which is now a crucial component of increasing customer interaction (Smith & Linden, 2017).

The number of times a customer clicks on the advertisement, the time they spend on the website, and the total number of visitors are all used to gauge customer engagement. In principle, AI-powered recommendations employ sophisticated data analysis techniques that examine vast amounts of user data, such as browsing and purchase histories, social media activity, and device usage habits, to generate precise consumer behavior models and predictions (Ricci 2015). These models are continuously improving to give recommendations that are more precise and actively adaptive to the shifting preferences of customers. Therefore, when customers visit the websites of marketers, the AI tools of apps give details of the customers shopping behavior to the marketing experts of the business houses i.e. beginning with the online opening of the app by the customers till they complete their purchase, AI tools keep record of the shopping behavior of buyers and use this information in guiding customers in their future purchases for example, giving recommendations to buyers to buy certain items or through online advertising, sending mails or any other mode of communication to provoke buyers to buy certain items (Sandrin, 2021). AI based recommender system judges the tastes, preferences, and likings of consumers based on their searches on the app and subsequently suggests items to buyers on the basis of their past search and purchase behavior, thereby enhancing the sales of the concerned items (Adomavicius et al., 2018). These AI models further incorporate metrics related to consumer involvement, including the amount of time spent on the website, interaction rates, and frequency of return visits (El Alam and Bitar, 2024). These metrics are crucial for e-commerce platforms because they help e-commerce platforms to directly relate to user engagement and interest levels, which in turn influence purchasing behavior.

In addition, marketers compete with each other to catch the attention of buyers by exposing them to marketing-related information. According to Carr (2021), an average buyer watched 500 to 1600 advertisements per day in the year 1970, via newspapers, billboards, magazines, and television, but now in 2021, an average buyer watches 6000 to 10000 advertisements every day, and customers avoid these advertisements by blocking certain sites, persons, unfollowing certain social media accounts, and by canceling subscriptions, etc. AI based recommender system helps to resolve the issue of information overload by separating irrelevant information and providing only relevant and to-the-point information to buyers (Schreiner et al., 2019).

METHODOLOGY

In this study, a qualitative approach has been used for searching, studying, and analyzing contributions of various researchers in this field. This review-based research paper aims to strike a balance between personalization and homogenization of AI-generated recommendations influencing consumer behavior. Google Scholar and the Google database help analysts to analyze and handle data successfully, as it has wider scope and enable sophisticated search features to narrow down data (Hallinger and Nguyen, 2020; Verma et al., 2021). 10,245 documents indexed in Google Scholar were identified using search terms including Artificial Intelligence, Machine Learning, Deep Learning, Neural Networks, Personalized Recommendations, Recommender System, Consumer Behavior, Involvement, Buying Decision, Click Through Rate, Customization and Generative AI in e-Commerce. The identification and screening steps follow the reporting structure of the Preferred Reporting Items for Systematic Reviews and Meta-Analyses (Moher et al., 2010) and are set out in Figure 2. The review is narrative rather than systematic in the strict sense, because no protocol was registered in advance and no formal quality appraisal instrument was applied.

Figure 2. Preferred Reporting Items for Systematic Reviews and Meta-Analyses (PRISMA) in the identification and screening of sources.

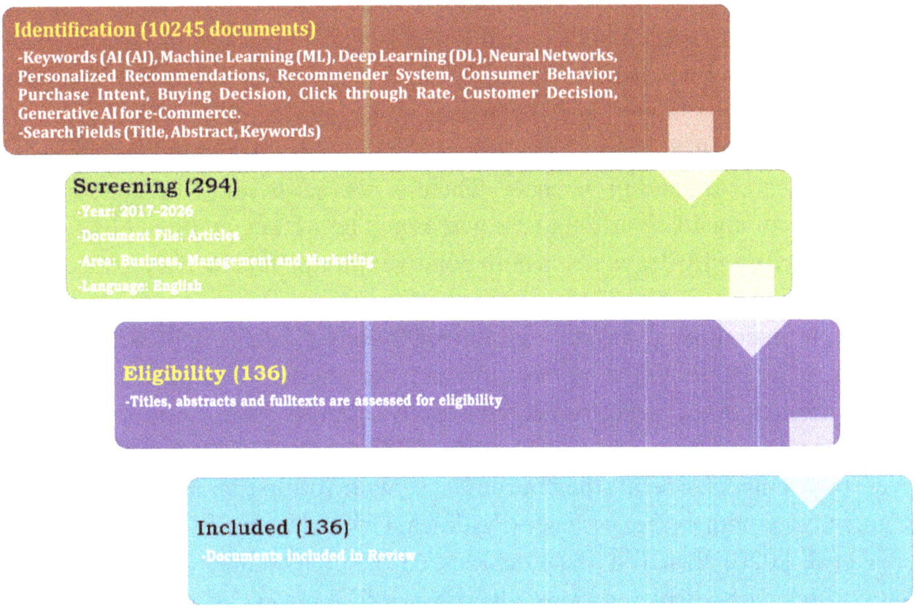

In the second step of screening, documents published between 2017 and 2026 in business, management and marketing, in English, were considered, and 294 articles were selected for further study. In the next two steps the authors read the titles, abstracts and full texts, and the review was narrowed to 136 sources. The inclusion criterion was the quality and standard of the work. Alongside the peer-reviewed literature, the review also draws on industry and practitioner sources, including consultancy reports, vendor case studies and trade publications. These are cited where they are the only available account of a named company's practice, and they are used to describe what firms report doing rather than as evidence of effect.

THE IMPACT OF AI-DRIVEN RECOMMENDATION SYSTEMS ON PERSONALIZATION

Various systems can provide recommendations to consumers; one is a collaborative recommendation system, or collaborative filtering, in which consumers are divided into groups based on their heterogeneity, and persons within the same group are homogeneous, and consumers in the same group are given recommendations based on the interests of the consumers in the same group. This collaborative filtering algorithm is very effective, but this approach does not suggest novel items or items that are very little discussed among buyers (Chinchanachokchai et al., 2021). This approach does not take into account features, characteristics, and attributes of items (Srivastava et al., 2020). While content-based filtering approach of recommender system gives recommendations and suggestions to buyers by matching features of the product with the buyers' profile (Jannach and Jugovac, 2019). This approach takes into consideration the fact that every individual is unique and everyone has his or her own tastes and preferences. There is another hybrid filtering approach that gives recommendations to buyers while buying. Molaie and Lee (2022) have revealed that diversity decreases in collaborative filtering and increases in content-based filtering.

AI driven recommender system has altered the buyers' decision-making process (Sharma et al., 2023). When buyers buy items for pleasure or enjoyment, i.e., for hedonic needs, they are engaged in impulsive buying and are satisfied with their post-purchase experience (Kimiagari and Malafe, 2021; Wu et al., 2021), and sometimes buyers buy items considering their purpose, i.e., with a utilitarian approach, and they are not satisfied with their experience (Festinger, 1957; Morvan and O'Connor, 2017; Akbar et al., 2020). Based on past purchases, AI-driven recommendation systems in digital selling apps display various advertisements to buyers as well as offer them discounts, gifts, deals, etc., based on the items in their wish list or added to the cart but not yet ordered; i.e., customized offers are generated by the recommendation system to provoke customers to buy the concerned items (Redine et al., 2023). But many times, after buying items on the basis of recommendations, customers feel dissatisfied because products bought by them on the basis of AI-driven recommendations do not match their expectations (Akbar et al., 2020; Chen et al., 2021).

This system recommends products to buyers on the basis of their browsing history and purchase history. AI-enabled personalization operates through five main strategies.

Customized recommendations. Based on the browsing history and past purchases of buyers, AI driven recommender system recommends products to customers to provide them with a customized shopping experience. This strategy is based on two features, i.e., customer tastes & preferences and technology, which enhance the shopping experience of buyers (Personalized Pricing, 2022).

Customized content on apps. AI-driven websites and shopping apps, as well as portals of business houses, customize the homepage of the online shopping apps and portals based on the search history and buying history of buyers to provide them with a personalized shopping experience. Customers are also offered customized offers on the basis of items in their wish list and carts (Muthuri, 2023).

Personalized pricing strategy. The AI-driven shopping apps customize the prices of items for customers based on their preferences, search history, and sometimes based on geographical location to maximize the profit of the seller. This strategy is also referred to as dynamic pricing (Personalized Pricing, 2022).

Reducing Information Load on Customers. The large number of products available online and their variability have made the decision-making process of buyers extremely difficult (Ghose and Ipeirotis, 2010), and to address this issue, AI-based tools are being employed to integrate and encapsulate the search results (Proserpio and Zervas, 2017). With the use of algorithm-based AI recommendation systems, the way in which search results are generated by search engines has changed radically and drastically, and it has an unforeseen influence on buyers' buying behavior; it also reduces information overload on buyers. In addition to this, AI has the feature of condensing the reviews of various customers into a single paragraph. This feature is known as the AI-based summary feature (Alavi and Nozari, 2023).

More Satisfying Shopping Experience. AI based recommender system has significantly changed buyers' buying behavior. They are now making informed buying decisions with the help of recommender system (Kim and Gupta, 2012). The AI tools enhance customer service and satisfaction as well as reduce cost and customer waiting time by attending to several customers at a time. This enhances customers' loyalty. All this will increase the efficiency of the concerned business house, and it will also reduce the number of employees in the organization, which would also save the cost of business house (Misra et al., 2024). Buyers' access to a vast amount of online information is restricted; they are connected to an 'echo chamber' generated by AI-based algorithms, and these algorithms limit the search engine results based on the buyers' interests (Xiao and Benbasat, 2013; Danaher et al., 2017). With the help of AI-based tools, businesses can provide a better experience to customers and can have an edge in digital marketing (Misra et al., 2024).

OVER-PERSONALIZATION, CONSUMER DECISION-MAKING AND CUSTOMER SATISFACTION

Recommender system is essential and has an enduring impact on customers in buying various items and services. Facebook, Netflix & Google News etc., have an effect on buyers' thoughts and opinions. This system has a great impact on buyers' involvement, retention, and purchases. But these recommender systems lack diversity; i.e., these systems suggest similar items to every buyer as well as the same items to the same buyer at the next purchase, which leads to homogeneity (Fleder et al., 2011). The excessive usage of AI in the recommendation system can have a detrimental effect on buyers' satisfaction. One school of thought highlights that AI based recommender system generates same type of suggestions to various consumers, due to which diversity in their buying has reduced and there is homogenization in their buying habits. This is referred to as the "Matthew Effect" (Lee and Hosanagar, 2019; Li et al., 2022).

The other school of thought, referred to as the "Internet's Long Tail," highlights that this recommender system shows varied items to buyers and enhances diversity in sales by showing every type of item to online buyers (Brynjolfsson et al., 2011; Holtz et al., 2020; Donnelly et al., 2021). Pariser (2011) has given the concept of a 'filter bubble', i.e., a system in which AI based recommender system suggests similar or homogeneous items to the same buyers. So, there is homogenization in-person but diversity across consumers or buyers. Another viewpoint has been given by Hosanagar et al. (2014) and Moller et al. (2018), which highlights that there is homogenization in the buying habits of varied buyers i.e., there is commonality among varied buyers, but the same buyers do not buy the same type of item time and again, so there is diversity in individual buying style.

Reconciling the Evidence: Level of Analysis as the Missing Variable

The four positions above are often read as four competing answers to one question, but they are not. They differ in the level at which diversity is measured. The Matthew effect and the long tail both concern concentration across the catalogue, that is, whether sales spread out or bunch up in aggregate. The filter bubble and the fragmentation argument concern something else entirely, namely the relationship between what a single consumer sees over time and what different consumers see relative to one another, and on that question the two positions point in opposite directions. Table 1 sets the four out side by side.

Table 1. The four positions on personalization and diversity, by level of measurement

Position	Core claim	Level at which diversity is measured	Principal evidence cited
Matthew effect and concentration bias	Recommenders narrow what is bought and reinforce items that are already popular	Aggregate, across the catalogue	Fleder et al. (2011); Adamopoulos and Tuzhilin (2014); Lee and Hosanagar (2019); Li et al. (2022)
Internet's long tail	Recommenders widen sales into rare and hard to find items	Aggregate, across the catalogue	Brynjolfsson et al. (2011); Holtz et al. (2020); Donnelly et al. (2021)
Filter bubble	The individual is shown an ever narrower set, while different individuals are shown different sets	Narrowing within the individual, widening across individuals	Pariser (2011)
Fragmentation reversed	Individuals keep varied consumption over time, while different individuals converge on the same items	Widening within the individual, narrowing across individuals	Hosanagar et al. (2014); Möller et al. (2018)

Read this way, the apparent contradiction in the literature largely dissolves. A recommender can concentrate aggregate sales while still widening what an individual encounters, and it can narrow an individual's field of view while pushing different individuals further apart. Two consequences follow for this chapter's central question. First, any claim that personalization increases or reduces diversity is incomplete until the level of measurement is stated, and much of the disagreement in the field is a disagreement about measurement rather than about mechanism. Second, the balance a brand should strike depends on which risk it is managing. A retailer worried about catalogue concentration and the visibility of small suppliers faces a different design problem from a platform worried that its customers are becoming indistinguishable from one another, and the same intervention will not serve both.

This homogeneity or similarity has a damaging impact on ecosystem-level goals.

1. **Reduction in diversity:** Recommender systems recommend the same item to every individual, as well as same buyers are offered the same item time and again, which leads to homogeneity (Fleder et al., 2011). This leads to concentration bias, i.e., recommender systems suggest the same items to everyone, which is unfair, wrongful, and ungenerous with other items (Adamopoulos and Tuzhilin, 2014). This is also known as popularity bias (Abdollahpouri et al., 2019) because it recommends popular items and services to buyers. So, reduction in diversity is a serious issue in recommender systems (Kunaver and Požrl, 2017). Recommender system never recommends unpopular items (Hong, 2020).

2. **Relies on historical data:** For new buyers and customers of online shopping platforms, the recommendations on the basis of past purchases of buyers are of no use. This problem is also known as data sparsity. Suggestions are given on the basis of mass popularity, which is not beneficial for new buyers, and these types of recommendations reduce buyers' delight and joy (Adamopoulos and Tuzhilin, 2014). This is known as the 'cold start problem' because the new items and products are not popular, so these items are not recommended by AI-based algorithms, and therefore these novel items are not noticed by many customers.
3. **Outcome criteria or indicators**: The programmer of AI based recommender system defines outcome criteria. The program developer has entire control over the working of the program, and the result of these programs influences buyers. The popularity of any item can be judged on the basis of likes and purchases of the item, and if the item is out of stock, it can be added to the wish list by interested buyers. To prevent malicious social assaults, AI based recommender systems do not reveal their exact configuration and parameters (Lang et al., 2010). Hong (2020) pointed out that when buyers rely on outcome criteria, they would select the items that are already popular. This would lead to popularity bias and would also lead to a reduction in sales of unpopular items, and this would also reduce diversity in recommender system. So, there is a challenge that the system can make any product popular because there is a lack of transparency. The programmer of the recommender system can design the program as per the need because he has sole authority over the customers' evaluation process.
4. **Company and social media influence:** Popularity bias is added by the programmer at the request of the company for whom the program is being created because the company has the ultimate authority. Moreover, this recommendation system is the part and parcel of social media platforms like Facebook, Twitter & Amazon feeds, etc., so financial benefits and incentives can be offered by the business houses to these social media platforms. In return, the social sites influence their recommendation systems. That is why recommendation systems lead to homogeneity in buyers' selection. To remove this problem, buyers must be suggested other items as per their needs, requirements, and interests so that diversity can be promoted.

Constant algorithmic observation of the buyer shapes and narrows the buying experience. These algorithms recommend items on the basis of the experience of buyers. So, instead of enhancing the buyers' experience, it may increase the risk of reducing variety options for buyers by shortlisting items based on the past purchase behavior of consumers, which may also compromise the personal tastes and desires of buyers. It also discourages diversity in buyers' buying behavior (Horkheimer, Adorno and Noeri, 2002). That is why consumers' choices are guided by algorithmic predictions of AI based recommender system. These algorithms recommend items of already established concerns which are in high market demand, but it proves disadvantageous for new & small concerns and also hinders innovations as well as hides creative items in an AI-controlled environment. Moreover, it enhances the turnover and profitability of large concerns. This recommendation system manipulates the buyers' buying behavior, and these AI-based customized recommendations have led to wider social repercussions.

LEVERAGING GENERATIVE AI FOR A MORE HETEROGENEOUS AND INCLUSIVE SHOPPING EXPERIENCE

Very recently, the evolution of Generative AI tools such as ChatGPT has shown remarkable influence on the e-commerce sector. Generative AI recommends items to buyers not only on the basis of their search history and past purchases, but it also considers recent digital market trends to provide an individualized shopping experience to buyers (Sag, 2023). Shopping apps have the capability to recognize customers based on their past purchase history and suggest items and give them promotional offers, which influence the buying behavior of 91% of buyers (Morgan, 2020; Xashimov and Khaydarova, 2023). Chatbots and virtual assistants are online assistants that help shoppers when they have any issues. Buyers can type their issue, and AI-based virtual assistants respond to the queries of online shoppers, and there are no human assistants to attend to the queries of buyers. These chatbots and virtual assistants respond to queries, and buyers' demand for instant responses is met (Nicolescu and Tudorache, 2022). These assistants perform a variety of tasks, such as receiving orders, sorting orders, and replying to the queries of buyers and other such tasks. These assistants perform their tasks in less time compared to human beings, as well as at a lower cost (Yang, 2023). Therefore, the business reliance on human agents is decreasing, and their reliance on virtual agents is increasing (Pillarisetty and Mishra, 2022). With the aid of virtual assistants and chatbots, employees of the organization don't feel stressed, and their work-life balance improves (Misra et al., 2024).

In fact, we have entered into a new era of customer engagement called Conversational AI powered by Generative AI, taking chatbot-based interactions to the next level where human conversations are made more realistic using Natural Language Processing (Bleich, 2026). While on the one hand, Conversational AI provides a hyper-personalized experience to customers, on the other hand, it brings exceptional results for corporates. For example, employing Conversational Shopping agent on Black Friday Sale, TFG, one of the largest South African Fashion & Retail brand, recorded a 35.2 percent online conversion rate leading to an increase of 39.8% in revenue per visit of customer engaging with the agent. In addition, the use of a Conversational Shopping agent reduced the exit rates by 28.1% (Bleich, 2026). Generative AI is also being used to create dynamic content, including customized emails, social media advertisements, and product descriptions based on the interests and browsing habits of each individual client (Kanumarlapudi, 2025). Also, AI can quickly create product images in a variety of urban, minimalist, or lifestyle-focused environments, saving money and time while the Virtual Try-On Technology based on Generative AI powered Augmented reality allows customers to "try before they buy.", thereby providing a precise, real-time depiction of how things appear on the customer, whether they are lipstick, sunglasses, or sneakers, clothes, hairstyles, jewelry etc. (Stark Digital, 2026). In order to personalize feeds of influencer material or user-generated style photographs, some fashion stores include AI in their apps. For instance, a user who is interested in streetwear might see more streetwear looks and how others are wearing specific things. Generative AI therefore enables merchants to provide what was previously only achievable in a boutique with attentive sales staff, frequently motivating customers to add additional things to their cart (Selvaraj, 2025). The key to be fast evolution of Generative AI-based recommendation systems is their revolutionary ability of real time adaptation to user's actions, in a systematic manner, rather than simply relying on predefined shopping and behavioral patterns from past experiences. Moreover, AI models can also integrate individual behavior with broader patterns and context. A strong AI may "predict what the shopper will want before they even know it" by analyzing not only an individual's personal preferences but also elements like seasonality, stock levels, and current trends (Selvaraj, 2025).

Agentic AI is another revolutionary technology that is enabling customers to achieve their shopping goals in a unique and personalized manner. Agentic AI uses Machine Learning, Natural Language Processing, and Large Language Models to evaluate problems, come up with answers, and act without human intervention, in contrast to standard AI tools that depend on explicit prompts to produce results. These agents work with a very sophisticated autonomy within agentic AI systems, managing tasks, analyzing data, and making real-time adjustments to maximize results. Agentic AI is being utilized in the e-commerce industry to make hyper-personalized recommendations, to act as virtual stylists, consultants offering seamless and hassle-free checkout experiences, even offering payment or shipping suggestions based on past behavior (Bleich, 2026). Interestingly, AI agents have created an entirely new paradigm, one in which discovery takes place prior to a user ever visiting your website. Consumers now brief rather than browse, and the rest is taken care of by the AI agent (Nederhorst, 2026). Such a unique strategy will not only change the way we search online shopping sites but also turn the search task into the ultimate comparison task while redefining loyalty (Pattern, 2025). The trend has been shifting to using third-party "objective" agents implemented in AI platforms including Perplexity, ChatGPT, and Gemini, etc. These agents deeply explore vendor websites, compile listings, analyze pricing, read reviews, and provide product recommendations. In fact, over the past year, ChatGPT shopping referrals have more than doubled in the US, France, the UK, and Germany, according to figures from Similarweb, a digital marketing analytics firm (Cheris et al., 2025). So, retailers must start designing their systems for machine interpretation rather than just optimizing for human browsing if they want to stay discoverable. This may be achieved through interoperable infrastructure, dependable commerce signals, and high-quality product data. AI agents like Sparky in ChatGPT are being investigated by brands like Walmart, Shopify, and Amazon to transform product discovery and shopping experiences in conversational interfaces (Nederhorst, 2026).

In another strategy to achieve personalization goals, attempts have been made to develop MultiVariate User Interfaces (MultiUI), offering different layouts of user Interfaces (UI) for diverse customer groups in contrast to the commonly adopted one-size-fits-all (Single UI) strategy in e-commerce (Wasilewski and Kolaczek, 2024; Wasilewski et al., 2025). This is important because a majority of online stores provide a single interface for all users due to some technical limitations, compromising diversity in expectations and preferences of the customers and adding to the homogeneity. MultiUI approach allows creating multiple UIs customized and tailored to suit different customer groups, thereby optimizing the shopping experience as per the specific characteristics, inclinations, and behavior of individual customers (Miraz et al., 2021). MultiUI layouts can be designed in a static manner where UI variants are predefined for different groups of customers based on certain underlying decision rules. This approach seems to be simple in implementation but suffers from the challenge of predefining the type and the number of user groups, as well as lacking flexibility in adapting to ever-evolving customer behaviors. In addition, it is always difficult and costly to design and maintain a larger number of static UIs (Wasilewski et al., 2025). A more dynamic strategy to achieve personalization is one that enables the creation of dynamic UIs based upon real-time customer behaviors and decisions (Alipour et al., 2023).

IMPLICATIONS, RISKS AND OPEN CONCERNS

Now, advancements like big data and the Internet of Things have revolutionized the marketing world (Del Vecchio et al., 2018; Trabucchi, Buganza, Dell'Era and Pellizzoni, 2018; Trabucchi and Buganza, 2019) by providing insights for innovating new products, services, and production processes (Del Vecchio et al., 2018). Building long-lasting client relationships is a top priority for any e-commerce company, and personalized recommendations are thought to be essential to achieving this (Grewal et al., 2017). The precision of AI-powered product recommendations influences customer decision-making processes as well as builds a perception of the business as being aware of and responsive to each customer's specific needs. A more engaging and fulfilling shopping experience results from customers feeling that they are getting personalized care, which increases their trust and satisfaction (El Alam and Bitar, 2024). Hyper-personalization achieved through Generative AI helps to minimize homogeneity in recommendations by creating a unique experience for individual customers, as no two customers view the same online store (Selvaraj, 2025).

However, like other technologies AI-based personalized recommendations are surrounded by concerns related to data privacy, security, transparency, and ethical handling of customer information (El Alam and Bitar, 2024). Establishing strong data governance structures and making sure that pertinent laws are followed are crucial for gaining the trust of clients and safeguarding their private information (Vashishth et al., 2024). In addition, buyers are also concerned about the reliability of recommendations as well as the relevance and accuracy of the recommendations. The adoption of AI-based technologies would lead to technological complexities; existing infrastructure might not support technological advancements, and there is also a lack of expertise to handle such technology improvements, which might lead to loss of market share for the concerned business house and reduced competitive strengths (Cakir et al., 2021).

Moreover, in the beginning, buyers adopt such technologies in excitement, but it is very difficult to maintain such behavior in the future (Bandura, 2001). Business houses are also concerned about cost and data management. No doubt, customers' engagement and conversion rate increase as a result of personalized product recommendations and individualized offers and promotions, but the criteria of dynamic pricing may create negativity and doubts among buyers (Mohamed, 2024). Nonetheless, it is crucial to thoroughly examine the wider impacts on long-term loyalty, consumer engagement, and brand perception. It is important to carefully balance the levels of attention and reaction that a brand seems to have, which are made possible by AI-driven recommendations, against the risks of data misuse and consumer mistrust (Amil, 2024). Sales, conversion rates, and customer retention could all increase significantly using AI-based recommendations (Kim et al., 2021).

Another issue is the precision of AI-powered suggestions and how they subsequently affect how customers make decisions. To enhance purchase intent, these tailored interventions must take into account the intricacies of human preferences, subtle cultural variations, and the potential for inadvertent bias (Ricci, 2015). The necessity to constantly communicate with customers to ensure that advice remains pertinent and responsive to changing customer needs makes the task much more challenging. Personalized recommendations have a broad effect that extends beyond the technological realm, influencing consumer behavior and corporate results in ways that are not always advantageous. Nguyen et al. (2018) caution against depending too heavily on algorithmic recommendations since this may restrict customer options (leading to homogeneity) and lessen the chance of an unexpected discovery.

SOLUTIONS AND RECOMMENDATIONS

Three recommendations follow from the review. First, brands should state which diversity problem they are solving before choosing a remedy, because the interventions that broaden a catalogue and the interventions that keep customers distinguishable from one another are not the same. Second, diversity should be measured on both axes at once, within the individual and across the customer base, since a system can improve one while quietly degrading the other. Third, where a recommender is deliberately introducing novelty, that fact should be visible to the customer, because the same unexpected suggestion reads as discovery when it is explained and as error when it is not. The multivariant interface work of Wasilewski and Kolaczek (2024) and the generative approaches described by Selvaraj (2025) both offer practical routes, but neither substitutes for deciding first which kind of sameness the brand is trying to avoid.

FUTURE RESEARCH DIRECTIONS

With ongoing developments in AI, machine learning, and data analytics, personalized marketing appears to have a bright future. It is anticipated that hyper-personalization-in which companies employ real-time data to produce even more accurate and dynamic personalized experiences-will increase. New opportunities for developing immersive, customized experiences will also arise from the incorporation of personalization into cutting-edge technologies like augmented reality (AR) and virtual reality (VR). However, the potential of AI-enabled personalization can only be explored in totality if brands invest in AI knowledge, infrastructure, and data management solutions to have a competitive edge. Big corporates are already moving in this direction, but for small and medium-sized retailers, integrating AI, particularly Generative AI, is a great challenge and requires the introduction of more cost-effective AI-based solutions. Researchers also need to take into consideration societal, cultural, technological, and infrastructural differences among different countries to develop more customized AI platforms to address such significant differences, particularly in terms of AI exposure, Digital literacy, cultural attributes, age groups, etc. to adopt automation and their influence on user behavior in emerging markets (Xie, 2026). Moreover, finding a right balance between brand consistency and personalization is another major challenge. Customizing communications to suit individual preferences is crucial, but organizations also need to make sure that these customized messages complement their broader brand identity. The use of Agentic AI is reshaping retailing by acting as third-party agents (e.g., Perplexity), on-site (e.g., Amazon's Rufus), and off-site (e.g., Amazon's "Buy for me") retailing agents (Cheris et al., 2025). However, these Agentic AI technologies are in their initial stages and need to cross the reliability mark, especially the third-party agents. These technologies hold the future, especially in achieving personalization without homogenization. However, their ability to provide choices from multiple vendors with greater transparency in prices can make the market much more competitive for retailers while lowering their margins (Cheris et al., 2025). Therefore, future research should be focused on striking the right balance between personalization, satisfaction, and price effectiveness for consumers and sustainable profitability for brands while strategically aligning with their business goals.

CONCLUSION

AI-based decision-making is logical, statistical, and computational intelligence-based, while the human decision-making process is influenced by emotions, reactions, socio-cultural dimensions, and reasoning, etc. (Arkhipova, 2024). Basically, a balance between AI based recommender system and human intelligence can enhance buyers' buying experience as well as business profitability, turnover, and reputation (Lau and Lee, 2019). The emergence of new strategies such as dynamic MultiUI layouts together with Generative AI-based recommendation systems, Virtual Assistants/AI Agents, etc. can prove to be a game changer by overcoming the impact of "information cocoon" that often leads to homogeneity in buying, thereby achieving a holistic shopping experience for the customers.

REFERENCES

Abdollahpouri, H., Burke, R., & Mobasher, B. (2019). Managing popularity bias in recommender systems with personalized re-ranking. *arXiv preprint arXiv:1901.07555*. https://doi.org//arXiv.1901.07555DOI: 10.48550

Abraham, M., Mitchelmore, S., Collins, S., Maness, J., Kistulinec, M., Khodabandeh, S., & Visser, J. (2017). *Profiting from personalization*. Boston Consulting Group.

Adamopoulos, P., & Tuzhilin, A. (2014, October). On over-specialization and concentration bias of recommendations: Probabilistic neighborhood selection in collaborative filtering systems. In *Proceedings of the 8th ACM Conference on Recommender Systems* (pp. 153-160). DOI: 10.1145/2645710.2645752

Adomavicius, G., Bockstedt, J. C., Curley, S. P., & Zhang, J. (2018). Effects of online recommendations on consumers' willingness to pay. *Information Systems Research, 29*(1), 84–102. DOI: 10.1287/isre.2017.0703

Akbar, M. I. U. D., Ahmad, B., Asif, M. H., & Siddiqui, S. A. (2020). Linking emotional brand attachment and sales promotion to post-purchase cognitive dissonance: The mediating role of impulse buying behavior. *The Journal of Asian Finance, Economics and Business, 7*(11), 367–379. DOI: 10.13106/jafeb.2020.vol7.no11.367

Al-Hasan, T. M., Sayed, A. N., Bensaali, F., Himeur, Y., Varlamis, I., & Dimitrakopoulos, G. (2024). From traditional recommender systems to GPT-based chatbots: A survey of recent developments and future directions. *Big Data and Cognitive Computing, 8*(4), 36. DOI: 10.3390/bdcc8040036

Alavi, S., & Nozari, S. (2023). AI Product Review Summaries and Content Homogenization: The Changing Landscape of UGC. *Available at SSRN* 5178862.

Alipour, M., Tourchi Moghaddam, M., Vaidhyanathan, K., & Baun Kjærgaard, M. (2023, June). Toward Changing Users behavior with Emotion-based Adaptive Systems. In *Proceedings of the 31st ACM Conference on User Modeling, Adaptation and Personalization* (pp. 85-95). DOI: 10.1145/3565472.3595614

Amil, Y. (2024). The Impact of AI-Driven Personalization Tools on Privacy Concerns and Consumer Trust in E-commerce.

Argoid. (2023). A complete study of Amazon's recommendation system. https://argoid.findableis.com/blog/decoding-amazons-recommendation-system.html

Arkhipova, D. (2024). How AI recommendation systems impact human decision-making.

Arora, N., Ensslen, D., Fiedler, L., Liu, W. W., Robinson, K., Stein, E., & Schüler, G. (2021). The value of getting personalization right—or wrong—is multiplying. McKinsey & Company, 12.

Bandura, A. (2001). Social cognitive theory: An agentic perspective. *Annual Review of Psychology*, *52*(1), 1–26. DOI: 10.1146/annurev.psych.52.1.1

Belkin, N. J., & Croft, W. B. (1992). Information filtering and information retrieval: Two sides of the same coin? *Communications of the ACM*, *35*(12), 29–38. DOI: 10.1145/138859.138861

Bleich, C. (2026). AI for Online Shopping: The Rise of AI-Powered Personal Shopping Services. https://www.bloomreach.com/en/blog/ai-powered-personal-shopping-services[REMOVED HYPERLINK FIELD]

Brynjolfsson, E., Hu, Y., & Simester, D. (2011). Goodbye pareto principle, hello long tail: The effect of search costs on the concentration of product sales. *Management Science*, *57*(8), 1373–1386. DOI: 10.1287/mnsc.1110.1371

Cakir, G., Iftikhar, R., Bielozorov, A., Pourzolfaghar, Z., & Helfert, M. (2021). Omnichannel retailing: Digital transformation of a medium-sized retailer. *Journal of Information Technology Teaching Cases*, *11*(2), 122–126. DOI: 10.1177/2043886920959803

Carr, S. (2021). How many ads do we see a day in 2021? https://www.lunio.ai/blog/how-many-ads-do-we-see-a-day retrieved on 30.04.2025[REMOVED HYPERLINK FIELD]

Chandra, S., Verma, S., Lim, W. M., Kumar, S., & Donthu, N. (2022). Personalization in personalized marketing: Trends and ways forward. *Psychology and Marketing*, *39*(8), 1529–1562. DOI: 10.1002/mar.21670

Chen, W. K., Chen, C. K., & Silalahi, A. D. K. (2021, August). Understanding Consumers' post-purchase behavior by cognitive dissonance and emotions in the online impulse buying context. In*2021 IEEE 22nd International Conference on Information Reuse and Integration for Data Science (IRI)* (pp. 390-394). IEEE. DOI: 10.1109/IRI51335.2021.00061

Cheng, H. T., Koc, L., Harmsen, J., Shaked, T., Chandra, T., Aradhye, H., & Shah, H. (2016, September). Wide & deep learning for recommender systems. In *Proceedings of the 1st workshop on deep learning for recommender systems* (pp. 7-10). DOI: 10.1145/2988450.2988454

Cheris, A., Kamel, M., Vu, M., Koszyk, S., Burns, M., & Lewis, R. (2025). *Agentic AI in retail: How autonomous shopping is redefining the customer journey*. Bain & Company.

Chinchanachokchai, S., Thontirawong, P., & Chinchanachokchai, P. (2021). A tale of two recommender systems: The moderating role of consumer expertise on AI based product recommendations. *Journal of Retailing and Consumer Services, 61*, 102528. DOI: 10.1016/j.jretconser.2021.102528

Covington, P., Adams, J., & Sargin, E. (2016, September). Deep neural networks for youtube recommendations. In *Proceedings of the 10th ACM conference on recommender systems* (pp. 191-198). DOI: 10.1145/2959100.2959190

Danaher, J., Hogan, M. J., Noone, C., Kennedy, R., Behan, A., De Paor, A., Felzmann, H., Haklay, M., Khoo, S.-M., Morison, J., Murphy, M. H., O'Brolchain, N., Schafer, B., & Shankar, K. (2017). Algorithmic governance: Developing a research agenda through the power of collective intelligence. *Big Data & Society*, *4*(2), 2053951717726554. DOI: 10.1177/2053951717726554

Del Vecchio, P., Di Minin, A., Petruzzelli, A. M., Panniello, U., & Pirri, S. (2018). Big data for open innovation in SMEs and large corporations: Trends, opportunities, and challenges. *Creativity and Innovation Management*, *27*(1), 6–22. DOI: 10.1111/caim.12224

Dollarhide M.E., Anderson S. (2020), Mass customization, Investopedia, 20/04/2025.

Dong, Z., Wang, Z., Xu, J., Tang, R., & Wen, J. (2022). A brief history of recommender systems.*arXiv preprint arXiv:2209.01860*. https://doi.org//arXiv.2209.01860DOI: 10.48550

Donnelly, R., Kanodia, A., & Morozov, I. (2021). The long tail effect of personalized rankings. *Available at SSRN,*3649342.

El Alam, R., & Bitar, M. O. (2024). "Unveiling the Influence of AI's Product Recommendation on Consumer Purchase Intent": A Quantitative Study Investigating The Role of AI product recommendations on Consumer Purchase intent.

Festinger, L. (1957). *A theory of cognitive dissonance*. Stanford University Press., DOI: 10.1515/9781503620766

Fleder, D., Hosanagar, K., & Buja, A. (2011). Recommender systems and their effects on consumers. DOI: 10.1145/1807342.1807378

Ghose, A., & Ipeirotis, P. G. (2010). Estimating the helpfulness and economic impact of product reviews: Mining text and reviewer characteristics. *IEEE Transactions on Knowledge and Data Engineering*, *23*(10), 1498–1512. DOI: 10.1109/TKDE.2010.188

Goldberg, D., Nichols, D., Oki, B. M., & Terry, D. (1992). Using collaborative filtering to weave an information tapestry. *Communications of the ACM*, *35*(12), 61–70. DOI: 10.1145/138859.138867

Gomez-Uribe, C. A., & Hunt, N. (2016). The Netflix recommender system: Algorithms, business value, and innovation. *ACM Transactions on Management Information Systems*, *6*(4), 1–19. DOI: 10.1145/2843948

Grewal, D., Levy, M., & Kumar, V. (2017). Customer experience management in retailing: An organizing framework. *Journal of Retailing*, *93*(1), 1–14. DOI: 10.1016/j.jretai.2016.12.008

Guan, Y., Wei, Q., & Chen, G. (2019). Deep learning based personalized recommendation with multi-view information integration. *Decision Support Systems*, *118*, 58–69. DOI: 10.1016/j.dss.2019.01.003

Guo, H., Tang, R., Ye, Y., Li, Z., He, X., & Dong, Z. (2018). Deepfm: An end-to-end wide & deep learning framework for CTR prediction.*arXiv preprint arXiv:1804.04950*. https://doi.org//arXiv.1804.04950DOI: 10.48550

Hallinger, P., & Nguyen, V. T. (2020). Mapping the landscape and structure of research on education for sustainable development: A bibliometric review. *Sustainability (Basel)*, *12*(5), 1947. DOI: 10.3390/su12051947

Hart, C. W. (1995). Mass customization: Conceptual underpinnings, opportunities and limits. *International Journal of Service Industry Management*, *6*(2), 36–45. DOI: 10.1108/09564239510084932

Harzer, T. S. (2013). *Value creation through mass customization: An empirical analysis of the requisite strategic capabilities* (Doctoral dissertation, Aachen, Techn. Hochsch., Diss., 2013).

Ho, E. (2024). Rule-Based vs. AI-Powered Recommendation: Which Should You Pick For Your Shopify Store? https://blog.boostcommerce.net/posts/rule-based-ai-powered-recommendation[REMOVED HYPERLINK FIELD]

Holtz, D., Carterette, B., Chandar, P., Nazari, Z., Cramer, H., & Aral, S. (2020). The engagement-diversity connection: Evidence from a field experiment on spotify. arXiv preprint arXiv:2003.08203. /arXiv.2003.08203DOI: 10.1145/3391403.3399532

Hong, C. (2020). An Approach to de-homogenizing recommender systems (Doctoral dissertation, Massachusetts Institute of Technology).

Horkheimer, M., Adorno, T. W., & Noeri, G. (2002). *Dialectic of enlightenment.* Stanford University Press.

Hosanagar, K., Fleder, D., Lee, D., & Buja, A. (2014). Will the global village fracture into tribes? Recommender systems and their effects on consumer fragmentation. *Management Science, 60*(4), 805–823. DOI: 10.1287/mnsc.2013.1808

Hue, T. T., & Hung, T. H. (2025). Impact of artificial intelligence on branding: A bibliometric review and future research directions. *Humanities & Social Sciences Communications, 12*(1), 209. DOI: 10.1057/s41599-025-04488-6

Jannach, D., & Jugovac, M. (2019). Measuring the business value of recommender systems. [TMIS]. *ACM Transactions on Management Information Systems, 10*(4), 1–23. DOI: 10.1145/3370082

Juan, Y., Zhuang, Y., Chin, W. S., & Lin, C. J. (2016, September). Field-aware factorization machines for CTR prediction. In *Proceedings of the 10th ACM conference on recommender systems* (pp. 43-50). DOI: 10.1145/2959100.2959134

Kanumarlapudi, P. K., & Ballamudi, S. (2025). Enhancing Generative AI Shopping Assistants through Advanced Multi-Attribute Decision Making Technique. *Journal of Artificial Intelligence and Machine Learning, 3*(2), 1–7. DOI: 10.55124/jaim.v3i2.267

Katrandjiev, H., Naydenov, A., & Dinev, A. (2025). THE ROLE OF AI IN MODERN BRAND MANAGEMENT.*Časopis za ekonomiju*, 397.

Kay, M. J. (1993). Making mass customization happen: Lessons for implementation. *Planning Review, 21*(4), 14–18. DOI: 10.1108/eb054421

Kim, J., Giroux, M., & Lee, J. C. (2021). When do you trust AI? The effect of number presentation detail on consumer trust and acceptance of AI recommendations. *Psychology and Marketing, 38*(7), 1140–1155. DOI: 10.1002/mar.21498

Kim, J., & Gupta, P. (2012). Emotional expressions in online user reviews: How they influence consumers' product evaluations. *Journal of Business Research, 65*(7), 985–992. DOI: 10.1016/j.jbusres.2011.04.013

Kim, J. K., Cho, Y. H., Kim, W. J., Kim, J. R., & Suh, J. H. (2002). A personalized recommendation procedure for Internet shopping support. *Electronic Commerce Research and Applications, 1*(3-4), 301–313. DOI: 10.1016/S1567-4223(02)00022-4

Kimiagari, S., & Malafe, N. S. A. (2021). The role of cognitive and affective responses in the relationship between internal and external stimuli on online impulse buying behavior. *Journal of Retailing and Consumer Services, 61*, 102567. DOI: 10.1016/j.jretconser.2021.102567

Klover.ai. (2025). Starbucks' AI strategy: Analysis of dominance in coffee. https://www.klover.ai/starbucks-ai-strategy-analysis-of-dominance-in-coffee/

Koren, Y. (2008, August). Factorization meets the neighborhood: a multifaceted collaborative filtering model. In *Proceedings of the 14th ACM SIGKDD international conference on Knowledge discovery and data mining* (pp. 426-434). DOI: 10.1145/1401890.1401944

Koren, Y. (2009, June). Collaborative filtering with temporal dynamics. In *Proceedings of the 15th ACM SIGKDD international conference on Knowledge discovery and data mining* (pp. 447-456). DOI: 10.1145/1557019.1557072

Kotler, P. (1989). From mass marketing to mass customization. *Planning review,17*(5), 10-47. DOI: 10.1108/eb054267

Kunaver, M., & Požrl, T. (2017). Diversity in recommender systems–A survey. *Knowledge-Based Systems, 123*, 154–162. DOI: 10.1016/j.knosys.2017.02.009

Lambrecht, A., & Tucker, C. (2019). Algorithmic bias? An empirical study of apparent gender-based discrimination in the display of STEM career ads. *Management Science, 65*(7), 2966–2981. DOI: 10.1287/mnsc.2018.3093

Lang, J., Spear, M., & Wu, S. F. (2010). Social manipulation of online recommender systems. In *Social Informatics: Second International Conference, SocInfo 2010, Laxenburg, Austria, October 27-29, 2010. Proceedings 2*(pp. 125-139). Springer Berlin Heidelberg. DOI: 10.1007/978-3-642-16567-2_10

Lau, K. W., & Lee, P. Y. (2019). Shopping in virtual reality: A study on consumers' shopping experience in a stereoscopic virtual reality. *Virtual Reality (Waltham Cross), 23*(3), 255–268. DOI: 10.1007/s10055-018-0362-3

Lee, D., & Hosanagar, K. (2019). How do recommender systems affect sales diversity? A cross-category investigation via randomized field experiment. *Information Systems Research, 30*(1), 239–259. DOI: 10.1287/isre.2018.0800

Li, X., Grahl, J., & Hinz, O. (2022). How do recommender systems lead to consumer purchases? A causal mediation analysis of a field experiment. *Information Systems Research, 33*(2), 620–637. DOI: 10.1287/isre.2021.1074

Lim, G. G., Kang, J. Y., Lee, J. K., & Lee, D. C. (2011). Rule-based personalized comparison shopping including delivery cost. *Electronic Commerce Research and Applications, 10*(6), 637–649. DOI: 10.1016/j.elerap.2011.07.002

Marketing with Dave. (2026). Case study: Amazon's recommendation engine — the personalization powerhouse driving 35% of sales. https://marketingwithdave.com/case-study-amazons-recommendation-engine-the-personalization-powerhouse-driving-35-%-of-sales

McKinsey & Company. (2023). What is Personalization? https://www.mckinsey.com/featured-insights/mckinsey-explainers/what-is-personalization

Konstan, J. A., & ACM Conference on Recommender Systems. 2007. *RecSys' 07: Proceedings of the 2007 ACM Conference on Recommender Systems:* Minneapolis, M. N. USA, October 19-20, 2007. Association for Computing Machinery. https://dl.acm.org/doi/proceedings/10.1145/1297231

Miraz, M. H., Ali, M., & Excell, P. S. (2021). Adaptive user interfaces and universal usability through plasticity of user interface design. *Computer Science Review, 40*, 100363. DOI: 10.1016/j.cosrev.2021.100363

Misra, R. R., Kapoor, S., & Sanjeev, M. A. (2024). The impact of personalisation algorithms on consumer engagement and purchase behavior in AI-enhanced virtual shopping assistants. DOI: 10.21203/rs.3.rs-3970797/v1

Mohamed, A. (2024). Assessing AI-Powered Personalization Strategies for Mid-Sized Finnish Fashion E-commerce: Enhancing Consumer Engagement and Conversion Rates

Moher, D., Liberati, A., Tetzlaff, J., & Altman, D. G.Prisma Group. (2010). Preferred reporting items for systematic reviews and meta-analyses: The PRISMA statement. *International Journal of Surgery, 8*(5), 336–341. DOI: 10.1016/j.ijsu.2010.02.007

Molaie, M. M., & Lee, W. (2022). Economic corollaries of personalized recommendations. *Journal of Retailing and Consumer Services, 68*, 103003. DOI: 10.1016/j.jretconser.2022.103003

Moller, J., Trilling, D., Helberger, N., & van Es, B. (2018). Do not blame it on the algorithm: An empirical assessment of multiple recommender systems and their impact on content diversity. *Information Communication and Society, 21*(7), 959–977. DOI: 10.1080/1369118X.2018.1444076

Morgan, B. (2020). 50 Stats Showing The Power Of Personalization. https://www.forbes.com/sites/blakemorgan/2020/02/18/50-stats-showing-the-power-of-personalization/[REMOVED HYPERLINK FIELD]

Morvan, C., & O'Connor, A. (2017). *An analysis of Leon Festinger's a theory of cognitive dissonance*. Macat Library.

Muthuri, D. (2023). Content Personalization: What It Is & How to Do It. URL: https://www.semrush.com/blog/personalized-content/ Accessed: 1 May 2025.

Nederhorst, L. (2026). How Do Retailers Stay Visible with AI Shopping Agents Choosing Products? https://www.ml6.eu/en/blog/how-do-retailers-stay-visible-with-ai-shopping-agents-choosing-products[REMOVED HYPERLINK FIELD]

Nguyen, T. T., Maxwell Harper, F., Terveen, L., & Konstan, J. A. (2018). User personality and user satisfaction with recommender systems. *Information Systems Frontiers, 20*(6), 1173–1189. DOI: 10.1007/s10796-017-9782-y

Nicolescu, L., & Tudorache, M. T. (2022). Human-computer interaction in customer service: The experience with AI chatbots—a systematic literature review. *Electronics (Basel), 11*(10), 1579. DOI: 10.3390/electronics11101579

Pariser, E. (2011). *The filter bubble: What the Internet is hiding from you*. penguin UK.

Pattern. (2025). Agentic shopping: the future of ecommerce is here. https://www.pattern.com/blog/agentic-shopping-agents

Personalized Pricing. (2022). *European Parliament's committee on Internal Market and Consumer Protection.*

Pillarisetty, R., & Mishra, P. (2022). A review of AI (AI) tools and customer experience in online fashion retail. [IJEBR]. *International Journal of E-Business Research, 18*(2), 1–12. DOI: 10.4018/IJEBR.294111

Pine, B. J. (1993). Mass customizing products and services. *Planning review,21*(4), 6-55. DOI: 10.1108/eb054420

Pine, B. J., & Gilmore, J. H. (2013). The experience economy: past, present and future. In *Handbook on the experience economy* (pp. 21–44). Edward Elgar Publishing., DOI: 10.4337/9781781004227.00007

Plus Info, A. I. (2026). AI & data-driven Starbucks-Deep Brew. https://www.aiplusinfo.com/blog/ai-data-driven-starbucks-deep-brew/

Proserpio, D., & Zervas, G. (2017). Online reputation management: Estimating the impact of management responses on consumer reviews. *Marketing Science, 36*(5), 645–665. DOI: 10.1287/mksc.2017.1043

Rashid, A. M., Albert, I., Cosley, D., Lam, S. K., McNee, S. M., Konstan, J. A., & Riedl, J. (2002). Getting to know you: learning new user preferences in recommender systems. In *Proceedings of the 7th international conference on Intelligent user interfaces* (pp. 127-134). DOI: 10.1145/502716.502737

Rebuy Engine. (2022). See what's next: How Netflix uses personalization to drive billions in revenue. https://www.rebuyengine.com/blog/netflix

Rebuy Engine. (n.d.). The Amazon effect: Using personalization to generate billions. https://www.rebuyengine.com/blog/the-amazon-effect[REMOVED HYPERLINK FIELD]

Redine, A., Deshpande, S., Jebarajakirthy, C., & Surachartkumtonkun, J. (2023). Impulse buying: A systematic literature review and future research directions. *International Journal of Consumer Studies, 47*(1), 3–41. DOI: 10.1111/ijcs.12862

Rendle, S. (2010, December). Factorization machines. In*2010 IEEE International conference on data mining* (pp. 995-1000). IEEE. DOI: 10.1109/ICDM.2010.127

Resnick, P., Iacovou, N., Suchak, M., Bergstrom, P., & Riedl, J. (1994, October). Grouplens: An open architecture for collaborative filtering of netnews. In *Proceedings of the 1994 ACM conference on Computer supported cooperative work* (pp. 175-186). DOI: 10.1145/192844.192905

Ricci, F. (2015). Recommender Systems: Introduction and Challenges. Recommender Systems Handbook, 1-34. DOI: 10.1007/978-1-4899-7637-6_1

Richardson, M., Dominowska, E., & Ragno, R. (2007, May). Predicting clicks: estimating the click-through rate for new ads. In *Proceedings of the 16th international conference on World Wide Web* (pp. 521-530). DOI: 10.1145/1242572.1242643

Riedl, J. (2013). Fine Tuning the Social Web. https://research.umn.edu/news/fine-tuning-social-web-john-riedl[REMOVED HYPERLINK FIELD]

Sag, M. (2023). Copyright safety for generative AI. *Houston Law Review, 61*, 295.

Sandrin, V. (2021). The Struggle between Human-centredness and Intelligent Technologies: a Critical Discussion on the Use of Customer Data in Marketing Practice-A Survey Analysis of the RIR Clusters in Veneto.

Schafer, J. B., Konstan, J., & Riedl, J. (1999, November). Recommender systems in e-commerce. In *Proceedings of the 1st ACM conference on Electronic commerce* (pp. 158-166). https://dl.acm.org/doi/pdf/10.1145/336992.337035

Schreiner, T., Rese, A., & Baier, D. (2019). Multichannel personalization: Identifying consumer preferences for product recommendations in advertisements across different media channels. *Journal of Retailing and Consumer Services*, *48*, 87–99. DOI: 10.1016/j.jretconser.2019.02.010

Selvaraj, T. (2025). Generative AI: Fashion's New Personal Shopper. https://medium.com/@tselvaraj/generative-ai-fashions-new-personal-shopper-425fefa68fe2[REMOVED HYPERLINK FIELD]

Shardanand, U., & Maes, P. (1995, May). Social information filtering: Algorithms for automating "word of mouth". In *Proceedings of the SIGCHI conference on Human factors in computing systems* (pp. 210-217). DOI: 10.1145/223904.223931

Sharma, P., Ueno, A., Dennis, C., & Turan, C. P. (2023). Emerging digital technologies and consumer decision-making in retail sector: Towards an integrative conceptual framework. *Computers in Human Behavior*, *148*, 107913. DOI: 10.1016/j.chb.2023.107913

Sheth, J. N., Sisodia, R. S., & Sharma, A. (2000). The antecedents and consequences of customer-centric marketing. *Journal of the Academy of Marketing Science*, *28*(1), 55–66. DOI: 10.1177/0092070300281006

Smith, B., & Linden, G. (2017). Two decades of recommender systems at Amazon.com. *IEEE Internet Computing*, *21*(3), 12–18. DOI: 10.1109/MIC.2017.72

Srivastava, A., Bala, P. K., & Kumar, B. (2020). New perspectives on gray sheep behavior in E-commerce recommendations. *Journal of Retailing and Consumer Services*, *53*, 101764. DOI: 10.1016/j.jretconser.2019.02.018

Stark Digital. (2026). Generative AI in Retail: The Future of Personalized Shopping. https://www.starkdigital.net/insights/generative-ai-in-retail-the-future-of-personalized-shopping

Stein, E., Robinson, K., Wolfer, A., Almeida, G., & Huang, W. (2025). Unlocking the next frontier of personalized marketing. *The McKinsey Quarterly*.

Stevenson, M. (2019). Design thinking for business: personalization,https://uxdesign.cc/design-thinking-for-business-personalisation-39f4b96ee1b7, 03/05/2025.[REMOVED HYPERLINK FIELD]

Stratoflow. (2025a). Amazon product recommendation system: How does Amazon's algorithm work? https://stratoflow.com/amazon-recommendation-system/

Stratoflow. (2025b). How Netflix's recommendation algorithm works. https://stratoflow.com/how-netflix-recommendation-algorithm-work/

Trabucchi, D., & Buganza, T. (2019). Data-driven innovation: Switching the perspective on Big Data. *European Journal of Innovation Management*, *22*(1), 23–40. DOI: 10.1108/EJIM-01-2018-0017

Trabucchi, D., Buganza, T., Dell'Era, C., & Pellizzoni, E. (2018). Exploring the inbound and outbound strategies enabled by user generated big data: Evidence from leading smartphone applications. *Creativity and Innovation Management*, *27*(1), 42–55. DOI: 10.1111/caim.12241

Tseng, M. M., & Jiao, J. (2001). Mass customization. *Handbook of industrial engineering,3*, 684-709.

Vashishth, T. K., Sharma, K. K., Kumar, B., Chaudhary, S., & Panwar, R. (2024). Enhancing customer experience through AI-enabled content personalization in e-commerce marketing. Advances in digital marketing in the era of AI, 7-32. DOI: 10.1201/9781003450443-2

Verma, S., Sharma, R., Deb, S., & Maitra, D. (2021). AI in marketing: Systematic review and future research direction. *International Journal of Information Management Data Insights*, *1*(1), 100002. DOI: 10.1016/j.jjimei.2020.100002

Virilio, P. (1986). Speed and politics: An essay on dromology, trans. *Mark Polizzotti, New York: Semiotext (e),52*.

VWO. (n.d.). How does Amazon & Netflix personalization work? https://vwo.com/blog/deliver-personalized-recommendations-the-amazon-netflix-way/[REMOVED HYPERLINK FIELD]

Wang, R., Fu, B., Fu, G., & Wang, M. (2017). Deep & cross network for ad click predictions. *Proceedings of the ADKDD*, *17*, 1–7. DOI: 10.1145/3124749.3124754

Wang, R., Shivanna, R., Cheng, D., Jain, S., Lin, D., Hong, L., & Chi, E. (2021, April). Dcn v2: Improved deep & cross network and practical lessons for web-scale learning to rank systems. In *Proceedings of the web conference 2021*(pp. 1785-1797). DOI: 10.1145/3442381.3450078

Wasilewski, A., Chawla, Y., & Pralat, E. (2025). *Enhanced E-Commerce Personalization Through AI-Powered Content Generation Tools*. IEEE., DOI: 10.1109/ACCESS.2025.3550956

Wasilewski, A., & Kolaczek, G. (2024). *One size does not fit all: multivariant user interface personalization in e-commerce*. IEEE., DOI: 10.1109/ACCESS.2024.3398192

Westbrook, R., & Williamson, P. (1993). Mass customization: Japan's new frontier. *European Management Journal*, *11*(1), 38–45. DOI: 10.1016/0263-2373(93)90022-A

Wu, Y., Xin, L., Li, D., Yu, J., & Guo, J. (2021). How does scarcity promotion lead to impulse purchase in the online market? A field experiment. *Information & Management, 58*(1), 103283. DOI: 10.1016/j.im.2020.103283

Xashimov, B., & Khaydarova, D. (2023). Using and development of AI on the process of accounting, 1(5), 219–223. DOI: 10.47689/STARS.university-5-pp219-223

Xiao, B., & Benbasat, I. (2013). Research on the use, characteristics, and impact of e-commerce product recommendation agents: A review and update for 2007–2012. *Handbook of strategic e-business management*, 403-431. DOI: 10.1007/978-3-642-39747-9_18

Xie, G. (2026). The impact of generative AI shopping assistants on E-commerce consumer motivation and behavior: Consumer-AI interaction design. *International Journal of Information Management, 86*, 102983. DOI: 10.1016/j.ijinfomgt.2025.102983

Yang, X. (2023). The effects of AI service quality and AI function-customer ability fit on customer's overall co-creation experience. *Industrial Management & Data Systems, 123*(6), 1717–1735. DOI: 10.1108/IMDS-08-2022-0500

Yi, X., Yang, J., Hong, L., Cheng, D. Z., Heldt, L., Kumthekar, A., & Chi, E. (2019, September). Sampling-bias-corrected neural modeling for large corpus item recommendations. In *Proceedings of the 13th ACM conference on recommender systems* (pp. 269-277). DOI: 10.1145/3298689.3346996

Zhou, G., Mou, N., Fan, Y., Pi, Q., Bian, W., Zhou, C., & Gai, K. (2019, July). Deep interest evolution network for click-through rate prediction. In *Proceedings of the AAAI conference on AI* (Vol. 33, No. 01, pp. 5941-5948). DOI: 10.1609/aaai.v33i01.33015941

Zhou, G., Zhu, X., Song, C., Fan, Y., Zhu, H., Ma, X., & Gai, K. (2018, July). Deep interest network for click-through rate prediction. In *Proceedings of the 24th ACM SIGKDD international conference on knowledge discovery & data mining* (pp. 1059-1068). DOI: 10.1145/3219819.3219823

KEY TERMS AND DEFINITIONS

Consumer behavior: Consumer behavior is the cognitive, sentimental, psychological and physiological processes that help an individual or a group of individuals to select, purchase, utilize and discard goods, services and notions.

Filter bubble: E-Commerce algorithms suggest items to buyers on the basis of their past search behavior, click-throughs, and shield buyers from searching for new items, intensify their confirmation, and help them to make quick decisions, thereby reducing their decision fatigue.

Generative AI: Generative AI is a branch of artificial intelligence focused on creating new, original content such as text, images, audio, video, or code by learning patterns from vast datasets and generating outputs that resemble human-created work.

Homogenization: Homogenization is the practice of producing the same item by competing business houses to mimic each other.

Internet long tail effect: It means that only online stores can maintain a huge variety of rare, uncommon, difficult-to-find items; i.e., one can easily find and purchase a particular item of one's taste and preference at an online store or in the internet space.

Matthew effect: In consumer behavior, the Matthew effect is based on the principle of 'rich get richer', i.e., a product or a company which is already popular gets more attention from consumers because they do not want to take risks, and due to this fact they never try new and less popular items.

Personalization: Personalization is the practice of leveraging personal data to customize a product, offering, service, an activity, or experience to each person's unique needs and requirements, behavior, patterns, and choices.

Recommender system: A recommender or recommendation system is a machine learning intelligent tool that studies the buyer's or individual's click-throughs, wish list, purchase pattern, watch history, ratings, and analyzes all this information and suggests items on the basis of these analyzed patterns.

Chapter 6
Habit Loops vs. Serendipity:
Machine Learning Algorithms in Consumer Decision-Making

Suman Vij
http://orcid.org/0000-0002-1565-9161
Shree Guru Gobind Singh Tricentenary University, Gurugram, India

ABSTRACT

This chapter examines how machine learning algorithms increasingly shape consumer decision-making within AI-mediated marketplaces. Focusing on the tension between algorithmically reinforced habit loops and the declining space for serendipitous discovery, the chapter integrates insights from behavioral science, marketing theory, and artificial intelligence. It explores how recommendation engines, predictive analytics, and personalized digital ecosystems optimize engagement by reinforcing existing consumer behaviors, potentially limiting exposure to new brands and alternative choices. Building upon marketing science concepts such as mental availability, brand salience, and consumer memory structures, the chapter analyzes how algorithmic personalization influences brand growth, consumer autonomy, and switching behavior. Through cross-regional examples and theoretical analysis, it proposes a strategic framework balancing predictive personalization with engineered serendipity.

DOI: 10.4018/979-8-3373-9589-0.ch006

INTRODUCTION

AI-Mediated Consumer Environments

Artificial Intelligence (AI) is transforming the modern world by building digital ecosystems that affect consumer search, evaluation, and purchase behavior. Personalization is one of the pivotal technologies of platforms such as e-commerce, streaming, social media, and mobile commerce, and machine learning algorithms play a central role, analyzing large data sets on consumer behavior—browsing history, click patterns, watch times, purchase frequency, and other interaction metrics—to more accurately predict consumer preferences. The consumer environment has evolved from a passive space of information into a highly adaptive, intelligent space that continuously learns from consumer behavior (Pandey, 2025).

The consumer journey is changing greatly with the rise of AI marketplaces. Earlier theories of consumer decision-making were based on information seeking, product comparison, and rational evaluation before choice. Today, however, algorithmic systems are central to filtering and prioritizing the options most likely to engage consumers, who are increasingly exposed to curated recommendations rather than exploring products on their own. Recommendation systems on streaming, e-commerce, and social commerce platforms shape what users see first, what remains visible, and how alternatives are evaluated. This has made the digital platform a hidden middleman in the decision-making process, quietly shaping consumer choice.

One fundamental shift in digital commerce is the transition from "search" to "recommendation"-driven consumption. The earlier online world was largely consumer-driven, with search beginning only once a need was clear. AI-powered systems, however, can predict preferences and make recommendations before consumers even ask, saving users the mental effort of searching and making them more loyal, engaged visitors. Chiriatti et al. (2026) suggested that AI systems increasingly influence consumer attention by regulating exposure to digital content and focusing attention on preferred products, brands, and content. Recommendation systems are no longer simply reacting to consumer preferences—they are increasingly shaping them.

Algorithmic Consumer Decision-Making

Today's consumer markets are characteristically shaped by algorithmic decisions. Machine learning recommendation systems personalize using collaborative, content-based, and predictive techniques, recognizing patterns in user behavior from large-scale data. Fu et al. (2023) noted that recommender systems have progressed from predicting preferences to maximizing engagement by balancing relevance, novelty, and personalization, with deep learning increasingly used for this purpose. These systems are used across retail, entertainment, travel, finance, and social networking, significantly shaping everyday consumer product discovery.

Predictive personalization algorithms depend on collecting extensive behavioral and real-time analytics data to leverage consumer interactions—tracking products bought, time spent on a site, scroll depth, searches without purchase, and emotional engagement with products. This data-driven architecture lets platforms continually improve accuracy and build highly responsive digital ecosystems. Abdullah (2025) found that AI-driven personalization can greatly improve customer loyalty and convenience, reducing the complexity of e-commerce choice. This has created a new competitive edge for companies and a growing expectation of personalization among digital consumers.

Platforms are also shaping consumer choice itself, as new platform-mediated decision architectures take over. Consumers increasingly see products and brands recommended based on what algorithms predict will engage them, not necessarily what they are genuinely interested in—creating systems where visibility depends on ranking near the top of results. Marchand et al. (2025) argued that in AI-powered marketing systems, consumer subjectivity is continuously formed through surveillance capitalism, via the monitoring and targeting of consumer behavior. Consumers' autonomy is thus a partial construct within algorithmic infrastructures aimed at maximizing commercial outcomes.

Habit Loops versus Serendipitous Discovery

Algorithmic personalization first reinforces consumer habits. Machine learning systems detect patterns and deliver the most effective recommendations for established preferences. As people grow used to a product, they rely on it more, forming digital habit loops around the same brands, content, and products. Şenyapar (2025) reported that this subtle behavioral engineering drives repeated actions and reduces behavioral uncertainty.

Habitual reinforcement increases convenience and efficiency but can reduce the chances of serendipitous discovery. In the past, consumers found new products and brands through browsing, social interaction, or incidental search in the physical environment. Recommendation systems, however, tend to prioritize relevance over exposing users to unfamiliar alternatives. Nalis et al. (2024) identified a persistent trade-off in recommender systems between recommending what users like and what they might like—personalization boosts short-term enjoyment but can limit long-term variety.

Balancing efficiency against exploratory consumption is a key challenge in AI-driven markets. As people rely more on personalized recommendations to cut down information overload, decisions become easier, but an over-optimized filter bubble can present a consistent stream of the same products and ideas, limiting opportunities for meaningful discovery. Fu et al. (2023) highlighted that recommendation systems are beginning to incorporate mechanisms that reduce repetitive consumption by considering serendipity, leaving platforms and brands caught between predictive accuracy and discovery, novelty, and exploration.

Objectives and Scope of the Chapter

This chapter explores the effect machine learning algorithms have on consumer decision-making in AI-powered digital marketplaces, examining the tension between serendipitous discovery and the reinforcement of habitual consumption. It adopts a multi-disciplinary perspective, drawing on behavioral science, marketing theory, and AI research to illuminate implications for consumer autonomy, brand visibility, and market dynamics, and to explore how predictive personalization is transforming consumer autonomy, brand visibility, and market competition.

One main goal of this chapter is to examine algorithmic systems' consequences for brand growth and consumer decisions. While traditional marketing theory emphasizes mental availability, wide market penetration, and consumer memory structures for brand success, these components take on a different character as more brands rely on AI-driven personalization, which focuses on what a consumer is buying now and has bought before—potentially reducing exposure to new brands and alternatives. The chapter thus assesses whether algorithmic recommendation systems contribute to market concentration, giving already-dominant brands structural advantages.

The chapter also aims to develop a balanced approach to personalization and serendipity in intelligent digital ecosystems, focusing not on whether AI recommendation systems are positive or negative but on how companies can design them to balance efficiency with exploration. Intelligent adaptive environments will increasingly be characterized by coexistence models where optimizing technology aligns with human-centered goals (Mokhtar & Manganelli, 2026). Wrench and Elmoudden (2025) likewise noted the growing importance of AI literacy for consumers to critically engage with algorithmically-mediated environments. This chapter therefore suggests that the path forward requires balancing predictive intelligence with meaningful discovery and autonomous choice.

BACKGROUND: THEORETICAL FOUNDATIONS OF AI-DRIVEN CONSUMER BEHAVIOR

Behavioral Science and Habit Formation

Behavioral science helps explain how AI systems shape consumer behavior by building habits through repeated digital interactions. Habit formation typically follows cue-routine-reward components, where a consumer reacts to a personalized notification or recommendation and, given a specific cue, acts again. Over time these interactions become automated patterns that lessen conscious evaluation before a purchase (Dharini, 2025).

These patterns build on foundational behavioral economics research. Simon (1955) argued that decision-makers operate under bounded rationality, relying on simplified heuristics rather than exhaustive evaluation due to limited information, time, and cognitive capacity; recommendation algorithms can be understood as exploiting this tendency by pre-narrowing the choice set to a small number of familiar options. Choice architecture research similarly shows that how options are presented predictably shapes choices without removing alternatives outright (Thaler & Sunstein, 2008), closely paralleling how recommendation interfaces default consumers toward algorithmically favored products.

Machine learning systems adapt to customer behavior to reinforce habits through digital reinforcement cycles: each click, purchase, or view becomes training data that teaches the algorithm to push ever more familiar products. Wang (2025) noted that predictive systems reduce uncertainty and add convenience to consumer choices, meaning customers increasingly rely on AI-powered suggestions rather than seeking other options.

Predictive systems are increasingly central to consumers' digital lives. AI algorithms drive user experience and decision-making across e-commerce, streaming, and social media, influencing everyday consumption habits and producing highly personalized, engaging digital experiences that shift consumer behavior (Pattnaik & Mohanty).

Machine Learning in Digital Marketplaces

Digital marketplaces' 'operational core' is now powered by machine learning technologies. Collaborative filtering and recommendation algorithms determine the similarity of users' behaviors and suggest similar products, while content-based recommendation systems focus on product content itself to suggest items similar to those already consumed (George, 2025).

Predictive analytics and behavioral targeting help companies use browsing patterns, purchases, and interactions to forecast future behavior. AI systems increasingly influence consumers through real-time, personalized ads and product suggestions (Ismaliyanto et al., 2026), engaging users while enhancing digital marketing efforts.

Engagement optimization models focus on increasing metrics like click-through rates, watch time, and repeat purchases. Bilgihan et al. (2025) found that AI-driven loyalty initiatives encourage consumer consistency and continuous engagement, strengthening the platform-user relationship.

Marketing Science Perspectives

Marketing science concepts such as mental availability and brand salience are highly relevant in AI-powered markets. Mental availability is the extent to which consumers recall a brand when making purchase decisions; recommendation systems continuously feed consumers' memory with brand and product suggestions, strengthening memory structures and visibility (Kovalenko et al., 2026).

As algorithmic ecosystems take hold, brand salience is no longer driven by advertising alone. Product positioning in feeds, search results, and recommendation sections is algorithmically determined; Dharini (2025) suggested that AI-driven systems shape consumer exposure and maintain familiarity, influencing consumer desire.

There is also a shift in penetration/loyalty dynamics in AI-based markets. Recommendation systems tend to focus on existing consumers' preferences and repeat actions, whereas traditional marketing theory emphasizes market penetration; Bilgihan et al. (2025) noted that AI-driven personalization fosters loyalty by continually reminding users to engage with familiar brands and services.

Consumer Autonomy and Algorithmic Gatekeeping

AI-based recommendation systems shape consumer interaction with information and products, affecting consumers' autonomy as they increasingly rely on algorithms to find and engage with content. The range of alternatives presented is reduced as algorithms prioritize products based on predicted engagement. Rana and Bhambri (2026) suggest predictive systems raise ethical questions by affecting consumer behavior indirectly through automated recommendations.

Algorithms can create filter bubbles that limit consumption by continually showing the same products and perspectives. Wang (2025) found that over-personalization can negatively affect exploratory behavior, narrowing exposure to unknown brands and alternatives, which can limit diversity in the marketplace.

Ethical issues in recommendation systems include transparency, privacy, manipulation, and behavior control. Kalpokas and Kalpokienė (2025) highlighted the societal and ethical implications of AI systems, where consumers may be less aware of their options while businesses gain greater influence. Moreno and Poudineh (2026) proposed that well-balanced policies, rather than total delegation of control to intelligent systems, are necessary to preserve the benefits of personalization without compromising consumer autonomy.

These concerns connect to two further strands of foundational theory. Attention economy scholarship treats consumer attention as a scarce, monetizable resource that organizations compete to capture and hold (Davenport & Beck, 2001), helping explain why engagement-maximizing algorithms are designed to hold attention rather than simply match preferences. Research on algorithmic governance similarly argues that recommender systems raise ethical and regulatory challenges that existing consumer-protection frameworks were not designed to address, calling for governance approaches specific to algorithmic decision-making (Milano, Taddeo, & Floridi, 2020).

ALGORITHMIC REINFORCEMENT AND HABIT LOOPS IN CONSUMER MARKETS

Personalized Recommendation Ecosystems

Personalized recommendation ecosystems have become central to contemporary digital commerce and platform-based consumption. Machine learning algorithms are increasingly common across streaming, e-commerce, and social media platforms, using collected data to maximize engagement and personalize experience. These systems track user behavior in real time—videos watched, scrolling, click rates, shopping habits, likes, and time spent—to deliver individualized suggestions, turning platforms into intelligent ecosystems that capture consumer attention and drive choices (Dharini, 2025).

One of the most evident examples of AI personalization is streaming platforms. Recommendation algorithms forecast user preferences for music, film, and digital entertainment services to ensure ongoing engagement, learning from past use to suggest similar content that keeps users subscribed. Avdić et al. (2025) noted that users increasingly accept and use platform recommendations over their own exploration, significantly affecting purchase and consumption decisions.

E-commerce recommendation systems function similarly to information retrieval systems. Collaborative filtering and predictive analytics provide product recommendations based on the purchase and navigation behavior of consumers and similar users, with suggestive selling, customer suggestions, and targeted ads aimed at improving conversions and repeat sales. S. Sharma et al. (2022) noted that reinforcement learning and collaborative filtering can further improve personalized loyalty programs by continually fine-tuning recommendations based on feedback, boosting both operational efficiency and behavioral consistency among users.

The role of social media content curators is another source of algorithmic influence over consumers. Platforms prioritize content based on predicted engagement metrics—likes, shares, watch time, and interactions—presenting consumers with highly filtered environments where algorithms determine visibility for certain products, influencers, ads, and opinions. Saxena (2025) argued that these programming algorithms have an immense power to shape consumer habits by consistently directing consumption and content preferences, cultivating routines and platform dependency over time.

Reinforcement of Existing Consumption Patterns

Machine learning systems are built to reinforce consumers' current practices, as predictive accuracy relies heavily on prior interactions and behavioral consistency. Recommendation algorithms focus on familiarity, repeatedly surfacing what a user has already liked, which algorithmically drives 'habitual buying' as consumers continue purchasing familiar product types. AI-driven marketing systems are becoming integral to consumer behavior in the digital era, minimizing uncertainty and easing the purchasing process through predictive recommendations (Sarin, 2025).

Frequent algorithmic exposure can also reduce consumers' switching behavior, as recommendation systems striving to maximize engagement and satisfaction make consumers more likely to stay with what they know rather than try something new. It is highlighted that AI personalization significantly affects purchasing behavior by building brand loyalty and repetitive buying behavior; personalized recommendations tend to be trusted more, reinforcing reliance on familiar digital environments.

Platform loyalty and repeated engagement are crucial outcomes of algorithmic reinforcement. AI systems provide suggestions that are increasingly specific and personalized, encouraging more engagement and repeat visits, creating positive feedback cycles in which engagement leads to better personalization and vice versa. Challoumis (2024) highlighted that AI systems can significantly affect consumers' purchasing patterns and interactions with digital platforms, building loyalty and platform dependency.

An alternative explanation for recommendation systems' emphasis on repeat interaction is economic. Budzinski et al. (2022) found that recommender services offer business benefits through higher efficiency of consumer attention and lower search expenses, easing decisions and increasing sales speed and duration. The same attributes that create this ease, however, can limit exposure to a variety of products and alternative uses, raising the question of how different recommendations can remain if they grow increasingly familiar and repetitive to consumers.

Implications for Brand Competition

In digital markets, algorithmic recommendation systems can be very influential, significantly shaping how products are placed in competition. Brands with high engagement rates gain substantial advantages by appearing prominently in recommendation ecosystems, as algorithms favor products with more engagement and better interaction history, dominating search results and curated feeds. Dharini (2025) claimed that AI-powered digital markets gradually influence consumer desire by orchestrating brand visibility and repetition patterns, giving established brands cumulative visibility that strengthens their market grip.

Discoverability problems affect emerging brands in algorithmically-curated environments. New products and smaller businesses are less likely to be recommended prominently because they lack extensive historical interaction data, which can lead to market concentration as algorithms favor recommendations from more popular, higher-engagement brands. AI recommendation engines may also contribute to a lack of variety in consumer choice, as algorithms continually prioritize familiar and commercially successful products (Enyiorji & Deloitte, 2023), placing smaller businesses at a disadvantage in discoverability and attracting new customers.

Another signature trait of algorithmically personalized digital ecosystems is attention concentration. Rather than competing solely for sales, social media platforms, streaming services, and online marketplaces increasingly compete for consumer attention. Content algorithms optimize visibility based on engagement, focusing attention on a few highly visible content creators, products, and brands (Saxena, 2025), while dampening attention toward lower-engagement content. This over-concentration of digital engagement can diminish market diversity and opportunities for exploratory consumption.

These developments raise key strategic issues for companies in AI-influenced environments. Brands face the challenge of optimizing products, ads, and digital interactions to align with platform recommendation systems, and those that fail to adjust risk losing relevance and visibility in the competitive digital landscape. Meanwhile, over-optimization of algorithmic prioritization can diminish market dynamism as consumer focus narrows toward a limited number of dominant players.

Consumer Convenience versus Choice Diversity

A major benefit of AI-based recommendation systems is streamlining consumer decision-making. Personalized recommendations cut down information overload by showing products and services similar to those consumers have already chosen, helping consumers navigate e-markets efficiently without extensive search and evaluation. Golchha and Nagariya (2025) reported that AI personalization is becoming a significant factor in consumer shopping habits, with growing influence on decision-making processes.

But the same systems that create convenience can also reduce exploratory shopping. Familiarity boosts both engagement and recommendation accuracy, making it increasingly common to recommend products similar to those interacted with previously; over time, consumers come to expect ever more personalized suggestions and may feel less need to experiment. Avdić (2025) found that AI-driven recommendation systems can profoundly affect repetitive consumption behaviors in subscription-based services, where consumers rely more on personalized recommendations than on actively seeking alternatives.

Lower exploratory behavior extends to consumers' long-term diversity of choice. Engagement- and retention-driven algorithms can inadvertently create commercial filter bubbles, leading consumers to repeatedly see the same products, brands, and viewpoints. Enyiorji and Deloitte (2023) suggest that AI recommendation systems may reduce choice diversity in financial and commercial products by presenting only familiar options.

SERENDIPITY AND DISCOVERY IN AI-CURATED ENVIRONMENTS

Understanding Serendipitous Consumption

In the past, consumer exposure to new products in physical marketplaces, bookstores, retail stores, and social environments was largely a matter of chance. In digital ecosystems, algorithms increasingly play a key role in consumer discovery, ensuring relevance and engagement. Dharini (2025) suggested that AI-driven digital markets actively shape consumer attention toward content expected to match existing consumption habits, changing how consumers discover content.

Exploratory purchasing behavior relates to curiosity, novelty-seeking, and experimentation. It can satisfy consumers by fulfilling desired products while also revealing new products that enrich their preferences and experiences. Manolovitz (2022) showed that repeated exposure to novel stimuli can gradually increase consumer acceptance and engagement, underscoring novelty's role in future consumer behavior. In business terms, exploratory consumption can diversify markets and create opportunities for new brands to reach consumers outside traditional consumption patterns.

Novelty is also important for the diffusion of innovation and long-term brand growth. New products and less popular brands often depend on happenstance encounters and exploratory behavior to become familiar to consumers, but AI-based recommendation systems tend to favor familiarity because it increases predictability of engagement. Marchand et al. (2025) theorized that consumer subjectivity is progressively formed through surveillance capitalism and algorithmic marketing systems that focus attention on commercial interests. As recommendation systems become more precise in behavioral prediction, opportunities for accidental discovery may accordingly shrink.

Declining Consumer Exploration

One major impact of algorithmic narrowing of product exposure is heightened personalization. Recommendation engines continuously learn from past interactions, focusing on products, brands, and content similar to those already consumed, which enhances relevance and convenience but can limit exposure to a variety of possibilities. Avdić (2025) found that on subscription-based platforms, recommendation systems strongly reinforce repeated engagement with familiar content, making exploration of new content less likely.

Repetitive consumption patterns are further reinforced by predictiveness and familiarity bias, since click-through and watch time are easier to achieve through familiar recommendations than unfamiliar ones—leading consumers to see the same products and opinions repeatedly across digital platforms. Tavares (2025) found that platforms like TikTok strongly influence purchase intentions by engaging consumers emotionally and delivering personalized content that keeps them within algorithmic consumption loops.

Commercial filter bubbles arise when recommendation systems continually narrow toward a user's preferred behavior patterns, exposing them to fewer alternative products or opinions and creating highly individualized consumption environments based mainly on previous consumption. Dharini (2025) also highlighted how algorithmic systems influence consumer desire by determining who sees what and how; such filter bubbles can, over time, reduce market diversity and exploratory consumer behavior.

Despite AI's role in creative spaces, Peng et al. (2025) maintained that novel and diverse inputs remain crucial to inspiration and ideation. By emphasizing predictability too strongly, there is a risk that consumers could miss the chance for discovery and learning that might occur if they weren't shown only the most popular item—creating inherent tension between efficiency and the human need to explore, be curious, and encounter variety.

Strategic Importance of Engineered Serendipity

With escalating concerns over repetitive consumption and limited exposure, online platforms are increasingly exploring engineered serendipity—the intentional design of a recommender system to surface novel, surprising items alongside relevant, personalized ones. These systems don't simply push new products, categories, or viewpoints, but do so strategically to fit the recommendation context. Kim et al. (2025) showed that incorporating a serendipity algorithm into recommender systems can enhance user satisfaction by balancing familiarity and exploration.

Discovery-oriented recommendation design aims to keep consumers interested while maintaining engagement efficiency. Platforms can add novelty by welcoming new brands, diversifying product catalogs, and recommending different products, allowing users to discover new possibilities without losing personalization's benefits. Dorigo et al. (2025) argued that AI systems should serve more general, human-centered applications rather than being limited to optimization and prediction—meaning recommendation systems in consumer markets must deliver both convenience and meaningful exploration. Figure 1 sets out the conceptual framework.

Figure 1. Conceptual framework of habit reinforcement and engineered serendipity.

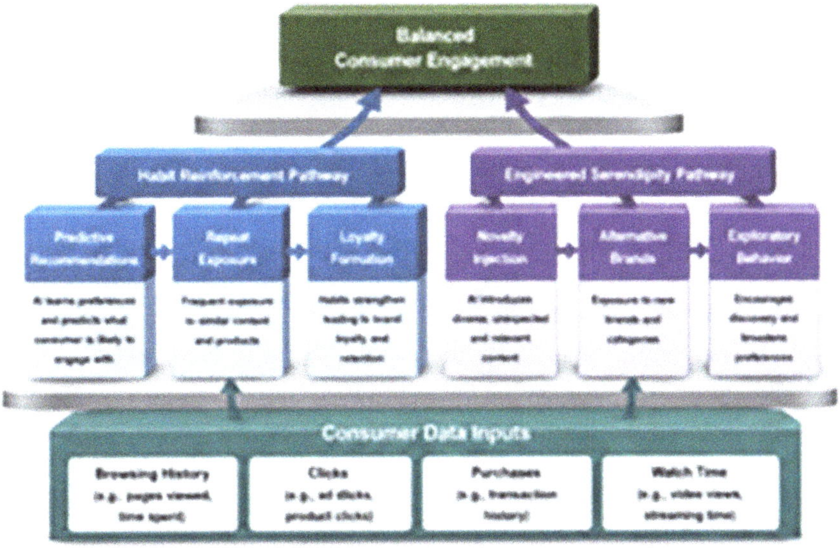

The figure shows two paths by which AI-based recommendation systems affect consumer behavior: personalization that drives repetition, exposure, and loyalty; and novelty that drives exploration, consumption, and discovery of alternative brands. It illustrates that balanced recommendation architectures can simultaneously capture consumer engagement while preserving opportunities for discovery and market diversification.

The need for relevance and novelty is gaining significance for sustainable digital ecosystems. Personalization can boost in-the-moment engagement but take a longer-term toll on consumer diversity and exposure to innovation. Wachtel (2023) asserted that open-mindedness may be necessary for meaningful human experience, including encounters with the unknown; similarly, environments that allow for accidental interaction with materials or ideas may foster greater creativity, experimentation, and independent choice.

There is thus considerable strategic and ethical value in enhancing consumers' exploratory experiences on digital platforms. Brands need to move beyond algorithmic popularity and past interactions to gain visibility. Recommendation systems that incorporate discovery-oriented attributes can help build healthier digital ecosystems where personalization aids, rather than hinders, consumer discovery.

CROSS-REGIONAL CASE STUDIES OF ALGORITHMIC PERSONALIZATION

North America Streaming Platforms and Habitual Consumption

North America is one of the most advanced markets for AI-powered personalization, particularly in streaming and subscription services. Recommendation systems leverage browsing history, user interactions, and time spent to deliver highly personalized content recommendations aimed at maximizing retention and ongoing platform use. Weerasinghe et al. (2025) noted that algorithmic music recommendations can contribute to behavioral biases by continuously suggesting the same content.

Consuming large amounts of content over short periods now characterizes engagement-based recommendation systems, with autoplay, sequential recommendations, and personalized playlists keeping viewers engaged without actively searching. Caliskan et al. (2025) argued that digital platforms are becoming increasingly efficient at optimizing commercial outcomes through algorithmic visibility management and behavioral prediction, giving recommendation systems significant influence over consumers' attention and entertainment behaviors in North American markets.

Europe: Ethical AI and Consumer Transparency

Accountability, explainability, and responsible AI use are key elements of European regulatory frameworks, which strive to balance technological advancement with consumer safeguards and ethical considerations (Ullagaddi, 2025).

Personalization in Europe is shaped by consumer trust and privacy concerns, with users often expecting greater clarity around data collection and recommendation processes

Asia: Hyper-Personalized Super App Ecosystems

Asian markets are defined by highly integrated super-app ecosystems combining commerce, payments, communication, and entertainment on a single platform, with AI-powered behavioral analytics and predictive personalization as key components. Depari (2024) explained that business analytics has driven the expansion of adaptive, AI-powered business ecosystems in the region.

AI-powered predictive consumption is particularly strong in mobile-first economies, where users rely on apps for daily business and life activities. Kulothungan and Gupta (2025) noted that Asian governance models emphasize innovation and scalability alongside regulatory adaptation, translating into a strong presence of personalization in the region's daily digital interactions.

Middle East: Smart Retail Ecosystems on the Rise

AI-driven retail ecosystems are growing fast in the Middle East, fueled by digital transformation and rising mobile commerce. AI has become central to retail, enabling one-to-one customer interactions, intelligent engagement systems, and targeted promotions across platforms.

The luxury and lifestyle retail sector has seen substantial AI impact in the region. Slama and Ghodbane (2026) noted that real-time AI customization systems can improve personalization quality and retail performance in digital commerce. Fintech solutions and intelligent retail technologies are positioning the Middle East as a new hotspot for AI-powered retail and personalized digital experiences.

EMPIRICAL STUDY: CONSUMER PERCEPTIONS OF MACHINE LEARNING RECOMMENDATIONS AND SERENDIPITOUS DISCOVERY

Study Objectives

The empirical study aimed to investigate the impact of machine learning-based recommender systems on consumer behavior in AI-driven digital marketplaces, focusing on how much consumers rely on algorithmic recommendations while streaming content, purchasing goods online, and consuming social media content. The study also explored the potential of personalized recommendation systems to reduce exploratory behavior and interaction with other brands and products, with particular emphasis on consumers' perception of decreasing spontaneous discovery in highly personalized digital spaces. It further sought to uncover demographic and regional differences in consumer behavior to understand how algorithmic personalization affects consumer engagement and brand visibility.

Research Design and Methodology

This study adopted a quantitative, cross-sectional survey design to investigate consumer perceptions of AI recommendation systems and exploratory consumption, collecting data from 412 respondents across India, UAE, USA, UK, and Singapore—regions selected to reflect a spectrum of digital platform adoption and attitudes toward personalization technologies. The survey was distributed via convenience and snowball sampling to active users of streaming, e-commerce, and social commerce platforms.

The questionnaire used structured, closed-ended questions on a 5-point Likert scale from strongly disagree to strongly agree, designed in Google Forms and shared via social networking groups, academic networks, and online consumer communities. The research design measured consumer dependence on AI recommendations, tendency to repeat purchases, exploratory behavior, and trust in personalization systems. Figure 2 summarizes the research design.

Figure 2. Research methodology flowchart.

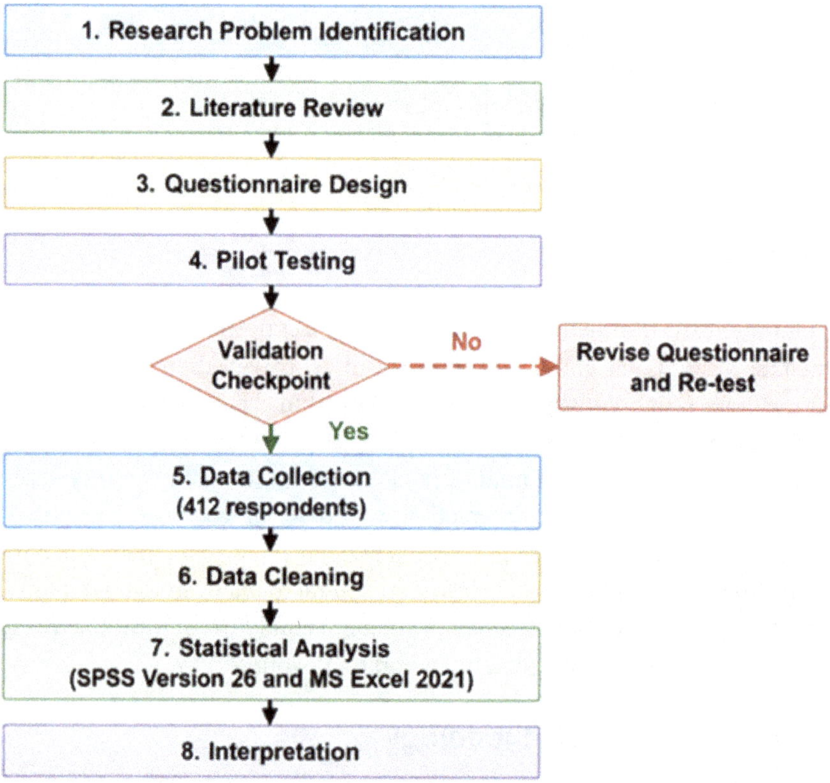

The flowchart illustrates the research process: identifying the research problem, literature search, questionnaire design, pilot testing, data collection, data cleaning, analysis, and interpretation of results, reflecting the systematic quantitative approach used to assess consumer perceptions of machine learning recommendations and serendipitous discovery.

Variables and Measurement

The study included several behavioral and perceptual variables. Recommendation dependency measured how much consumers relied on AI recommendations when purchasing and consuming content. Habitual buying tendency captured the likelihood of repeat purchases following algorithmic exposure. Perceived decrease in discovery measured whether consumers felt personalized systems reduced their discovery of new products and brands. Consumer exploration orientation captured willingness to try new products or categories beyond algorithmic suggestions. Consumer trust in AI recommendations focused on perceived relevance, reliability, and usefulness of personalized suggestions.

Multi-item scales, adapted to the AI-mediated marketplace context, were used to assess all variables. Higher scores reflected greater dependence, engagement, and trust in recommendation systems, while lower scores reflected stronger interest in independent exploration and diversified consumption.

The internal consistency of all multi-item scales was assessed using Cronbach's alpha prior to correlation analysis. Table 1 reports the reliability coefficients for each construct.

Table 1. Cronbach's alpha reliability coefficients for multi-item scales.

Construct	No. of Items	Cronbach's α	Interpretation
Recommendation Dependency	5	0.84	Good
Habitual Buying Tendency	5	0.81	Good
Perceived Decrease in Discovery	4	0.79	Acceptable
Consumer Exploration Orientation	4	0.82	Good
Consumer Trust in AI Recommendations	5	0.87	Good

Cronbach's alpha was in the range of 0.79–0.87 for all five constructs, which is above the commonly accepted threshold of 0.70 (as suggested by Nunnally, 1978). The internal consistencies were highest for Consumer Trust in AI Recommendations ($\alpha = 0.87$), Recommendation Dependency ($\alpha = 0.84$), and Consumer Exploration Orientation ($\alpha = 0.82$). The reliabilities of the other two constructs Habitual Buying Tendency ($\alpha = 0.81$) and Perceived Decrease in Discovery ($\alpha = 0.79$) showed good results. These results also indicated that each scale successfully measured the construct it was designed for, which lends validity to the correlation analysis.

Tools and Software Used

Data were analyzed using IBM SPSS Statistics (version 26) and Microsoft Excel 2021. Descriptive statistics—means, standard deviations, frequencies, and percentages—summarized respondent behavior and perceptions. Correlation analysis examined the relationship between recommendation dependence and purchasing habits, cross-tabulation compared usage patterns across platforms, and independent-sample t-tests examined regional differences in attitudes toward AI-based personalization.

Ethical Considerations and Informed Consent

This research was done in an ethical framework of research involving human subjects. A statement describing the purpose of the study and that the participation was voluntary, and that the respondents could withdraw at any time without consequences, was presented to all respondents at the beginning of the online questionnaire. Thus, informed consent was achieved with all of the respondents before data collection began. No personal data was gathered, all responses were anonymous and only aggregated. All data was kept confidential and only for the purpose of this study.

Results and Analysis

Consumer Dependence on Recommendation Systems

Results indicated high consumer dependence on AI-driven suggestions: 74% reported relying on personalized recommendations often or very often when choosing products, entertainment, or online services. Dependence was significantly stronger among younger consumers, with those aged 18–34 showing the heaviest use, reflecting greater familiarity with digital ecosystems and constant use of streaming and social media platforms. Figure 3 shows this pattern across age groups.

Figure 3. Consumer dependence on AI recommendations across age groups.

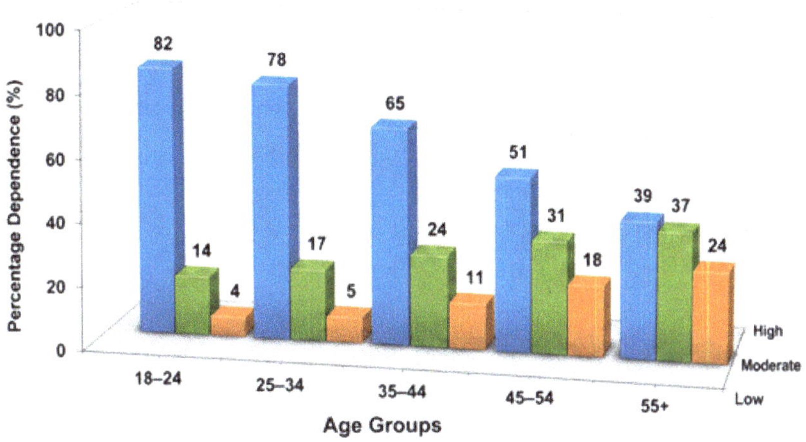

The figure shows a significant difference in dependence across age groups, with reliance on AI recommendations gradually decreasing as age increases, suggesting more deeply embedded algorithmic reliance among younger consumer segments. Table 2 gives the frequency distribution.

Table 2. Frequency distribution of recommendation usage.

Recommendation Usage Frequency	**Frequency**	**Percentage (%)**
Very Frequently	168	40.8
Frequently	137	33.3
Occasionally	61	14.8
Rarely	31	7.5
Never	15	3.6
Total	**412**	**100.0**

The table shows that most respondents actively interact with personalized recommendations very often, reflecting high usage of AI in decision-making and the integration of recommendation systems into consumers' daily lives.

Habit Reinforcement and Repeat Consumption

Analysis showed a strong relationship between exposure to recommendations and repeated buying behavior. Consumers who interacted with recommendation systems were more likely to repurchase familiar recommended products and services, and constant algorithmic exposure enhanced platform loyalty by increasing familiarity and reducing decision-making uncertainty. Figure 4 plots this relationship.

Figure 4. Relationship between recommendation exposure and repeat purchases.

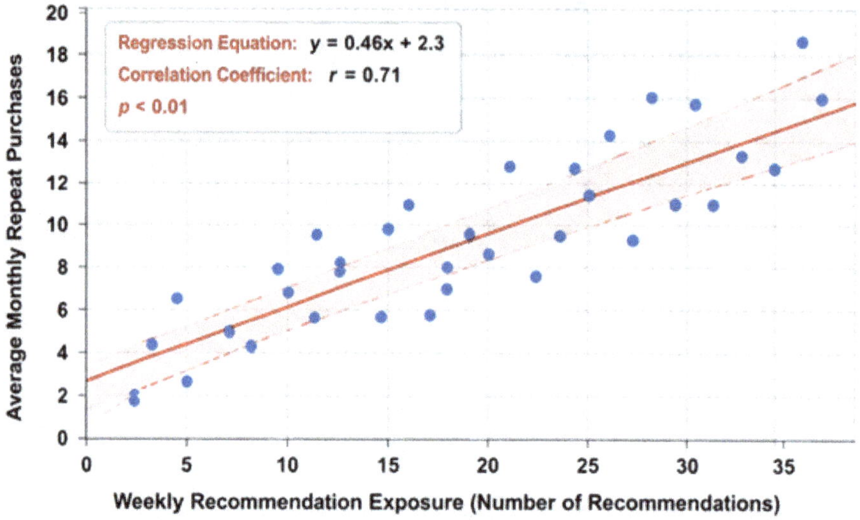

The figure shows a positive correlation between recommendation frequency and repeat purchases: consumers exposed to more personalized recommendations showed greater consumption regularity and reliance on familiar digital environments. Table 3 reports the associated statistics.

Table 3. Relationships between recommendation dependence and purchase frequency.

Variables	Mean	Standard Deviation	Correlation (r)	Significance (p-value)
Recommendation Dependence	4.12	0.71	0.71	0.000
Habitual Buying Behavior	3.96	0.83	0.71	0.000
Platform Loyalty	3.88	0.79	0.64	< 0.001
Exploratory Purchasing	3.28	0.74	-0.53	< 0.001

Note. Correlations are Pearson coefficients between each listed variable and overall recommendation usage frequency, as reported in the frequency distribution table above. All coefficients are based on the full sample of 412 respondents.

The table shows a statistically significant positive correlation between recommendation dependence and purchasing habits, suggesting that greater use of AI-generated suggestions is associated with more repetitive behavior and stronger platform loyalty.

Algorithmic Impact on Customer Purchase Frequency

Findings confirmed that repeat purchases increased with higher exposure to recommendations across platform categories, with subscription-based streaming and social commerce applications showing higher habitual usage than other marketplace applications—the more consumers were exposed to algorithmic suggestions, the more likely they were to continue buying familiar products and using preferred services. Figure 5 shows average monthly repeat purchases.

Figure 5. Average monthly repeat purchases influenced by algorithms.

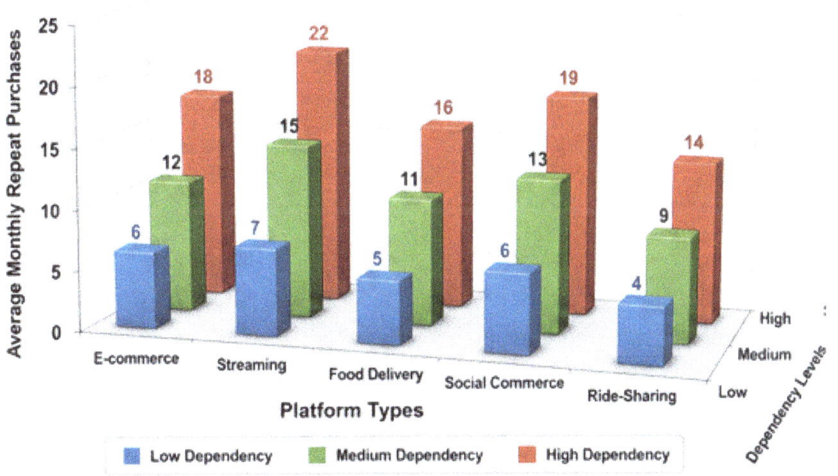

The figure shows that consumers highly dependent on recommendations have significantly higher repeat purchasing rates, particularly in streaming and social commerce contexts where recommendation systems are in constant use.

Decline in Serendipitous Brand Discovery

Most respondents felt that personalized recommendation systems lower exposure to new brands and alternative product categories. Many noted seeing similar recommended products repeatedly while browsing, reducing opportunities for discovery, and algorithmically-curated recommendations also decreased respondents' willingness to seek out alternatives on their own. Figure 6 shows the perceived reduction in discovery.

Figure 6. Perceived reduction in new brand discovery.

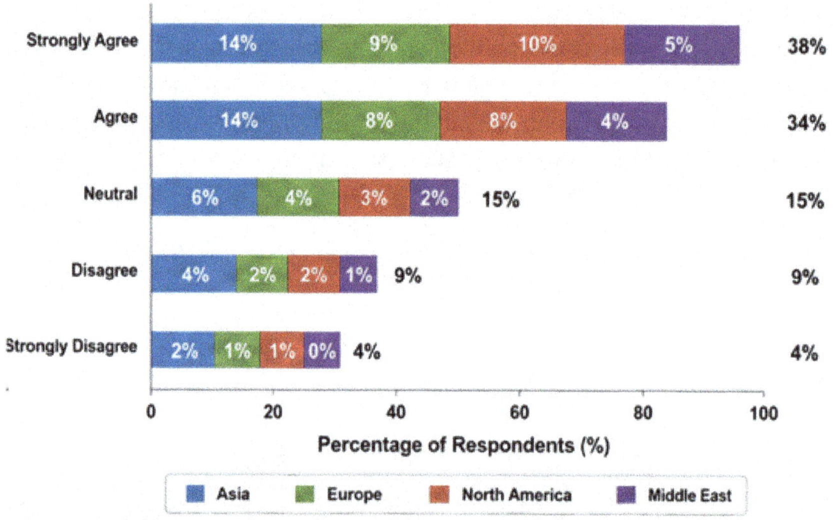

The figure shows that a significant share of respondents feel AI personalization decreases their chances of finding new brands and products, suggesting recommendation systems' negative effects on exploration are becoming more apparent to consumers. Table 4 cross-tabulates platform usage against discovery behavior.

Table 4. Cross-tabulation of platform usage and discovery behavior.

Platform Type	High Discovery Behavior	Moderate Discovery Behavior	Low Discovery Behavior	Total Respondents
E-commerce Platforms	74	39	21	134
Streaming Platforms	19	41	58	118
Social Media Commerce	28	46	37	111
Food Delivery Applications	11	17	21	49
Total	**132**	**143**	137	412

Consumer Exploration Across Digital Platforms

Analysis showed significant differences in exploratory consumption by platform type. Streaming and social media app users showed low experimentation levels due to personalized recommendation systems, while users of marketplaces with wider product scope showed relatively higher interest in trying new products and categories, reflecting greater variety and search flexibility. Figure 7 compares exploration tendency across platforms.

Figure 7. Consumer exploration tendency by digital platform.

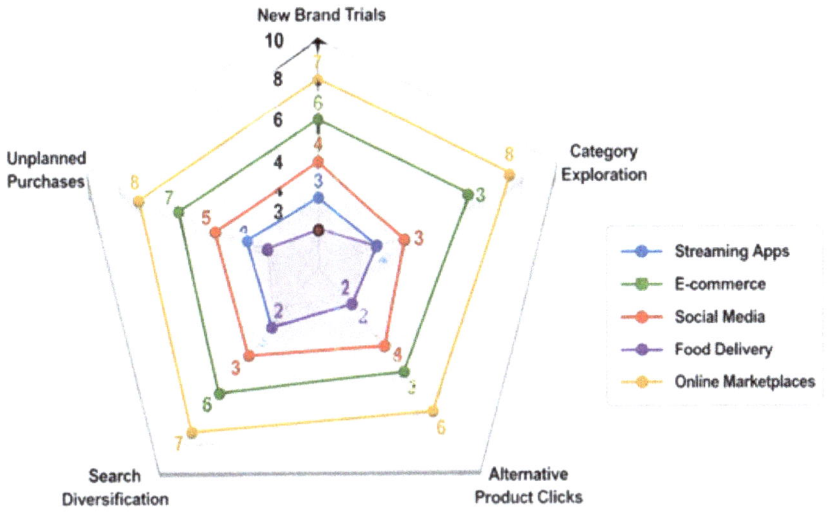

The figure compares exploratory consumption behavior across platform types, showing marketplace platforms as relatively more experimental than highly personalized streaming or social media platforms, where users tend to stick to a few sites and services.

Regional Differences in Consumer Attitudes

There was regional variation in consumer perceptions of algorithmic personalization: Asian respondents were more accepting of recommendation systems and trusted AI personalization more, while European respondents showed greater concern about algorithmic impact, transparency, and privacy issues. Figure 8 compares trust in AI recommendations by region.

Figure 8. Regional comparison of trust in AI recommendations.

Figure 8

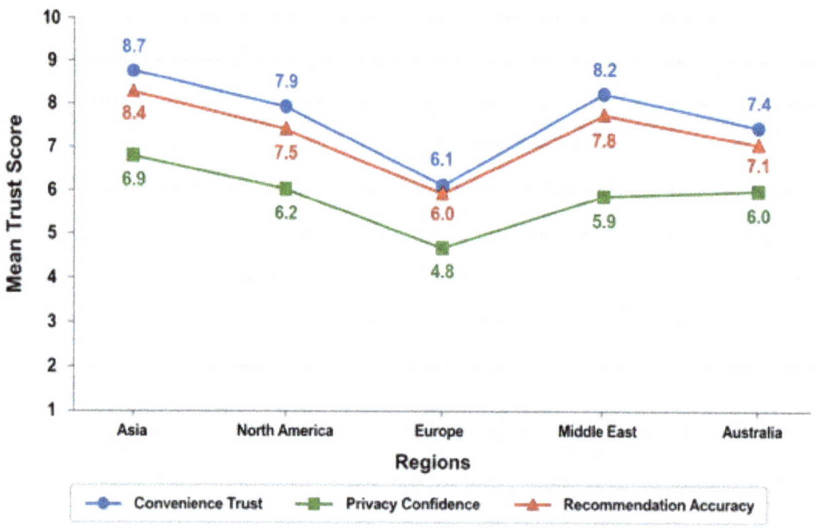

The figure shows regional variation in trust in AI recommender systems: Asian respondents had the highest trust and convenience scores, while European respondents scored comparatively lower, reflecting privacy and algorithmic transparency concerns. Table 5 reports the regional means.

Table 5. Consumer attitudes by region.

Region	Trust in AI Recommendations	Perceived Convenience	Concern About Reduced Choice	Preference for Exploratory Discovery	n	t (df)	p
Asia	4.20	4.35	2.60	3.05	170	6.30	0.001
North America	3.75	3.95	3.20	3.40	100	2.34	0.021
Europe	3.00	3.05	4.05	3.80	62	-9.32	0.001
Middle East	3.90	4.10	2.95	3.25	80	0.54	0.25

The table shows stark regional differences in convenience perception, trust in AI recommendations, and concern about reduced choice, indicating that cultural and regulatory factors shape consumer acceptance of algorithmic systems.

Discussion of Findings

Empirical results show that machine learning recommendation systems produce a strong reinforcement effect, continuously presenting consumers with known products, services, and experiences that increase repetition in consumption. Customized suggestions streamline user experience and minimize choices, increasing loyalty and engagement regularity, but personalization also has negative consequences for serendipitous discovery and exploratory consumption, especially in highly curated streaming and social media environments.

The study also reflects key regional differences in consumer attitudes toward AI-driven personalization. European respondents were more concerned than Asian respondents about privacy, transparency, and algorithmic impact on autonomy, while Asian consumers were more accepting of predictive systems. Achieving a balance between personalization and discovery mechanisms will remain crucial for maintaining consumer variety, market innovation, and long-term brand growth in AI-mediated digital markets.

SOLUTIONS AND RECOMMENDATIONS: A STRATEGIC APPROACH TO BALANCING PERSONALIZATION AND SERENDIPITY

Recommendation Systems: Designing Systems to Discover

As AI-driven personalization becomes more prevalent in digital marketplaces, companies and platform designers increasingly recognize the need to incorporate discovery-based mechanisms into recommendation systems, since over-personalization can perpetuate over-consumption and restrict opportunities to discover new products, brands, and opinions. Recommendation architectures therefore need to go beyond optimizing for engagement to balance relevance and exploratory discovery. Reviglio (2023) suggested that serendipity can serve as a basic design concept in personalization systems, since positive experiences for consumers can arise unexpectedly rather than being guaranteed by frequency of system contact.

One approach is controlled novelty insertion—deliberately introducing novel items into the recommendation environment without disrupting its natural dynamics. Systems can proactively surface new products, brands, or categories into personalized feeds without sacrificing relevance, introducing consumers to new experiences while maintaining recommendation quality. Chen et al. (2024) explained that shaping novelty exposure through thoughtful, strategic system design—both predictive and relevant—can achieve artificial serendipity, allowing platforms to maintain engagement while fostering curiosity and experimentation among users.

Dynamic exposure diversification further improves discovery-oriented recommendation systems by avoiding excessive repetition of similar content and products. Algorithms can be varied to diversify recommendations across categories, price ranges, creators, and brands, rather than continuously reinforcing previous interactions. Lin et al. (2025) stressed that a recommendation system incorporating serendipity perspectives can maintain user engagement while enhancing the discovery experience. Such diversification tactics can also lower the chance of commercial filter bubbles and provide more equitable visibility for new brands.

Hybrid recommendation strategies balance personalization and exploratory recommendation logic to enhance the digital experience, incorporating metrics like novelty, diversity, and discovery scores alongside engagement scores. Jiang et al. (2025) advocated for systematically defining and optimizing serendipity in recommendations through a data-driven method considering novelty, relevance, and consumer satisfaction together, making hybrid recommendation systems a practical approach for balancing algorithmic efficiency with meaningful exploratory opportunities.

Nalis et al. (2024) showed that consumer trust is important to the effectiveness of serendipitous recommendation systems, since platforms perceived as reliable and transparent are more likely to have new recommendations accepted by users. Future recommendation systems need to optimize personalization while ensuring consumers retain trust when introduced to new products to explore.

Effects on Brand Managers

AI-powered recommendation engines have profound implications for brand management strategies. Algorithmic curation environments drive digital visibility, determining whether consumers encounter certain brands during their purchase and consumption journeys, making it important for brand managers to build strong digital brand salience. Continual exposure through custom feeds, social media algorithms, and recommendation systems reinforces consumer memory structures and the likelihood of future selection.

For emerging and challenger brands, discoverability in the AI ecosystem is equally crucial, since smaller brands often struggle to compete against established brands' visibility due to the recommendation system's emphasis on engagement history and familiarity. To overcome this, companies need content strategies, interaction models, and digital engagement methods aligned with platform algorithms. Tuominen (2025) noted that strategic digital content management can optimize brand reach and engagement on algorithmically-driven platforms like YouTube and social commerce.

Combining familiarity and novelty is increasingly crucial in consumer engagement, since the former can cause consumer fatigue while the latter can reduce relevance and trust. Effective AI-driven branding therefore requires balancing brand familiarity with creative, adventurous customer experiences. Kim and Baek (2025) noted that culturally competent, emotionally resonant digital content boosts brand engagement and consumer attachment on social media.

In the current digital landscape, visibility depends less on advertising spend than on algorithmic compatibility, engagement optimization, and behavioral responsiveness. Brand managers therefore need data-driven tactics that stay relevant amid fast-changing recommendation systems while retaining authenticity and consumer trust.

Ethical and Consumer-Centric AI Personalization

As AI personalization systems become more prevalent, ethical issues grow more acute where they influence consumer behavior, lack transparency, and constrain freedom of choice. Recommendations increasingly drive what users see, consider, and buy, often without users understanding how many decisions are made algorithmically. Transparency and explainability are therefore critical to ethical AI personalization: recommendation systems are more effective when they clearly explain their recommendation process and data sources.

Consumer control mechanisms are also important for building more responsible personalization environments. Platforms can enhance consumer autonomy by letting users set recommendation preferences, control personalization levels, and manage data-sharing practices. Smets (2025) noted that the conundrum of artificial serendipity lies in balancing algorithmic intervention with genuine consumer exploration—excessive algorithmic control can produce sub-optimal discovery experiences, while too little control fails to provide sufficient personalization for relevance and usability. Ethical personalization systems therefore need to preserve freedom of exploration, choice, and informed decision-making.

Responsible algorithmic branding, however, involves more than optimizing for engagement. Beyond maximizing interaction metrics, AI systems should support consumer wellbeing, diversity of exposure, and even competition in the marketplace. Reviglio (2023) argued that serendipity-based personalization can build diversity, openness, and exploratory interaction, helping create healthier digital ecosystems and reducing the negative consequences of commercial filter bubbles and consumption loops.

As AI systems become more embedded in everyday decision-making, consumer-centric strategies grow increasingly crucial. Charette (2025) noted that digital technologies are already shaping many aspects of people's experiences, behaviors, and perceptions; in consumer markets, recommendation systems similarly influence attention, brand exposure, and purchasing behavior. Ethical, responsible applications of AI in digital ecosystems will therefore be essential to preserving consumer autonomy, trust, and diversity going forward.

FUTURE RESEARCH DIRECTIONS

Future research should further explore how continuous experience with a recommendation system affects customer behavior over time, since prior studies have largely relied on cross-sectional snapshots that cannot capture how algorithmic reinforcement gradually affects behavior, brand loyalty, exploration, and long-term brand preference. Morales-Muñoz et al. (2026) stressed the need to further explore the changing dynamics of AI-consumer relationships in social media contexts; longitudinal studies could offer deeper insight into the long-term impacts of repeated algorithmic exposure on consumer decision-making and market diversity.

As generative AI technologies continue to evolve, they will likely reshape recommendation systems, ushering in personalization models that prioritize adaptability, conversational interaction, and context-awareness. Future systems could combine multimodal information, emotion recognition, and real-time behavioral adaptation to make digital experiences more responsive. Chatterjee and Das (2025) reported that generative AI is becoming integral to adaptive recommendation systems capable of adjusting recommendations in real time based on context and user behavior, while Borimnejad and Borimnejad (2025) suggested future research into AI-powered customer engagement and marketing should focus on generative AI.

Cross-cultural differences in algorithmic response are another crucial area for future study, since personalization systems can elicit varied consumer reactions depending on cultural, social, and regional context, technological familiarity, privacy expectations, and trust perceptions. Hari (2025) found that transparency mechanisms affect algorithmic trust differently across cultures, and Sun (2025) showed that algorithmic purchase prediction systems function differently in cross-cultural e-commerce. Further comparative research is needed to explore how cultural dimensions shape consumer trust, exploratory behavior, and acceptance of AI-driven personalization.

As recommendation systems grow more complex and autonomous, studying AI explainability and consumer trust becomes increasingly critical, since users are more inclined to rely on AI suggestions when platforms are transparent about how recommendations are developed and what actions users can take. Dang and Li (2026) found that technological, psychological, and cultural factors all shape an AI system's trustworthiness, while Zhang et al. (2026) found that algorithm features and generational differences significantly affect user acceptance of recommendation systems. Given persistent concerns about manipulation, privacy, and algorithmic bias, future research could examine the long-term implications of explainability features for consumer autonomy, trust-building, and continued interaction with AI-powered platforms.

CONCLUSION

This chapter examined the rise of machine learning recommendation systems in the lives of consumers in AI-powered marketplaces. It demonstrated that algorithmic personalization, combined with engagement optimization and repeated exposure, helps build consumption habits. While these customized systems ease choice and decision-making, they can also reduce opportunities for serendipitous discovery and exploratory consumption. AI systems also shape brand visibility, competition, and consumer engagement more broadly.

The future of consumer choice will likely be more locked into intelligent digital ecosystems that continually predict preferences and make consumption an interactive process, with recommendation systems becoming more adaptable, cohesive, and responsive across streaming, e-commerce, social media, and mobile commerce.

This growth in AI personalization, however, carries serious consequences: greater reliance on algorithmic recommendations, commercial filter bubbles, and restricted consumer access to a range of possibilities.

Ensuring opportunities for discovery is therefore critical to keeping markets diverse, maintaining consumer interest, and facilitating innovation diffusion over time. Relevance and novelty are key factors in designing recommendation systems that encourage serendipity; actively encouraging exploratory interaction may contribute to healthier digital ecosystems, where personalization enhances rather than diminishes the consumer experience and discovery of brands.

Ethical challenges around algorithmic power and consumer autonomy were also highlighted, including growing concerns about attention being shaped by AI systems through mechanisms that are not always visible or well understood by consumers. As markets grow more intelligent, keeping them transparent, explainable, and consumer-centered will become increasingly crucial to sustaining trust and responsible digital engagement. The future viability of AI-mediated consumption environments will depend on reconciling technological efficiency with ethical responsibility, consumer diversity, and opportunities for autonomous exploration.

REFERENCES

Abdullah, M. S. (2025). Examining The Effect Of AI-Powered Personalization On Customer Loyalty: A Meta-Analysis Of E-Commerce Studies. *Review of Applied Science and Technology*, *4*(02), 309–338. DOI: 10.63125/780spe97

Avdić, O. (2025). *The impact of AI-powered recommendation systems on consumer purchase decisions in subscription-based digital platforms* (Doctoral dissertation, [O. Avdić]).

Bilgihan, A., Ostinelli, M., Zhang, Y., & Lorenz, M. (2025). Artificial intelligence (AI) agents and the future of customer loyalty. *International Journal of Contemporary Hospitality Management*, *37*(9), 3240–3262. DOI: 10.1108/IJCHM-03-2025-0373

Borimnejad, H., & Borimnejad, V. (2025). Emerging trends challenges and research opportunities in artificial intelligence applications in marketing. *Discover Artificial Intelligence*, *6*(1), 9. Advance online publication. DOI: 10.1007/s44163-025-00705-y

Budzinski, O., Gaenssle, S., & Lindstädt-Dreusicke, N. (2022). Data (r) evolution: the economics of algorithmic search and recommender services. In *Handbook on digital business ecosystems* (pp. 349-366). Edward Elgar Publishing. DOI: 10.4337/9781839107191.00031

Caliskan, K., MacKenzie, D., & Callon, M. (2025). Stacked economization: A research program for the study of platforms. *Journal of Cultural Economics*, *18*(2), 304–331. DOI: 10.1080/17530350.2024.2423687

Challoumis, C. (2024, October). Navigating the financial landscape-the impact of AI on consumer spending. In *XVI International Scientific Conference* (pp. 62-93).

Charette, M. G. (2025). Chronic Pain Beyond Measure: E-Health and the Politics of Pain Care.

Chatterjee, P., & Das, A. (2025). Adaptive Financial Recommendation Systems Using Generative AI and Multimodal Data. *Journal of Knowledge Learning and Science Technology ISSN: 2959-6386 (online)*, *4*(1), 112-120. DOI: 10.60087/jklst.v4.n1.012

Chen, X., Lin, A., & Webber, S. (2024, June). Designing artificial serendipity. In *International Conference on Human-Computer Interaction* (pp. 28-45). Cham: Springer Nature Switzerland. DOI: 10.1007/978-3-031-60405-8_3

Chiriatti, M., Ganapini, M. B., Panai, E., & Riva, G. (2026). Attention is not all you need: How AI is reshaping consumer attention and the future of brand strategy. *Harvard Data Science Review, 8*(2). Advance online publication. DOI: 10.1162/99608f92.53f091e6

Dang, Q., & Li, G. (2026). Unveiling trust in AI: The interplay of antecedents, consequences, and cultural dynamics. *AI & Society, 41*(1), 669–692. DOI: 10.1007/s00146-025-02477-6

Davenport, T. H., & Beck, J. C. (2001). *The attention economy: Understanding the new currency of business*. Harvard Business School Press.

Depari, G. S. (2024). How is the Implementation of Business Analytics in Asia. *Global Journal Indexing*, 2142-2159.

Dharini, M. G. (2025). THE ALGORITHMIC CONSUMER: HOW AI SHAPES DESIRE AND DECISION IN DIGITAL MARKETS. *Global Dimensions of Multidisciplinary Research*, 237.

Dorigo, T., Brown, G. D., Casonato, C., Cerdà, A., Ciarrochi, J., Da Lio, M., D'Souza, N., Gauger, N. R., Hayes, S. C., Hofmann, S. G., Johansson, R., Liwicki, M., Lotte, F., Nieto, J. J., Olivato, G., Parnes, P., Perry, G., Plebe, A., Rao, I. M., & Yazdanpanah, N. (2025). Artificial intelligence in science and society: The vision of USERN. *IEEE Access : Practical Innovations, Open Solutions, 13*, 15993–16054. DOI: 10.1109/ACCESS.2025.3529357

Enyiorji, P., & Deloitte, L. (2023). Does widespread use of AI recommendation engines reduce consumer financial choice diversity. *International Journal of Science and Engineering Applications, 12*(4), 163–173.

Fu, Z., Niu, X., & Maher, M. L. (2023). Deep learning models for serendipity recommendations: A survey and new perspectives. *ACM Computing Surveys, 56*(1), 1–26. DOI: 10.1145/3605145

George, A. S. (2025). How AI Agents Are Reshaping the Internet from Human-Centered to Machine-Mediated Commerce. *Partners Universal International Innovation Journal, 3*(4), 52–65.

Golchha, C., & Nagariya, R. J. (2025). Exploring consumer choices and shopping patterns: Examining influences on consumer choices. In *Cultural Sensitivity, Cross-Border Logistics, and E-Commerce in Global Marketing* (pp. 181-214). IGI Global Scientific Publishing.

Hari, M. K. (2025). A Cross-Cultural Framework for Algorithmic Trust: How Data Transparency Mechanisms Influence Consumer Confidence in AI-Driven Marketing. *Journal of International Commercial Law and Technology*, *6*, 727–743.

Ismaliyanto, J., Sudjaniah, D., Afiat, D. D., Jacobalis, R. J., Hastuti, W., Rahayu, S., & Andayani, R. (2026). *CONSUMER BEHAVIOR IN THE DIGITAL ERA*. Mawadra Lestari Enterprise.

Jiang, W., Li, S., Li, X., Li, K., & Wu, J. (2025). Uncovering Recommendation Serendipity with Objective Data-driven Factor Investigation. *ACM Transactions on Information Systems*, *43*(6), 1–33. DOI: 10.1145/3758092

Kalpokas, I., & Kalpokienė, J. (2025). *Societies at an AI Crossroads: Choices and Value Conflicts*. Routledge. DOI: 10.4324/9781003715849

Kim, M., & Baek, T. H. (2025). Fostering brand love through branded memes on social media. *Journal of Product and Brand Management*, *34*(4), 486–499. DOI: 10.1108/JPBM-02-2024-5002

Kim, Y., Oh, S., Noh, C., Hong, E., & Park, S. (2025). Design of a serendipity-incorporated recommender system. *Electronics (Basel)*, *14*(4), 821. DOI: 10.3390/electronics14040821

Kovalenko, Y., Nikitin, A., & Kuzina, Y. (2026). Value Creation in the Algorithmic Age: A Systematic Review of How AI, Data Privacy, and Platform Ecosystems Are Reshaping Marketing Theory. *American Impact Review*, *1*(1), e2026018–e2026018. DOI: 10.66308/air.e2026018

Kulothungan, V., & Gupta, D. (2025, May). Towards adaptive AI governance: Comparative insights from the US, EU, and Asia. In *2025 IEEE 11th Conference on Big Data Security on Cloud (BigDataSecurity)* (pp. 32-38). IEEE. DOI: 10.1109/BigDataSecurity66063.2025.00018

Lin, Y. L., Zheng, Y. X., & Ku, Y. C. (2025). Augmenting micro-moment recommendations with group and serendipity perspectives. *Decision Support Systems*, *193*, 114454. DOI: 10.1016/j.dss.2025.114454

Manolovitz, B. (2022). *Effects of Repetition of Unfamiliar Music on Listening Behavior and Neural Responses* (Doctoral dissertation, University of Miami).

Marchand, É., Durand, T., & Dubois, M. (2025). Surveillance Capitalism, Consumer Subjectivity and Marketing in the Age of Artificial Intelligence. *Social Science Chronicle*, *5*(1), 01-18. DOI: 10.56106/ssc.2025.01

Milano, S., Taddeo, M., & Floridi, L. (2020). Recommender systems and their ethical challenges. *AI & Society, 35*(4), 957–967. DOI: 10.1007/s00146-020-00950-y

Mokhtar, T., & Manganelli, J. (2026). *Coexistence and Coevolution of Humans and Intelligent, Adaptive Environments*. CRC Press., DOI: 10.1201/9781003441953

Morales-Muñoz, A., Iniesta-Bonillo, M. Á., Estrella-Ramón, A., & Herrada-Lores, S. (2026). Artificial Intelligence and Consumer Behavior in Social Media: Systematic Literature Review and Future Research Agenda. *International Journal of Consumer Studies, 50*(1), e70173. DOI: 10.1111/ijcs.70173

Moreno, V. K., & Poudineh, R. (2026). *Reshaping the consumer-energy relationship through AI: Opportunities, risks and regulatory outlook* (No. 62). OIES Paper: EL

Nalis, I., Sippl, T., Kolb, T. E., & Neidhardt, J. (2024, June). Navigating serendipity-an experimental user study on the interplay of trust and serendipity in recommender systems. In *Adjunct Proceedings of the 32nd ACM conference on user modeling, adaptation and personalization* (pp. 386-393). DOI: 10.1145/3631700.3664901

Pandey, D. (2025). Al-Driven Consumer Behavior and. *Adapting Global Communication and Marketing Strategies to Generative AI*, 113.

Pattnaik, A., & Mohanty, M. (n.d.). The Role of AI in Transforming Consumer Behavior and Market Trends. Innovate to Dominate: AI and Sustainability in Business, 1.

Peng, C., Qian, A., Jin, L., Chen, J., Han, E. X., Liang, P. P., . . . Hsieh, J. (2025). Exploring Opportunities to Support Novice Visual Artists' Inspiration and Ideation with Generative AI. *arXiv preprint arXiv:2509.24167.*

Rana, R., & Bhambri, P. (2026). AI, Predictive Analytics, and Automated Influence: Ethical Frontiers in Algorithmic Marketing. In *Surveillance, Trust, and the New Politics of Digital Marketing* (pp. 53-98). IGI Global Scientific Publishing.

Reviglio, U. (2023). Serendipity as a design principle of personalization systems—theoretical distinctions. In *Serendipity science: An emerging field and its methods* (pp. 145–165). Springer International Publishing., DOI: 10.1007/978-3-031-33529-7_8

Sarin, A. B. (2025). The evolution of consumer behavior and the role of artificial intelligence in shaping it: AI in marketing. In *Decoding Consumer Behavior Using the Insight Equation and AI Marketing* (pp. 21–40). IGI Global Scientific Publishing., DOI: 10.4018/979-8-3693-8588-3.ch002

Saxena, S. (2025). ALGORITHMS & ATTENTION: HOW TECH INFLUENCES CONSUMER HABITS. *International Journal of Applied Mathematics, 38*(4). Advance online publication. DOI: 10.12732/ijam.v38i4.11

Şenyapar, H. N. D. (2025). Artificial Intelligence and Behavioral Engineering: Hidden Societal Costs and Design Challenges in Consumer Contexts. *Balkan Journal of Electrical and Computer Engineering*, *13*(4), 445–460. DOI: 10.17694/bajece.1712706

Sharma, A., Patel, N., & Gupta, R. (2022). Enhancing Personalized Loyalty Programs through Reinforcement Learning and Collaborative Filtering Algorithms. *European Advanced AI Journal, 11*(10).

Simon, H. A. (1955). A behavioral model of rational choice. *The Quarterly Journal of Economics*, *69*(1), 99–118. DOI: 10.2307/1884852

Slama, W. B., & Ghodbane, S. B. (2026). Real-Time Customization and Artificial Intelligence Performance Drivers in Quick Commerce. In *Revolutionizing Quick Commerce With AI Tools and Technologies* (pp. 23–52). IGI Global Scientific Publishing., DOI: 10.4018/979-8-3373-3486-8.ch002

Smets, A. (2025). Intended, afforded, and experienced serendipity: Overcoming the paradox of artificial serendipity. *Ethics and Information Technology*, *27*(3), 33. DOI: 10.1007/s10676-025-09841-6

Sun, M. (2025). AI-Driven Cross-Cultural Consumer Purchase Intention Prediction Methods for E-commerce Platforms: An Applied Research Approach. *Spectrum of Research, 5*(2).

Tavares, A. C. D. (2025). *How TikTok Influences Purchase Intention: The Role of Purchase Condition, Perceived Personalization and Emotional Engagement* (Master's thesis, Universidade NOVA de Lisboa (Portugal)).

Thaler, R. H., & Sunstein, C. R. (2008). *Nudge: Improving decisions about health, wealth, and happiness.* Yale University Press.

Tuominen, D. (2025). Strategic Use of YouTube for Business Development in China and Europe: Case study of "Very Venture China".

Ullagaddi, P. (2025). Cross-regional analysis of global AI healthcare regulation. *J Computer Commun*, *13*(5), 66–83. DOI: 10.4236/jcc.2025.135005

Wachtel, P. L. (2023). *Making room for the disavowed: Reclaiming the self in psychotherapy*. Guilford Publications.

Wang, Z. (2025). The influence of AI on consumer behavior: Shaping choices and preferences in the digital marketplace. *Systems and Soft Computing*, *200397*, 200397. Advance online publication. DOI: 10.1016/j.sasc.2025.200397

Weerasinghe, S., Malik, M., Andargoli, A., Morrow, G., Jayaraman, P. P., & Forkan, A. (2025). Are Algorithmic Biases in AI-Based Recommendations Real? An Activity Theory Framing of Digital Music Streaming. *An Activity Theory Framing of Digital Music Streaming (November 22, 2025).*

Wrench, J. S., & Elmoudden, S. (2025). AI in Personal Life. *The Future is Now: Empowering Society Through AI Literacy.*

Zhang, Y., Di, Y., & Liu, L. (2026). Beyond Accuracy: How Algorithm Characteristics and Digital Generational Differences Affect User Interaction and Acceptance in Fashion Recommendation Systems. *International Journal of Human-Computer Interaction*, •••, 1–24. DOI: 10.1080/10447318.2026.2628995

KEY TERMS AND DEFINITIONS

Algorithmic Gatekeeping: The influence exerted by automated ranking and recommendation mechanisms over which products, brands, information, or content become visible to consumers.

Algorithmic Personalization: The use of machine learning to tailor products, services, content, or messages to an individual based on observed or inferred preferences.

Commercial Filter Bubble: A personalized digital environment in which repeated algorithmic filtering narrows exposure to alternatives, potentially limiting diversity of consumer choice.

Consumer Autonomy: A consumer's capacity to make informed and voluntary choices without undue dependence on opaque algorithmic recommendations or commercial influence.

Engineered Serendipity: The deliberate incorporation of novelty and unexpected but relevant alternatives into a recommendation system to support exploration.

Exploratory Consumption: A consumer's willingness to investigate, compare, and try products, brands, or categories beyond familiar or algorithmically suggested choices.

Habit Loop: A repeated pattern in which a digital cue triggers a familiar consumer action and produces a reinforcing outcome, increasing the likelihood of repetition.

Recommendation Dependency: The extent to which a consumer relies on algorithmically generated suggestions when choosing products, services, or digital content.

Recommendation Transparency: The degree to which a platform communicates understandable information about why recommendations are presented and how personalization affects user exposure.

Serendipitous Discovery: The experience of encountering a relevant or valuable product, brand, content item, or idea that was not part of the consumer's original search intention.

Chapter 7
The Impact of Homepage Algorithmic Innovation on Switching Behavior in Indian Quick Commerce Platforms

Roselyn James
http://orcid.org/0009-0005-0171-3058
Christ University, Bangalore, India

N. Elangovan
http://orcid.org/0000-0002-4551-6081
Christ University, Bangalore, India

L. Ganesh
http://orcid.org/0000-0003-1114-2461
Christ University, Bangalore, India

T. Dheepa
http://orcid.org/0000-0001-9636-5503
Christ University, Bangalore, India

ABSTRACT

The homepage of a quick-commerce app is a dynamic, algorithmically composed surface rebuilt for each user using purchase history, browsing, time, and inferred signals. This chapter examines how homepage algorithmic innovation in Indian quick-commerce platforms shapes perceptions of platform intelligence and relevance, reducing switching to rivals. It argues that homepage algorithms enable continuous

DOI: 10.4018/979-8-3373-9589-0.ch007

ambient personalization, anticipatory intelligence that surfaces needs before they are articulated, and accumulating preference data that raises invisible yet salient switching costs. Drawing on relationship marketing, technology acceptance, and behavioral economics, and using evidence from India's leading platforms, it introduces "platform intelligence perception" and "compounding personalization," positioning homepage algorithmic quality as an undertheorized driver of platform brand equity.

INTRODUCTION

When a consumer opens Blinkit on a Tuesday morning after a long weekend, they do not see the same homepage that a stranger in the same apartment complex sees. They see a surface that has been reconstructed, within the application's rendering cycle, from a model of who they are as a consumer: what they have bought, when they have bought it, what they have browsed without purchasing, and how those patterns compare with consumers whose preferences resemble theirs. The morning after a long weekend, that surface might feature bottled water and electrolyte drinks near the top, because the platform has learned, across millions of similar sessions, that such sessions tend to follow periods of elevated social activity. It might feature a reorder prompt for the coffee brand the consumer buys every ten days, because the purchase cycle has been modeled and the next replenishment window has opened. It might also feature a new product in a category the consumer has explored recently, because the algorithm has identified a latent interest that has not yet crystallized into a purchase.

This is homepage algorithmic innovation: the systematic deployment of machine learning and real-time data processing to construct a consumer-facing interface that is continuously, dynamically, and specifically relevant to the individual user. In the Indian quick commerce context, where Blinkit, Zepto, bigbasket, Flipkart Minutes, and Swiggy Instamart compete for the attention and loyalty of an increasingly sophisticated urban consumer base, the homepage has become the primary arena of what might properly be called autonomous decision-making: a system that makes thousands of consumer-facing presentation decisions per second without human review, operating on learned models of individual preference. It is where the platform makes its most consequential claim on the consumer's perception: the claim that it understands them.

The relationship between that claim and consumer switching behavior is the subject of this chapter. Switching behavior in digital platform contexts refers to the decision to migrate from a currently used platform to an alternative. It is one of the most consequential outcomes studied in the services marketing and information systems literatures (Bansal & Taylor, 1999; Keaveney, 1995). In quick commerce, where the cost of any individual order is modest and the activation cost of a competing platform requires little more than a download, switching is structurally easy. What prevents it, this chapter argues, is not contractual lock-in or pricing advantage alone, but a construct termed here platform intelligence perception: the consumer's accumulated sense that the current platform understands their needs in a way that a competitor has not yet earned the data to replicate.

The chapter is structured as follows. The background section surveys the relevant literatures on algorithmic personalization, platform loyalty, and consumer switching behavior, with particular attention to the Indian quick commerce market and the brand equity implications of algorithm-driven consumer experience. The main analytical sections develop the argument in sequence: that homepage algorithms construct a perception of platform intelligence; that the most advanced platforms extend this into anticipatory intelligence; and that repeated algorithmically personalized encounters generate a compounding loyalty effect that makes switching psychologically and cognitively costly. These sections formalize the argument as four propositions (P1-P4) stated where each is developed. The proposed conceptual framework is depicted in Figure 1. The chapter closes with a discussion of theoretical contributions, strategic implications, and directions for future research.

LITERATURE REVIEW AND BACKGROUND

The following review draws on peer-reviewed articles published between 2000 and 2024, retrieved from Web of Science, Scopus, and Google Scholar using the search terms "algorithmic recommendation," "platform switching," "personalization and loyalty," "quick commerce," and "consumer-AI interaction." Foundational theoretical works predating this window are included where they remain the definitive source for a specific construct. Records were included when they (a) appeared in peer-reviewed journals or edited scholarly volumes, (b) addressed personalization, recommendation systems, platform loyalty, or switching behavior in consumer-facing digital contexts, and (c) offered constructs or findings transferable to the quick commerce setting; purely technical treatments of recommender system engineering without consumer-behavior implications were excluded, as were practitioner commentaries without an identifiable method. A large initial pool of records was screened at the title and abstract level against these criteria, and a substantially smaller subset was read in full. Of that subset, the sources retained in the reference list below are those that supply a foundational construct, definition, or finding directly load-bearing for the chapter's argument, consistent with the space constraints and synthesis aims of a conceptual book chapter rather than a full systematic review. The review is organized across four bodies of literature (quick commerce in India, homepage algorithm architecture, personalization and consumer behavior, and switching behavior) before an integrative paragraph establishes the chapter's primary theoretical orientation.

Quick Commerce in India: The Stakes of the Homepage

India's quick commerce market has, over roughly four years, grown from a niche experiment in hyperlocal grocery delivery to one of the defining retail formats of the urban Indian consumer economy. The sector's growth has been underpinned by a confluence of structural enablers: the navigability and density of Indian cities, a large and flexible two-wheeler delivery workforce, the rapid proliferation of smartphones and affordable mobile data, and the post-pandemic acceleration of digital commerce adoption across income segments (IAMAI, 2023; RedSeer, 2023). Blinkit, Zepto, and Swiggy Instamart, the three platforms that have emerged as dominant players following a period of intense competition and consolidation, collectively process tens of millions of orders each month, primarily in India's top twenty metropolitan areas. bigbasket and Flipkart Minutes remain credible competitors, particularly in planned-basket and value-oriented shopping occasions. The analysis in this chapter nevertheless concentrates on Blinkit, Zepto, and Swiggy Instamart because they account for the substantial majority of quick commerce order volume in the metropolitan markets under discussion and because their ecosystem-level data positions are the most extensively documented in public sources (RedSeer, 2023).

What distinguishes Indian quick commerce from its counterparts in other markets is the particular intensity of competition for consumer attention and loyalty. Unlike Western markets where quick commerce often supplements an established supermarket relationship, Indian urban consumers have, in many cases, migrated substantial portions of their grocery and daily essentials spending directly to these platforms (Bain & Company, 2023). In this environment, the homepage carries disproportionate strategic weight: it is the first surface the consumer encounters on each visit, the primary means by which the platform makes its case for relevance, and the page that most directly determines whether the consumer finds what they need quickly or abandons the session in frustration. As delivery times are reported to have converged toward a common operational floor of approximately ten to fifteen minutes across the leading platforms, and as catalog breadth has, by these industry estimates, approached functional parity (RedSeer, 2023; Zomato, 2024), the homepage, and the algorithm that constructs it, has arguably become the primary dimension along which meaningful differentiation remains possible.

Homepage Algorithms: Architecture and Objectives

The homepage algorithm of a mature quick commerce platform is not a single system but an ensemble of interoperating machine learning models, each responsible for a distinct decision in the construction of the consumer-facing surface. At the most general level, these decisions concern ranking and selection: which products, categories, and promotional surfaces should be shown to a given consumer at a given moment, in which order, and in which format. The inputs to these decisions span multiple timescales and signal types, from the long-horizon purchase history that informs the preference model to the real-time session behavior (the products tapped, the categories scrolled, the search terms entered) that enables within-session adaptation (Jannach & Jugovac, 2019).

Collaborative filtering, the technique that underlies the most widely understood form of algorithmic recommendation, identifies consumers with similar purchase patterns and uses group preferences to inform individual recommendations. In quick commerce, collaborative filtering remains an important component of the recommendation stack, but it is supplemented by content-based filtering, which characterizes products by their attributes and matches those attributes to demonstrated preferences, and by contextual bandits, which balance exploration of new recommendations against exploitation of known preferences. More recently, deep learning models have been applied to embed products and consumers in high-dimensional representation spaces, where proximity captures preference affinity in ways that simpler models cannot (Ricci et al., 2015; Covington et al., 2016).

The objectives that homepage algorithms optimize are themselves a product of strategic choice. The most obvious objective is immediate conversion: maximizing the probability that the consumer adds a product to their cart. Platforms have learned, however, that optimizing purely for conversion tends to surface products already purchased rather than introducing new categories that could expand engagement. The more mature algorithmic objective is a composite that balances immediate relevance (the consumer finds what they need quickly) with discovery and long-horizon loyalty, such that the consumer's engagement with the platform deepens over time (Kaminskas & Bridge, 2016). The increasing capacity of these systems to pursue such composite objectives without human intervention is precisely what qualifies them as autonomous decision systems in the sense foregrounded by this volume (De Bruyn et al., 2020).

Personalization and Consumer Behavior: Theoretical Foundations

The relationship between personalization and consumer behavior has been studied extensively in the marketing and information systems literatures, with a consistent finding that consumers respond positively to experiences tailored to their individual preferences, provided that the tailoring is perceived as helpful rather than intrusive (Vesanen, 2007; Tam & Ho, 2006). From relationship marketing, the concept of partner quality, the consumer's perception that a service provider understands and responds to their needs, has been shown to be a significant predictor of relationship commitment and loyalty (Fournier, 1998; Morgan & Hunt, 1994). From information systems, the technology acceptance literature has demonstrated that perceived usefulness, the belief that a system helps one accomplish goals more effectively, is the primary driver of continued system use (Davis, 1989). In the context of digital platforms, personalization contributes simultaneously to both constructs: a homepage that surfaces relevant products reduces effort (perceived usefulness) and demonstrates attentiveness (partner quality).

Recent research on consumer responses to artificial intelligence has added important nuance to this picture. Puntoni et al. (2021) demonstrate that consumers experience AI-driven interactions through a distinctly experiential lens: the same algorithmic output can be received as either helpfully attentive or invasively mechanical depending on contextual framing. A related body of work has examined the tendency of consumers to attribute human-like qualities to algorithmic systems that consistently anticipate their needs, a process of anthropomorphization that generates trust and positive affect similar to that produced by a competent human advisor (Epley et al., 2007). Separately, Labrecque (2014) has shown that sustained, responsive digital interactions can generate parasocial intimacy, a sense of relational closeness with a non-human platform that predicts loyalty behaviors typically associated with interpersonal relationships. Algorithmic trust, a third but distinct construct, refers specifically to the willingness to rely on an automated system's outputs based on its track record of accurate prediction. It accumulates gradually through repeated positive confirmation (Komiak & Benbasat, 2006). The relationship is not one-directional, however: Dietvorst et al. (2015) show that trust in an algorithm is disproportionately fragile once it is seen to err, a vulnerability that carries direct implications for how platforms should handle visible personalization failures. Together, these three mechanisms (anthropomorphization, parasocial intimacy, and algorithmic trust) explain why homepage algorithms that consistently demonstrate understanding of consumer preferences generate loyalty responses that exceed what their purely utilitarian value would predict.

The personalization literature also distinguishes between surface-level personalization (the insertion of the consumer's name or the display of recently viewed items) and deep personalization, which requires genuine modeling of preferences, context, and behavioral trajectory. Awad and Krishnan (2006) find that surface-level personalization can backfire when consumers perceive it as tokenistic, producing what has become known as the personalization paradox: the simultaneous desire for personalized experience and resistance to the data collection that enables it. Deep personalization, by contrast, produces what this chapter terms a service intelligence effect (the consumer's recognition that the system has anticipated a need they were not yet consciously aware of), which is associated with unusually strong positive affect and sustained loyalty. The effect builds on Rust and Huang's (2014) broader account of how information technology enables progressively deeper, more personalized service relationships, and on Huang and Rust's (2018) later distinction between mechanical, analytical, intuitive, and empathetic forms of AI-driven service intelligence.

Switching Behavior in Platform Contexts

Switching behavior in digital platform contexts has been studied extensively through the push-pull-mooring framework, originally developed in the service switching literature (Bansal et al., 2005). Push factors drive consumers away from a current provider: dissatisfaction, unfair pricing, repeated service failures. Pull factors attract them toward an alternative: superior features, promotional offers, peer recommendations. Mooring factors anchor consumers to their current provider even when push and pull forces are present: these include accumulated interaction history, habitual use, the investment of time in learning a platform's interface, and the social embeddedness of one's network on a given service (Keaveney, 1995; Bhattacherjee, 2001; Chou & Cheng, 2012). In quick commerce, where push and pull dynamics are structurally intense (platforms routinely offer new-user incentives that pull consumers toward experimentation), the strength and nature of mooring factors are of particular theoretical and practical interest.

The central argument of this chapter is that homepage algorithmic quality represents a distinct and previously undertheorized mooring factor in quick commerce: one that operates through the accumulation of personalization data and the consumer's perception that switching would forfeit an intelligence advantage the current platform has earned through sustained interaction. This mooring factor is qualitatively different from simple habit or inertia because it is grounded in genuine platform capability rather than mere familiarity. A consumer who remains with a well-personalized platform is not simply choosing the path of least resistance; they are making a reasoned assessment that the platform's demonstrated understanding of their preferences constitutes a form of value that a competitor, however attractive in other respects, cannot immediately replicate.

Theoretical Integration

This chapter is grounded primarily in relationship marketing theory, using Fournier's (1998) partner quality construct and Morgan and Hunt's (1994) commitment-trust framework as the primary lens through which homepage algorithm quality is connected to consumer loyalty. The technology acceptance framework (Davis, 1989) provides the usability pathway, explaining why relevance reduces friction and increases continued use. Behavioral economics, specifically the endowment effect (Thaler, 1980) and expectation-confirmation theory (Bhattacherjee, 2001), provides the switching cost pathway, explaining why accumulated personalization data generates reluctance to defect. Social psychology contributes the mechanisms of anthropomorphization, parasocial intimacy, and algorithmic trust through which these rational dynamics are amplified by affective processes. These frameworks are not competing explanations but complementary layers in a multi-level account of how homepage algorithm quality generates switching resistance.

Homepage Algorithmic Innovation as a Driver of Platform Brand Equity

Although this chapter focuses on switching behavior as its primary dependent construct, the mechanisms through which homepage algorithms reduce switching are fundamentally brand mechanisms: they build attachment, trust, and a sense of being understood that is, in brand theory terms, a form of perceived partner quality and brand intimacy. Keller's (1993) customer-based brand equity framework identifies consumer associations (functional, emotional, and self-expressive) as the building blocks of brand equity. In the quick commerce context, the associations generated by a consistently well-personalized homepage are all three: functionally, the platform helps the consumer find what they need efficiently; emotionally, it generates the positive affect associated with feeling understood; and self-expressively, it reinforces the consumer's sense of their own preferences through the mirror of an accurate recommendation.

Sharp's (2010) concept of mental availability, the probability that a brand will come to mind in a buying situation, is equally relevant to the homepage algorithm argument. A platform whose homepage has, over many visits, consistently surfaced the right product at the right moment builds a strong and distinctive memory structure around the buying situation: when the consumer needs something quickly, the well-personalized platform comes to mind first, not because of advertising but because of the accumulated experience of relevant, attentive, and occasionally surprising interaction. Homepage algorithmic quality is, in this sense, an investment in mental availability as much as in operational efficiency. This framing positions the chapter's argument within the broader evidence-based brand growth science that the present volume foregrounds, and suggests that investment in homepage algorithm sophistication should be evaluated not only as a conversion optimization initiative but as a brand-building one.

Figure 1. Proposed framework: Homepage algorithmic quality, platform intelligence perception, and switching behavior. Propositions P1-P4 are stated in the sections where each is developed.

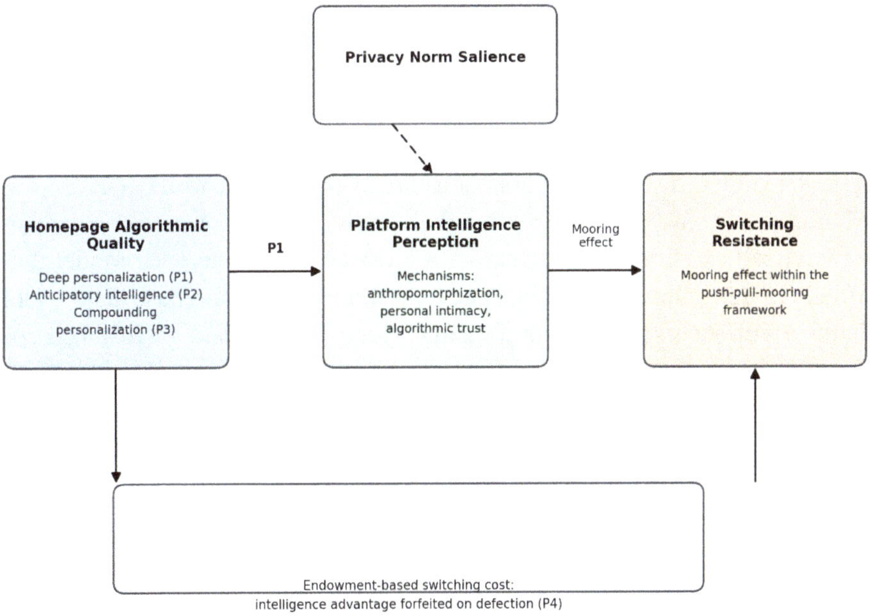

HOMEPAGE ALGORITHMS AND THE PERCEPTION OF PLATFORM INTELLIGENCE

From Catalog to Conversation: The Algorithmic Transformation of the Homepage

The conceptual shift that homepage algorithmic innovation represents is, at its deepest level, a shift from the homepage as catalog to the homepage as conversation. A catalog is a static presentation of available goods, organized by category and designed to be navigated by a consumer who arrives with a defined intention. A conversation is a dynamic exchange in which each party responds to signals from the other, adjusting the interaction in real time. When a quick commerce homepage is reconstructed on every visit based on what the algorithm knows and infers about the consumer's current context, it engages in something that, from the consumer's experiential perspective, closely resembles a conversation even though no human is on the other side (Puntoni et al., 2021). The autonomous nature of this process (decisions made at scale, in real time, without human review) is precisely what gives these systems their distinctive character as brand-building instruments.

Platforms that have integrated data signals across multiple consumer touchpoints are theoretically positioned to construct a cross-context preference model that is materially more comprehensive than one built from grocery purchase history alone. A platform with access to its parent company's food delivery data, for instance, could leverage dining preference signals (the cuisines ordered, the meal occasions, the frequency of social dining) to inform grocery homepage personalization in ways that anticipate needs the consumer has not explicitly expressed on the grocery platform. Where such integration has been publicly reported, as with Blinkit's position within the Zomato ecosystem noted in the annual report (Zomato, 2024), the theoretical advantage is substantial: the system develops a theory of the consumer that extends across purchase contexts rather than within a single category.

Platforms that weight real-time session behavior heavily, rather than relying primarily on long-horizon purchase history, pursue a complementary strategy. In such systems, signals that emerge within the first moments of a visit (which product thumbnails attract a momentary pause, which categories are scrolled without tapping, which search terms are entered and then revised) recalibrate the surface in near-real time. The result, for a consumer who has spent time with the platform, is an interface that adapts to the current mood or intent signal rather than the historical baseline alone. This within-session adaptation reflects the contextual bandit architecture described in the preceding section and represents a form of continuous, low-latency autonomous decision-making that distinguishes mature quick commerce platforms from simpler catalog-display applications (Covington et al., 2016).

Platforms built within an ecosystem that spans both restaurant food delivery and grocery commerce possess a particular form of data advantage: the capacity to infer a household's broader food culture (the cuisines, ingredients, and dietary patterns that characterize its consumption) from the combination of restaurant ordering and grocery purchase signals. A homepage that reflects this broader culinary identity, surfacing regional staples, specialty condiments, or brand preferences aligned with the household's revealed food culture, creates an experience of cultural resonance that a generic grocery catalog cannot achieve. Swiggy Instamart's position within the Swiggy food delivery ecosystem provides this form of cross-signal advantage (RedSeer, 2023), though the precise extent of current integration is not publicly detailed at a technical level. Table 1 sets out the proposed data advantage, algorithmic orientation, and loyalty mechanism associated with each of the leading Indian quick commerce platforms.

Table 1. Proposed Homepage Algorithmic Strategies and Loyalty Mechanisms of Leading Indian Quick Commerce Platforms

Platform	Proposed Data Advantage	Algorithmic Orientation	Proposed Loyalty Mechanism	Autonomy Characteristic
Blinkit (Zomato)	Cross-platform dining and grocery signal integration (Zomato, 2024)	Long-horizon cross-context preference modeling	Anticipatory relevance; cognitive lock-in through accumulated multi-context data	Real-time reconstruction without human curation
Zepto	Dense real-time session signal data from high-frequency urban users	Within-session real-time surface recalibration	Intent-moment matching; affective lock-in through consistent relevance	Autonomous within-session adaptation without query
Swiggy Instamart	Food delivery ecosystem providing culinary identity signals (RedSeer, 2023)	Culinary identity inference and category alignment	Cultural resonance; identity-expressive lock-in through food culture matching	Autonomous cross-app inference and surface construction

Note. Algorithmic strategies are theoretically proposed based on publicly available ecosystem information. Technical implementation details are not publicly disclosed by these platforms at the level of individual algorithm architecture.

The Perception of Being Understood: Psychological Mechanisms and the Mooring Effect

These operational strategies have measurable psychological consequences. The transition from platform-level algorithmic design to its effect on the individual consumer runs through a set of well-documented psychological mechanisms that collectively explain why the perception of platform intelligence is a more powerful loyalty driver than delivery speed or pricing alone. The following paragraphs examine these mechanisms and connect them explicitly to the mooring dimension of the push-pull-mooring framework introduced in the literature review.

The experience of being known and understood, whether by a service provider or, by extension, by an autonomous system, is intrinsically rewarding, generating positive affect, increased trust, and stronger relational commitment (Reis et al., 2004). This is the construct this chapter terms platform intelligence perception: the consumer's subjective assessment of the platform's capacity to understand and anticipate their needs, formed through repeated algorithmically personalized interactions. Platform intelligence perception is formally distinct from perceived personalization (Vesanen, 2007), which refers to the consumer's awareness that content has been tailored to them, and from perceived usefulness (Davis, 1989), which captures functional efficiency. Platform intelligence perception adds an evaluative dimension: not merely "this has been tailored for me" but "this platform genuinely understands me."

Platform intelligence perception influences switching behavior as a mooring factor through two distinct pathways. The first is the trust pathway: a platform that consistently demonstrates accurate understanding generates trust that future needs will be similarly well served, reducing the anxiety associated with continued reliance and elevating the perceived risk of migrating to an untested alternative. The consumer reasoning here is essentially Bayesian: repeated evidence of platform competence raises the posterior probability of continued good performance, while a competing platform, however attractive its promotional offers, carries the uncertainty of an unproven track record (Morgan & Hunt, 1994).

The second pathway operates through what Thaler (1980) terms the endowment effect: the tendency to value things more highly once acquired than one would have predicted before acquisition. In the context of platform personalization, the relevant endowment is the accumulated preference model the platform has built through sustained interaction. This model is a genuine asset: it makes the platform more useful and more relevant than it was at the start of the consumer-platform relationship. However, it is an asset that exists only within the platform and cannot be transferred to a competitor, who would have to rebuild it from scratch through a period of reduced relevance and elevated friction. This endowment-based switching cost is invisible during normal platform use (the consumer does not think about it) but becomes salient precisely at the moment of contemplated defection, functioning as a powerful mooring force that the push-pull-mooring framework would classify as a relationship investment cost. The core mediating claim of the chapter can accordingly be stated as its first proposition:

P1: Deep homepage personalization generates platform intelligence perception, the consumer's evaluative judgment that the platform genuinely understands their needs, which functions as a mooring force against switching within the push-pull-mooring framework.

Anticipatory Intelligence: Surfacing Needs Before They Are Articulated

The most consequential frontier of homepage algorithmic innovation in quick commerce is what this chapter terms anticipatory intelligence: the capacity of the platform to surface a consumer's needs before the consumer has consciously registered them. Reactive personalization (showing products related to what the consumer has previously purchased) is now a baseline capability across all three leading platforms. The competitive differentiation that matters at the frontier is the move from reactive to anticipatory: knowing not just what the consumer has wanted but what they will want next, and surfacing that on the homepage before the want has been consciously formulated.

Anticipatory intelligence in quick commerce rests on several distinct forecasting capabilities. The first is consumption cycle modeling: the identification of the replenishment rhythms that govern a household's purchase of staples, from a ten-day coffee cycle to a monthly dishwasher tablet cycle. By modeling these rhythms from purchase history data and tracking the elapsed time since the last purchase in each category, the algorithm can identify with reasonable precision when a replenishment window is opening and surface the relevant product prominently on the homepage. The consumer who opens the application and finds their usual coffee brand featured at the top on day nine of their typical purchase cycle experiences a small but genuine convenience: the platform has anticipated a need they were about to register themselves, and has saved them the effort of searching.

The second component of anticipatory intelligence is seasonal and contextual forecasting. Quick commerce platforms in India operate in an environment of intense seasonal variation. The approach of Diwali generates predictable demand for sweets, dry fruits, and gifting items. The onset of the monsoon generates demand for rainwear and preventive healthcare products. Major cricket tournaments generate demand for snacks and beverages calibrated to the viewing occasion. An algorithm that can anticipate these contextual shifts and surface relevant products before the consumer has connected an upcoming occasion to a specific purchasing need is doing something qualitatively more valuable than simple reactive recommendation.

The third component is need-state forecasting based on life-event signals embedded in purchase history. The sudden appearance of infant nutritional products in a household that has never previously purchased them is a life-event signal of considerable predictive value. The transition from meat products to plant-based alternatives may signal a dietary shift. The first purchase of sports nutrition products may signal a fitness resolution. A platform whose algorithms can identify these signals and gradually adjust the homepage surface accordingly (introducing products relevant to the new life context while maintaining continuity with established preferences) creates an experience of a platform that develops alongside the consumer rather than remaining static. Consider, as a theoretical illustration, a scenario in which a consumer who regularly books restaurant celebrations through a linked food delivery application encounters, in the days preceding a booked occasion, a homepage surface featuring relevant celebration supplies and ingredient staples. Were cross-application data integrated to this depth, such anticipatory relevance would represent a qualitative departure from catalog-based retailing toward something approaching ambient consumer intelligence. The distinctive loyalty consequence of this capability is stated formally as the second proposition:

P2: Anticipatory intelligence, the surfacing of needs before they are consciously registered, produces expectation-exceeding service intelligence moments that generate disproportionately greater loyalty and switching resistance than reactive personalization of equivalent technical sophistication.

THE COMPOUND LOYALTY EFFECT OF REPEATED PERSONALIZED ENCOUNTERS

How Personalization Accumulates Over Time

One of the most important but least discussed properties of homepage algorithmic personalization is its compounding nature, what this chapter formalizes as the compounding personalization construct. The relevance of the homepage to a given consumer is not a fixed function of the algorithm's sophistication; it improves over time as the algorithm accumulates more observations of that consumer's preferences, purchase cycles, and contextual patterns. This is a consumer-specific capability accumulation dynamic in the sense described by Murray and Häubl (2007), who show that platform-specific skill and history create cognitive lock-in that grows with tenure. The present chapter extends their argument by identifying personalization data accumulation as a structurally similar but distinct mechanism: not the consumer's investment in learning the platform, but the platform's investment in learning the consumer.

The relationship between personalization and switching costs has been noted in adjacent literatures: Murray and Häubl (2007) describe "customer-specific capability accumulation" in interface learning contexts, and Bhattacherjee (2001) identifies confirmation of prior expectations as a driver of continuance. To the authors' knowledge, the present chapter is among the first to formalize personalization data accumulation as a compounding dynamic and to apply it to the quick commerce context. The key distinction is directional: prior work focuses on what the consumer learns about the platform; this chapter focuses on what the platform learns about the consumer, and on the switching cost implications of that platform-held asset.

The compounding effect is amplified by the interaction between homepage personalization and broader platform engagement. A consumer whose homepage is well personalized will, on average, explore more categories, encounter more discovery moments, and generate more behavioral signal data, which further refines the preference model, which generates additional relevance on subsequent visits. This virtuous cycle deepens the consumer-platform relationship at an accelerating rate. Platforms that have invested most in homepage algorithm quality are thereby creating a self-reinforcing loyalty dynamic that compounds over time in ways that operational investments in delivery logistics or pricing cannot replicate. This dynamic is stated formally as the third proposition:

P3: The personalization data asset underlying platform intelligence perception compounds with platform tenure, such that the switching cost, defined as the intelligence advantage forfeited on defection, grows invisibly and persistently over the consumer-platform relationship.

The Role of Surprise and Delight in Sustained Loyalty

The relationship between personalization and loyalty is not linear. The satisfaction literature has established a threshold structure in the performance-loyalty relationship: performance below a minimum threshold generates active dissatisfaction; performance at the expected level generates satisfaction but not strong loyalty; performance that exceeds expectations generates the positive surprise that is the most reliable driver of deep loyalty (Oliver, 1999; Anderson & Mittal, 2000). Applied to homepage algorithmic personalization, this finding implies that meeting the consumer's expectation of relevance (surfacing products they were already planning to buy) generates satisfaction but not the deeper loyalty associated with the unexpected. The service intelligence effect described by Rust and Huang (2014), the consumer's recognition that the system has anticipated a need they were not yet consciously aware of, is precisely the kind of expectation-exceeding performance that produces disproportionate loyalty returns.

Moments of anticipatory accuracy are disproportionately memorable and disproportionately influential on long-term loyalty because they confirm the consumer's implicit model of the platform as a sophisticated and attentive partner rather than a generic tool (Fournier, 1998). A consumer who opens a quick commerce application the afternoon before a dinner gathering and finds the homepage has surfaced a curated selection of the specific cooking ingredients most congruent with their established food preferences, without any dinner-related search, experiences something more than satisfaction. They experience a sense of being genuinely understood, which is intrinsically rewarding and generates the kind of positive attribution that builds durable relational loyalty.

At the same time, the most effective homepage algorithms are those that balance exploitation of known preferences with exploration of adjacent possibilities, ensuring that consumers consistently find what they expect while occasionally discovering something they did not know they wanted. Algorithms optimized purely for exploitation (converging entirely on known preferences) risk producing a filter-bubble effect in which the consumer perceives the homepage as a reflection of the past rather than a discovery surface for the future. Kaminskas and Bridge (2016) identify this serendipity-accuracy trade-off as one of the central design challenges in recommender systems, and its resolution requires an explicit algorithmic objective that values discovery and novelty alongside relevance.

Navigating the Personalization Paradox: The Curvilinear Boundary Condition

The relationship between personalization depth and the consumer's experience of platform intelligence is not uniformly positive; it exhibits a curvilinear structure that the existing literature has described as the personalization paradox (Awad & Krishnan, 2006; Norberg et al., 2007). At low levels of personalization depth, the homepage is experienced as generic and the platform is perceived as inattentive. As personalization depth increases, the experience becomes progressively more relevant and attentive, generating rising platform intelligence perception. However, at high levels of personalization depth (particularly when the algorithm surfaces data that the consumer had forgotten they shared, or when the precision of the recommendation makes the underlying surveillance mechanism visible), the experience tips from attentive to intrusive, and platform intelligence perception declines.

The moderating variable that governs where on this curvilinear path a given consumer sits is their privacy norm salience: the degree to which concerns about data collection and algorithmic profiling are actively present in their evaluative frame at the moment of platform interaction (Norberg et al., 2007). Consumers with low privacy norm salience experience the personalization-loyalty relationship as approximately linear in the relevant range, while consumers with high privacy norm salience encounter the inverted-U more steeply and at lower levels of personalization depth. For platform designers, this suggests that the optimal personalization depth is not the maximum technically achievable, but the level that maximizes perceived intelligence while remaining below the intrusiveness threshold for the target consumer segment. This boundary condition is stated formally as the fourth proposition:

P4: Privacy norm salience moderates the relationship between personalization depth and platform intelligence perception, such that the relationship follows an inverted-U, with the downturn occurring at lower levels of personalization depth for consumers with high privacy norm salience.

Practically, this boundary condition has implications for the use of cross-platform data in homepage personalization. Integration of data from a food delivery application into a grocery homepage may be technically straightforward and algorithmically advantageous, but it crosses a contextual boundary that consumers may experience as unexpected or privacy-violating if not transparently communicated. Lobschat et al. (2021) argue that corporate digital responsibility, the ethical management of consumer data and algorithmic decision-making, is increasingly a source of brand equity in its own right, and that platforms that communicate their data practices transparently can shift the privacy norm salience threshold, enabling deeper personalization without triggering intrusiveness responses. The mooring value of personalization is thus highest when it is grounded in consumer-perceived legitimacy.

DISCUSSION

Theoretical Contributions

This chapter makes three contributions to the theoretical literatures on algorithmic personalization, platform loyalty, and consumer switching behavior. The first is the conceptualization of platform intelligence perception as a formally defined mediating construct between homepage algorithm quality and switching behavior. Platform intelligence perception is distinguished from perceived personalization (the awareness that content has been tailored), from perceived usefulness (the functional efficiency of the platform), and from the established constructs of anthropomorphization, parasocial intimacy, and algorithmic trust, each of which represents a specific mechanism through which platform intelligence perception is generated. The construct is defined by its evaluative dimension (the consumer's judgment that the platform genuinely understands their needs), and its theoretical antecedents include personalization depth, anticipatory accuracy, and the cumulative history of confirmed predictions. Table 2 summarizes the chapter's three focal constructs (their definitions, theoretical antecedents, and nearest neighboring constructs) as a foundation for the scale development work called for in the Future Research Directions section.

Table 2. Summary of Focal Constructs: Definitions, Antecedents, and Nearest Neighboring Constructs

Construct	Definition	Theoretical Antecedents	Nearest Neighboring Constructs and Point of Distinction
Platform intelligence perception	The consumer's subjective, evaluative assessment of a platform's capacity to understand, anticipate, and respond to their needs, formed through repeated algorithmically personalized interactions.	Personalization depth; anticipatory accuracy; cumulative history of confirmed predictions.	Perceived personalization (Vesanen, 2007): awareness that content is tailored, without the evaluative judgment of being understood. Perceived usefulness (Davis, 1989): functional efficiency, without the relational dimension. Algorithmic trust (Komiak & Benbasat, 2006): willingness to rely on system outputs, a mechanism through which the perception forms, not the perception itself.
Anticipatory intelligence	The platform's capacity to identify and surface a consumer's needs before those needs are consciously registered or explicitly communicated.	Consumption cycle modeling; seasonal and contextual forecasting; life-event inference from purchase signals.	Reactive personalization: responds to expressed history rather than forecasting latent needs. Predictive analytics: a technical capability; anticipatory intelligence denotes its consumer-facing experiential expression.
Compounding personalization	The property whereby recommendation relevance for a given consumer improves with accumulated observations, creating a platform-held data asset whose switching-cost value grows with tenure.	Interaction frequency; platform tenure; breadth of integrated data signals.	Cognitive lock-in (Murray & Häubl, 2007): grounded in the consumer's accumulated skill; compounding personalization is grounded in the platform's accumulated knowledge of the consumer. Expectation-confirmation continuance (Bhattacherjee, 2001): consumer belief updating rather than platform-side asset accumulation.

The second contribution is the formalization of compounding personalization as a distinct switching cost mechanism. Prior work on cognitive lock-in (Murray & Häubl, 2007) and expectation confirmation (Bhattacherjee, 2001) provides the theoretical foundation. This chapter extends those frameworks by identifying the platform-held personalization data asset, rather than the consumer's accumulated interface skill, as the primary source of lock-in in the quick commerce context. The compounding dynamic implies that switching costs grow with platform tenure in a way that is invisible during normal use and becomes salient only at the moment of contemplated defection, producing the asymmetric loyalty pattern that characterizes mature platform-consumer relationships.

The third contribution is the positioning of homepage algorithmic quality as a driver of platform brand equity and mental availability. By connecting the personalization literature to Keller's (1993) customer-based brand equity framework and Sharp's (2010) mental availability concept, the chapter expands the theoretical scope of brand building to include algorithm-mediated consumer experience as a primary brand asset, not merely a conversion optimization tool. This framing is relevant to the broader argument of the present volume: that autonomous decision systems are not ancillary to brand strategy but constitutive of it.

Strategic Implications for Indian Quick Commerce Platforms

For the leadership teams of Indian quick commerce platforms, the analysis suggests three strategic orientations. The first is the reframing of homepage algorithm investment as a brand equity investment rather than a conversion rate optimization exercise. The two objectives are often aligned in the short term but diverge in ways that matter for long-term platform health: an algorithm optimized solely for immediate conversion will make conservative recommendations, surfacing products the consumer has already bought; an algorithm optimized for long-term loyalty will balance safety with discovery, accepting some short-term conversion risk in exchange for the service intelligence moments that generate durable attachment.

The second strategic orientation concerns data quality and ecosystem breadth. The most sophisticated recommendation model is constrained by the quality and range of the signals it receives. Platforms that invest in broadening the consumer signals available to the homepage algorithm (through cross-platform integration, contextual data partnerships, or richer in-session behavioral tracking) can generate homepage experiences that are qualitatively different from competitors rather than merely incrementally better.

The third orientation is the adoption of what might be termed a Homepage Algorithm Maturity Model: a staged progression framework for platform managers, in which each stage carries an observable diagnostic signal indicating that it has been reached; the full progression is summarized in Table 3. This maturity progression is proposed as a practical framework for platform investment prioritization, with each stage producing incrementally greater mooring value and platform intelligence perception.

Table 3. Homepage Algorithm Maturity Model: Stage, Capability, and Diagnostic Signal

Stage	Capability	Diagnostic Signal
Stage 1: Reactive Catalog	Reorder prompts for recently purchased items and basic category navigation.	Reorder prompt adoption: share of orders initiated from a homepage reorder prompt.
Stage 2: Collaborative Filtering	Pattern-based recommendation; consumers with similar histories are used to surface relevant discoveries.	Discovery conversion: share of purchases originating from recommended items outside the consumer's prior purchase history.
Stage 3: Contextual Awareness	Time of day, weather, and seasonal signals modulate recommendations.	Contextual uplift: incremental click-through and conversion of context-modulated placements over a non-contextual baseline.
Stage 4: Anticipatory Intelligence	Consumption cycle modeling and life-event inference surface needs before they are expressed.	Forecast hit rate: proportion of surfaced replenishment prompts converted within the predicted window.
Stage 5: Cross-Context Integration	Full compounding personalization effect; the platform holds a complete model of the consumer's food culture, social occasions, and household life stage.	Cross-context conversion: purchases attributable to signals originating outside the grocery purchase history itself.

Note. Stages are cumulative; a platform at Stage 4 is assumed to retain the capabilities and diagnostic signals of Stages 1–3.

The implication that follows from the maturity model is a clear strategic priority for platforms that have not yet reached Stage 4 or 5: in a market where industry reporting suggests that delivery times and catalog breadth have largely converged across the leading platforms (RedSeer, 2023; Zomato, 2024), the homepage algorithm is arguably the primary remaining axis of competitive differentiation. Platforms that invest most seriously in advancing through these maturity stages are not merely improving a technical system; they are building the most durable form of brand loyalty available in the attention economy of instant commerce: the loyalty of consumers who remain because the platform genuinely understands them, and who recognize that understanding was earned through time.

A necessary qualification to these orientations concerns the tension between advertising monetization and platform intelligence perception. Indian quick commerce platforms operate substantial retail media businesses, and a meaningful share of the homepage surface is consequently paid placement rather than organically ranked recommendation. Sponsored tiles can work directly against the perception of intelligence this chapter describes: a consumer who senses that a slot was sold rather than earned receives a signal of commercial motive precisely where the personalization narrative promises attentiveness, and the attribution of understanding that underpins platform intelligence perception weakens accordingly. The strategic response is not to forgo retail media revenue but to manage it under an explicit relevance constraint: imposing a relevance floor on sponsored placements so that paid tiles are drawn from the set of products the preference model would plausibly have surfaced organically; capping the sponsored share of the first visible screen; labeling sponsored content transparently; and treating platform intelligence perception as a guardrail metric in retail media yield management, accepting reduced short-term advertising yield where the alternative is measurable erosion of the perception asset on which long-run mooring depends.

Finally, platform intelligence perception should be instrumented, not merely theorized. The most direct instrument is the within-app rating prompt (a single-item measure, presented periodically at the close of a session, asking how well the day's homepage matched what the consumer needed), supplemented by short survey intercepts administered to a rotating panel of active users. Behavioral proxies available in existing analytics infrastructure provide convergent evidence: the share of add-to-cart events initiated from homepage surfaces rather than search, scroll depth to first engagement, and repeat-visit intervals. Tracked alongside conversion as a standing guardrail metric, these measures give a brand or product manager a concrete answer to whether algorithmic investment is translating into perceived intelligence. They also operationalize, in managerial form, the measurement agenda developed in the Future Research Directions section.

FUTURE RESEARCH DIRECTIONS

The arguments developed in this chapter are primarily theoretical and point toward a substantial agenda of empirical research. The most immediate priority is the measurement of platform intelligence perception as a consumer attitude construct and the quantitative examination of its relationship with switching intentions. A survey-based study that measures consumers' perceptions of their primary quick commerce platform's intelligence, drawing on scale development methodologies consistent with those used in the perceived personalization literature (Vesanen, 2007), alongside their intention to switch and actual switching behavior over a subsequent period, would provide the foundational empirical evidence for the chapter's central claim.

Longitudinal and panel research designs are particularly well suited to investigating the compounding personalization hypothesis. A study that tracks the homepage relevance experience (measured, for instance, through within-app rating prompts or periodic survey intercepts) alongside switching intentions and behaviors over a twelve- to eighteen-month period would be able to test whether the personalization-loyalty relationship does indeed strengthen with platform tenure. Such research would also be positioned to identify any inflection point at which the accumulated personalization advantage becomes a sufficient anchor to retain consumers even against significant competitive inducement, the theoretical equivalent of the customer lifetime value threshold in subscription services.

The curvilinear personalization paradox model proposed in this chapter requires dedicated empirical investigation of its own. Experimental designs that manipulate personalization depth (for instance, through simulated homepage conditions presented to research participants) and measure the resulting platform intelligence perception and intrusiveness ratings across different levels of privacy norm salience would enable a direct test of the boundary condition model. Qualitative follow-up, using in-depth interviews or experience-sampling methods with regular quick commerce users, would illuminate the specific design and communication features that shift the intrusiveness threshold.

Finally, the cross-platform comparative research that would most directly validate the chapter's argument would require a measure of homepage personalization quality comparable across platforms. A conjoint analysis or discrete choice experiment that presents consumers with simulated homepage variants of varying personalization sophistication (controlling for delivery time, pricing, and visual design) would isolate the specific contribution of algorithmic relevance to switching intention, producing the cleanest test of the chapter's central proposition.

CONCLUSION

The homepage of a quick commerce application is, in the most consequential sense, the place where the platform's brand promise is either confirmed or eroded on every single visit. A homepage that feels generic communicates that the platform does not know the consumer. A homepage that feels relevant, attentive, and occasionally surprising communicates something more valuable than any advertising campaign: that the platform has been paying attention, has been learning, and has developed a model of the consumer's needs that is genuinely useful.

This chapter has argued that the algorithmic innovation that makes the latter kind of homepage possible is, in the Indian quick commerce context, an undertheorized but powerful mechanism through which platforms reduce consumer switching behavior. The argument rests on four formal propositions developed in the body of the chapter. First (P1), homepage algorithms that achieve deep personalization generate platform intelligence perception, the consumer's judgment that the platform understands their needs, which functions as a mooring force in the push-pull-mooring framework of switching behavior. Second (P2), the most advanced platforms have extended personalization into anticipation, surfacing needs before they are consciously registered and thereby producing the service intelligence moments that generate disproportionate loyalty returns. Third (P3), the data asset underlying this personalization compounds with platform tenure, making the switching cost, defined as the intelligence advantage forfeited, grow invisibly and persistently, anchoring consumers against defection. Fourth (P4), the mooring value of personalization is bounded: privacy norm salience moderates the relationship between personalization depth and platform intelligence perception in an inverted-U pattern, so that the deepest technically achievable personalization is not necessarily the most loyalty-productive.

Positioned within the broader argument of this volume, the chapter's contribution is to demonstrate that autonomous decision systems, the homepage algorithms that make these personalization capabilities possible, are not ancillary tools serving a brand strategy determined elsewhere. They are themselves the primary brand-building mechanism in the quick commerce context, constructing consumer associations, driving mental availability, and generating the form of loyalty that is most durable precisely because it is grounded in genuine intelligence rather than promotional incentive.

REFERENCES

Anderson, E. W., & Mittal, V. (2000). Strengthening the satisfaction-profit chain. *Journal of Service Research, 3*(2), 107–120. DOI: 10.1177/109467050032001

Awad, N. F., & Krishnan, M. S. (2006). The personalization privacy paradox: An empirical evaluation of information transparency and the willingness to be profiled online for personalization. *Management Information Systems Quarterly, 30*(1), 13–28. DOI: 10.2307/25148715

Bain & Company. (2023). *India quick commerce report 2023*. Bain & Company India.

Bansal, H. S., & Taylor, S. F. (1999). The service provider switching model (SPSM): A model of consumer switching behavior in the services industry. *Journal of Service Research, 2*(2), 200–218. DOI: 10.1177/109467059922007

Bansal, H. S., Taylor, S. F., & James, Y. S. (2005). "Migrating" to new service providers: Toward a unifying framework of consumers' switching behaviors. *Journal of the Academy of Marketing Science, 33*(1), 96–115. DOI: 10.1177/0092070304267928

Bhattacherjee, A. (2001). Understanding information systems continuance: An expectation-confirmation model. *Management Information Systems Quarterly, 25*(3), 351–370. DOI: 10.2307/3250921

Chou, S., & Cheng, C. (2012). Exploring the continuance intentions of consumers for B2C online shopping: Perspectives of fairness and trust. *Online Information Review, 36*(1), 104–125. DOI: 10.1108/14684521211209572

Covington, P., Adams, J., & Sargin, E. (2016). Deep neural networks for YouTube recommendations. *Proceedings of the 10th ACM Conference on Recommender Systems*, 191–198. DOI: 10.1145/2959100.2959190

Davis, F. D. (1989). Perceived usefulness, perceived ease of use, and user acceptance of information technology. *Management Information Systems Quarterly, 13*(3), 319–340. DOI: 10.2307/249008

De Bruyn, A., Viswanathan, V., Beh, Y. S., Brock, J. K.-U., & von Wangenheim, F. (2020). Artificial intelligence and marketing: Pitfalls and opportunities. *Journal of Interactive Marketing, 51*(1), 91–105. DOI: 10.1016/j.intmar.2020.04.007

Dietvorst, B. J., Simmons, J. P., & Massey, C. (2015). Algorithm aversion: People erroneously avoid algorithms after seeing them err. *Journal of Experimental Psychology. General, 144*(1), 114–126. DOI: 10.1037/xge0000033 PMID: 25401381

Epley, N., Waytz, A., & Cacioppo, J. T. (2007). On seeing the human: A three-factor theory of anthropomorphism. *Psychological Review, 114*(4), 864–886. DOI: 10.1037/0033-295X.114.4.864 PMID: 17907867

Fournier, S. (1998). Consumers and their brands: Developing relationship theory in consumer research. *The Journal of Consumer Research, 24*(4), 343–373. DOI: 10.1086/209515

Huang, M.-H., & Rust, R. T. (2018). Artificial intelligence in service. *Journal of Service Research, 21*(2), 155–172. DOI: 10.1177/1094670517752459

IAMAI. (2023). *India internet report 2023*. Internet and Mobile Association of India.

Jannach, D., & Jugovac, M. (2019). Measuring the business value of recommender systems. *ACM Transactions on Management Information Systems, 10*(4), 1–23. DOI: 10.1145/3370082

Kaminskas, M., & Bridge, D. (2016). Diversity, serendipity, novelty, and coverage: A survey and empirical analysis of beyond-accuracy objectives in recommender systems. *ACM Transactions on Interactive Intelligent Systems, 7*(1), 1–42. DOI: 10.1145/2926720

Keaveney, S. M. (1995). Customer switching behavior in service industries: An exploratory study. *Journal of Marketing, 59*(2), 71–82. DOI: 10.1177/002224299505900206

Keller, K. L. (1993). Conceptualizing, measuring, and managing customer-based brand equity. *Journal of Marketing, 57*(1), 1–22. DOI: 10.1177/002224299305700101

Komiak, S. Y. X., & Benbasat, I. (2006). The effects of personalization and familiarity on trust and adoption of recommendation agents. *Management Information Systems Quarterly, 30*(4), 941–960. DOI: 10.2307/25148760

Labrecque, L. I. (2014). Fostering consumer-brand relationships in social media environments: The role of parasocial interaction. *Journal of Interactive Marketing, 28*(2), 134–148. DOI: 10.1016/j.intmar.2013.12.003

Lobschat, L., Mueller, B., Eggers, F., Brandimarte, L., Diefenbach, S., Kroschke, M., & Wirtz, J. (2021). Corporate digital responsibility. *Journal of Business Research, 122*, 875–888. DOI: 10.1016/j.jbusres.2019.10.006

Morgan, R. M., & Hunt, S. D. (1994). The commitment-trust theory of relationship marketing. *Journal of Marketing, 58*(3), 20–38. DOI: 10.1177/002224299405800302

Murray, K. B., & Häubl, G. (2007). Explaining cognitive lock-in: The role of skill-based habits of use in consumer choice. *The Journal of Consumer Research, 34*(1), 77–88. DOI: 10.1086/513048

Norberg, P. A., Horne, D. R., & Horne, D. A. (2007). The privacy paradox: Personal information disclosure intentions versus behaviors. *The Journal of Consumer Affairs, 41*(1), 100–126. DOI: 10.1111/j.1745-6606.2006.00070.x

Oliver, R. L. (1999). Whence consumer loyalty? *Journal of Marketing, 63*(4, suppl1), 33–44. DOI: 10.1177/00222429990634s105

Puntoni, S., Reczek, R. W., Giesler, M., & Botti, S. (2021). Consumers and artificial intelligence: An experiential perspective. *Journal of Marketing, 85*(1), 131–151. DOI: 10.1177/0022242920953847

RedSeer. (2023). *Quick commerce in India: The next frontier*. RedSeer Strategy Consultants.

Reis, H. T., Clark, M. S., & Holmes, J. G. (2004). Perceived partner responsiveness as an organizing construct in the study of intimacy and closeness. In Mashek, D. J., & Aron, A. P. (Eds.), *Handbook of closeness and intimacy* (pp. 201–225). Lawrence Erlbaum Associates.

Ricci, F., Rokach, L., & Shapira, B. (2015). Recommender systems: Introduction and challenges. In Ricci, F., Rokach, L., & Shapira, B. (Eds.), *Recommender systems handbook* (2nd ed., pp. 1–34). Springer., DOI: 10.1007/978-1-4899-7637-6_1

Rust, R. T., & Huang, M. H. (2014). The service revolution and the transformation of marketing science. *Marketing Science, 33*(2), 206–221. DOI: 10.1287/mksc.2013.0836

Sharp, B. (2010). *How brands grow: What marketers don't know*. Oxford University Press.

Tam, K. Y., & Ho, S. Y. (2006). Understanding the impact of web personalization on user information processing and decision outcomes. *Management Information Systems Quarterly, 30*(4), 865–890. DOI: 10.2307/25148757

Thaler, R. (1980). Toward a positive theory of consumer choice. *Journal of Economic Behavior & Organization, 1*(1), 39–60. DOI: 10.1016/0167-2681(80)90051-7

Vesanen, J. (2007). What is personalization? A conceptual framework. *European Journal of Marketing, 41*(5/6), 409–418. DOI: 10.1108/03090560710737534

Zomato. (2024). *Annual report 2023–24*. Zomato Ltd.

ADDITIONAL READING

Aaker, D. A. (1996). *Building strong brands*. Free Press.

Acquisti, A., Brandimarte, L., & Loewenstein, G. (2015). Privacy and human behavior in the age of information. *Science*, *347*(6221), 509–514. DOI: 10.1126/science.aaa1465 PMID: 25635091

Grewal, D., Motyka, S., & Levy, M. (2018). The evolution and future of retailing and retailing research. *Journal of Retailing*, *94*(1), 6–12. DOI: 10.1016/j.jretai.2021.02.004

Hamilton, R., Ferraro, R., Haws, K. L., & Mukhopadhyay, A. (2021). Traveling with companions: The social customer journey. *Journal of Marketing*, *85*(1), 68–92. DOI: 10.1177/0022242920908227

Matz, S. C., Kosinski, M., Nave, G., & Stillwell, D. J. (2017). Psychological targeting as an effective approach to digital mass persuasion. *Proceedings of the National Academy of Sciences of the United States of America*, *114*(48), 12714–12719. DOI: 10.1073/pnas.1710966114 PMID: 29133409

Shankar, V., Grewal, D., Sunder, S., Fossen, B., Peters, K., & Agarwal, A. (2022). Digital marketing communication in global marketplaces: A review of extant research, future directions, and potential approaches. *International Journal of Research in Marketing*, *39*(2), 541–565. DOI: 10.1016/j.ijresmar.2021.09.005

van Doorn, J., Mende, M., Noble, S. M., Hulland, J., Ostrom, A. L., Grewal, D., & Petersen, J. A. (2017). Domo arigato Mr. Roboto: Emergence of automated social presence in organizational frontlines and customers' service experiences. *Journal of Service Research*, *20*(1), 43–58. DOI: 10.1177/1094670516679272

Verhoef, P. C., Broekhuizen, T., Bart, Y., Bhattacharya, A., Qi Dong, J., Fabian, N., & Haenlein, M. (2021). Digital transformation: A multidisciplinary reflection and research agenda. *Journal of Business Research*, *122*, 889–901. DOI: 10.1016/j.jbusres.2019.09.022

KEY TERMS AND DEFINITIONS

Anticipatory Intelligence: The capacity of a platform's algorithmic systems to identify and surface a consumer's needs before those needs have been consciously registered or explicitly communicated, based on modeling of purchase cycles, contextual patterns, and life-event signals embedded in long-horizon behavioral data.

Autonomous Decision System: An algorithmic system that makes consequential, consumer-facing decisions at scale in real time without human review, operating on learned models of individual and aggregate behavior. In the quick commerce context, the homepage algorithm is the primary autonomous decision system mediating the consumer experience.

Compounding Personalization: The property of homepage recommendation algorithms whereby the relevance and predictive accuracy of recommendations for a given consumer improves over time as the underlying preference model is refined through additional consumer-specific observations, creating a platform-held data asset that grows in switching-cost value with platform tenure.

Homepage Algorithm: The ensemble of machine learning models and data processing systems responsible for constructing the consumer-facing homepage of a digital platform in real time, determining which products, categories, and promotional surfaces are presented to a given consumer at a given moment based on a combination of historical preference modeling and real-time contextual signals.

Platform Brand Equity: The set of consumer associations (functional, emotional, and self-expressive) built around a digital platform through repeated interactions, which increases the consumer's willingness to use, recommend, and remain loyal to that platform. In quick commerce, homepage algorithmic quality is identified as a primary driver of platform brand equity.

Platform Intelligence Perception: A consumer's subjective evaluative assessment of a digital platform's capacity to understand, anticipate, and respond to their preferences and needs. Formally distinguished from perceived personalization (awareness of tailoring) and perceived usefulness (functional efficiency), platform intelligence perception adds the relational dimension of feeling genuinely understood.

Privacy Norm Salience: The degree to which concerns about data collection and algorithmic profiling are actively present in a consumer's evaluative frame at the moment of platform interaction, moderating the point at which deep personalization tips from being experienced as attentive to being experienced as intrusive.

Quick Commerce: A retail delivery model in which consumer goods (primarily groceries and daily essentials) are delivered to the consumer within ten to thirty minutes of order placement, enabled by a network of urban micro-fulfillment centers known as dark stores.

Switching Behavior: The decision by a consumer to cease using their current service provider or digital platform and migrate to a competing alternative, driven by a combination of push factors (dissatisfaction) and pull factors (alternative attractiveness), and moderated by mooring factors (switching costs, accumulated history, relational investment) that resist defection.

Section 3
Brand Assets, Salience, and Machine Visibility

Brand assets were crafted to resonate with human perception. This section examines what becomes of them once selection is performed by a machine, transforming the inquiry into a measurement-based question: how do sonic assets perform when no consumer is listening at the moment of selection, and how should salience be conceptualized when it must operate through both human and algorithmic channels simultaneously?

Chapter 8
Sonic Branding and Audio Brand Assets for AI-Mediated Voice Interfaces

Shawn Mathew
http://orcid.org/0000-0002-5190-657X
Middlesex University Dubai, UAE

Esther Bassil Sleilati
http://orcid.org/0000-0002-2092-8741
Notre Dame University, Zouk Mosbeh, Lebanon

Prama Vishnoi
http://orcid.org/0000-0003-0885-9955
Delhi Technological University, India

ABSTRACT

Conversational artificial intelligence has opened a gap in brand communication that theory has been slow to close. When a consumer speaks to a voice assistant, the visual cues that have carried brand recognition across page, screen, and shelf fall away, and sound becomes the only register in which the brand is present. This chapter rethinks sonic branding under that constraint. It synthesizes the Ehrenberg-Bass account of distinctive assets and mental availability, psychoacoustic and crossmodal research on how sound carries meaning, sound-symbolism findings on the link between phonemes and perception, and conditioning models of how audio acquires brand associations. From this synthesis the chapter develops the Sonic Distinctiveness Hierarchy, an original framework that ranks brand voice personas,

DOI: 10.4018/979-8-3373-9589-0.ch008

sonic logos, notification sounds, and ambient audio by their capacity to encode distinctive brand associations when the visual channel is absent. Four propositions formalize the framework and anchor a closing research agenda.

INTRODUCTION

Brands have used sound to identify themselves for as long as they have advertised, in jingles, anthems, and the short signatures now called sonic logos. The communicative load that sound must carry has, however, increased substantially. In little more than a decade, conversational assistants have developed from novelty into habit (Hildebrand et al., 2020; McLean & Osei-Frimpong, 2019), and they now sit between brand and consumer at moments of choice. Consumers now reorder coffee through smart speakers and book rooms through in-car assistants, and in each case the brand judgment is made without visual contact. The visual identity that managers have spent careers refining is unavailable at that moment, and the brand is represented instead by the sonic logo, the answering voice, the small confirming sounds, and the prosody of the reply. Whether audio alone can carry the recognizable, emotionally resonant associations that brand theory treats as the basis of equity (Aaker, 1996; Keller, 1993) is therefore both a practical problem for managers and an open question for the literature.

The Ehrenberg-Bass tradition supplies the most useful evaluative standard. Brands grow by building mental availability, the ease with which a name comes to mind across the situations in which people buy, and they build it by deploying assets distinctive to the brand and useful where category needs arise, consistently and at reach (Romaniuk & Sharp, 2004). Sonic logos, brand voices, and recurring acoustic motifs are the audio counterparts of visual distinctive assets, and the same demands of consistency, reach, and category relevance apply (Romaniuk & Sharp, 2004). The voice interface differs in one respect that carries far-reaching consequences, because the audio operates alone. No logo, color, or package stands beside it, so the acoustic design carries a load it never carried in multimodal settings, and it must achieve a precision in which few brands have thought to invest (Spence & Keller, 2024).

This chapter makes four contributions. First, it draws the parent literatures into a single account organized around mechanism rather than channel. Second, it introduces the Sonic Distinctiveness Hierarchy, which ranks audio assets by their capacity to encode distinctiveness under voice-first conditions and provides managers with a basis for prioritizing sonic-branding investment. Third, four propositions make the framework testable, each tying a tier to an empirical claim. Fourth, a closing agenda identifies where evidence remains thin. The chapter proceeds from the field's conceptual foundations, through the mechanisms by which sound encodes brand meaning, to the voice-first context and the framework, and then to industry variations, technology, ethical considerations, and future research directions.

By a voice-first or screenless interaction, the chapter means any exchange in which the consumer receives the brand through sound with no synchronous visual display, whether a smart-speaker query or an in-car assistant. Such interfaces are by now an established object of study whose acoustic signal can be measured at scale (Hildebrand et al., 2020; McLean & Osei-Frimpong, 2019). The screenless condition is treated here as the boundary case in which the value of sonic assets is most clearly visible, though most real journeys remain mixed.

LITERATURE REVIEW / BACKGROUND

Defining Sonic Branding

Definitions in the field have shifted as the range of branded sound has expanded. The earliest treatments framed music as a marketing stimulus working on mood and attention in advertising and on the retail floor (Bruner, 1990). Attention then moved to designed, brand-owned assets, above all the sonic logo, read as the auditory counterpart of a visual mark (Krishnan et al., 2012). Graakjær and Bonde (2018) extended the construct further, showing that non-musical sound, including interface tones and environmental sound, also acquires brand meaning when it recurs in brand settings. The newest reviews describe a field at the intersection of art and science, where craft traditions meet a growing experimental record (Spence & Keller, 2024), as earlier consumer-oriented reviews anticipated (Gustafsson, 2015). Table 1 summarizes this progression, which follows changes in the media environment. Broadcast advertising rewarded the memorable song, shorter and more crowded spots compressed musical identity into the few-second sonic logo, and the migration of listening to devices has extended brand sound into interface tones, product sounds, and the answering voice (Bruner, 1990; Graakjær & Bonde, 2018; Krishnan et al., 2012). Research has followed practice, moving from conditioning experiments treating music as an affective stimulus (Gorn, 1982) and jingles as mnemonics for slogans (Yalch, 1991), to designed assets brought under experimental control (Krishnan et al., 2012; Scott et al., 2022), to the registrable sound trademark and the assistant's answering voice (McLean & Osei-Frimpong, 2019; Zhang, 2021).

Table 1. Selected Milestones in Sonic Branding and Related Research

Period	Conceptual focus	Representative source
1982	Music as a classical-conditioning stimulus in advertising	Gorn (1982)
1990	Music as a managerial stimulus shaping mood and response	Bruner (1990)
2000–2004	Phonetic meaning and sound symbolism in brand names	Klink (2000); Yorkston and Menon (2004)
2012	Sonic logos as designed, measurable brand assets	Krishnan et al. (2012)
2018	Non-musical sound as a brand asset	Graakjær and Bonde (2018)
2024	Sonic branding as an art-and-science field	Spence and Keller (2024)

Note. Source: Authors.

The working definition adopted here is broad enough to encompass these strands. Sonic branding is the strategic design, deployment, and management of auditory brand assets that build distinctiveness, semantic meaning, and consumer outcomes across every touchpoint at which the brand is heard. Three developments have made the topic pressing. Brand contact continues to migrate toward screenless touchpoints, where audio is the only cue available (Hildebrand et al., 2020; McLean & Osei-Frimpong, 2019). The making of audio assets is being industrialized by generative voice and music tools, which cut the cost of creation while raising the risk of sameness (Efthymiou et al., 2024). In addition, distinctive sonic assets now receive recognition as protectable sound trademarks in major jurisdictions, adding a legal rationale to the commercial one (Zhang, 2021). Managers therefore need to know which auditory elements count as assets worth designing, protecting, and measuring. The evidence drawn on throughout is peer-reviewed work in marketing, consumer psychology, and human-computer interaction across four decades, weighting experimental and review findings ahead of practitioner commentary.

A Taxonomy of Sonic Brand Assets

Audio brand assets are heterogeneous, and treating them as a single category obscures consequential design choices. Six components warrant separate treatment. Sonic logos are brief designed phrases that mark a brand as a visual logo does (Krishnan et al., 2012). Brand voice personas are the recorded or synthesized voices in which a brand speaks (Melzner & Raghubir, 2023). Brand anthems and longer themes are deployed with the brand across campaigns (Allan, 2008). Ambient soundscapes furnish the acoustic settings in which brand decisions are made (Garlin & Owen, 2006). Functional earcons and notification architectures signal events inside an interface (Garzonis et al., 2009). Consequential product sounds, the sounds a product makes in use, come to identify the product even when they were not designed as brand assets (Ringler et al., 2021). Table 2 presents the six components and the primary mechanism on which each relies. Under voice-first conditions they consolidate into the four classes ranked below. Anthems fold into ambient and musical audio, since extended music rarely plays inside an assistant exchange, and consequential product sounds join notification signals as repetition-learned cues.

Table 2. A Six-Component Taxonomy of Sonic Brand Assets

Component	Function	Primary mechanism	Anchor study
Sonic logos	Rapid brand identification	Processing fluency, psychoacoustic structure	Krishnan et al. (2012)
Brand voice personas	Personality and trust in interaction	Prosody, anthropomorphism	Melzner and Raghubir (2023)
Brand anthems and themes	Affective association across campaigns	Conditioning, musical fit	Allan (2008)
Ambient soundscapes	Shaping the decision context	Mood and arousal	Garlin and Owen (2006)
Earcons and notification sounds	Functional signaling and reinforcement	Repetition, learnability	Garzonis et al. (2009)
Consequential product sounds	Implicit identification in use	Co-occurrence and inference	Ringler et al. (2021)

Note. Source: Authors.

Sound offers capabilities that visual identity does not. It reaches a listener without demanding that attention be pointed at any surface, so it operates while visual attention is engaged elsewhere. It carries affective information at high density, so a motif of one or two seconds can establish a mood. It can convey semantic content as well as identify a source, because phonetic and acoustic structure map onto perception in ways that are not arbitrary (Spence, 2012; Yorkston & Menon, 2004). Once a distinctive sound can be registered as a trademark, it becomes property that can be owned and defended (Zhang, 2021). These properties are advantageous in any channel and become decisive when sound is the only channel available.

Sonic Branding Across the Customer Journey

Sound contributes value at every stage of the path to purchase, which is why managed investment is warranted. Early on, distinctive sonic assets build recognition and mental availability, so the brand surfaces when a category need appears, and a sung or musical cue tends to be retrieved more readily than a spoken one (Romaniuk & Sharp, 2004; Yalch, 1991). At the point of choice, a recognized sonic logo speeds identification and can shift the decision toward the brand already known (Anglada-Tort et al., 2022; Krishnan et al., 2012). During the experience itself, ambient music and consequential product sounds influence mood, perceived quality, and satisfaction

(Garlin & Owen, 2006; Ringler et al., 2021). Over repeated encounters, consistent audio may contribute to recognition, continuity, and loyalty-related responses (Graakjær & Bonde, 2018; Kemp et al., 2024). This chapter examines what becomes of this accumulated value once the setting becomes voice-first.

Brand Equity and the Distinctive-Asset Standard

Two traditions define what audio assets are being asked to deliver. The customer-based view defines brand equity as the differential effect of brand knowledge on consumer response, built from awareness and from strong, favorable, and unique associations held in memory (Keller, 1993). Under this view, an audio asset contributes by adding a recognizable, positive association the consumer can retrieve. The Ehrenberg-Bass tradition recasts the problem as retrieval rather than persuasion. Brands grow by being easy to notice and to call to mind across buying situations, and distinctive assets are the non-product elements, visual or auditory, that trigger brand retrieval at those moments (Romaniuk & Sharp, 2004). In this tradition an asset derives its value from its uniqueness to the brand and its fame across the customer base, and it operates by becoming linked to category entry points, the cues and situations that prompt a buyer to think of the category (Romaniuk & Sharp, 2004). A sonic logo, a brand voice, or a recurring motif counts as distinctive only when it satisfies both criteria, a standard more demanding than mere presence. The traditions do differ, since Keller requires favorable meaning while distinctive-asset theory requires only that the asset identify the brand, yet for audio they converge on one practical standard. An asset is worth having to the degree that it is distinctive to one brand rather than generic to a category, deployed consistently enough to be learned, and present where a category need is cued. This standard is especially demanding in a voice interface, where a weak asset receives no visual support and the absence of a learned cue exposes the brand to the platform default.

Mechanisms of Sonic Brand Effects

Three families of mechanism underlie the effects of audio assets, and each can operate with little deliberate attention. The first family is psychoacoustic, in that acoustic descriptors carry meaning and the timbral character of a sound informs the personality consumers attribute to a brand. Across 10 studies, Melzner and Raghubir (2023) find that timbral quality, the roughness or smoothness of an audio logo, shifts judgments of brand personality toward ruggedness or sophistication, an effect strong enough to move perceptions of well-known brands. Tone count bears on willingness to pay through processing ease (Krishnan et al., 2012), while tempo, mode, and sound frequency alter how consumers respond and decide (Hahn & Hwang, 1999;

Knoeferle et al., 2012; Sunaga, 2018). Intensity, pitch, and pace orient attention and shape the emotional response (Mas et al., 2021). The instrument carrying the melody operates similarly, since instrumental timbre can move brand perceptions toward ruggedness or sophistication independently of the melody (Puligadda & VanBergen, 2023). Placement also carries measurable consequences, because a logo at the close of an advertisement produces a different emotional response than the same logo at the opening (Scott et al., 2022).

A second set of effects is crossmodal. Auditory cues map onto visual, gustatory, olfactory, and tactile attributes through correspondences stable across people (Spence, 2012). Sound frequency maps onto color lightness and can direct visual attention, with high-frequency sounds drawing attention toward light objects and low-frequency sounds toward dark ones (Hagtvedt & Brasel, 2016). Acoustic features shift the perceived crispness, healthfulness, and taste of food (Reinoso Carvalho et al., 2016; Techawachirakul et al., 2022). Sound meaning can direct visual search toward a congruent brand (Knoeferle et al., 2016), and the principle extends to olfaction, where soundscapes are composed to match a fragrance (Spence et al., 2024). Within a voice interface these correspondences operate in one direction only, since the consumer hears but cannot see yet still forms judgments about color, texture, and quality.

The third family is sound symbolism, whose evidence concerns spoken brand names rather than logos or ambient sound. Phonemes carry non-arbitrary associations with size, shape, taste, and emotion that recur across languages, so the sound of a name shapes perception before any explicit message is read (Klink, 2000; Yorkston & Menon, 2004). Voiced consonants are perceived as larger, rougher, and more masculine, while voiceless consonants and high-front vowels are perceived as smaller, lighter, and softer (Pathak et al., 2020). The position of sound-symbolic elements within a name, and their combination, moderates the effect (Klink & Wu, 2014), and devices such as reduplication bring associations of approachability and warmth (Motoki et al., 2025). Recent electrophysiological work shows these associations modulate neural activity during brand-name processing, pointing to a perceptual root rather than learned association alone (Glim & Hillje, 2025).

Review Method and Corpus

The corpus behind the synthesis was assembled through a two-round search of Google Scholar and the publisher websites of the journals identified there, with 122 queries in the first round and 25 targeted queries in the second. Queries spanned sonic branding, sonic logo, brand voice, servicescape music, sound symbolism, and cognate terms. Sources were eligible if peer reviewed, in English, and published from 1999 onward, with seven earlier seminal studies, published between 1968 and

1996, retained for theoretical anchoring. Candidates were screened for scholarly impact, operationalized as publication in a peer-reviewed outlet together with citation performance relative to the age of the work. Backward and forward citation tracking extended the pool to a corpus of 100 articles. The chapter cites the subset bearing most directly on brand strategy under voice-first conditions, with foundational works from consumer psychology. The eight streams in Table 3 were derived by clustering the retained articles by dominant construct, mechanism, and setting.

Eight Thematic Streams in the Existing Literature

The field has developed along eight streams that rarely intersect. The first examines sonic logos and brand identity, the designed mark and its acoustic parameters (Krishnan et al., 2012; Mas et al., 2021). The second examines music in advertising and how musical stimuli influence attitude and choice (Allan, 2008; Bruner, 1990; Gorn, 1982; Park & Young, 1986). The third, on voice and AI, treats the assistant as interface and brand at once (Hildebrand et al., 2020; McLean & Osei-Frimpong, 2019). The fourth, servicescape research, examines ambient music in retail and service settings (Garlin & Owen, 2006; North et al., 1999). The fifth traces crossmodal correspondences across the senses (Hagtvedt & Brasel, 2016; Spence, 2012). The sixth, neuromarketing, measures implicit response to sound (Bosshard & Walla, 2023). The seventh attends to consequential and functional product sounds (Garzonis et al., 2009; Ringler et al., 2021). The eighth comprises newer work on podcasts, short-video advertising, and inclusive soundtracks (Palencia-Lefler, 2024; Yang et al., 2025). Table 3 lists each stream with its anchor sources and its principal unresolved question. Recent reviews synthesize across the streams (Spence & Keller, 2024), but none ranks the assets for investment purposes, and the framework introduced below addresses this gap. Figure 1 shows the temporal distribution of the cited evidence.

Table 3. Eight Thematic Streams and an Unanswered Question in Each

Stream	Anchor sources	Open question
Sonic logos and identity	Krishnan et al. (2012); Mas et al. (2021)	Which acoustic parameters survive voice-assistant playback?
Music in advertising	Allan (2008); Bruner (1990); Gorn (1982); Park and Young (1986)	How do conditioning effects transfer to AI service contact?
Voice and AI-mediated brand voice	Hildebrand et al. (2020); McLean and Osei-Frimpong (2019)	Which prosodic settings build trust across categories?
Servicescape and ambient music	Garlin and Owen (2006); Knoeferle et al. (2012); North et al. (1999)	Does ambient design matter when the room is uncontrolled?

continued on following page

Table 3. Continued

Stream	Anchor sources	Open question
Crossmodal and multisensory	Hagtvedt and Brasel (2016); Spence (2012)	Do correspondences hold under audio-only access?
Neuromarketing of sound	Bosshard and Walla (2023)	Can implicit measures predict field recognition?
Product and functional sound	Garzonis et al. (2009); Ringler et al. (2021)	When do incidental sounds become brand assets?
Emerging streams	Palencia-Lefler (2024); Yang et al. (2025)	How is sonic identity built on attention-scarce platforms and for excluded audiences?

Note. Source: Authors.

Figure 1. Temporal distribution of the cited evidence base.

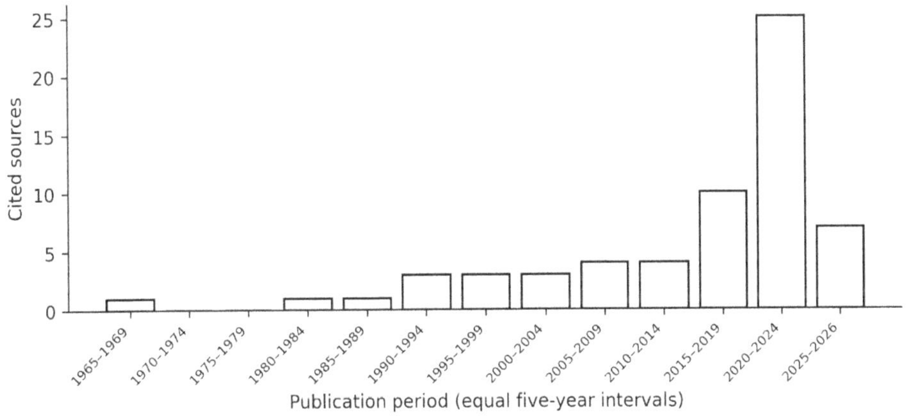

THE VOICE-FIRST CONTEXT

Sound as the Sole Carrier of Identity

When the screen is removed, audio ceases to be a supporting cue and becomes the brand's entire perceptual surface. The crossmodal correspondences set out above continue to operate, but in one direction only. The consumer hears a voice or a logo and from that alone infers the color, texture, quality, and warmth making up the brand, with nothing visual to confirm or correct the inference (Spence, 2012; Spence & Keller, 2024). The acoustic parameters of a voice or a sonic logo become consequential to a degree they do not reach when a package or screen is present, because they constitute the identity rather than accenting a visual one.

This shift places on sound a design burden that most brands have not previously carried. In a voice interface a brand voice has no redundancy, so small choices about rate, pitch, and warmth carry the whole weight of personality transmission (Mas et al., 2021; Melzner & Raghubir, 2023). The consequences for memory follow from conditioning principles. A sonic asset takes on associative value through repeated pairing with brand experience, so a logo or voice accompanying smooth, satisfying interactions builds a warmer conditioned response than one tied to friction (Gorn, 1982; Krishnan et al., 2012). Controlled evidence that initially neutral brands pick up measurable evaluative shifts after audio pairing supports this account (Bosshard & Walla, 2023). The mood created by music can transfer to choices made while it plays, operating at the brand level rather than the advertisement level (Bruner, 1990).

The Restructured Consideration Set

Voice assistants restructure the consideration set presented to the consumer. A web page lays out many options at once for the eye, whereas a voice interface reads them out one after another and often volunteers a single default (McLean & Osei-Frimpong, 2019). Requesting further options requires more effort than scanning a shelf, so the first acceptable answer is accepted more often. This serialization raises the value of recognition, since a consumer who places a brand from a brief audio cue can accept it and search no further. Anglada-Tort et al. (2022) show that recognizing the music attached to a brand shifts choice toward it, with the recognition advantage operating through sound rather than sight.

Within Ehrenberg-Bass theory these developments change which cue carries mental availability rather than the underlying logic of growth. Brands still grow by being easy to bring to mind when a category need arises, but inside a voice interface the operative cue is auditory (Romaniuk & Sharp, 2004). The category entry point becomes the spoken request itself, the moment a consumer asks aloud for a coffee, a bank, or a song, and the asset that secures the brand's place in the answer is the audio cue the consumer has learned to recognize. A brand with no auditory route to mental availability is therefore exposed in voice commerce in a way it is not on a shelf, since the platform may furnish its own default where no strong brand cue exists (Khamis & Keogh, 2021). The advantage accrues to assets that remain identifiable through the degraded, compressed audio common in assistant playback.

The Brand Voice as a Designed Asset

The voice that answers a branded assistant serves simultaneously as a functional channel and a brand character, and its prosody, the rate, the pitch movement, the warmth, the expressiveness of delivery, encodes the personality the consumer attributes to the brand (Melzner & Raghubir, 2023). Digitally manipulating vocal tract length shifts product congruency and advertising performance, making the brand voice a designable parameter rather than a fixed recording (Efthymiou et al., 2024). Voice pitch produces measurable effects even in contexts as specific as destination promotion (Au et al., 2025).

Three effects of voice design operate jointly in the branded voice. The first is anthropomorphism, since human-like voices and social-presence cues lead consumers to grant the agent, and the brand behind it, human characteristics (Cherif & Lemoine, 2019; Vernuccio et al., 2023). The second is trust, since acoustic features combine with perceived competence and authenticity to set how far the agent is trusted, and synthetic and pre-recorded voices differ in the brand anthropomorphism and equity they generate (Knödler & Rudeloff, 2024; Rawool et al., 2025). The third is the erasure of the line between intentional and incidental branding, because a voice on a smart speaker is interface signal, service medium, and brand asset at once (Hildebrand et al., 2020). This convergence carries risk as well as benefit, since consumers report unease when humanization is taken too far, so calibration matters more than maximization. The design objective is a voice that is recognized and trusted rather than one that is merely lifelike (Knödler & Rudeloff, 2024; Monteverde et al., 2025).

THE SONIC DISTINCTIVENESS HIERARCHY

The literatures reviewed so far offer managers limited guidance on where to invest first when sound must carry the brand alone. The Sonic Distinctiveness Hierarchy addresses this gap. It ranks four families of audio asset by how well each encodes distinctive, durable brand associations under voice-interface conditions, judging each on three dimensions. Brand-design control captures the extent to which the brand can specify the asset rather than inherit it. Distinctiveness-encoding capacity captures the amount of brand-specific association the asset can hold at a strength sufficient to trigger identification. Scalability captures how well the asset survives transfer across channels without losing its distinctive features. Figure 2 presents the hierarchy and the three dimensions. The ranking follows the standard that already governs visual distinctive assets, namely that an asset qualifies by being controllable, distinctive, and deployable consistently at scale (Romaniuk & Sharp, 2004; Spence & Keller, 2024). Figure 3 situates the framework within the wider logic, from the mechanisms of sonic meaning through the asset tiers to brand outcomes under screenless interaction. The three dimensions do not always align. The sonic logo is the most portable of the four yet ranks below the voice persona because the persona matches it on design control and leads on encoding capacity. The ranking therefore reflects net standing rather than any single dimension, and it constitutes a default ordering for investment rather than a judgment that lower tiers are dispensable. Table 4 makes the mapping explicit, scoring each class on each dimension on a three-point scale, so the ordering is transparent and open to challenge.

Table 4. Scoring the Four Asset Classes on the Three Ranking Dimensions

Asset class	Brand-design control	Distinctiveness-encoding capacity	Scalability	Tier	Anchor evidence
Brand voice persona	High	High	Medium	1	Efthymiou et al. (2024); Melzner and Raghubir (2023); Rawool et al. (2025)
Sonic logo	High	Medium	High	2	Anglada-Tort et al. (2022); Krishnan et al. (2012); Scott et al. (2022)
Notification and interface sounds	Medium	Medium	Medium	3	Garzonis et al. (2009); Nees and Liebman (2023); Ringler et al. (2021)
Ambient and environmental audio	Low	Low	Low	4	Garlin and Owen (2006); North et al. (1999); Spence (2012)

Note. High on brand-design control denotes that the brand can specify the asset's acoustic parameters in full before deployment, High on distinctiveness-encoding capacity denotes that the asset can carry a brand-identifying association retrievable without visual support, and High on scalability denotes that the asset retains its distinctive features across channels and playback conditions. Low denotes the converse and Medium partial satisfaction, with assignments anchored to the evidence listed in the final column. Tier order follows net standing across the three dimensions under voice-first conditions, and where net standing ties, distinctiveness-encoding capacity takes precedence, because identification without visual support is the criterion the voice-first channel makes binding. Source: Authors.

A boundary condition concerns who owns the answering voice. On brand-owned surfaces, a branded application, a proprietary in-car assistant, or a dedicated device, the brand specifies the voice persona in full and the hierarchy applies as stated. On third-party surfaces such as general-purpose smart speakers, the answering voice belongs to the platform, and the brand controls little beyond its sonic logo, notification sounds, and supplied audio (Hildebrand et al., 2020; Khamis & Keogh, 2021). The hierarchy then effectively begins at Tier 2, and the budgeting implication is that investment in a proprietary voice persona is justified only where the brand commands the surface on which it speaks. Proposition 1 is therefore scoped to brand-owned surfaces, since on third-party surfaces the persona is not the brand's to design.

Figure 2. The Sonic Distinctiveness Hierarchy.

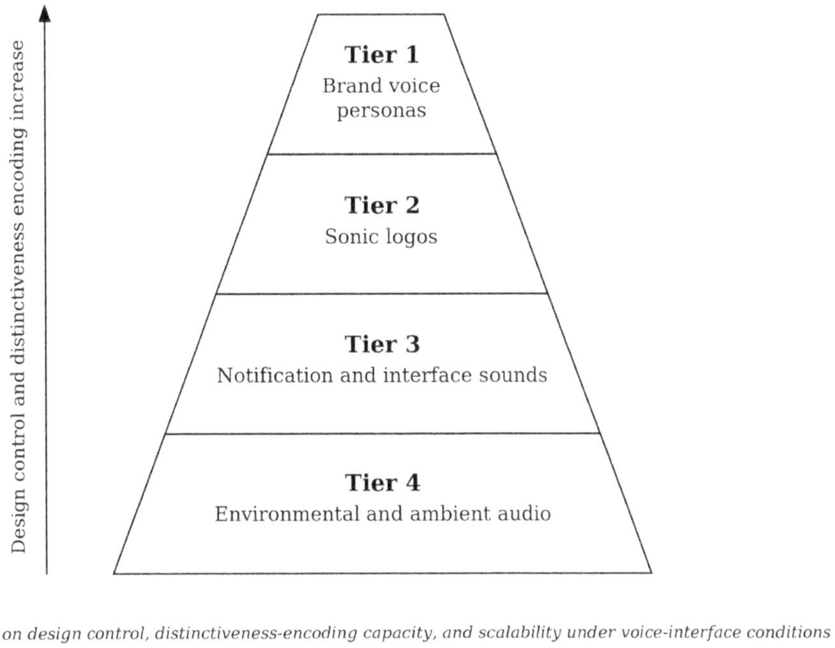

Figure 3. From mechanism to brand equity under voice-first conditions.

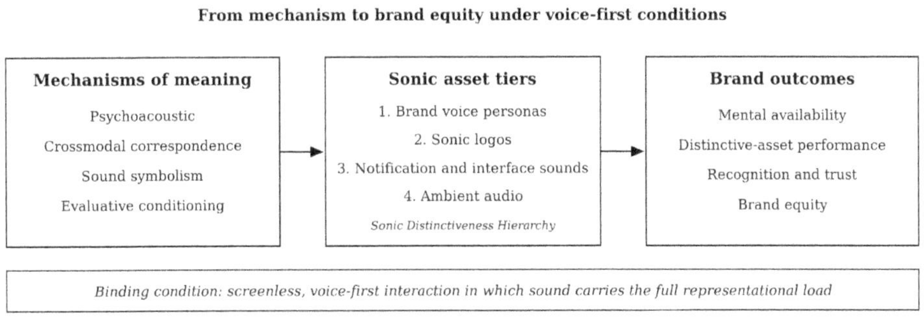

Tier 1: Brand Voice Personas

Brand voice personas occupy the first tier because in an AI-mediated exchange they are the primary and most sustained signal through which the consumer encounters the brand. The prosodic parameters defining a voice, its rate, pitch contour, warmth, and expressiveness, fall within the brand's design control and encode personality, competence, and trustworthiness directly (Efthymiou et al., 2024; Melzner & Raghubir, 2023). A voice gathers associative weight through repeated functional contact, answering both the distinctive-asset demand for consistent, broad deployment and the conditioning demand for consistent valence in the paired experience (Krishnan et al., 2012; Romaniuk & Sharp, 2004). The persona also bears the heaviest relational load, since the warmth and competence a listener hears feed into trust in the agent and the brand behind it, and into the anthropomorphic inferences framing the relationship (Rawool et al., 2025; Vernuccio et al., 2023). The persona ranks above the logo on informational bandwidth as much as on presence, since prosody encodes personality continuously across a long interaction whereas the logo encodes a brief signature. The ordering is a conceptual prior that the research agenda below marks for empirical testing. Platform voices such as Alexa and Siri illustrate the tier as platform-owned personas, while branded banking and in-car assistants show that a brand can specify its own persona as deliberately as any visual mark.

Proposition 1. In AI-mediated voice contexts on brand-owned surfaces, the brand voice persona is the highest-leverage sonic distinctive asset, and its prosodic parameters predict brand personality perception and trust over and above the contribution of the sonic logo.

Tier 2: Sonic Logos

Sonic logos occupy the second tier. Their brevity and distinctive structure make them highly efficient identification devices, working much as a visual logo does (Krishnan et al., 2012; Scott et al., 2022). The effects operate through specific acoustic features. Timbre moves brand personality perceptions toward ruggedness or sophistication (Melzner & Raghubir, 2023; Puligadda & VanBergen, 2023). Tone count influences willingness to pay through processing fluency (Krishnan et al., 2012). Intensity, pitch, and pace orient attention and carry personality (Mas et al., 2021). The logo ranks below the voice persona because it carries a narrower band of brand information in a shorter window, not because any single exposure is weak. At the point of choice, its recognition advantage is decisive, and recognizing a brand's music has been shown to shift choice toward that brand (Anglada-Tort et al., 2022). Illustrative cases range from Intel's five-note signature to Netflix's opening ident and the McDonald's motif that Graakjær (2019) traces. In Proposition 2, the recognition advantage denotes the probability that the brand is identified from the cue alone, and the persuasion advantage denotes the attitude shift an exposure produces once the source is known. The tone-count evidence on willingness to pay does not conflict with the proposition, because fluency operates within a single exposure while distinctiveness governs identification across exposures (Krishnan et al., 2012).

Proposition 2. Sonic-logo effectiveness in voice-first contexts is determined more by acoustic distinctiveness than by length or melodic complexity, and the recognition advantage outweighs the persuasion advantage when the consideration set is serialized.

Tier 3: Notification and Interface Sound Architectures

Notification and interface earcons, the short designed sounds marking an event such as a confirmation or an alert, rank third. They give steady, low-salience reinforcement across the high-frequency micro-interactions of ordinary device use, and their value builds through repetition rather than any one exposure (Garzonis et al., 2009; Nees & Liebman, 2023). The principal design challenge at this tier is learnability. Comparative evidence on brief audio alerts shows that well-designed earcons and auditory icons, the latter being everyday sounds resembling the event they stand for, outperform arbitrary tones (Garzonis et al., 2009; Nees & Liebman, 2023). Consequential product sounds, a payment chime or an app's opening flourish, come to identify the platform through repeated co-occurrence even where they were never designed as brand assets (Ringler et al., 2021). They mark the point at which the line between intentional and incidental branding is least distinct. Mastercard's transaction chime illustrates the designed case, and the payment and unlock sounds of everyday devices illustrate the incidental case. Design control is rated Medium rather than High because deployment runs through platform notification frameworks, user sound settings, and operating-system playback constraints outside the brand's control. For testing, the mere-exposure baseline in Proposition 3 is an acoustically matched but nondistinctive control tone, equated for loudness, duration, and timbre class on the same exposure schedule, so any lift reflects distinctiveness rather than the familiarity repeated exposure alone produces (Zajonc, 1968).

Proposition 3. Distinctiveness in notification architecture produces a measurable lift in implicit brand attitude above a mere-exposure baseline, and the lift is larger under the high-frequency micro-interaction conditions typical of mobile and voice platforms.

Tier 4: Environmental and Ambient Audio Design

Environmental and ambient audio occupies the fourth tier because it offers context rather than identity encoding. Ambient music sets the emotional frame within which brand decisions are made, an effect on record since the classic field study in which French or German in-store music shifted wine purchases toward the matching country (North et al., 1999). It can also influence impulse buying and variety seeking (Garlin & Owen, 2006; Manzoor, 2024; Sun et al., 2023). Crossmodal correspondences between ambient acoustic features and product attributes can likewise steer perception (Reinoso Carvalho et al., 2016; Spence, 2012). Ambient audio is also the most channel-fragile of the four tiers, since a brand cannot govern the acoustic surroundings in which a voice query is made, so it must design assets that remain effective under interference. Ambient audio therefore falls last in voice-first allocation decisions, because it cannot secure brand identification when a consumer asks an assistant to choose.

Proposition 4. Ambient audio raises brand-related affect and momentary evaluation but does not improve unaided brand identification under voice-only conditions, so its marginal contribution to distinctive-asset strength falls below that of the upper three tiers.

INDUSTRY VARIATIONS AND MULTICHANNEL INTEGRATION

The Domain Landscape

Sectors differ in sonic-branding practice, because the dominant asset and the binding constraint vary from one category to the next. Table 5 maps seven sectors against their leading asset and principal constraint. In quick-service restaurants and packaged goods, frequent repeat exposure rewards short sonic logos, and discourse analysis tracks how the McDonald's logo has been varied across 15 years of advertising while still reading as the same mark (Graakjær, 2019). In financial services the constraint is trust, so the voice persona leads and acoustic design is weighed against perceived competence and authenticity (Mas et al., 2021; Rawool et al., 2025). In healthcare, sonic logos can raise perceived competence and trust while easing negative emotion (Kemp et al., 2023). In advertising more broadly, they generate positive emotion and engagement, particularly for consumers who rely on affect when deciding (Kemp et al., 2024). Luxury and hospitality lean toward restrained themes and ambient soundscapes that signal exclusivity (Garlin & Owen, 2006; Khamis & Keogh, 2021). In automotive and telecommunications, in-car interfaces and consequential product sounds carry the identity (Cherif &

Lemoine, 2019; Ringler et al., 2021). On technology platforms, short-video and music-video advertising raise fresh questions under the feed's attention dynamics (Mandolfo et al., 2024; Yang et al., 2025). Sport spans these sectors, using music and sonic identity to build emotional connection in the stadium and in broadcast coverage (Ballouli & Heere, 2015). One pattern holds across Table 5, in that the dominant asset follows the binding constraint of the channel.

Table 5. Sonic Branding Across Sectors

Sector	Dominant asset	Principal constraint	Evidence
Quick service and packaged goods	Short sonic logo	Consistency across years	Graakjær (2019)
Financial services	Brand voice persona	Trust	Mas et al. (2021); Rawool et al. (2025)
Healthcare	Sonic logo for reassurance	Competence and empathy	Kemp et al. (2023)
Luxury and hospitality	Ambient theme (indicative)	Atmosphere and exclusivity	Garlin and Owen (2006); Khamis and Keogh (2021)
Automotive and telecommunications	Consequential and interface sound	In-car attention	Cherif and Lemoine (2019); Ringler et al. (2021)
Multi-platform advertising	Sonic logo in advertising	Emotional fit	Kemp et al. (2024); Silas et al. (2024)
Technology platforms	Short-video sonic strategy	Attention scarcity	Mandolfo et al. (2024); Yang et al. (2025)

Note. Source: Authors.

Multichannel Integration

Brands distribute sonic assets across broadcast, online video, podcasts, social platforms, voice assistants, and apps, and integrating them into one coherent identity is a central structural problem. Three challenges recur across channels. The first is acoustic format adaptation, since a logo built for full-bandwidth television must survive compressed mobile playback and assistant output without losing its distinctive features (Silas et al., 2024). The second is contextual congruence, since the soundscape suiting a luxury hotel will not suit a waiting room or stadium, so assets must keep their identity across settings (Ballouli & Heere, 2015; Kemp et al., 2023). The third is consistency, which strengthens identification through processing fluency, and music that fits the brand and message outperforms music that does not (Anglada-Tort et al., 2022; Knoeferle et al., 2012; Lavack et al., 2008). The hierarchy implies a sequencing logic in which the voice persona is integrated first for its design control, the sonic logo second for its portability, and the notification and ambient layers last as the most channel-fragile. Where journeys mix screen and voice, the sequencing adjusts rather than reverses. The persona still leads on owned surfaces, the sonic logo takes precedence wherever visual identity shares the load, and investment should be weighted toward the persona in proportion to the share of contact that is screenless.

TECHNOLOGY STACK FOR SONIC ASSET CREATION AND MEASUREMENT

The toolkit for making and measuring audio assets has expanded rapidly, and it comprises the four layers set out in Table 6. The base layer is music production and acoustic modeling, the established craft of composing and engineering brand sound. The second layer is voice synthesis and neural text-to-speech, which allows a brand voice to be specified parametrically, including vocal tract length, to tune product congruency (Efthymiou et al., 2024). The third layer is computational modeling, where machine learning analyzes and represents sonic assets, including unsupervised audio embeddings that surface emotional and semantic structure in branding music and large-scale analysis of how music shapes response to video advertising (Silas et al., 2024; Silas et al., 2026). The top layer is measurement, reaching from neuromarketing tools such as electroencephalography and implicit reaction time to the acoustic feature-extraction pipelines of voice analytics (Bosshard & Walla, 2023; Hildebrand et al., 2020). Generative production changes the economics of asset creation, because a brand can synthesize voices and music cheaply, which lowers the cost of creation and raises the risk of generic sameness (Efthymiou et al., 2024; Knödler & Rudeloff, 2024). Because the tools that make a distinctive voice affordable also lower the cost of undifferentiated output, measurement supplies the discipline that preserves distinctiveness in creation. The available tools have outpaced the supply of evidence-based design guidance, and this gap frames the research agenda below.

Two published cases illustrate these methods in application. Efthymiou et al. (2024) manipulate digital vocal tract length in synthesized speech, a parametric intervention in the acoustics of the voice itself, and demonstrate downstream effects on product congruency and advertising performance. Silas et al. (2026) apply unsupervised feature selection to branding music and recover emotional-semantic dimensions on which any brand's music can be positioned and compared computationally. Both cases illustrate a pattern common to modern audio systems, in which a model learns a representation of sound and then exposes controllable parameters to the designer.

The same measurement discipline can be implemented without a laboratory. Aided and unaided recognition of the sonic logo and the brand voice can be carried in standard brand-tracking waves, and distinctive-asset strength can be judged on the uniqueness and fame standard that already governs visual assets (Romaniuk & Sharp, 2004). Linkage between sonic assets and category entry points can be probed with cued-recall questions, and cross-channel consistency can be audited by cataloging every touchpoint at which each asset sounds.

Table 6. Technology Stack for Sonic Asset Creation and Measurement

Layer	Tool category	Application	Anchor evidence
1. Production and acoustic modeling	Composition and sound design	Asset creation	Spence and Keller (2024)
2. Voice synthesis and TTS	Parametric brand voice	Vocal-tract-length tuning	Efthymiou et al. (2024)
3. Computational modeling	Machine-learning analysis and representation	Emotional-semantic structure	Silas et al. (2024); Silas et al. (2026)
4. Measurement	EEG, implicit reaction time, voice analytics	Implicit response and feature extraction	Bosshard and Walla (2023); Hildebrand et al. (2020)

Note. Source: Authors.

STAKEHOLDERS AND ETHICAL CONSIDERATIONS

The turn to voice-first branding raises questions that extend beyond the brand and the consumer. Voice interfaces gather biometrically distinctive audio, and consent, retention, and reuse practices remain inconsistent across jurisdictions, making privacy a first-order design concern (Monteverde et al., 2025). Synthetic-voice technology can reproduce a brand voice without the original speaker, and the cues signaling authenticity can themselves be engineered, so a consumer may have no way to tell human contact from a synthesized brand voice (Efthymiou et al., 2024; Knödler & Rudeloff, 2024). Accessibility carries direct design consequences, because sonic assets can include or exclude audiences, and inclusive soundtrack design shapes how listeners with conditions such as tinnitus experience an advertisement (Palencia-Lefler, 2024). The regulatory framework is also changing, since distinctive sounds now count as protectable trademarks in the European Union and the United States, which sets up both an incentive to invest and a requirement to design for registrability (Zhang, 2021).

For the brand manager these questions carry a governance implication. The same prosodic engineering that builds a warm, trusted voice can also manufacture a false impression of human contact, which puts disclosure of synthetic voicing squarely inside responsible design (Knödler & Rudeloff, 2024). Qualitative evidence records consumer unease about over-humanized assistants, a sense of intrusion and a blurring of the line between tool and companion (Monteverde et al., 2025). A defensible program therefore treats privacy, disclosure, accessibility, and trademark protection as design constraints established at the outset rather than as compliance checks added afterward.

FUTURE RESEARCH DIRECTIONS

The framework generates empirical questions, which Table 7 organizes by theoretical lens, method, and priority. Six questions warrant particular attention. First, the strength of sonic distinctive assets under voice mediation is unestablished, since no study has compared recognition and memory for a sonic logo heard through an assistant against the same logo on broadcast media (Graakjær & Bonde, 2018; Spence & Keller, 2024). Second, the boundary conditions for AI brand voice remain underspecified, because the interactions among voice parameters, brand category, and consumer segment are unmapped (Efthymiou et al., 2024; Melzner & Raghubir, 2023). Third, crossmodal transfer in voice-first contexts is untested, so it is not known whether a strong sonic identity sharpens later visual and tactile judgments in an omnichannel journey (Spence & Keller, 2024). Fourth, the formation of category entry points through repeated voice interaction invites priming and implicit-association methods (Glim & Hillje, 2025). Fifth, the conditions under which an assistant's algorithmic default overrides learned brand recognition require direct study, since this interaction determines the value of sonic equity in voice commerce. Sixth, inclusive sonic design for visually impaired and neurodiverse audiences needs direct attention (Palencia-Lefler, 2024). In fully agentic commerce, an AI agent selects the brand and no human hears anything at the moment of choice, so sonic equity shapes the outcome only through preferences formed beforehand. The hierarchy therefore governs interactions a listener hears, and the transmission of sonic equity into agent-mediated choice remains open.

Table 7. Research-Agenda Matrix

Open question	Theoretical lens	Method	Priority
Asset strength under voice mediation	Distinctive assets	Recognition and memory experiment	High
AI brand-voice boundary conditions	Psychoacoustic	Factorial experiment	High
Crossmodal transfer in voice-first journeys	Crossmodal	Cross-modal priming	Medium
Category-entry-point formation via voice	Conditioning and memory	Priming, implicit association, neuroimaging	High
Default bias versus learned recognition	Distinctive assets	Choice experiment and field study	High
Inclusive sonic design	Accessibility	Mixed methods and field study	Medium

Note. Source: Authors.

Two methodological considerations apply across the agenda. The first consideration concerns measurement. Several of the questions turn on implicit and memory-based outcomes that self-report captures poorly, so progress will depend on pairing behavioral choice data with implicit measures and, where it is warranted, neural ones, in the way recent neuromarketing and voice-analytics work has begun to show (Bosshard & Walla, 2023; Hildebrand et al., 2020). The second consideration concerns stimulus control. Because the effects depend on fine acoustic detail, studies will need to share their audio materials so findings can be reproduced and parameters compared, something computational modeling now makes feasible (Silas et al., 2024; Silas et al., 2026).

CONCLUSION

Voice-first interfaces have compressed the brand's multimodal identity into a single sensory register, and this chapter has argued that the change obliges brand managers to treat audio assets as primary equity vehicles rather than decoration. The synthesis organized the parent literatures around mechanism, tracing how sound comes to carry brand meaning. The Sonic Distinctiveness Hierarchy turned that synthesis into a prioritization framework, ranking brand voice personas, sonic logos, notification architectures, and ambient audio by design control, distinctiveness-encoding capacity, and scalability. Four propositions stated its testable claims, and the agenda marked where evidence is missing. The practical implication is conditional on surface ownership. A brand that owns its interaction surfaces should invest in its voice persona first, its sonic logo second, its notification architecture third, and its ambient design last, because that order follows the three ranking dimensions under screenless interaction. A brand operating on third-party surfaces should begin at the sonic logo. The argument carries three limitations. The framework is conceptual and awaits direct tests, the ranking is calibrated to voice-first conditions and would shift wherever visual cues remain, and parts of the evidence base are recent and not yet replicated. Within these limits, sound has become the brand's perceptual surface rather than an accessory to it across a growing share of consumer contact. The discipline long reserved for visual identity must now extend to sound.

Disclosure

The authors declare the use of generative artificial intelligence in the research and writing process. Under full human supervision, the following tasks were delegated to generative AI tools: literature organization, language editing, proofreading and editing, and reformatting. The models used were Claude Opus 4.7 and 4.8. Responsibility for the final manuscript lies entirely with the authors. The generative AI tools are not listed as authors and do not bear responsibility for the final outcomes. The authors received no specific funding for this chapter and declare no conflicts of interest. Declaration submitted by the authors.

REFERENCES

Aaker, D. A. (1996). Measuring brand equity across products and markets. *California Management Review*, *38*(3), 102–120. DOI: 10.2307/41165845

Allan, D. (2008). A content analysis of music placement in prime-time television advertising. *Journal of Advertising Research*, *48*(3), 404–417. DOI: 10.2501/S0021849908080434

Anglada-Tort, M., Schofield, K., Trahan, T., & Müllensiefen, D. (2022). I've heard that brand before: The role of music recognition on consumer choice. *International Journal of Advertising*, *41*(8), 1567–1587. DOI: 10.1080/02650487.2022.2060568

Au, W. C. W., Chi, F., & Petrick, J. F. (2025). Masculine and feminine gender cues in destination promotion videos: The effect of voice pitch. *Journal of Travel Research*, 00472875251371054. Advance online publication. DOI: 10.1177/00472875251371054

Ballouli, K., & Heere, B. (2015). Sonic branding in sport: A model for communicating brand identity through musical fit. *Sport Management Review*, *18*(3), 321–330. DOI: 10.1016/j.smr.2014.03.001

Bosshard, S. S., & Walla, P. (2023). Sonic influence on initially neutral brands: Using EEG to unveil the secrets of audio evaluative conditioning. *Brain Sciences*, *13*(10), 1393. Advance online publication. DOI: 10.3390/brainsci13101393

Bruner, G. C.II. (1990). Music, mood, and marketing. *Journal of Marketing*, *54*(4), 94–104. DOI: 10.1177/002224299005400408

Cherif, E., & Lemoine, J.-F. (2019). Anthropomorphic virtual assistants and the reactions of Internet users: An experiment on the assistant's voice. [English Edition]. *Recherche et Applications en Marketing*, *34*(1), 28–47. DOI: 10.1177/2051570719829432

Efthymiou, F., Hildebrand, C., de Bellis, E., & Hampton, W. H. (2024). The power of AI-generated voices: How digital vocal tract length shapes product congruency and ad performance. *Journal of Interactive Marketing*, *59*(2), 117–134. DOI: 10.1177/10949968231194905

Garlin, F. V., & Owen, K. (2006). Setting the tone with the tune: A meta-analytic review of the effects of background music in retail settings. *Journal of Business Research*, *59*(6), 755–764. DOI: 10.1016/j.jbusres.2006.01.013

Garzonis, S., Jones, S., Jay, T., & O'Neill, E. (2009). Auditory icon and earcon mobile service notifications: Intuitiveness, learnability, memorability and preference. In *Proceedings of the SIGCHI Conference on Human Factors in Computing Systems* (pp. 1513–1522). Association for Computing Machinery. https://doi.org/ DOI: 10.1145/1518701.1518932

Glim, S., & Hillje, A. (2025). Neural processing of sound-symbolic associations in product branding. *Journal of Neuroscience, Psychology, and Economics, 18*(3), 113–125. DOI: 10.1037/npe0000204

Gorn, G. J. (1982). The effects of music in advertising on choice behavior: A classical conditioning approach. *Journal of Marketing, 46*(1), 94–101. DOI: 10.1177/002224298204600109

Graakjær, N. J. (2019). Sounding out 'I'm lovin' it': A multimodal discourse analysis of the sonic logo in commercials for McDonald's 2003–2018. *Critical Discourse Studies, 16*(5), 569–582. DOI: 10.1080/17405904.2019.1624184

Graakjær, N. J., & Bonde, A. (2018). Non-musical sound branding: A conceptualisation and research overview. *European Journal of Marketing, 52*(7/8), 1505–1525. DOI: 10.1108/EJM-09-2017-0609

Gustafsson, C. (2015). Sonic branding: A consumer-oriented literature review. *Journal of Brand Management, 22*(1), 20–37. DOI: 10.1057/bm.2015.5

Hagtvedt, H., & Brasel, S. A. (2016). Cross-modal communication: Sound frequency influences consumer responses to color lightness. *JMR, Journal of Marketing Research, 53*(4), 551–562. DOI: 10.1509/jmr.14.0414

Hahn, M., & Hwang, I. (1999). Effects of tempo and familiarity of background music on message processing in TV advertising: A resource-matching perspective. *Psychology and Marketing, 16*(8), 659–675. DOI: 10.1002/(SICI)1520-6793(199912)16:8<659::AID-MAR3>3.0.CO;2-S

Hildebrand, C., Efthymiou, F., Busquet, F., Hampton, W. H., Hoffman, D. L., & Novak, T. P. (2020). Voice analytics in business research: Conceptual foundations, acoustic feature extraction, and applications. *Journal of Business Research, 121*, 364–374. DOI: 10.1016/j.jbusres.2020.09.020

Keller, K. L. (1993). Conceptualizing, measuring, and managing customer-based brand equity. *Journal of Marketing, 57*(1), 1–22. DOI: 10.1177/002224299305700101

Kemp, E., Cho, Y.-N., Bui, M., & Kintzer, A. (2024). Music to the ears: The role of sonic branding in advertising. *International Journal of Advertising, 43*(6), 1039–1059. DOI: 10.1080/02650487.2023.2273645

Kemp, E., Kopp, S. W., & Bui, M. (2023). Healthcare brands sound off: Evaluating the influence of sonic branding in shaping consumer perceptions. *International Journal of Pharmaceutical and Healthcare Marketing, 17*(3), 340–352. DOI: 10.1108/IJPHM-10-2022-0093

Khamis, S., & Keogh, B. (2021). Sonic branding and the aesthetic infrastructure of everyday consumption. *Popular Music, 40*(2), 281–296. DOI: 10.1017/S0261143021000118

Klink, R. R. (2000). Creating brand names with meaning: The use of sound symbolism. *Marketing Letters, 11*(1), 5–20. DOI: 10.1023/A:1008184423824

Klink, R. R., & Wu, L. (2014). The role of position, type, and combination of sound symbolism imbeds in brand names. *Marketing Letters, 25*(1), 13–24. DOI: 10.1007/s11002-013-9236-3

Knödler, L., & Rudeloff, C. (2024). Look who's talking now: The effects of prerecorded and AI-generated synthetic brand voices on brand anthropomorphism and brand equity. *Journal of Creative Communications, 19*(3), 295–311. DOI: 10.1177/09732586241253651

Knoeferle, K. M., Knoeferle, P., Velasco, C., & Spence, C. (2016). Multisensory brand search: How the meaning of sounds guides consumers' visual attention. *Journal of Experimental Psychology. Applied, 22*(2), 196–210. DOI: 10.1037/xap0000084

Knoeferle, K. M., Spangenberg, E. R., Herrmann, A., & Landwehr, J. R. (2012). It is all in the mix: The interactive effect of music tempo and mode on in-store sales. *Marketing Letters, 23*(1), 325–337. DOI: 10.1007/s11002-011-9156-z

Krishnan, V., Kellaris, J. J., & Aurand, T. W. (2012). Sonic logos: Can sound influence willingness to pay? *Journal of Product and Brand Management, 21*(4), 275–284. DOI: 10.1108/10610421211246685

Lavack, A. M., Thakor, M. V., & Bottausci, I. (2008). Music-brand congruency in high- and low-cognition radio advertising. *International Journal of Advertising, 27*(4), 549–568. DOI: 10.2501/S0265048708080141

Mandolfo, M., Di Dalmazi, M., & Lamberti, L. (2024). Now you see me: Evaluating visual and auditory brand placement disclosures in music videos. *Journal of Marketing Communications, 30*(5), 553–575. DOI: 10.1080/13527266.2022.2152475

Manzoor, A. (2024). Impact of ambient music on consumer perceptions and impulse buying behavior with the moderating role of gender. *SAGE Open, 14*(2), 21582440241259001. Advance online publication. DOI: 10.1177/21582440241259001

Mas, L., Bolls, P., Rodero, E., Barreda-Ángeles, M., & Churchill, A. (2021). The impact of the sonic logo's acoustic features on orienting responses, emotions and brand personality transmission. *Journal of Product and Brand Management, 30*(5), 740–753. DOI: 10.1108/JPBM-05-2019-2370

McLean, G., & Osei-Frimpong, K. (2019). Hey Alexa … examine the variables influencing the use of artificial intelligent in-home voice assistants. *Computers in Human Behavior, 99*, 28–37. DOI: 10.1016/j.chb.2019.05.009

Melzner, J., & Raghubir, P. (2023). The sound of music: The effect of timbral sound quality in audio logos on brand personality perception. *JMR, Journal of Marketing Research, 60*(5), 932–949. DOI: 10.1177/00222437221135188

Monteverde, G., Cammarota, A., Serafini, L., & Quadri, M. (2025). Are we human or are we voice assistants? Revealing the interplay between anthropomorphism and consumer concerns. *Journal of Marketing Management, 41*(1–2), 200–235. DOI: 10.1080/0267257X.2025.2475231

Motoki, K., Iseki, S., & Pathak, A. (2025). Sounds cute: Exploring the role of sound reduplication in brand names. *International Journal of Research in Marketing, 42*(4), 1305–1322. DOI: 10.1016/j.ijresmar.2025.02.002

Nees, M. A., & Liebman, E. (2023). Auditory icons, earcons, spearcons, and speech: A systematic review and meta-analysis of brief audio alerts in human-machine interfaces. *Auditory Perception & Cognition, 6*(3–4), 300–329. DOI: 10.1080/25742442.2023.2219201

North, A. C., Hargreaves, D. J., & McKendrick, J. (1999). The influence of in-store music on wine selections. *The Journal of Applied Psychology, 84*(2), 271–276. DOI: 10.1037/0021-9010.84.2.271

Palencia-Lefler, M. (2024). Inclusive advertising through the soundtrack: Insights from people with tinnitus. *Journal of Marketing Communications, 30*(1), 102–122. DOI: 10.1080/13527266.2022.2103584

Park, C. W., & Young, S. M. (1986). Consumer response to television commercials: The impact of involvement and background music on brand attitude formation. *JMR, Journal of Marketing Research, 23*(1), 11–24. DOI: 10.1177/002224378602300102

Pathak, A., Calvert, G. A., & Lim, L. K. S. (2020). Harsh voices, sound branding: How voiced consonants in a brand's name can alter its perceived attributes. *Psychology and Marketing, 37*(6), 837–847. DOI: 10.1002/mar.21346

Puligadda, S., & VanBergen, N. (2023). The influence of sound logo instruments on brand personality perceptions: An investigation of brand ruggedness and sophistication. *Journal of Business Research, 156*, 113531. Advance online publication. DOI: 10.1016/j.jbusres.2022.113531

Rawool, V., Foroudi, P., & Palazzo, M. (2025). AI-powered voice assistants: Developing a framework for building consumer trust and fostering brand loyalty. *Electronic Commerce Research, 25*(6), 4471–4503. DOI: 10.1007/s10660-024-09850-5

Reinoso Carvalho, F., Wang, Q. J., van Ee, R., & Spence, C. (2016). Music influences hedonic and taste ratings in beer. *Frontiers in Psychology, 7*, 636. Advance online publication. DOI: 10.3389/fpsyg.2016.00636

Ringler, C., Sirianni, N. J., & Christenson, B. (2021). The power of consequential product sounds. *Journal of Retailing, 97*(2), 288–300. DOI: 10.1016/j.jretai.2020.09.002

Romaniuk, J., & Sharp, B. (2004). Conceptualizing and measuring brand salience. *Marketing Theory, 4*(4), 327–342. DOI: 10.1177/1470593104047643

Scott, S. P., Sheinin, D., & Labrecque, L. I. (2022). Small sounds, big impact: Sonic logos and their effect on consumer attitudes, emotions, brands and advertising placement. *Journal of Product and Brand Management, 31*(7), 1091–1103. DOI: 10.1108/JPBM-06-2021-3507

Silas, S., Baker, D., Sachet, A., & Müllensiefen, D. (2026). An unsupervised feature selection approach for finding diverse emotional-semantic representations in sonic branding music. *Journal of New Music Research, 54*(2–3), 107–124. DOI: 10.1080/09298215.2025.2607362

Silas, S., Baker, D. J., & Müllensiefen, D. (2024). Musical manipulation of visual scenes in video, film, and TV advertisements: A large-scale investigation into the implicit effects of sonic branding. *Journal of Advertising Research, 64*(2), 192–212. DOI: 10.2501/JAR-2024-013

Spence, C. (2012). Managing sensory expectations concerning products and brands: Capitalizing on the potential of sound and shape symbolism. *Journal of Consumer Psychology, 22*(1), 37–54. DOI: 10.1016/j.jcps.2011.09.004

Spence, C., Di Stefano, N., Reinoso-Carvalho, F., & Velasco, C. (2024). Marketing sonified fragrance: Designing soundscapes for scent. *IPerception, 15*(4), 20416695241259714. Advance online publication. DOI: 10.1177/20416695241259714

Spence, C., & Keller, S. (2024). Sonic branding: A narrative review at the intersection of art and science. *Psychology and Marketing, 41*(7), 1530–1548. DOI: 10.1002/mar.21995

Sun, W., Chang, E.-C., & Xu, Y. (2023). The effects of background music tempo on consumer variety-seeking behavior: The mediating role of arousal. *Frontiers in Psychology, 14*, 1236006. Advance online publication. DOI: 10.3389/fpsyg.2023.1236006

Sunaga, T. (2018). How the sound frequency of background music influences consumers' perceptions and decision making. *Psychology and Marketing, 35*(4), 253–267. DOI: 10.1002/mar.21084

Techawachirakul, M., Pathak, A., & Calvert, G. A. (2022). That sounds healthy! Audio and visual frequency differences in brand sound logos modify the perception of food healthfulness. *Food Quality and Preference, 99*, 104544. Advance online publication. DOI: 10.1016/j.foodqual.2022.104544

Vernuccio, M., Patrizi, M., Šerić, M., & Pastore, A. (2023). The perceptual antecedents of brand anthropomorphism in the name-brand voice assistant context. *Journal of Brand Management, 30*(4), 302–317. DOI: 10.1057/s41262-022-00305-6

Yalch, R. F. (1991). Memory in a jingle jungle: Music as a mnemonic device in communicating advertising slogans. *The Journal of Applied Psychology, 76*(2), 268–275. DOI: 10.1037/0021-9010.76.2.268

Yang, Q., Wang, Y., Song, M., Jiang, Y., & Li, Q. (2025). Sonic strategies: Unveiling the impact of sound features in short video ads on enterprise market entry performance. *Journal of Business-To-Business Marketing, 32*(1), 95–116. DOI: 10.1080/1051712X.2024.2396966

Yorkston, E., & Menon, G. (2004). A sound idea: Phonetic effects of brand names on consumer judgments. *The Journal of Consumer Research, 31*(1), 43–51. DOI: 10.1086/383422

Zajonc, R. B. (1968). Attitudinal effects of mere exposure. *Journal of Personality and Social Psychology, 9*(2, Pt. 2), 1–27. DOI: 10.1037/h0025848

Zhang, X. (2021). From audio branding to sound trademark: A comparative study in the EU and the US. *Beijing Law Review, 12*(2), 409–424. DOI: 10.4236/blr.2021.122023

ADDITIONAL READING

Aaker, D. A. (1991). *Managing brand equity: Capitalizing on the value of a brand name*. The Free Press.

Allan, D. (2022). *Super sonic logos: The power of audio branding*. Business Expert Press.

Jackson, D. M. (2003). *Sonic branding: An introduction*. Palgrave Macmillan., DOI: 10.1057/9780230503267

Romaniuk, J. (2018). *Building distinctive brand assets*. Oxford University Press.

Sharp, B. (2010). *How brands grow: What marketers don't know*. Oxford University Press.

KEY TERMS AND DEFINITIONS

Brand voice persona: The intentionally designed recorded or synthesized voice through which a brand communicates in voice-mediated interactions.

Crossmodal correspondence: A systematic perceptual mapping between attributes in different sensory modalities, such as the mapping between sound frequency and color lightness.

Distinctive brand asset: A non-product brand element, visual or auditory, that is consistently linked to the brand and able to trigger brand identification in buying situations (after Romaniuk & Sharp, 2004).

Earcon: A short, structured sound used to convey a specific functional event in a user interface.

Mental availability: The propensity of a brand to be brought to mind across the situations in which people buy (Romaniuk & Sharp, 2004).

Sonic branding: The strategic design, deployment, and management of auditory brand assets that build distinctiveness, semantic meaning, and consumer outcomes across every touchpoint at which the brand is heard.

Sonic Distinctiveness Hierarchy: The four-tier framework introduced in this chapter for prioritizing sonic-asset investment under voice-interface conditions.

Sonic logo: A brief, intentionally designed acoustic phrase that functions as the auditory equivalent of a visual logo.

Sound symbolism: A non-arbitrary mapping between phonemes and meaning that recurs across languages.

Chapter 9
Dual-Channel Brand Salience in AI-Curated Markets:
Bridging Cognitive Accessibility and Algorithmic Visibility

Jose M. Jomon
http://orcid.org/0009-0003-4341-9936
Sahrdaya Institute of Management Studies,Thrissur, India

Jyothis Rachel Mathews
http://orcid.org/0009-0003-8279-6080
Ahalia School of Management, Palakkad, Kerala, India

ABSTRACT

Accelerating adoption of artificial intelligence (AI) across commercial ecosystems is fundamentally reconfiguring how brands attain recognition and sustain competitive positioning within digitally mediated markets. This study introduces and theorizes dual-channel brand salience — a construct that captures the simultaneous pursuit of cognitive accessibility among consumers and algorithmic discoverability within machine-driven systems. Drawing on brand growth theory, mental availability research, autonomous decision-system models, and the Stimulus-Organism-Response (S-O-R) framework, the paper examines how conversational agents, recommendation architectures, predictive filtering, and autonomous purchasing technologies collectively reshape brand encounter and consumer selection behavior.

DOI: 10.4018/979-8-3373-9589-0.ch009

INTRODUCTION

Commercial ecosystems are being reshaped by the pervasive integration of artificial intelligence into nearly every stage of the consumer journey. Sophisticated recommender engines, voice-activated assistants, predictive behavioral analytics, and increasingly autonomous purchasing tools have jointly changed how consumers find, evaluate, and commit to brands. Rather than relying solely on direct marketing exposure, today's consumers increasingly encounter offerings that have already been ranked, filtered, and prioritized by algorithmic intermediaries, often without their explicit awareness (Huang & Rust, 2021). This move toward algorithmically mediated consumption is among the most consequential shifts in the history of brand management, and it calls for a matching evolution in theory and strategy.

The strategic importance of AI in marketing now reaches well past operational efficiency gains. Platforms such as Amazon, TikTok, Netflix, and voice-commerce ecosystems function as recommendation infrastructures that actively shape consumer consideration sets. Competitive advantage no longer flows only to brands that build strong psychological associations with consumers; it increasingly flows to brands that satisfy the evaluation logic of machine-learning systems acting as digital gatekeepers (Davenport et al., 2020; Kozinets, 2022). Appealing simultaneously to human cognition and algorithmic classification is an emergent, still under-theorized dimension of brand strategy.

Established branding frameworks offer useful but incomplete guidance here. The Ehrenberg-Bass tradition, which grounds brand growth in broad penetration and strong mental and physical availability, was developed for markets governed chiefly by human attention and mass-media reach (Sharp, 2010). Its conceptual core remains valuable, but it needs meaningful extension to address conditions in which algorithms partly decide which brands even reach consumer consideration (Hue & Hung, 2025; Deryl et al., 2023). Once recommendation systems curate what consumers see, availability itself changes character: a brand can be cognitively strong yet functionally invisible if its digital signals are not machine-readable.

This chapter proposes the construct of dual-channel brand salience to address that gap. It holds that durable brand visibility in AI-curated markets depends on the synchronized strengthening of two channels: a human cognitive channel built from memory structures, emotional associations, and recognition-based retrieval, and a machine algorithmic channel built from semantic metadata, recommendation compatibility, engagement-signal quality, and structured digital identity. Neither channel alone is sufficient; each reinforces the other through a continuous feedback loop.

Four questions organize the inquiry: (1) through what mechanisms do autonomous decision systems shape brand salience and consumer choice; (2) which organizational and content factors determine a brand's recognizability within algorithmic environments; (3) how can firms pursue emotional branding and algorithmic optimization together without sacrificing either; and (4) what are the longer-run consequences of AI-mediated branding for brand equity, market penetration, and consumer trust? Engaging these questions extends the scholarly conversation on AI-driven marketing while offering practical direction to brand managers operating in increasingly autonomous consumer ecosystems.

The remainder of the chapter is organized as follows. The next section traces branding's evolution from traditional paradigms to the current AI-mediated landscape. Subsequent sections lay out the theoretical foundations underlying the dual-channel construct; develop the dual-channel brand salience framework itself, including its antecedents, mediating constructs, moderators, and outcomes; examine how AI reshapes consumer decision-making across the purchase journey; consider the changing strategic role of distinctive brand assets in algorithmically governed settings; draw out managerial implications for AI-ready brand strategy; review industry cases and regional comparisons; set out a future research agenda; and conclude.

THE EVOLUTIONARY TRAJECTORY OF BRANDING IN INTELLIGENT DIGITAL ECOSYSTEMS

Branding has always evolved alongside the technological, economic, and communicative structures dominant in each era. In its earliest commercial form, branding functioned mainly as a product-identification device, distinguishing one manufacturer's goods from another's. As mass-media infrastructures matured across the twentieth century, firms used broadcast advertising, retail design, and public relations to build layered symbolic meaning around brands. This period saw brand equity emerge as a formal construct — a strategic intangible through which awareness, perceived quality, psychological association, and loyalty translated into measurable financial value (Aaker, 1991; Keller, 1993).

Emotional branding followed as firms recognized that functional claims alone could not sustain differentiation in saturated categories. Brands began engineering affective experiences, aspirational narratives, and identity resonance intended to embed themselves in consumers' self-concepts (Gobé, 2001). The rise of consumer-centric approaches further elevated personalization, co-creation, and relationship depth, aided by data-collection technologies that let firms tailor interactions at the individual level (Prahalad & Ramaswamy, 2004). Social media accelerated this shift by redistributing communicative power, letting consumers shape brand narratives through peer discussion and public advocacy.

The arrival of AI in marketing marks a qualitatively different break in this sequence. Earlier technologies mainly extended the reach or efficiency of communication aimed at human audiences; AI systems, by contrast, increasingly act as autonomous participants in consumer-brand encounters. Machine-learning systems ingest behavioral data — browsing sequences, transaction histories, dwell time, social signals — to build probabilistic consumer profiles and generate recommendations with notable predictive accuracy (Davenport et al., 2020; Hue & Hung, 2025). Brands must now earn recognition not only in consumer memory but within the classification logic of these systems.

Recommendation platforms sit at the center of this shift. Collaborative filtering, content-based models, and hybrid deep-learning architectures used by leading e-commerce and streaming platforms continuously recalibrate which offerings become visible to each individual consumer (Gentsch, 2019). Conversational systems such as Siri and Alexa add further complexity by narrowing recommendation scope: whereas visual interfaces typically present several alternatives at once, spoken interfaces usually return only one or two options, concentrating competitive stakes at the point of algorithmic selection (Huang & Rust, 2021).

Predictive personalization has reshaped brand exposure further still. Highly targeted communication can raise relevance and conversion, but it also produces filter-bubble effects that limit spontaneous brand discovery and favor brands that already have strong behavioral signal histories (Pariser, 2011). Autonomous shopping systems, including IoT-linked replenishment tools, push this logic to its endpoint by delegating routine purchasing to algorithms entirely. In such settings, the decisive competitive dimension is no longer human attention alone but algorithmic preference — the likelihood that a brand's digital profile satisfies the selection criteria built into autonomous systems.

This landscape calls for a reconceived branding practice, one that neither discards established cognitive and emotional principles nor treats them as adequate on their own. The task is to integrate human psychological foundations with the structural requirements of machine recognition, recognizing that brand visibility is now co-produced by consumer cognition and algorithmic mediation operating in recursive interdependence (Kozinets, 2022; Deryl et al., 2023).

As a conceptual book chapter, this study does not draw on primary empirical data; instead, it develops its framework through a structured synthesis of literature spanning branding, artificial intelligence, consumer behavior, digital marketing, recommendation systems, technology adoption, and strategic management. Relevant sources were identified through searches of major academic databases — Scopus, Web of Science, ScienceDirect, SpringerLink, Emerald Insight, Wiley Online Library, and Google Scholar — using keyword combinations such as AI branding, brand salience, mental availability, algorithmic recommendation systems, consumer decision-making, voice commerce, generative AI, algorithmic visibility, and AI-driven marketing. Priority was given to peer-reviewed articles, seminal texts, highly cited theoretical work, and recent publications capturing the rapid evolution of AI-enabled marketing.

Selection emphasized studies bearing on the chapter's core theoretical domains — Ehrenberg-Bass brand-growth theory, mental availability theory, the Stimulus–Organism–Response framework, technology acceptance and trust models, brand equity theory, and emerging work on AI-powered recommendation systems. These sources were compared to surface conceptual overlaps, theoretical gaps, and unresolved questions about brand visibility in AI-curated markets, and this synthesis informed the proposed Dual-Channel Brand Salience Framework and its six research propositions, offering a theoretically grounded basis for future empirical work and managerial application.

THEORETICAL FOUNDATIONS

Ehrenberg-Bass Brand Growth Theory

The Ehrenberg-Bass framework is a foundational reference point here, capturing the empirical regularities that govern brand growth in competitive markets. Its central claim — that penetration among light and occasional buyers drives category growth more than deepening loyalty within a narrow base — carries clear implications for AI-curated environments (Sharp, 2010). Penetration logic, applied algorithmically, implies that brands need broad algorithmic reach: they must be retrievable by recommendation systems serving diverse behavioral segments, not merely familiar to existing buyers. In digital contexts, physical availability translates into search discoverability, recommendation compatibility, and structured digital accessibility, extending the original construct into the algorithmic domain (Hue & Hung, 2025).

Mental Availability Theory

Mental availability, as developed within the Ehrenberg-Bass tradition and elaborated by Romaniuk and Sharp (2004), refers to the probability that a brand will be mentally retrieved during a purchase decision. That probability depends on the richness, breadth, and recency of the associative networks linking a brand to varied needs, occasions, and emotional states. In low-involvement or cognitively demanding settings, brands with stronger, more widely distributed memory structures enjoy a retrieval advantage. In AI-curated markets, the processes that build these memory structures are themselves partly mediated by recommendation exposure: algorithms that repeatedly surface a brand in relevant contexts deepen associative networks through incidental reinforcement (Broughton, 2026). Mental availability therefore remains essential, but should now be understood as a product of both deliberate communication and algorithmic exposure patterns.

Autonomous Decision Systems

Autonomous decision systems comprise the machine-learning models, algorithmic filters, and predictive engines that increasingly mediate consumer information environments (Russell & Norvig, 2021). Recommendation engines work through collaborative filtering — matching users by behavioral similarity — content-based filtering, and hybrid architectures blending several signal types. In doing so they act as algorithmic gatekeepers, determining which brands enter personalized consideration sets and exercising a market influence once reserved for institutional retailers or mass-media gatekeepers (Torthienchai & Chuaikaew, 2025). These systems also learn continuously from interaction data, so consumer engagement with recommended brands feeds back into and refines future recommendation logic.

Stimulus–Organism–Response Framework

The S-O-R model, originally developed to explain environmental influences on consumer behavior (Mehrabian & Russell, 1974), offers a useful structure for mapping AI-mediated brand encounters. Algorithmic recommendations, personalized ads, and voice-assistant outputs form the stimulus layer that structures the information environment consumers inhabit. These stimuli activate internal cognitive and affective states — attention, familiarity, trust, evaluative affect — that constitute the organism layer, which in turn produces behavioral responses such as continued search, brand engagement, purchase intention, and repeat acquisition. This lens helps explain how algorithmic stimuli can generate meaningful consumer responses even when consumers are only partly aware of the recommendation mechanisms shaping their experience (Liang, 2026).

Technology Acceptance and Trust Perspectives

Consumers' willingness to rely on AI-generated recommendations is heavily shaped by perceived usefulness, ease of use, and trustworthiness (Davis, 1989). Trust in algorithmic recommendations operates across several dimensions: belief in their accuracy, confidence in data-privacy practices, perceptions of fairness, and transparency about the basis for personalization (Pasquale, 2015; Liang, 2026). Where recommendation systems are seen as opaque or potentially manipulative, skepticism toward algorithmically surfaced brands can emerge and reverse visibility advantages.

Ethical AI governance and explainable recommendation mechanisms are thus strategic brand-building variables, not merely compliance concerns (Pasquale, 2015).

Brand Equity Theory

Brand equity theory illuminates the asset value embedded in consumer associations, perceived quality, and loyalty (Aaker, 1991; Keller, 1993). In AI-curated markets, equity operates at two levels at once. At the consumer level, strong equity produces the cognitive accessibility and preference that let brands be actively sought rather than merely recommended. At the algorithmic level, high-equity brands tend to generate the engagement signals — click-through rates, completed purchases, repeat visits, review volume — that recommendation systems read as relevance indicators, producing a self-reinforcing visibility dynamic. Brand equity cannot, however, substitute for machine-readable brand infrastructure: firms that neglect structured digital identity may see their cognitive advantages undercut by weak algorithmic discoverability (Deryl et al., 2023).

CONCEPTUALIZING DUAL-CHANNEL BRAND SALIENCE

Core Construct Definition

This chapter defines dual-channel brand salience as a brand's integrated capacity to achieve simultaneous visibility and accessibility within both human cognitive systems and machine-driven recommendation architectures in AI-curated marketplaces. The human cognitive channel covers the psychological infrastructure of recall — associative memory networks, emotional valence, distinctive-asset recognition, and situational retrieval cues. The machine algorithmic channel covers the digital infrastructure of discoverability — semantic metadata coherence, recommendation-system compatibility, search visibility, engagement-signal quality, and voice-interface responsiveness. Neither dimension alone sustains competitiveness in today's environment; their synchronized strength produces disproportionately greater market impact than either does independently (Broughton, 2026; Hue & Hung, 2025).

Comparison With Existing AI Branding Frameworks

Existing literature on AI-driven branding recognizes artificial intelligence as a transformative force for personalizing customer experience, deepening engagement, and improving marketing effectiveness (Davenport et al., 2020; Huang & Rust, 2021). Among the most comprehensive contributions, Deryl et al. (2023) propose an integrated framework explaining AI-driven branding through the interaction of technological capability, consumer-brand relationships, and organizational value creation. Their model positions AI persuasively as a strategic enabler of branding, but it focuses more on how AI supports branding activity than on how AI systems themselves shape brand visibility and consumer choice.

The Dual-Channel Brand Salience Framework extends this literature by arguing that competitiveness in AI-curated markets depends on optimizing two complementary but distinct dimensions at once. The first, human mental salience, draws on established branding constructs – memory structures, emotional association, brand recall (Romaniuk & Sharp, 2004; Sharp, 2010). The second, machine algorithmic salience, captures a brand's visibility within AI-powered recommendation systems through metadata quality, semantic optimization, engagement signals, search visibility, and recommendation compatibility. Where earlier AI-branding frameworks tend to treat AI primarily as a branding tool, this chapter treats it also as an algorithmic market gatekeeper that actively determines whether brands become visible during digitally mediated decision-making (Kozinets, 2022; Deryl et al., 2023).

A further distinction concerns causal structure. Existing frameworks identify important antecedents and consequences of AI adoption but say less about the mechanisms through which algorithmic visibility translates into consumer behavior and long-run brand performance. This chapter addresses that gap with a four-layer architecture – antecedents, mediating constructs, moderating variables, behavioral outcomes – plus a dynamic feedback loop explaining the reciprocal relationship between consumer engagement and algorithmic learning, extending traditional brand salience theory into intelligent digital environments.

The chapter also advances six empirically testable propositions specifying expected relationships among human-centric branding activity, AI-centric optimization, dual-channel salience, consumer trust, purchase intention, and long-term brand equity, giving researchers a measurable model that can be operationalized through survey research, digital analytics, experiments, and structural equation modeling. Key comparative features of existing AI branding frameworks and the proposed Dual-Channel Brand Salience Framework are set out in Table 1.

Table 1. Comparison of Existing AI Branding Frameworks and the Proposed Dual-Channel Brand Salience Framework

Dimension	Existing AI Branding Framework (Deryl et al., 2023)	Dual-Channel Brand Salience Framework (Present Chapter)
Primary focus	AI-enabled branding and digital transformation	Simultaneous optimization of human cognitive salience and machine algorithmic salience
Conceptual perspective	AI as a branding capability	AI as both a branding capability and an algorithmic market gatekeeper
Core construct	General AI-driven branding	Dual-Channel Brand Salience (new conceptual construct)
Consumer perspective	Customer engagement and personalization	Human memory, emotional recall, and AI-mediated discoverability
Algorithmic perspective	General AI integration	Recommendation systems, metadata optimization, search visibility, conversational AI, algorithmic recognition
Framework architecture	Broad conceptual relationships	Four-layer framework with antecedents, mediators, moderators, outcomes, and feedback loop
Measurement orientation	Limited operational guidance	Clearly measurable human and machine salience constructs
Research propositions	No formal propositions	Six theoretically derived propositions for empirical testing
Primary theoretical contribution	Explains AI's role in branding	Integrates branding theory with algorithmic visibility and consumer cognition
Managerial implication	AI adoption for branding effectiveness	Development of AI-ready brand architectures balancing emotional branding and algorithmic optimization

Source: Developed by the authors.

The proposed framework complements rather than replaces existing AI-branding theory. Where prior work establishes AI's strategic importance for branding, this chapter offers a lens for explaining how brands compete in AI-mediated markets where visibility depends jointly on consumer cognition and algorithmic evaluation, extending branding theory and providing a firmer foundation for empirical research and managerial decision-making in AI-curated marketplaces.

Human Mental Salience Mechanisms

Within the human cognitive channel, emotional branding is a primary driver of salience. Brands that build narrative depth, experiential richness, and symbolic resonance create memory structures with broader associative reach, linking themselves to a wider range of consumer occasions, aspirations, and identity dimensions – which raises retrieval probability across more purchasing contexts. Distinctive brand assets, such as logos, color systems, sonic identities, and packaging design, act as perceptual anchors that speed recognition and reduce cognitive effort at the point of decision. In high-noise digital environments marked by rapid content flow and short attention spans, assets that trigger instant recognition confer a real competitive advantage (Sharp, 2010; Roach, 2025).

Familiarity, built through repeated encounters across touchpoints, further strengthens associative networks and lowers the perceived uncertainty of brand choice. This mechanism matters particularly in AI-curated settings because recommendation exposure itself generates the incidental repetition that reinforces memory. The two salience channels are therefore interdependent: algorithmic visibility produces the repeated encounters that deepen human memory structures, while strong memory structures generate the engagement behavior that signals brand relevance back to algorithmic systems.

Machine Algorithmic Salience Mechanisms

Within the machine algorithmic channel, metadata architecture forms the foundational infrastructure of discoverability. Structured product descriptions, semantic keyword integration, schema markup, and taxonomic consistency together determine how effectively search and recommendation algorithms categorize and surface brand-related content. Brands with coherent, richly structured digital identities across platforms achieve higher algorithmic legibility, reducing the uncertainty with which AI systems assign relevance scores (Hue & Hung, 2025).

AI-readable brand assets extend this logic to visual and audio domains. Machine-vision systems analyze brand visual material to support classification and contextual placement, so brands that design for structural clarity, cross-platform consistency, and machine-interpretable convention improve how accurately algorithms identify and prioritize them. In voice commerce, where systems process spoken queries through natural-language understanding, phonetic clarity, semantic associativity, and conversational keyword compatibility determine whether a brand appears within the narrow output typical of voice-assistant interactions (Huang & Rust, 2021).

Engagement-signal quality is a third algorithmic salience mechanism. Recommendation systems treat click-through rates, session depth, purchase completion, review engagement, and repeat visits as implicit relevance signals that feed future recommendation logic. Brands generating high-quality engagement signals accumulate a form of algorithmic capital – a self-reinforcing positioning advantage. Strategically, cultivating genuine engagement pays twice: it deepens human salience through experiential reinforcement and improves machine salience through behavioral signal generation.

Integrated Framework Architecture

Figure 1 depicts the Dual-Channel Brand Salience Framework as a dynamic system of four structural layers. The antecedent layer splits into human-centric drivers – emotional branding investment, distinctive-asset development, advertising breadth, experiential touchpoint design, and familiarity cultivation – and AI-centric drivers – metadata optimization, recommendation-system compatibility, search-visibility management, engagement-signal strategy, and structured digital-identity maintenance. These feed the mediating construct of dual-channel brand salience, comprising human mental salience (operationalized as top-of-mind awareness, emotional recall intensity, and cross-situational recognition) and machine algorithmic salience (operationalized as recommendation frequency, search-ranking prominence, and voice-interface prioritization).

Figure 1. Dual-Channel Brand Salience Framework

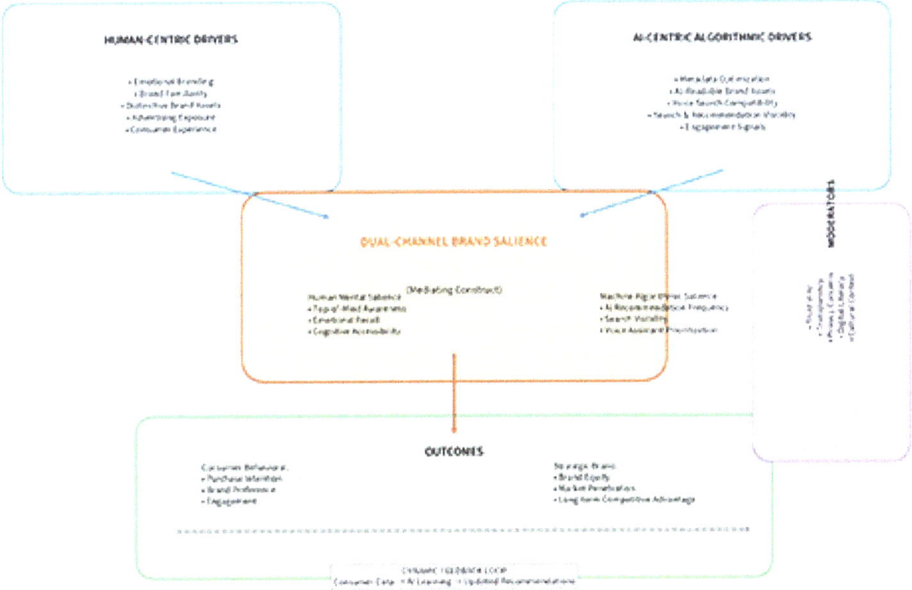

Source: Developed by the authors.

Moderating variables include consumer trust in algorithmic systems, perceived transparency of recommendation mechanisms, digital literacy, cultural orientation toward technology adoption, and market-level AI diffusion. These moderators condition how both salience dimensions convert into the framework's output layer: behavioral outcomes such as purchase intention, preference formation, engagement depth, and repeat acquisition, and strategic outcomes such as brand equity appreciation, market-penetration growth, and sustained competitive positioning within AI-governed categories.

The framework also incorporates a dynamic feedback loop linking consumer interaction data, algorithmic learning and refinement, evolving recommendation structures, and resulting exposure patterns – reflecting the recursive, co-evolutionary nature of human-algorithmic brand encounters: consumer behavior shapes algorithm behavior, which reshapes exposure, which shapes consumer behavior again. Brand managers must accordingly monitor and respond to algorithmic signal quality continuously rather than treat digital infrastructure as a one-time deployment.

Research Propositions and Directions for Empirical Validation

The proposed framework provides a conceptual foundation for future empirical work by integrating traditional branding theory with AI-driven marketing. The six propositions below identify expected relationships among its constructs and suggest possible validation approaches.

Proposition 1 (P1): Human-centric branding activities positively influence human mental salience. Sustained investment in emotional branding, distinctive brand assets, and integrated marketing communication strengthens memory structures and raises brand recall and recognition (Keller, 1993; Sharp, 2010). Human mental salience could be measured via top-of-mind awareness, unaided recall, and recognition scales, with structural equation modeling (SEM) as a suitable analytical approach.

Proposition 2 (P2): AI-centric brand optimization positively influences machine algorithmic salience. Firms that build structured metadata, semantic content, and AI-readable digital assets are expected to gain visibility within recommendation systems, search engines, and conversational AI platforms (Huang & Rust, 2021; Kozinets, 2022). This could be measured via search visibility, recommendation frequency, and voice-search inclusion, validated through SEM or regression analysis.

Proposition 3 (P3): The joint presence of high human mental salience and high machine algorithmic salience positively influences purchase intention. Brands that are both cognitively accessible and algorithmically recommended are more likely to enter consumers' consideration sets, raising purchase likelihood (Romaniuk & Sharp, 2004). Purchase intention could be captured with established behavioral-intention scales, with interaction effects examined through moderated SEM.

Proposition 4 (P4): Machine algorithmic salience mediates the relationship between digital brand optimization and market visibility. Digital optimization improves AI readiness, but its market impact depends on how effectively AI systems recognize and recommend the brand (Deryl et al., 2023). This mediation could be tested using metadata quality, recommendation frequency, and digital-visibility indicators via SEM with bootstrapping.

Proposition 5 (P5): Consumer trust in AI recommendation systems positively moderates the relationship between machine algorithmic salience and consumer behavioral outcomes. Consumers with higher trust in AI recommendations are more likely to accept algorithmically suggested brands, strengthening the effect of machine salience on purchase intention and engagement (Gefen et al., 2003; Liang, 2026). Moderated regression or PROCESS analysis could validate this relationship.

Proposition 6 (P6): Dual-channel brand salience positively contributes to long-term brand equity through continuous consumer engagement and algorithmic reinforcement. Repeated interactions generate behavioral signals that improve future recommendations while also strengthening brand awareness, loyalty, and perceived quality (Aaker, 1991; Keller, 1993). Longitudinal studies could examine this using brand equity measures and customer lifetime value, with longitudinal SEM as a suitable technique.

Together, these propositions render the framework empirically testable by naming measurable constructs, expected relationships, and appropriate analytical methods, offering a practical agenda for research on branding effectiveness in AI-curated markets.

AI-CURATED CONSUMER BEHAVIOR AND BRAND DECISION-MAKING

Artificial intelligence has reconstituted the consumer journey, turning the discovery and evaluation stages from largely consumer-directed activity into hybrid processes co-shaped by algorithmic curation. Traditional journey models – linear sequences running from awareness through consideration, purchase, and post-purchase evaluation – assumed consumers actively navigated choice environments using self-gathered information (Lemon & Verhoef, 2016). Contemporary AI-mediated environments invert much of that agency: rather than consumers seeking brands out, algorithmic systems increasingly position brands in front of consumers based on predicted preference profiles drawn from behavioral history (Deryl et al., 2023; Yin et al., 2025).

Recommendation systems are the most pervasive mechanism behind this shift. Collaborative filtering identifies behavioral similarities across users, while content-based models match product attributes to individual taste profiles; hybrid architectures augmented with deep learning achieve a precision that consumers often experience as uncannily relevant (Ricci et al., 2015; Torthienchai & Chuaikaew, 2025). For brands, algorithmic placement functions as a form of mediated shelf positioning: top recommendation slots bring exposure advantages structurally similar to prime physical retail placement, but awarded on the basis of behavioral data rather than commercial negotiation.

Voice commerce concentrates competitive dynamics further, into a single recommendation output. Where visual interfaces present several brands for simultaneous evaluation, conversational systems typically voice just one or two recommendations per query, sharply compressing competitive space (Kumar et al., 2019). A consumer asking a voice assistant to reorder a household item effectively hands brand selection to the algorithm – a setting in which simply being included in the recommendation set matters more than relative ranking within it. Brands with phonetically accessible names and robust natural-language representation in their metadata are disproportionately likely to occupy this narrow space (Huang & Rust, 2021; Kumar et al., 2019).

The interplay between algorithmic recommendation and emotional consumer choice creates a real tension in AI-curated markets. Emotionally differentiated brands retain meaningful influence, particularly in categories carrying symbolic, hedonic, or identity-expressive weight; consumers buying luxury goods, fashion, or experiential services are less likely to delegate selection to algorithms than those buying commodities (Gobé, 2001; Hue & Hung, 2025). Even in emotionally engaged categories, however, algorithms still shape which brands are encountered and evaluated, so emotional differentiation is necessary but not sufficient for sustained visibility. Firms that invest only in emotional positioning while ignoring algorithmic infrastructure risk becoming invisible within algorithmically mediated discovery.

Filter bubbles are a structurally significant pathology of recommendation-dominated environments. When algorithms optimize for predicted preference alignment based on prior behavior, they inherently limit exposure to novel brands or categories outside a consumer's established behavioral signature (Pariser, 2011). This reinforces incumbent brands with rich signal histories in a self-perpetuating cycle, while creating a real entry barrier for challengers and new entrants navigating behavioral path dependence. Future brand strategy must confront this asymmetry, potentially through broad advertising investment aimed at building the initial behavioral signal mass needed to activate recommendation-system consideration (Pariser, 2011; Hue & Hung, 2025).

Consumer trust is the psychological infrastructure on which AI-mediated brand encounters depend. When recommendation systems are seen as accurate, fair, and respectful of personal data, consumers apply less cognitive effort in evaluating algorithmically surfaced alternatives, effectively extending implicit endorsement to recommended brands and lowering purchase resistance (Gefen et al., 2003; Liang, 2026). Where algorithmic opacity breeds uncertainty about recommendation motives, or where privacy concerns trigger defensive processing, consumers may actively discount or resist algorithmic guidance. Trust is thus a systemic condition governing the effectiveness of machine salience as a brand-building mechanism, not merely a satisfaction metric.

Autonomous purchasing delegation deserves particular attention as AI capability advances. Replenishment automation, subscription-based algorithmic purchasing, and IoT-triggered procurement sit at the far end of a continuum of consumer-AI agency transfer, where routine brand selection migrates from deliberate choice to embedded algorithmic preference. Within such systems, brand selection is effectively locked in at the point of configuration, giving outsized strategic weight to whichever brand first enters the automated purchase loop. Both cognitive and algorithmic first-mover advantages are amplified in autonomous purchasing contexts because switching costs there are structural, not merely psychological (Hue & Hung, 2025) – meaning early placement within AI adoption cohorts may generate compounding loyalty effects as repeated behavioral reinforcement entrenches the initial choice.

Generational and demographic variation in AI-mediated decision delegation adds further complexity. Digital-native cohorts with extensive platform experience tend to show greater comfort with algorithmic recommendation, higher trust in personalization systems, and a more sophisticated grasp of recommendation mechanics; some actively configure AI systems to reflect their brand preferences, generating intentional algorithmic salience for trusted brands. Older cohorts, by contrast, may retain a stronger preference for human-directed discovery, leaning more on established mental availability than on algorithmic surfacing. Brand strategy in AI-curated markets must therefore segment not only by product preference but by algorithmic engagement orientation – how actively or passively different populations engage with recommendation architectures (Hue & Hung, 2025).

AI Answer Engines and Conversational Brand Discovery

Generative AI answer engines – ChatGPT, Perplexity AI, Google AI Overviews, Claude, and Microsoft Copilot among them – are fundamentally changing how consumers discover brands and products. Unlike traditional search engines, which return ranked lists of webpages, these platforms generate synthesized answers by retrieving, evaluating, and integrating information across multiple authoritative sources. Brand visibility increasingly depends not just on search engine optimization (SEO) but on Answer Engine Optimization (AEO) – making brand information understandable, trustworthy, and retrievable by large language models (Huang & Rust, 2021; OpenAI, 2025).

This represents a further evolution from traditional SEO through AI-powered recommendation systems to generative answer engines, where discovery is influenced by source credibility, structured content, semantic metadata, schema markup, and knowledge-graph integration. Brands with consistent digital identities, high-quality citations, and authoritative content are more likely to be referenced by AI systems, strengthening both machine algorithmic salience and consumer trust (Kozinets, 2022; Deryl et al., 2023). Firms therefore need to extend conventional digital marketing to include AEO practices that improve AI interpretability and conversational discoverability, sustaining visibility across increasingly AI-mediated consumer journeys.

DISTINCTIVE BRAND ASSETS IN AI-GOVERNED ENVIRONMENTS

Evolving Strategic Role of Brand Assets

Distinctive brand assets have long served as perceptual shortcuts that enable rapid identification under cognitive load and competitive clutter. Logos, color systems, typography, sonic signatures, packaging, and brand characters consolidate associative networks by providing consistent sensory anchors that trigger recognition across contexts (Sharp, 2010). In AI-curated environments these assets take on a second function: they act as machine-interpretable signals feeding visual recognition systems, natural-language understanding architectures, and cross-platform classification engines. Designing assets that serve cognitive and algorithmic functions simultaneously calls for a broader conception of brand-asset strategy than firms have traditionally applied (Roach, 2025; Hue & Hung, 2025).

Visual and Audio Assets in Algorithmic Contexts

Machine-vision systems embedded in search engines, recommendation platforms, and social media algorithms analyze visual content using pattern-recognition methods that differ meaningfully from human perception. While people respond to aesthetic originality, emotional tone, and cultural symbolism, algorithmic vision prioritizes structural consistency, categorical legibility, and cross-instance recognition accuracy. Brands whose visual identities are overly complex, irregular, or inconsistent across platforms may see reduced algorithmic recognition despite strong human appeal (Chiriatti et al., 2026), which implies a design discipline balancing creative distinctiveness — essential for human salience — with the structural standardization that supports machine interpretability.

Audio brand assets have grown in strategic importance alongside voice-interface adoption. Sonic logos, brand voice signatures, and jingles now operate within natural-language processing environments where phonetic distinctiveness and semantic associativity determine whether brands are accurately retrieved by voice recognition. The rise of smart speakers and voice-activated commerce has raised the strategic stakes of brand naming: names that are phonetically unambiguous, lexically unique, and categorically evocative perform more reliably in voice-search architectures than names optimized purely for visual or print use (Huang & Rust, 2021; Kumar et al., 2019).

Metadata and Structured Digital Identity

Metadata architecture is, in effect, the invisible brand infrastructure of the algorithmic era. Structured product information — semantic keyword schemas, descriptive taxonomies, schema.org markup, and platform-specific attribute completeness — determines how effectively search and recommendation systems categorize, contextualize, and surface brands within personalized environments. Firms that invest systematically in structured digital identity achieve higher algorithmic legibility: their representations are interpreted more accurately, matched more precisely to consumer behavioral profiles, and recommended more reliably across contexts (Deryl et al., 2023; Hue & Hung, 2025).

Managing metadata well requires continuous refinement, not a one-time deployment, as recommendation systems adopt new signal types and update their learning architectures. Brand managers need ongoing monitoring capability that tracks algorithmic performance indicators — recommendation frequency, search-ranking trajectories, click-through conversion — and iteratively adjusts digital identity structures in response.

Cross-platform digital identity coherence is a further metadata-governance priority many organizations underestimate. Inconsistencies in product naming, category assignment, attribute completeness, or descriptive language across platforms create ambiguity that algorithms resolve by lowering confidence in brand classification, which can depress recommendation priority. Firms operating across multiple e-commerce platforms, social ecosystems, and voice interfaces need centralized brand-data governance responsible for semantic coherence across their digital brand footprint — a function analogous to traditional brand-standards management, but applied to machine-readable data rather than visual style guides (Deryl et al., 2023).

Generative AI: Opportunity and Brand Integrity Risk

Generative AI presents both real creative opportunity and real risk to brand distinctiveness. Large language models, diffusion-based image generators, and synthetic voice systems let firms scale content production dramatically — personalizing outputs, accelerating campaign cycles, and sustaining cross-channel communication volume at efficiency levels previously out of reach, which is particularly valuable for maintaining the consistent engagement-signal generation that recommendation ecosystems reward.

The countervailing risk is that generative systems trained on population-scale data tend to produce outputs reflecting statistical norms — the aesthetic and linguistic conventions most common in their training data. Heavy reliance on AI-generated brand content can therefore erode creative distinctiveness as firms converge on algorithmically typical outputs, producing brand homogenization that undermines the differentiation both salience channels depend on (Chiriatti et al., 2026). Strategic discipline requires keeping human creative direction over brand voice, visual identity, and narrative architecture while deploying generative tools for content scaling and personalization execution.

Synthetic media, including deepfake video and audio, poses an acute threat to brand integrity in AI-curated environments. Widely accessible fabrication tools make it possible to produce and distribute counterfeit brand representations, fabricated executive communications, and deceptive endorsements at scale (Chesney & Citron, 2019). Organizations face growing reputational exposure from synthetic impersonation and need proactive protection — AI-powered content monitoring, digital watermarking, and authenticated communication channels. Governing brand authenticity in synthetic-media environments is an emerging dimension of brand management that existing frameworks address only inadequately.

STRATEGIC IMPLICATIONS FOR BRAND MANAGEMENT IN AI-CURATED MARKETS

Building AI-Ready Brand Architectures

AI-readiness requires firms to extend traditional brand management into algorithmic infrastructure development. AI-ready brands maintain coherent digital identity systems that work across the full range of algorithmic environments they inhabit — consistent semantic representation on e-commerce platforms, conversational compatibility within voice assistants, visual legibility for machine-vision systems, and engagement-signal quality across social recommendation architectures (Deryl et al., 2023; Kozinets, 2022). Achieving this coherence requires cross-functional collaboration among brand strategists, data scientists, digital platform specialists, and AI governance professionals — an integration many firms have not yet institutionalized.

Natural-language and conversational optimization are increasingly central to AI-ready brand strategy. As consumer interaction migrates toward voice- and chat-mediated interfaces, brand communication needs a linguistic architecture designed with natural-language-processing constraints in mind. Product descriptions, FAQ structures, and narrative elements that anticipate conversational query patterns improve accurate retrieval and prioritized recommendation in voice-commerce environments — though this optimization must be balanced against the risk of content that is algorithmically legible but humanly sterile, undermining the emotional resonance human salience depends on (Huang & Rust, 2021).

Balancing Market Reach and Personalization Depth

A structural tension in AI-curated marketing concerns how firms allocate resources between broad market reach and deep personalization. The Ehrenberg-Bass tradition holds that sustainable brand growth depends on light-buyer acquisition through wide penetration — a logic favoring investment in broad visibility and category mental availability (Sharp, 2010). Algorithmic personalization, however, tends to optimize for behavioral relevance within narrow segments, concentrating exposure among audiences with established preference signals. Over-personalization risks creating brand bubbles in which existing consumers receive increasingly reinforced recommendations while potential new buyers go unexposed.

Resolving this tension requires portfolio thinking about communication objectives. Broad-reach investments — emotionally resonant advertising, culturally prominent sponsorships, mass-media brand building — generate the awareness and behavioral signal mass that support algorithmic consideration across diverse segments, while personalized engagement investment optimizes within-segment conversion and deepens relationships with active consumers. Effective strategy in AI-curated markets maintains both streams, since broad reach creates the population of potential algorithmic encounters while personalization depth converts those encounters into engagement, and engagement into algorithmic signal quality (Hue & Hung, 2025).

Ethical AI Branding and Governance

The ethical dimensions of AI-driven branding have moved from peripheral concern to strategic priority as consumers, regulators, and civil society scrutinize algorithmic marketing more closely. Privacy governance is the foundational requirement: firms collecting, storing, and deploying consumer behavioral data must do so within frameworks of informed consent, data minimization, and purpose limitation, not only to satisfy regulation but to sustain the trust that recommendation effectiveness depends on (Liang, 2026). Regulatory regimes including the GDPR and emerging AI governance instruments impose enforceable constraints on data-intensive branding, with compliance failures carrying financial and reputational cost.

Algorithmic transparency is a growing dimension of ethical AI branding. Consumers facing AI-generated recommendations often report uncertainty about the basis for personalization, uncertainty that can trigger skepticism and erode trust (Pasquale, 2015). Firms that build explainable recommendation interfaces — communicating in accessible terms why particular products are surfaced — may turn transparency into a trust-building mechanism that boosts brand credibility alongside algorithmic effectiveness, making it a differentiation strategy as much as a compliance stance: brands associated with ethical data stewardship may gain a preference advantage among privacy-aware segments.

Algorithmic bias is a further governance concern. Recommendation systems trained on historical behavioral data can encode and perpetuate demographic disparities in brand exposure, systematically steering categories toward or away from populations along lines of gender, geography, socioeconomic status, or cultural identity. Firms bear responsibility for auditing their recommendation systems for discriminatory outcomes and implementing proportionate bias-correction mechanisms; failing to address algorithmic bias exposes them to regulatory liability and to reputational consequences that digital media can amplify quickly (Dwivedi et al., 2023).

Evolving Brand Performance Measurement

Conventional brand measurement captures consumer-side brand health through aided and unaided awareness, attribute associations, net promoter scores, and purchase-incidence tracking. These instruments remain relevant for human mental salience, but they do not directly assess machine algorithmic salience — the dimension increasingly co-determining market access in AI-curated environments. Firms need expanded measurement architectures that add algorithmic performance indicators to traditional brand-health metrics (Kozinets, 2022).

Candidate algorithmic visibility metrics include recommendation frequency within relevant categories, search-rank position across target queries, voice-search response inclusion, recommendation click-through conversion, and engagement-signal quality indices. Integrating these into unified brand dashboards lets firms monitor dual-channel salience — spotting configurations where human mental salience is strong but machine algorithmic salience is deteriorating, or the reverse, and allocating corrective investment accordingly. Developing standardized algorithmic brand-visibility measurement frameworks is an important priority for both applied research and industry practice. Proposed metrics for measuring dual-channel brand salience are set out in Table 2.

Beyond measurement, forward-looking brand managers need organizational learning capability oriented toward algorithmic environment intelligence: tracking platform recommendation policy changes, algorithm update announcements, and emerging signal categories to enable proactive strategy adjustment before visibility losses occur. Firms with dedicated platform-intelligence functions — applying to algorithmic landscape evolution the same rigor typically reserved for competitive brand monitoring — should sustain algorithmic salience advantages through transitions that reactive firms navigate only after losses appear. Marketing intelligence functions must therefore expand beyond competitor and consumer monitoring to cover the algorithmic environments in which consumer-brand encounters now predominantly occur (Kozinets, 2022).

Table 2. Proposed Metrics for Measuring Dual-Channel Brand Salience

Metric	**Human Channel**	**Machine Channel**	**Primary Data Source**
Top-of-mind Brand Recall	Yes	–	Consumer Survey
Brand Awareness	Yes	–	Consumer Survey
Recommendation Frequency	–	Yes	E-commerce/Platform Analytics
Search Visibility	–	Yes	SEO & AEO Analytics (e.g., SEMrush, Google Search Console)
Voice Search Inclusion	–	Yes	Voice Assistant Testing (e.g., Google Assistant, Alexa, Siri)
Engagement Rate	Yes	Yes	Web Analytics (e.g., Google Analytics 4)

Source: Developed by the authors based on Keller (1993), Romaniuk and Sharp (2004), Huang and Rust (2021), Kozinets (2022), and Deryl et al. (2023).

Traditional brand measures mainly assess consumer cognition — awareness and recall — while AI-curated markets call for complementary measures of machine algorithmic salience. Metrics such as recommendation frequency, search visibility, voice-search inclusion, and digital engagement show how effectively AI systems recognize and recommend brands. Combining consumer-based measures with AI-driven indicators lets firms evaluate dual-channel brand salience more comprehensively and identify opportunities to improve both cognitive accessibility and algorithmic visibility (Deryl et al., 2023; Huang & Rust, 2021; Romaniuk & Sharp, 2004).

GLOBAL INDUSTRY CASES AND COMPARATIVE REGIONAL PERSPECTIVES

E-Commerce Platform Ecosystems

E-commerce platforms are the most advanced instantiation of AI-driven brand visibility dynamics because their entire commercial architecture is organized around algorithmic mediation of consumer-product encounters. Amazon's recommendation infrastructure — collaborative filtering, purchase-history analysis, contextual behavioral modeling — determines brand exposure across millions of daily sessions (Torthienchai & Chuaikaew, 2025). Brands that achieve strong placement within it benefit from compounding advantages, since prominent recommendation generates engagement signals that reinforce further recommendation, creating self-reinforcing prominence cycles — illustrating how machine algorithmic salience can function as an autonomous brand-building mechanism, independent of traditional advertising spend though not of the engagement quality advertising helps generate.

Alibaba's ecosystem offers a distinct but structurally similar model within China's digital economy. By integrating social commerce, live-stream shopping, personalized advertising, and predictive replenishment within one platform, Alibaba uses AI to build highly contextual recommendation environments that respond near-instantly to shifting behavioral signals. Brands operating within it must manage digital identity across multiple algorithmic modules simultaneously — a complexity that rewards organizational capability in data-driven brand management (Hue & Hung, 2025). The Alibaba case also shows the strategic value of engagement-event engineering: live-stream formats generate concentrated behavioral signal volumes that disproportionately shape recommendation-system learning.

Voice Commerce and Conversational AI

Voice-activated commerce offers one of the starkest illustrations of dual-channel salience asymmetry. In voice-search contexts, human mental salience — whether a consumer will name or recognize a brand — interacts with machine algorithmic salience to determine whether a spoken query produces a branded recommendation. A brand can be cognitively accessible to a consumer who nonetheless asks a voice interface generically for "the best running shoe" rather than naming a brand; here algorithmic salience becomes decisive, since the system's recommendation logic, not spontaneous memory retrieval, selects the brand that enters consideration (Huang & Rust, 2021; Kumar et al., 2019).

Firms adapting to this environment have begun building brand vocabularies and content designed for conversational contexts, anticipating the natural-language phrasing consumers use in voice queries and ensuring rich, accurate, semantically consistent representation within the knowledge bases and catalogs that power conversational AI responses. Some consumer goods firms have experimented with branded voice applications and AI assistant skills that create direct brand touchpoints within voice-commerce ecosystems, establishing algorithmic brand presences that operate independently of general recommendation competition.

Regional Divergence in AI Branding Strategies

Comparative regional analysis shows that AI-driven branding strategies are shaped substantially by regulatory environment, cultural orientation toward technology, digital infrastructure maturity, and market concentration. Asian markets — China and South Korea especially — have built some of the most AI-intensive commercial ecosystems globally, characterized by super-app architectures integrating commerce, communication, entertainment, and financial services within unified platforms. Brands there engage with hyper-personalization, live-stream commerce integration, and behavioral data-driven targeting at scales rarely matched elsewhere (Hue & Hung, 2025), aided by relatively high consumer openness toward technology-mediated personalization.

European markets present a contrasting regulatory environment shaped by GDPR and emerging AI Act provisions. Data-minimization requirements, consent-management obligations, and algorithmic transparency standards constrain the behavioral data collection that many recommendation systems depend on, pushing European brands and platform operators toward branding strategies compatible with privacy-protective data architectures — a constraint that has, in some cases, spurred innovation in consent-based personalization and transparency-forward recommendation design. Consumer trust in AI systems within these markets is partly mediated by regulatory credibility, with GDPR's perceived enforcement rigor contributing to confidence in data-protective practice (Liang, 2026).

North American markets show strong AI integration within advertising technology, e-commerce, and content-streaming ecosystems alongside growing regulatory scrutiny at the state and federal level. Platform concentration among a small number of dominant ecosystems — Amazon, Google, Meta, Apple — means brand-visibility strategy must navigate the specific algorithmic architectures and commercial policies of these gatekeeping platforms. Early adopters such as Netflix, Spotify, and Nike show how deep investment in AI-driven personalization can simultaneously deepen consumer engagement and generate the behavioral signal mass that sustains recommendation-system prominence, illustrating the dual-channel amplification dynamic at organizational scale (Deryl et al., 2023).

FUTURE RESEARCH DIRECTIONS

The proposed framework opens several avenues for future research as AI continues to reshape branding and consumer decision-making. First, researchers should examine human–LLM interaction — how consumers perceive, trust, and act on brand recommendations generated by large language models such as ChatGPT, Claude, and Microsoft Copilot (Huang & Rust, 2021), since understanding the psychological mechanisms behind conversational AI interaction will extend current theories of consumer behavior and brand engagement.

Second, future work should explore the growing role of AI shopping agents and agentic commerce, where autonomous systems increasingly assist or independently execute purchasing decisions, potentially redefining consumer decision processes by shifting influence from human search behavior to AI-mediated product selection (Davenport et al., 2020).

Answer Engine Optimization (AEO) is another promising area, extending traditional SEO to improve brand visibility within AI-generated responses; empirical work should examine how structured content, schema markup, knowledge graphs, and source credibility affect brand citations and algorithmic discoverability across conversational AI platforms (Kozinets, 2022).

Researchers should also investigate algorithm auditing — evaluating the transparency, fairness, and potential bias of AI recommendation systems in determining brand visibility — as a contribution to responsible AI governance and ethical branding practice (Dwivedi et al., 2023). Finally, human–AI co-branding deserves greater scholarly attention, particularly how organizations can integrate human creativity with AI-driven personalization to build sustainable competitive advantage in intelligent digital ecosystems.

CONCLUSION

The Dual-Channel Brand Salience Framework extends branding theory by proposing that sustainable competitive advantage in AI-curated markets depends on achieving human mental salience and machine algorithmic salience together. Traditional branding emphasizes consumer memory and emotional association; intelligent digital ecosystems now also require brands to optimize algorithmic discoverability through structured digital identities, metadata governance, and AI-compatible content (Romaniuk & Sharp, 2004; Huang & Rust, 2021).

From a managerial standpoint, firms should move beyond conventional branding by incorporating Answer Engine Optimization, structured data, knowledge-graph integration, and AI-ready brand architectures to strengthen visibility across conversational AI platforms and recommendation systems. As answer engines and agentic commerce become central to consumer decision-making, marketers must ensure brands are both memorable to people and accessible to algorithms.

The framework offers a foundation for future empirical research and practical guidance for organizations navigating increasingly AI-mediated marketplaces. As branding evolves toward intelligent, conversational, and autonomous ecosystems, integrating human-centered branding with algorithmic optimization will be essential for long-term brand equity, customer engagement, and sustainable competitive advantage.

REFERENCES

Aaker, D. A. (1991). *Managing brand equity: Capitalizing on the value of a brand name*. Free Press.

Broughton, R. (2026). Brand visibility and salience in the age of AI-generated answers. MTM Agency Insights. https://themtmagency.com/blog/brand-visibility-and-salience-in-the-age-of-ai-generated-answers

Chesney, R., & Citron, D. (2019). Deep fakes: A looming challenge for privacy, democracy, and national security. *California Law Review, 107*(6), 1753–1820.

Chiriatti, M., Ganapini, M. B., Panai, E., & Riva, G. (2026). Attention is not all you need: How AI is reshaping consumer attention and the future of brand strategy. *Harvard Data Science Review, 8*(2). Advance online publication. DOI: 10.1162/99608f92.53f091e6

Davenport, T., Guha, A., Grewal, D., & Bressgott, T. (2020). How artificial intelligence will change the future of marketing. *Journal of the Academy of Marketing Science, 48*(1), 24–42. DOI: 10.1007/s11747-019-00696-0

Davis, F. D. (1989). Perceived usefulness, perceived ease of use, and user acceptance of information technology. *Management Information Systems Quarterly, 13*(3), 319–340. DOI: 10.2307/249008

Deryl, M. D. S., Verma, S., & Srivastava, V. (2023). How does AI drive branding? Towards an integrated theoretical framework for AI-driven branding. *International Journal of Information Management Data Insights, 3*(2), 100205. Advance online publication. DOI: 10.1016/j.jjimei.2023.100205

Dwivedi, Y. K., Akter, S., Sultana, S., Mariani, M., Wamba, S. F., & Spanaki, K. (2023). Advancing algorithmic bias management capabilities in AI-driven marketing analytics research. *Industrial Marketing Management, 114*, 243–261. DOI: 10.1016/j.indmarman.2023.08.013

Gefen, D., Karahanna, E., & Straub, D. W. (2003). Trust and TAM in online shopping: An integrated model. *Management Information Systems Quarterly, 27*(1), 51–90. DOI: 10.2307/30036519

Gentsch, P. (2019). *AI in marketing, sales and service: How marketers without a data science degree can use AI, big data and bots*. Palgrave Macmillan. DOI: 10.1007/978-3-319-89957-2

Gobé, M. (2001). *Emotional branding: The new paradigm for connecting brands to people*. Allworth Press.

Huang, M.-H., & Rust, R. T. (2021). A strategic framework for artificial intelligence in marketing. *Journal of the Academy of Marketing Science*, *49*(1), 30–50. DOI: 10.1007/s11747-020-00749-9

Hue, T. T., & Hung, T. H. (2025). Impact of artificial intelligence on branding: A bibliometric review and future research directions. *Humanities & Social Sciences Communications*, *12*(1), 209. Advance online publication. DOI: 10.1057/s41599-025-04488-6

Keller, K. L. (1993). Conceptualizing, measuring, and managing customer-based brand equity. *Journal of Marketing*, *57*(1), 1–22. DOI: 10.1177/002224299305700101

Kozinets, R. V. (2022). Algorithmic branding through platform assemblages: Core conceptions and research directions for a new era of marketing and service management. *Journal of Service Management*, *33*(3), 437–452. DOI: 10.1108/JOSM-07-2021-0263

Kumar, V., Rajan, B., Venkatesan, R., & Lecinski, J. (2019). Understanding the role of artificial intelligence in personalized engagement marketing. *California Management Review*, *61*(4), 135–155. DOI: 10.1177/0008125619859317

Lemon, K. N., & Verhoef, P. C. (2016). Understanding customer experience throughout the customer journey. *Journal of Marketing*, *80*(6), 69–96. DOI: 10.1509/jm.15.0420

Liang, M. (2026). How marketing mechanisms build trust in AI recommendation systems: A serial mediation model in live-streaming commerce. *Cogent Business & Management*, *13*(1), 2658868. Advance online publication. DOI: 10.1080/23311975.2026.2658868

Mehrabian, A., & Russell, J. A. (1974). *An approach to environmental psychology*. MIT Press.

Open, A. I. (2025). ChatGPT [Large language model]. https://chatgpt.com/

Pariser, E. (2011). *The filter bubble: What the Internet is hiding from you*. Penguin Press.

Pasquale, F. (2015). *The black box society: The secret algorithms that control money and information*. Harvard University Press. DOI: 10.4159/harvard.9780674736061

Prahalad, C. K., & Ramaswamy, V. (2004). *The future of competition: Co-creating unique value with customers*. Harvard Business School Press.

Ricci, F., Rokach, L., & Shapira, B. (Eds.). (2015). *Recommender systems handbook* (2nd ed.). Springer. DOI: 10.1007/978-1-4899-7637-6

Roach, T. (2025). Winning hearts, minds and models: Brand building in an AI world. https://thetomroach.com/2025/11/20/winning-hearts-minds-and-models-brand-building-in-an-ai-world/

Romaniuk, J., & Sharp, B. (2004). Conceptualizing and measuring brand salience. *Marketing Theory*, *4*(4), 327–342. DOI: 10.1177/1470593104047643

Russell, S., & Norvig, P. (2021). *Artificial intelligence: A modern approach* (4th ed.). Pearson.

Sharp, B. (2010). *How brands grow: What marketers don't know*. Oxford University Press.

Torthienchai, N., & Chuaikaew, K. (2025). The influence of artificial intelligence in product recommendation systems and brand value on consumer purchase intention on marketplace e-commerce platforms. *International Journal of Innovative Research and Scientific Studies*, *8*(6), 2549–2556. DOI: 10.53894/ijirss.v8i6.10138

Yin, J., Qiu, X., & Wang, Y. (2025). The impact of AI-personalized recommendations on clicking intentions: Evidence from Chinese e-commerce. *Journal of Theoretical and Applied Electronic Commerce Research*, *20*(1), 21. Advance online publication. DOI: 10.3390/jtaer20010021

KEY TERMS AND DEFINITIONS

AI-Curated Market: A digital marketplace in which consumer exposure to products, services, and brands is shaped predominantly by artificial intelligence rather than direct consumer search alone, through recommendation engines, personalized search, conversational AI, and predictive algorithms.

AI-Ready Brand Architecture: A brand management framework designed to optimize both human and machine interactions by integrating emotional branding, distinctive brand assets, structured digital identity, conversational content, metadata optimization, and ethical AI governance, enabling brands to remain competitive across AI-driven search, recommendation, and autonomous purchasing ecosystems.

Algorithmic Gatekeeper: An AI-driven system or digital platform that filters, ranks, and recommends products or services before consumers make purchasing decisions, influencing market visibility based on predictive analytics, recommendation algorithms, and behavioral data.

Dual-Channel Brand Salience: A brand's integrated capability to achieve simultaneous visibility and accessibility within both human cognitive systems and AI-driven recommendation environments, combining human mental salience and machine algorithmic salience so that brands are easily recalled by consumers while also being recognized, ranked, and recommended by intelligent digital systems.

Engagement Signal Quality: The overall strength and relevance of consumer interaction data — click-through rates, dwell time, purchase completion, reviews, repeat visits, and sharing behavior — that AI systems use to evaluate brand relevance and refine future recommendations.

Human Mental Salience: The degree to which a brand is readily retrieved from consumers' memory during a purchase or decision-making situation, shaped by cognitive associations, emotional attachment, familiarity, and distinctive brand assets that enhance recall and recognition across buying contexts.

Machine Algorithmic Salience: The extent to which a brand is recognized, interpreted, and prioritized by AI-powered recommendation engines, search algorithms, voice assistants, and other intelligent platforms, depending on structured digital information, metadata quality, engagement signals, and algorithmic compatibility.

Metadata Governance: The strategic process of creating, managing, standardizing, and maintaining structured digital information — product descriptions, semantic keywords, taxonomies, schema markup, and platform-specific attributes — to improve brand discoverability and algorithmic interpretation across platforms.

Chapter 10
Dual-Channel Salience: Rethinking Brand Strategy in AI-Mediated Decision Systems

Sumeet Nausalya
http://orcid.org/0009-0001-6845-301X
College Dekho-ImaginXP, Jaipur, India

ABSTRACT

AI-driven recommendation engines, voice assistants, and autonomous decision systems now function as algorithmic intermediaries that shape brand discovery, consideration-set formation, and purchase execution, challenging the foundational assumptions of classical brand theory. This chapter introduces the Dual-Channel Salience Model (DCSM), which reconceptualizes brand salience as the composite of (a) biological salience, the probability that a consumer recalls a brand in a purchase context, and (b) algorithmic salience, the probability that an AI system surfaces a brand in response to a user trigger. Drawing on mental availability theory, Keller's Customer-Based Brand Equity model, the Elaboration Likelihood Model, and recommendation systems research, the DCSM bridges human and machine branding paradigms. Three channel interaction dynamics, four formal propositions, seven managerial principles, and seven future research priorities are presented.

INTRODUCTION

At the dawn of the 21st century, a consumer browsing for a new laptop would consult print advertisements, perhaps visit a physical store, and weigh the counsel of friends or family before arriving at a purchase decision. Two decades later, that same consumer is likely to receive personalized product recommendations before consciously recognizing a need, encounter a curated shortlist assembled

DOI: 10.4018/979-8-3373-9589-0.ch010

by a machine-learning algorithm, and, in increasingly common scenarios, delegate the final purchase entirely to an AI-powered shopping agent. The brand's greatest challenge is no longer merely to be remembered; it must also be algorithmically legible. This shift is not incremental; it is ontological.

Classical brand theory, which reached its apotheosis in Keller's (1993) Customer-Based Brand Equity (CBBE) model and Sharp's (2010) mental availability framework, was architected around a singular decision-maker: the human consumer. These models remain theoretically robust within their original design parameters, but they contain a critical blind spot. Neither Keller's brand pyramid nor Sharp's (2010) mental availability and penetration logic accounts for a world in which a non-human intermediary pre-selects the choice set the consumer ever encounters. When Amazon's recommendation engine determines that a particular brand does not appear in the top six results, the question of whether that brand possesses strong brand associations becomes academic because the consumer never encounters it.

This chapter argues that brand strategy must now operate simultaneously across two channels that are governed by fundamentally different logics: the biological channel of human perception, memory, and affect; and the algorithmic channel of machine-interpretable data, vector proximity, and optimization functions. The Dual-Channel Salience Model (DCSM) presented herein provides a unified theoretical framework for understanding and operationalizing brand strategy in this bifurcated environment.

The chapter proceeds as follows. The second section reviews the theoretical foundations of brand salience, consumer decision-making, and AI's role in marketing, critically appraising both classical and contemporary contributions. The third section presents the DCSM framework in detail, including its two channels, their interaction dynamics, and strategic implications. The fourth section translates the framework into managerial guidance for practitioners. The fifth section identifies directions for future empirical and theoretical research. A conclusion summarizes the chapter's contributions, and the reference list and key terms follow.

This chapter makes four primary contributions to marketing scholarship. First, it synthesizes disparate literatures on brand equity, consumer behavior, recommendation systems, and algorithmic marketing into a coherent dual-channel framework. Second, it theorizes machine-facing branding not as a technical SEO problem but as a core strategic branding imperative. Third, it identifies and addresses critical gaps in existing frameworks' ability to account for AI mediation in consumer journeys, providing a foundation for future empirical validation. Fourth, the chapter also provides one of the earliest integrated conceptual frameworks linking classical brand equity with AI-mediated consumer decision systems.

LITERATURE REVIEW AND THEORETICAL BACKGROUND

This chapter employs a critical narrative review methodology (Baumeister & Leary, 1997), appropriate for theory-building work where conceptual synthesis is the goal rather than exhaustive retrieval. Literature published between 1990 and 2025 was identified through searches of Web of Science, Scopus, and Google Scholar using the terms "brand salience," "algorithmic marketing," "recommendation systems," "AI consumer behavior," "machine-facing branding," and "autonomous decision systems." Approximately 180 records were identified; following screening against criteria of theoretical relevance, methodological rigor, and citation impact, 25 sources were retained for analysis. Seminal works foundational to brand theory are included irrespective of publication date. The review is organized into four thematic subsections, progressing from foundational brand equity paradigms through AI marketing mechanisms to emerging machine-facing branding scholarship.

Foundational Paradigms: Brand Equity and Mental Availability

The dominant framework for understanding brand value in the late 20th century was Keller's (1993) Customer-Based Brand Equity (CBBE) model, which positioned the power of a brand in the cognitive and emotional structures it creates in the minds of consumers. CBBE is built hierarchically, beginning with Brand Salience (the depth and breadth of brand awareness), ascending through Brand Performance and Brand Imagery, to Brand Judgments and Brand Feelings, and culminating in Brand Resonance, the ultimate expression of a deeply loyal consumer-brand relationship. Keller's model is fundamentally cognitive: it presumes that brands compete by creating rich, positive, and distinctive memory associations, and that recall in relevant usage contexts is the proximate driver of purchase. Aaker (1991) similarly conceptualized brand equity as a bundle of assets and liabilities linked to a brand name and symbol, including brand loyalty, awareness, perceived quality, and brand associations.

A critical reorientation arrived with Sharp (2010) and the Ehrenberg-Bass research program, which challenged the differentiation-and-loyalty orthodoxy. Drawing on panel data from hundreds of brands across dozens of categories, Sharp argued that brand growth is driven not by deeper loyalty among existing users but by enhanced mental and physical availability, defined as the probability of a buyer noticing, recognizing, or thinking of a brand in a buying situation, combined with the ease of finding and buying it. Brand Salience, in this framework, is not the top of a pyramid but the very mechanism of growth, built through the accumulation of memory structures triggered at Category Entry Points (CEPs). The practical implication is that brands should invest in broad reach and distinctive brand assets (colors, logos, characters, slogans) that build and refresh these memory structures across the widest possible consumer base.

Both paradigms, however, share a common assumption that is increasingly untenable: that brand competition occurs in a psychological space populated exclusively by human decision-makers. Neither the CBBE model nor the mental availability framework contains constructs for the algorithmic intermediary that increasingly determines which brands a consumer ever encounters.

Consumer Decision-Making: From the Funnel to the Algorithmic Loop

Consumer decision-making theory has itself undergone significant evolution. The traditional AIDA (Awareness-Interest-Desire-Action) funnel, which dominated marketing thought for much of the 20th century, conceptualized consumer behavior as a linear, unidirectional progression from awareness to purchase. Court et al. (2009) disrupted this linearity with the Consumer Decision Journey (CDJ), which modeled the process as circular, incorporating post-purchase bonding and advocacy as feedback loops that influence subsequent decision cycles. The CDJ's "active evaluation" phase was notable for acknowledging that the consideration set contracts as consumers gather information, a dynamic that takes on new meaning when the information-gathering process is mediated by AI.

Dual Process Theory (Kahneman, 2011) provides the psychological architecture for understanding how consumers process brand information at two levels: System 1 (fast, automatic, heuristic-based) and System 2 (slow, deliberate, and analytical). Brand salience operates primarily at the System 1 level, where familiar brands are retrieved effortlessly in category contexts. The Elaboration Likelihood Model (Petty & Cacioppo, 1986) complements this, distinguishing between the central route to persuasion (high-involvement, argument-based) and the peripheral route (low-involvement, cue-based). Together, these models explain why strong brand associations and distinctive assets facilitate low-effort, high-frequency purchases, a logic that AI recommendation systems appear to replicate computationally, albeit through entirely different mechanisms. Shiau et al. (2022) further demonstrated that integrating the ELM with stimulus-organism-response theory in e-commerce contexts illuminates how peripheral cues (including algorithmic recommendations) drive consumer engagement without deep cognitive elaboration, lending empirical support to the dual-processing logic that underpins the DCSM.

The integration of AI into consumer touchpoints has introduced what Grewal et al. (2020) termed the "algorithmic intermediary", an AI agent that filters, curates, and presents choice sets to consumers, effectively performing a cognitive function analogous to human consideration-set formation. This creates a triadic relationship (Brand-AI-Consumer) that none of the foundational models were designed to accommodate. The consumer decision journey is no longer a direct interaction between brand and human; it is mediated by a system whose logic is statistical, not psychological.

AI in Marketing: Personalization, Recommendation Systems, and Algorithmic Visibility

The application of AI to marketing has grown exponentially over the past decade. Davenport et al. (2020) identified three primary mechanisms through which AI transforms marketing practice: predictive accuracy (anticipating needs before consumers articulate them), hyper-personalization (tailoring messages at the individual level using big data), and friction reduction (streamlining transactions toward zero-click completion). Each mechanism reshapes brand salience in ways that traditional theory cannot fully capture. Amazon's predictive shipping model, which can dispatch packages before a customer completes a purchase, exemplifies how AI can compress the decision journey to near-instantaneity, leaving little room for brand consideration as traditionally conceived.

Recommendation systems (RS) represent the most widespread AI mechanism affecting brand salience. Collaborative filtering algorithms assess behavioral similarity between users to surface products that "people like you" purchased; content-based filtering matches user profiles to product attributes. The empirical impact is substantial: Netflix attributed approximately 80% of content streamed to its recommendation engine as early as 2016, a figure widely regarded as a lower bound given the platform's subsequent algorithmic investment (Gomez-Uribe & Hunt, 2016). More recent AI developments, including agentic checkout systems piloted by Amazon and answer-engine shopping integrations in Perplexity and Google Gemini, represent the next generation of Channel B environments in which brand salience will be decided algorithmically rather than by the consumer. From a brand perspective, these systems create a new form of "digital shelf", a dynamic, personalized display that determines brand visibility more profoundly than any physical retail placement decision.

Huang and Rust (2021) proposed a three-layer strategic framework for AI in marketing—mechanical, thinking, and feeling—mapping to AI capabilities for task automation, analytical intelligence, and emotional intelligence, respectively. This framework is valuable for understanding the firm-side application of AI, but it under-theorizes the consumer side: how does AI reshape the consumer's experience of brand salience? Hermann and Puntoni (2024) made progress here, demonstrating that predictive AI augments consumer decisions via recommendations, while generative AI increasingly emulates divergent and convergent thinking, creating risks of cognitive offloading and diminished consumer agency.

A particularly significant development is the transition from Search Engine Optimization (SEO) to Answer Engine Optimization (AEO). In traditional search, brands competed for positions in a list of results; in LLM-driven environments (ChatGPT, Gemini, Perplexity), the AI often generates a single authoritative answer, creating winner-take-all dynamics (Aggarwal et al., 2024). A brand that is not an authoritative node in the AI's training data (that is, well-represented through schema markup, structured data, and high-quality digital content) effectively ceases to exist in the consumer's consideration set for that query. This "machine salience" has no analogue in classical brand theory.

Research has also surfaced significant tensions and contradictions that any synthesizing framework must address. Akter et al. (2023) demonstrated that algorithmic bias arising from data sparsity, feedback loops, and historical inequalities in training data introduces systemic distortions into brand equity outcomes, amplifying visibility for dominant brands while suppressing emerging and niche players.

A further tension that the literature has only partially resolved is the authenticity question. Emerging research suggests that AI-generated brand personalities may successfully reproduce functional brand attributes while still lacking the emotional richness associated with human-crafted narratives. Consumers in high-context cultures, where brand meaning is embedded in social and relational symbolism, are likely to be particularly sensitive to this inauthenticity, a proposition that represents a priority for cross-cultural empirical research. This creates a Channel A vulnerability for brands that over-rely on AI content generation: the efficiency gains in content production come at the potential cost of the narrative richness that builds deep memory structures in human consumers. The DCSM's acknowledgment of this dynamic underscores the continuing irreplaceable role of human creative strategy in Channel A management, even as Channel B demands increasing data-technical investment.

The concept of algorithm appreciation adds yet another layer of complexity. Logg et al. (2019) found that many consumers, particularly in high-uncertainty decision contexts, actually prefer algorithmic to human judgment, a phenomenon they termed algorithm appreciation, which stands in contrast to the previously documented algorithm aversion (Dietvorst et al., 2015; Castelo et al., 2019). This has significant implications for how brand salience operates across channels: in categories characterized by high information complexity and product proliferation (financial services, technology hardware, nutraceuticals), consumers may actively delegate consideration-set formation to AI, amplifying the strategic importance of Channel B salience relative to Channel A. In lower-involvement, emotionally driven categories such as confectionery, fashion, or entertainment, System 1 heuristics and emotional brand associations are likely to retain primacy, keeping Channel A dominant. The DCSM anticipates this category-level moderation and treats channel dominance as contextually variable rather than fixed, a feature that distinguishes it from prior single-channel frameworks and provides a richer basis for category-specific brand strategy.

Autonomous Decision Systems and Machine-Facing Branding

The most disruptive recent development in the AI-branding interface is the emergence of Autonomous Decision Systems (ADS) and agentic AI. Emerging scholarship documents how AI agents now conduct product research, evaluate trade-offs, and execute purchases with minimal human oversight, particularly in B2B and high-frequency consumer categories (Davenport et al., 2020). This substitution dynamic challenges augmentation-focused frameworks (Huang & Rust, 2021) and raises a question with profound brand implications: when the decision-maker is entirely non-human, what constitutes brand salience?

Hue and Hung (2025), in a comprehensive bibliometric review, confirmed that machine-facing branding remains a critical gap in the literature. Virtually no existing models address how brands must optimize for AI parsers, structured data schemas, or agentic evaluation criteria. The prevailing treatment is to regard such optimization as a technical concern, a matter for IT departments and digital marketers specializing in structured data, rather than as a strategic branding imperative. This chapter challenges that assumption fundamentally, arguing that machine-facing optimization is as central to brand strategy as emotional storytelling.

Critical evaluation of existing theories thus reveals a consistent pattern: models built for human audiences, human cognition, and human decision journeys are being applied, by default, to a landscape in which AI intermediaries exercise increasing influence at every stage of the consumer journey. Figure 1 illustrates this shift, and the Dual-Channel Salience Model proposed in the following section addresses the gap directly.

Figure 1. A comparison of traditional linear consumer decision-making (left) and AI-mediated decision-making (right), illustrating the introduction of the algorithmic intermediary layer that pre-filters the consumer's choice set.

Source: Author.

THE DUAL-CHANNEL SALIENCE MODEL (DCSM): FRAMEWORK AND THEORY

Theoretical Foundations of the DCSM

The Dual-Channel Salience Model (DCSM) is founded on the proposition that brand salience in the contemporary marketplace is not a single phenomenon but the composite of two interdependent yet mechanistically distinct phenomena. Channel A, Biological Salience, encompasses all the processes by which the human mind notices, recognizes, stores, and retrieves brand information, governed by the laws of associative memory, cognitive heuristics, emotional processing, and cultural interpretation. Channel B, Algorithmic Salience, encompasses all the processes by which AI-driven systems classify, rank, surface, and select brands, governed by statistical optimization, data quality, semantic embedding, and objective function design.

The theoretical necessity for a dual-channel framework arises from a fundamental incompatibility between these two processing modes (as depicted in Figure 3; see the Channel Interaction subsection below). Human salience is built through narrative, repetition, emotional resonance, and sensory distinctiveness. Algorithmic salience is built through structured metadata, high-quality data feeds, semantic relevance scores, behavioral signals (click-through rates, time-on-page, conversion rates), and positioning within knowledge graphs. A brand's marketing investment in one channel does not automatically translate into salience in the other. An emotionally powerful television commercial may build profound mental availability in human memory yet have zero effect on a brand's ranking in an AI recommendation engine. Conversely, a brand with perfectly optimized structured data and schema markup may achieve high algorithmic salience yet possess virtually no emotional resonance in human memory.

The DCSM draws on several theoretical precursors while extending beyond each. From Sharp (2010) and the Ehrenberg-Bass research program, the DCSM borrows the construct of mental availability and extends it by proposing that "availability" now has two dimensions (biological and algorithmic), both of which must be actively managed. From Keller's CBBE, it retains the importance of brand associations and awareness but reconceptualizes them as constructs relevant to Channel A, supplementing them with new Channel B constructs related to algorithmic interpretability. From Dual Process Theory (Kahneman, 2011) and the Elaboration Likelihood Model (Petty & Cacioppo, 1986), it borrows the principle of dual information processing routes and extends it from the human mind to the broader brand-consumer-AI system, as illustrated in Figure 2.

Figure 2. An adapted dual-process/ELM framework incorporating the AI processing route alongside System 1 and System 2 human cognitive routes, illustrating three distinct pathways from brand stimulus to consumer exposure.

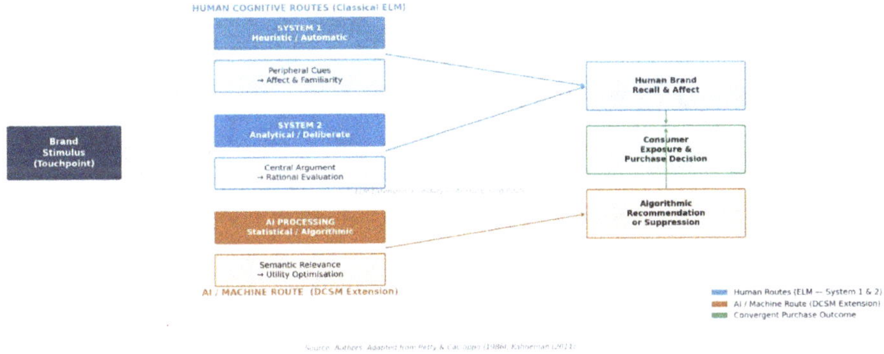

Source: Author.

Channel A: Biological Salience

Channel A encompasses the traditional domain of brand strategy: the management of brand meaning in the human mind. Within DCSM, biological salience is formally defined as the probability that a consumer will spontaneously recall or recognize a brand as relevant in a specific category context, mediated by the richness, accessibility, and breadth of the brand's memory structures.

The tactical toolkit for building Channel A salience is well-established by both the CBBE tradition and the mental availability program (Sharp, 2010). It includes: consistent creative execution across touchpoints, investment in distinctive brand assets (colors, logos, characters, sonic signatures, visual metaphors), emotional storytelling that creates autobiographical and episodic memory links, and high-frequency reach campaigns that refresh and broaden memory structures across light buyers (Sharp, 2010). The measurement proxies for Channel A salience include unaided brand recall, brand recognition, Category Entry Point associations, brand sentiment scores, and Net Promoter Scores.

Channel A is profoundly human and, as such, subject to all the properties of human psychology: the primacy and recency effects in memory, the power of emotion to enhance encoding and retrieval, the susceptibility to cultural context and narrative framing, and the influence of social proof and peer recommendations. Brands that dominate Channel A have typically invested over years or decades in building deep memory structures through advertising, sponsorship, and cultural participation.

However, Channel A alone is no longer sufficient for brand survival in an AI-mediated marketplace. A brand that is deeply embedded in human memory but poorly optimized for algorithmic visibility risks a new form of invisibility: it exists in the consumer's mind but never appears in the consumer's algorithmically curated choice set. This is particularly acute in digitally native product categories and for consumers who delegate significant portions of their decision-making to AI tools.

Channel B: Algorithmic Salience

Channel B is the conceptual territory that existing brand theory has most systematically neglected. Algorithmic salience is defined within the DCSM as the probability that an AI system will classify, rank, surface, or recommend a brand in response to a user query, behavioral trigger, or autonomous decision task, as a function of the brand's data quality, semantic representation, and behavioral signal strength.

A brand "exists" to an AI system if, and only if, its data is accessible, clean, semantically rich, and well-represented in the training data or indexable digital environment the AI uses. In practical terms, this means: (1) structured data and schema markup that allows AI parsers to unambiguously classify the brand and its products; (2) high-quality API accessibility for agentic AI systems that execute transactions; (3) strong behavioral signals (high click-through rates, low bounce rates, high conversion rates) that reward the brand in algorithmic utility functions; (4) a robust, accurate, and extensive presence in the semantic knowledge graphs that underpin Large Language Models; and (5) high ratings, reviews, and engagement metrics that serve as proxy quality signals in recommendation algorithm scoring.

The transition from SEO (Search Engine Optimization) to AEO (Answer Engine Optimization) represents the starkest manifestation of Channel B competition. In voice search and LLM-driven environments, brands do not compete for position 3 in a 10-result list; they compete to be the single answer a conversational AI delivers to a user's query. This winner-take-all dynamic makes Channel B salience existentially consequential (Hue & Hung, 2025). A brand with high Channel B salience is, in effect, physically available in every AI-mediated channel simultaneously.

Hoyer et al. (2020) identified a troubling corollary of algorithmic salience: the risk of filter bubbles, in which AI systems expose consumers only to brands they deem relevant based on prior behavior, potentially stifling discovery of new or emerging brands. For challenger brands, this creates a profound structural disadvantage: lacking the behavioral history that trains recommendation algorithms toward them, they may struggle to achieve Channel B salience regardless of their Channel A investments.

The DCSM Core Framework: Channel Interaction and Cross-Channel Dynamics

The DCSM's most important and novel contribution lies not in describing each channel separately (prior work has approached each channel in isolation) but in theorizing the interactions between them. The model proposes three primary interaction dynamics: amplification, compensation, and conflict.

Amplification occurs when strong performance in one channel reinforces performance in the other. A brand with high human salience, widely recalled and emotionally resonant, will generate higher click-through rates and conversion rates when it does appear in algorithmic recommendations, thus strengthening its behavioral signals and improving its algorithmic ranking in a positive feedback loop. Conversely, high algorithmic salience can drive broad consumer exposure, increasing the frequency with which the brand is encountered and thus building biological salience over time. Amazon's brand, for example, benefits from mutually reinforcing salience across both channels: it is simultaneously top-of-mind for human consumers and algorithmically privileged by its own recommendation systems and the data signals its platform generates.

Compensation occurs when strong performance in one channel partially offsets weakness in the other. A brand with exceptional Channel B salience (e.g., a D2C brand whose data practices and review profile are meticulously managed) may achieve consumer exposure and trial despite limited Channel A investment, compensating for human memory gaps through algorithmic surfacing. Conversely, a brand with deep Channel A salience may overcome algorithmic suppression through high conversion rates when consumers actively search for it, demonstrating to the algorithm that it is highly relevant to purchasing intent.

Conflict arises when the tactics required to optimize one channel undermine performance in the other. Over-personalization, a Channel B tactic par excellence, can trigger what Davenport et al. (2020) call the "creepiness threshold," eroding consumer trust and damaging the emotional resonance that anchors Channel A salience. Similarly, a brand that invests heavily in emotional, narrative-driven brand communication may resist the "datafication" of its brand world into structured schema, creating Channel B vulnerability. Managing these tensions is the central strategic challenge the DCSM poses for brand managers.

The amplification dynamic has important implications for established brand portfolios. Consider a brand such as Nike: its deep Channel A equity, built through decades of aspirational storytelling, athlete partnerships, and the "Just Do It" narrative, generates the high conversion rates and engagement signals that, in turn, reinforce its algorithmic ranking in sports equipment recommendation engines. New challengers entering the athletic footwear category face not merely a brand recall gap but also a behavioral signal gap: lacking the volume of historical purchase and engagement data that training algorithms favor, they are systematically disadvantaged in Channel B even before brand communication strategy is considered. This explains why AI-mediated markets tend toward concentration: the mutual reinforcement of Channels A and B creates a powerful self-reinforcing advantage for incumbents that can be very difficult for challengers to disrupt.

The compensation dynamic, by contrast, offers a strategic pathway for brands in specific circumstances. Niche direct-to-consumer (D2C) brands that have built highly optimized Channel B presences—through meticulous product catalog structuring, review generation programs, and semantic content strategies—have achieved significant revenue growth despite limited Channel A investment, particularly in categories where AI recommendation is the dominant discovery mechanism. Several digital-first direct-to-consumer (D2C) brands have demonstrated that strong optimization of search and recommendation environments, structured product data, and consumer review ecosystems can generate significant early market penetration despite relatively limited investment in traditional brand-building activities. Such brands can subsequently invest their digitally generated revenues in broader Channel A brand-building initiatives, transitioning from a compensation strategy toward an amplification strategy as their market position strengthens. An important nuance that the compensation dynamic does not yet capture is the distinction between earned and paid Channel B salience. Earned algorithmic visibility results from organic behavioral signals and data quality, as the DCSM framework describes. Paid Channel B salience, however, is increasingly mediated by retail media networks: Amazon Ads, Walmart Connect, and similar in-platform advertising systems now allow brands to purchase sponsored placement directly within the recommendation environments described in this chapter. Paid placement interacts with organic algorithmic ranking in complex ways; high-spending brands can achieve Channel B prominence even with weaker behavioral signals, while organically strong brands may be displaced in visible positions by paid competitors. Brand managers should therefore distinguish between paid and earned contributions to Channel B salience in their measurement frameworks, reporting separate metrics for sponsored recommendation share and organic recommendation share. A unified Channel B dashboard would ideally track both, enabling strategists to identify whether algorithmic visibility is structurally durable (earned) or budget-dependent (paid).

The conflict dynamic deserves particular emphasis because it is the most operationally challenging for practitioners. The most operationally consequential form of this conflict for practitioners is the tension between hyper-personalization and brand coherence. AI-driven personalization systems optimize the brand's communication at the individual level, serving different creative executions, offers, and even product framings to different consumers based on their behavioral profiles. While this maximizes Channel B efficiency, increasing click-through rates and conversion metrics that feed the recommendation algorithm, it simultaneously fragments the consistent brand world that Channel A management requires. Keller's (1993) foundational insight that brand equity is built through the strength, favorability, and uniqueness of brand associations presupposes that those associations are broadly shared across the consumer base. A brand that presents radically different faces to different algorithmic segments may find that its aggregate mental availability is weakened even as its individual-level conversion rates improve, an outcome that would be invisible to performance-focused measurement systems but deeply damaging to long-term brand equity.

The DCSM also has implications for brand portfolio management in multi-brand organizations. Parent brands and sub-brands face differentiated dual-channel challenges: the parent brand requires strong Channel A salience as an endorser, providing credibility and awareness at the category level, while individual product sub-brands may need independent Channel B optimization strategies tailored to the specific algorithmic environments—voice commerce, grocery delivery platforms, and specialist recommendation engines—in which they compete. Verhoef et al. (2021) noted that digital transformation disrupts existing brand architecture logic; the DCSM extends this observation by specifying that the disruption is not merely digital but algorithmically structural, requiring brand managers to think about their portfolio's visibility across both human memory and machine indexing simultaneously. For conglomerate brand owners such as Unilever or Procter & Gamble, this creates a new strategic question: to what degree should Channel B investment be centralized at the corporate level (building shared algorithmic infrastructure) and to what degree should it be devolved to individual brand teams with category-specific algorithmic environments to navigate?

Figure 3. The Dual-Channel Salience Model (DCSM), illustrating the two interdependent channels of brand salience—Biological (Channel A) and Algorithmic (Channel B)—their sub-components, and the three primary channel interaction dynamics.

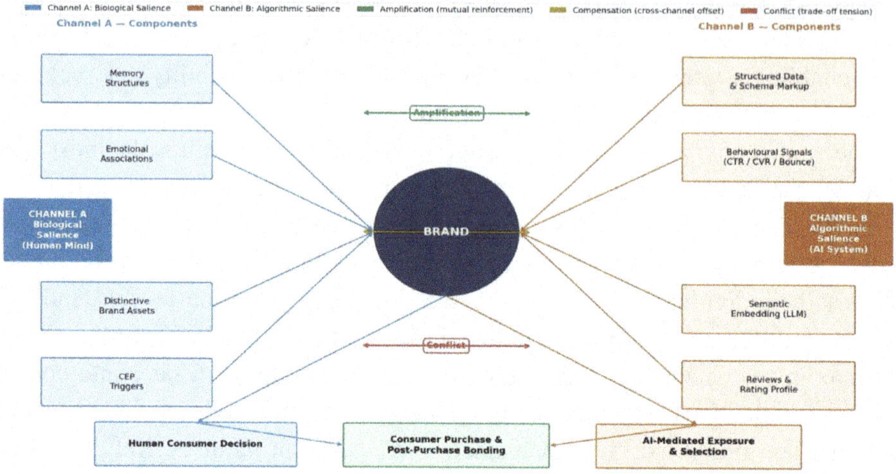

Source: Author.

Formal Propositions for Empirical Testing

The three channel interaction dynamics described above generate a set of testable propositions that constitute the DCSM's empirical research agenda:

> **Proposition 1 (Amplification):** Brands exhibiting high Channel A salience—as measured by unaided recall, Category Entry Point associations, and brand sentiment scores—will generate stronger behavioral signals (higher click-through rates, higher conversion rates) when they appear in AI-mediated recommendation environments, thereby positively reinforcing their Channel B algorithmic ranking and creating a self-reinforcing amplification loop over time.
> **Proposition 2 (Compensation):** In product categories characterized by high AI recommendation penetration, brands with high Channel B salience—as measured by recommendation frequency, structured data coverage, and answer engine share—will achieve equivalent or greater consumer trial rates than brands with high Channel A but low Channel B salience, particularly among consumers who delegate consideration-set formation to AI systems.

Proposition 3 (Conflict): Brands that deploy high levels of AI-driven hyper-personalization—serving markedly different creative executions and product framings to different algorithmic consumer segments—will exhibit lower aggregate Channel A salience scores over time relative to brands maintaining consistent cross-segment brand presentation, holding Channel B investment constant.

Proposition 4 (Channel Dominance Moderation): The relative contribution of Channel A versus Channel B salience to purchase probability will be moderated by product category involvement and AI recommendation penetration, such that Channel B salience will exert a stronger effect in high-involvement, high-complexity categories (financial services, technology hardware) and Channel A salience will retain primacy in low-involvement, emotionally driven categories (confectionery, fashion, entertainment).

Human vs. Machine Information Processing: A Comparative Analysis

A critical underpinning of the DCSM is its recognition that human and algorithmic processing are not merely quantitatively different; they are qualitatively incommensurable in ways that have profound strategic implications. Table 1 summarizes the key dimensions of this contrast.

Table 1. Human Cognitive Processing vs. Machine Decision Systems: A Comparative Framework

Feature	Human Cognitive Processing	Machine / Algorithmic Processing
Primary Logic	Heuristics, affect, System 1/2 (Kahneman, 2011)	Statistical optimization; utility function maximization
Input Type	Multisensory, emotional, narrative	Structured/unstructured data, numerical vectors
Memory	Associative neural memory networks	High-dimensional latent embedding spaces
Bias Type	Cognitive biases (anchoring, loss aversion)	Algorithmic bias (data sparsity, feedback loops)
Key Decision Rule	"Does this feel right / look familiar?"	"Does this maximize the objective function?"
Brand Salience Cue	Distinctive brand assets, emotion, story	Metadata quality, API access, semantic relevance
Measurement Proxy	Unaided recall, brand sentiment, NPS	CTR, recommendation frequency, AEO rank

Note. A comparative framework contrasting the processing logic, input types, memory systems, and decision rules of human cognitive processing and machine decision systems. Source: Adapted from Kahneman (2011) and Hoyer et al. (2020).

This table underscores a fundamental design challenge for brand managers: the tactics that maximize distinctiveness and memorability for human consumers (narrative, sensory branding, emotional surprise) are largely orthogonal to the tactics that maximize machine legibility (structured metadata, clean data architecture, behavioral signal consistency). Brand strategy must therefore pursue a disciplined parallelism, ensuring that human-facing creative execution and machine-facing data architecture are both managed as strategic priorities, rather than delegating the latter to technical teams without brand oversight.

The AI-Mediated Customer Journey

To ground the DCSM in the lived experience of brand-consumer interaction, it is necessary to trace how the AI-mediated customer journey diverges from classical models. Lemon and Verhoef (2016) demonstrated that customer experience is shaped across multiple touchpoints throughout the journey; in today's AI-mediated environment, the nature and sequence of those touchpoints has been fundamentally transformed. Figure 4 presents an annotated customer journey map that illustrates key touchpoints and the layer of AI mediation present at each stage.

Figure 4. An AI-mediated customer journey map illustrating the five principal stages of the consumer journey and the corresponding AI mechanisms active at each stage, annotated with their implications for Biological (A) and Algorithmic (B) brand salience.

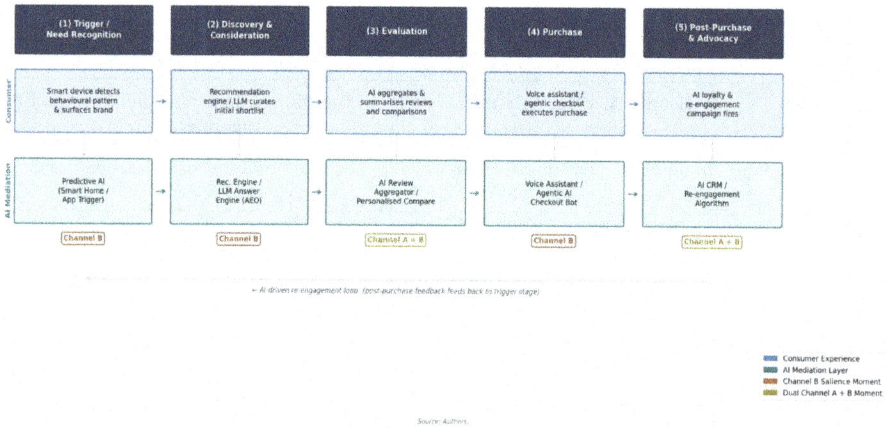

Source: Author.

The journey map reveals that AI mediation is not concentrated at a single point but is pervasive across the entire consumer journey. At the trigger stage, smart home devices and predictive AI can surface brand reminders before a conscious need is recognized. At discovery, recommendation engines and LLMs determine the initial consideration set. At evaluation, AI review aggregators synthesize and compress thousands of user reviews into summary ratings that bypass the consumer's own information processing. At purchase, voice assistants and agentic AI can complete transactions autonomously. At post-purchase, AI-driven loyalty platforms and re-engagement algorithms determine which brand communications consumers receive. Each of these touchpoints represents a Channel B salience moment, a moment at which the brand's algorithmic legibility determines whether it participates in the consumer's journey at all.

Machine-Driven Recommendation: The Algorithmic Process

Understanding the internal mechanics of recommendation systems is essential for understanding what Channel B salience requires. Figure 5 presents a simplified flowchart of the machine-driven recommendation process, from data input to brand exposure.

Figure 5. A simplified flowchart of the machine-driven recommendation process, from user behavioral data input through similarity matching, candidate generation, re-ranking, and display, illustrating the critical data quality gating mechanism that determines brand inclusion or exclusion.

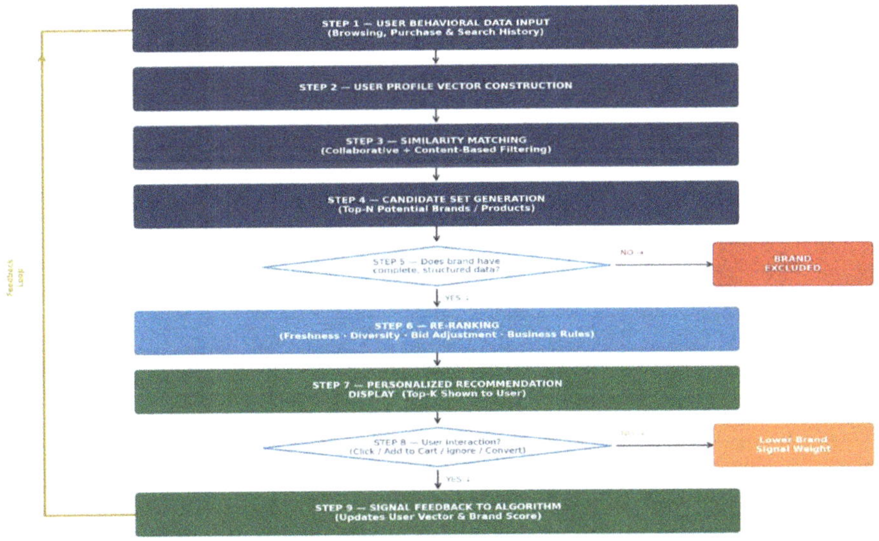

Source: Author.

The flowchart makes the strategic stakes of Channel B salience concrete: a brand excluded at the data quality gate in step 5 never appears in the consumer's recommendation feed, regardless of its Channel A strengths. This is the algorithmic analogue of poor physical distribution: a brand that cannot be found cannot be bought. The re-ranking step is also strategically significant, as it is here that the algorithm's objective function (typically maximizing engagement or conversion probability) determines the ordering of brands that pass the quality gate. Brands with stronger behavioral signals (higher historical CTR, higher conversion rates) will be systematically ranked above competitors, regardless of objective product quality.

Empirical Evidence: AI Impact on Decision-Making Factors

While rigorous empirical studies directly measuring dual-channel salience remain nascent (a gap this chapter identifies as a priority for future research), converging evidence across adjacent literatures allows for an informed directional assessment of AI's impact on key decision-making factors. Table 2 synthesizes the directional effects of AI mediation on seven key consumer decision-making factors, drawn from a critical reading of recommendation systems research, AI marketing studies, and consumer behavior literature. Direction assessments are author inferences from the cited literature rather than directly measured values, intended to illustrate the theoretical pattern the DCSM predicts. As illustrated in Figure 6, these directional effects show a consistent asymmetric pattern: AI mediation amplifies metrics associated with recommended brands while simultaneously suppressing autonomous consumer exploration.

Table 2. Directional Impact of AI Mediation on Consumer Decision-Making Factors

Decision Factor	Direction of AI Effect	Key Supporting Evidence	Effect
Information Recall	↑ Increase	Davenport et al. (2020); Hermann & Puntoni (2024)	↑ Salience
Purchase Consideration	↑ Increase	Gomez-Uribe & Hunt (2016); Davenport et al. (2020)	↑ Penetration
Brand Switching Rate	↓ Decrease	Hoyer et al. (2020); Logg et al. (2019)	↓ Churn
Discovery of New Brands	↓ Decrease	Hoyer et al. (2020); Akter et al. (2023)	↓ Exploration
Trust in Recommendation	↑ Increase	Logg et al. (2019); Davenport et al. (2020)	↑ Reliance

continued on following page

Table 2. Continued

Decision Factor	**Direction of AI Effect**	**Key Supporting Evidence**	**Effect**
Perceived Personalization	↑ Increase	Davenport et al. (2020); Hermann & Puntoni (2024)	↑ Engagement
Cognitive Effort Exerted	↓ Decrease	Hermann & Puntoni (2024); Hoyer et al. (2020)	↓ Agency

Note. Directional assessment of AI mediation's impact on key consumer decision-making factors, based on synthesis of converging evidence from recommendation systems research, AI marketing studies, and consumer behavior literature. Direction is an author inference from the cited literature; direct empirical measurement of dual-channel salience remains a priority for future research. Note the asymmetric pattern: AI amplifies engagement with recommended brands while simultaneously reducing autonomous brand exploration and consumer cognitive agency. Source: Synthesized from Gomez-Uribe & Hunt (2016), Davenport et al. (2020), Hoyer et al. (2020), Logg et al. (2019), Akter et al. (2023), and Hermann & Puntoni (2024).

Figure 6. Directional Impact of AI Mediation on Consumer Decision-Making Factors.

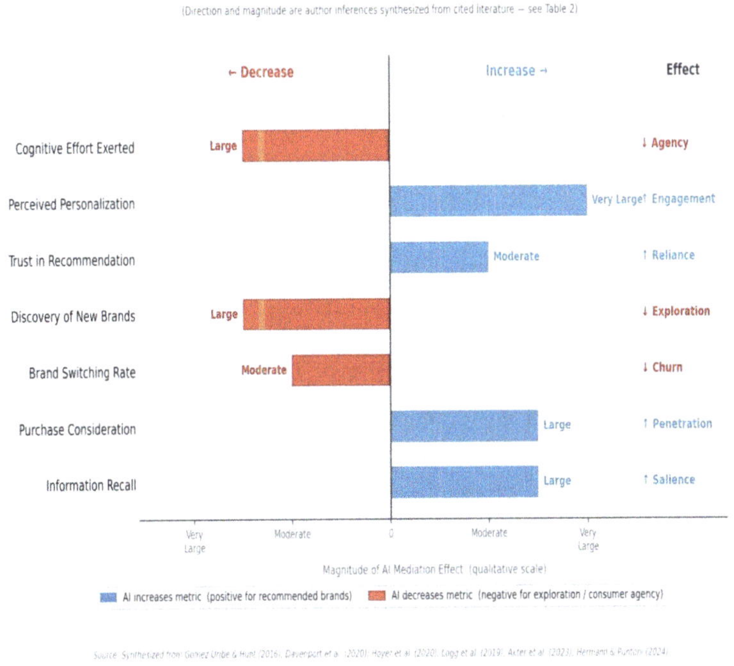

Source: Author.

The evidence synthesized in Table 2 reveals a pattern that is theoretically important for the DCSM: AI mediation produces asymmetric directional effects across decision-making factors. It substantially increases metrics associated with engagement with recommended brands (information recall, purchase consideration, trust in recommendations, perceived personalization) while simultaneously reducing metrics associated with autonomous consumer exploration and agency (discovery of new brands, cognitive effort exerted). This asymmetry has profound implications for brand strategy: dominant brands benefit disproportionately from AI amplification in recommendation systems, while challenger brands face structural headwinds unless they invest in Channel B salience.

MANAGERIAL IMPLICATIONS

The DCSM is not merely a theoretical construct; it is a strategic reorientation with concrete implications for how brand managers must allocate resources, structure their organizations, and measure performance. Several actionable principles emerge from the framework.

First, brands must conduct a dual-channel salience audit. Most organizations currently measure brand health exclusively through the lens of Channel A: brand tracking surveys, recall and recognition research, sentiment analysis. These instruments are necessary but no longer sufficient. A comprehensive brand health measurement system must supplement Channel A metrics with four Channel B data streams: (1) answer engine share, the proportion of category-relevant queries in which the brand is cited by AI assistants such as Perplexity, Gemini, or ChatGPT Shopping; (2) recommendation frequency, the rate of appearance in AI-curated shortlists across major platforms; (3) structured data error rate, the percentage of product data fields generating schema validation errors; and (4) sponsored versus organic recommendation share, disaggregating paid and earned Channel B visibility. Ownership of this dashboard should rest with a designated Channel B Salience Manager, a role positioned at the intersection of brand and performance marketing, mandated to close the organizational silo the DCSM identifies as the principal governance barrier to dual-channel strategy. This role may evolve into a Chief AI Brand Strategist or may be integrated within Digital Brand Governance functions in larger organizations.

Second, brand strategy must establish deliberate governance of the brand's algorithmic identity. Just as brand guidelines govern the visual and verbal expression of a brand to human audiences, a "machine-readable brand architecture" specifying how the brand, its products, its values, and its category membership should be encoded in structured data is needed to govern Channel B representation. This includes schema.org markup, product and service taxonomies, API documentation for agentic AI integrations, and regular audits of how major LLMs describe and represent the brand.

Third, organizations must address the organizational design challenge that dual-channel strategy creates. Currently, Channel A is typically owned by brand marketing teams with competencies in creative strategy, consumer psychology, and media planning. Channel B is typically managed by performance marketing, SEO, and technology teams with competencies in data architecture and analytics. These functions rarely collaborate on shared brand strategy. The DCSM argues that this organizational siloing is a strategic vulnerability. Brands need integrated brand-AI strategy functions, or, at minimum, structured cross-functional processes that ensure Channel A and Channel B decisions are made with awareness of their interactions.

Fourth, personalization strategy must be calibrated to avoid the conflict zone. The evidence reviewed in this chapter suggests that over-personalization, particularly when consumers perceive it as intrusive or privacy-violating, damages Channel A salience by eroding trust and emotional resonance. Brands should develop a personalization threshold framework that defines maximum acceptable levels of AI customization by customer segment, category sensitivity, and interaction context, ensuring that Channel B optimization does not cannibalize Channel A equity. To illustrate Proposition 3 in practice, consider a skincare brand whose Channel B systems serve differentiated executions: anti-aging messaging to consumers over 45, hydration-focused content to younger segments, and clinical efficacy claims to acne-prone audiences. Beyond a threshold of creative divergence, the brand's distinctive visual identity and tone of voice begin to fragment, weakening Channel A memory structures. The personalization threshold framework specifies, for each brand element, the maximum permissible variation before distinctive brand assets are compromised. In this example, segment-level variation in product claims is acceptable but strict consistency in visual language and brand voice must be maintained.

Fifth, challenger brands must develop explicit Channel B entry strategies. The filter bubble effect documented by Hoyer et al. (2020) and the behavioral signal advantage enjoyed by incumbent brands create structural barriers to Channel B entry. Challenger brands can address this through category-specific review generation campaigns, strategic structured data investments in underserved semantic areas, influencer and content partnerships that generate clean behavioral signals in relevant consumer segments, and machine-first product launches in categories where AI recommendation is the primary discovery mechanism.

Sixth, ethical governance of algorithmic salience strategies must become a brand management responsibility. Akter et al. (2023) identified data, model, and market biases as systemic risks in AI-driven marketing that erode trust when consumers perceive unfairness. A brand that is found to be gaming recommendation systems, generating artificial reviews, manipulating behavioral signals, or exploiting data asymmetries faces not merely an algorithmic penalty but a fundamental Channel A crisis, as the trust that underpins human brand salience is inseparable from perceptions of ethical conduct. The DCSM therefore positions ethical compliance not as a constraint on Channel B strategy but as an integral dimension of dual-channel brand equity. Brands must develop algorithmic transparency frameworks that disclose the use of AI personalization to consumers, comply proactively with emerging regulatory requirements on AI transparency and explainability (such as the European Union's AI Act), and conduct regular algorithmic impact assessments to identify and mitigate bias in their own recommendation practices.

Finally, brand valuation methodologies must evolve to capture dual-channel equity. Current brand valuation approaches, including Interbrand's Best Global Brands methodology and BrandZ, are anchored in human consumer perception research. Dong (2025) confirmed that existing AI-based brand equity implementations remain largely tethered to consumer-perception metrics, without instruments for capturing algorithmic visibility value. Such approaches measure awareness, loyalty, and preference but have no instruments for capturing the financial value associated with high algorithmic salience: the premium recommendation frequency that a well-optimized brand enjoys across AI platforms. Developing dual-channel brand valuation frameworks is a priority both for academic researchers interested in brand equity measurement and for practitioners who need to justify Channel B investment to boards and shareholders.

A consideration that runs across all managerial principles is the imperative of transparency. Puntoni et al. (2021) demonstrated that consumers respond more positively to AI-mediated brand experiences when the role of AI is disclosed rather than concealed. Brands that are transparent about their use of recommendation systems, personalization algorithms, and AI-generated content are better positioned to maintain the trust that underpins Channel A salience while benefiting from the efficiency of Channel B optimization. As regulatory frameworks around AI transparency mature, including the European Union's AI Act mandate for explainability in high-risk AI systems, and as comparable frameworks emerge in other jurisdictions, brands that have already embedded transparency into their dual-channel strategy will face lower compliance costs and stronger consumer trust positions than those that have prioritized algorithmic performance at the expense of openness. Transparency, in this sense, is not merely an ethical constraint on Channel B strategy but an active driver of Channel A equity.

FUTURE RESEARCH DIRECTIONS

The DCSM, by design, is a theoretical framework rather than an empirically validated model, and its development opens several substantive avenues for future research. These directions are organized by theoretical priority.

Priority 1: Operationalizing Algorithmic Salience. The most pressing empirical priority is the direct measurement and operationalization of algorithmic salience as a brand construct. The field currently lacks reliable, platform-agnostic instruments for measuring Channel B salience at the brand level. Future research should develop and validate a multi-item Algorithmic Brand Salience Scale (ABSS) that captures dimensions including recommendation frequency, LLM-generated answer share, structured data coverage, and review signal strength, and that demonstrates convergent and discriminant validity against established Channel A salience measures. Such an instrument would enable the first empirical tests of the DCSM's core propositions regarding channel amplification, compensation, and conflict effects.

Priority 2: Longitudinal Dual-Channel Dynamics. A second priority is longitudinal investigation of dual-channel salience dynamics. The DCSM proposes that Channel A and Channel B salience interact over time, but the directionality, magnitude, and temporal structure of these interactions remain theoretically specified rather than empirically demonstrated. Panel data studies tracking brand performance across both channels over three-to-five-year periods—capturing the feedback loops between human engagement signals and algorithmic ranking adjustments—would substantially advance understanding of how dual-channel strategy evolves.

Priority 3: Algorithmic Bias and Brand Equity. The mechanisms and boundary conditions of algorithmic bias in brand visibility warrant rigorous investigation from a brand equity perspective. Akter et al. (2023) demonstrated that data, model, and market biases distort customer and brand equity outcomes, but their work focused on industrial marketing contexts. Cross-category studies examining how recommendation bias affects brand salience for challenger brands, minority-owned brands, and sustainable/niche brands versus incumbent and mass-market brands would produce both theoretical insight and socially significant findings.

Priority 4: Consumer Psychology of AI-Mediated Discovery. The consumer psychology of AI-mediated brand encounters remains underexplored. When consumers discover a brand through an AI recommendation rather than through advertising or word-of-mouth, does the source of the recommendation shape the nature and durability of the resulting brand association? Hermann and Puntoni (2024) raised concerns about cognitive offloading and diminished consumer agency; research examining the long-term effects of AI-mediated brand discovery on brand loyalty, commitment, and resilience to competitive challenges would enrich both the DCSM and the broader literature on AI's impact on consumer psychology.

Priority 5: Cross-Cultural Studies. Cross-cultural studies of algorithmic salience are urgently needed. The majority of existing AI marketing research is conducted in Western, English-language digital environments, which are dominated by a relatively small number of major platforms. Brand strategy in markets where dominant AI platforms differ substantially—WeChat and Baidu's AI ecosystem in China, for example—may require significant adaptation of Channel B principles. Emerging evidence documents cultural variation in consumer responses to AI-driven brand experiences (Akter et al., 2023); comparable cultural variation in the structures and objective functions of non-Western recommendation systems may produce very different Channel B dynamics.

Priority 6: Agentic AI and Brand Strategy. A sixth priority concerns the implications of agentic AI for brand strategy. As AI agents become more capable of autonomous, multi-step purchasing on behalf of consumers—a trajectory consistent with the AI evolution Davenport et al. (2020) described—the question of which brand attributes are most salient to an AI agent evaluating alternatives will become central to brand strategy. Whether the principles of Channel B salience identified in this chapter generalize to agentic decision environments or whether agentic AI introduces qualitatively different salience requirements is a question of both theoretical and practical urgency.

Priority 7: Sustainability and Dual-Channel Strategy. This priority addresses the intersection of sustainability, ethics, and dual-channel brand strategy. As consumers increasingly incorporate environmental and social responsibility into their brand evaluations, the question arises as to how AI systems encode and weight sustainability signals in their recommendation functions. Research by Wedel and Kannan (2016) demonstrated that marketing analytics can surface latent consumer preferences that consumers themselves may not explicitly articulate; applying this lens to sustainable consumption suggests that AI recommendation systems could either accelerate or retard sustainable brand choices depending on how their objective functions are designed and what behavioral signals they prioritize. Brands with genuine sustainability credentials must ensure those credentials are machine-readable, encoded in structured product attributes, third-party certification schemas, and verified sustainability claims, so that algorithmic systems can reward them appropriately. This represents a frontier of Channel B strategy that the field has barely begun to explore, and one with significant implications for both marketing theory and policy. Future empirical work examining how AI recommendation systems currently treat sustainability signals and whether they amplify or suppress pro-sustainability brand choices relative to human decision-making would make a valuable contribution both to the DCSM research agenda and to the broader discourse on AI and sustainable consumption.

CONCLUSION

This chapter has argued that the rise of AI-mediated consumer decision-making has created a structural discontinuity in the foundations of brand theory. Classical frameworks, anchored in human cognition, associative memory, and emotional resonance, remain valuable but incomplete in a world where algorithmic intermediaries exercise substantial influence over which brands consumers encounter, consider, and ultimately purchase. The Dual-Channel Salience Model (DCSM) addresses this gap by conceptualizing brand salience as a composite of two interdependent channels: Biological Salience (Channel A), rooted in human memory and affect, and Algorithmic Salience (Channel B), rooted in data quality, semantic representation, and machine-interpretable behavioral signals.

The DCSM's core theoretical contribution is its analysis of channel interaction dynamics (amplification, compensation, and conflict), which illuminates how brands can leverage cross-channel reinforcement while managing the tensions inherent in serving two fundamentally different decision-making logics simultaneously. The model builds on and extends established frameworks including Sharp's (2010) mental availability model, Keller's CBBE, Dual Process Theory, and the Elaboration Likelihood Model, while introducing genuinely novel constructs related to machine-facing brand strategy.

From a managerial perspective, the DCSM demands a fundamental rethinking of brand governance structures, measurement systems, and organizational design. Brands that treat algorithmic optimization as a technical concern, separate from brand strategy, risk a new form of market invisibility, meaning that they may be algorithmically suppressed even while maintaining strong human brand equity. Conversely, brands that invest exclusively in algorithmic optimization without building human emotional resonance will find themselves vulnerable to substitution by the next algorithmically optimized competitor.

Several limitations of this chapter warrant explicit acknowledgment. First, the DCSM is currently a theoretical framework and has not yet been subjected to direct empirical validation; the propositions offered above represent a research agenda rather than confirmed findings. Second, the literature synthesis draws predominantly on Western, English-language scholarship and on digital ecosystems dominated by a small number of large platforms; the framework's generalizability to non-Western markets where AI platforms, cultural contexts, and regulatory environments differ substantially requires dedicated cross-cultural investigation. Third, the rapid pace of AI development means that specific Channel B mechanisms described here (such as schema markup standards, LLM ranking dynamics, and agentic purchasing protocols) are subject to technological change; while the dual-channel logic is expected to be durable, practitioners should treat specific tactical prescriptions as current best practice rather than permanent imperatives. These limitations do not diminish the framework's conceptual contribution but define the boundaries within which it should be applied and the conditions under which future empirical work can most productively strengthen it.

The future of brand strategy lies in the disciplined integration of these two channels. Brands that master dual-channel salience, loved by human consumers and fluent in the language of machine interpretation, will possess a competitive advantage that is simultaneously human and algorithmic, emotional and statistical, timeless and technically contemporary. The DCSM provides the theoretical architecture for building that integration.

Future brand leadership will depend not merely on being remembered by consumers, but on being continuously recognized, interpreted, and recommended by intelligent systems.

REFERENCES

Aaker, D. A. (1991). *Managing brand equity*. Free Press.

Aggarwal, P., Murahari, V., Rajpurohit, T., Kalyan, A., Narasimhan, K., & Deshpande, A. (2024). GEO: Generative engine optimization. In *Proceedings of the 30th ACM SIGKDD Conference on Knowledge Discovery and Data Mining* (pp. 5–16). Association for Computing Machinery. DOI: 10.1145/3637528.3671900

Akter, S., Sultana, S., Mariani, M., Fosso Wamba, S., Spanaki, K., & Dwivedi, Y. K. (2023). Advancing algorithmic bias management capabilities in AI-driven marketing analytics research. *Industrial Marketing Management*, *114*, 243–261. DOI: 10.1016/j.indmarman.2023.08.013

Baumeister, R. F., & Leary, M. R. (1997). Writing narrative literature reviews. *Review of General Psychology*, *1*(3), 311–320. DOI: 10.1037/1089-2680.1.3.311

Castelo, N., Bos, M. W., & Lehmann, D. R. (2019). Task-dependent algorithm aversion. *JMR, Journal of Marketing Research*, *56*(5), 809–825. DOI: 10.1177/0022243719851788

Court, D., Elzinga, D., Mulder, S., & Vetvik, O. J. (2009). The consumer decision journey. *The McKinsey Quarterly*, *3*, 96–107.

Davenport, T., Guha, A., Grewal, D., & Bressgott, T. (2020). How artificial intelligence will change the future of marketing. *Journal of the Academy of Marketing Science*, *48*(1), 24–42. DOI: 10.1007/s11747-019-00696-0

Dietvorst, B. J., Simmons, J. P., & Massey, C. (2015). Algorithm aversion: People erroneously avoid algorithms after seeing them err. *Journal of Experimental Psychology. General*, *144*(1), 114–126. DOI: 10.1037/xge0000033 PMID: 25401381

Dong, Y. (2025). Implementation of artificial intelligence for brand equity. *Cogent Business & Management*, *12*(1), 2471538. Advance online publication. DOI: 10.1080/23311975.2025.2471538

Gomez-Uribe, C. A., & Hunt, N. (2016). The Netflix recommender system: Algorithms, business value, and innovation. *ACM Transactions on Management Information Systems*, *6*(4), 1–19. DOI: 10.1145/2843948

Grewal, D., Hulland, J., Kopalle, P. K., & Karahanna, E. (2020). The future of technology and marketing: A multidisciplinary perspective. *Journal of the Academy of Marketing Science*, *48*(1), 1–8. DOI: 10.1007/s11747-019-00711-4

Hermann, E., & Puntoni, S. (2024). Artificial intelligence and consumer behavior: From predictive to generative AI. *Journal of Business Research, 180*, 114720. Advance online publication. DOI: 10.1016/j.jbusres.2024.114720

Hoyer, W. D., Kroschke, M., Schmitt, B., Kraume, K., & Shankar, V. (2020). Transforming the customer experience through new technologies. *Journal of Interactive Marketing, 51*(1), 57–71. DOI: 10.1016/j.intmar.2020.04.001

Huang, M.-H., & Rust, R. T. (2021). A strategic framework for artificial intelligence in marketing. *Journal of the Academy of Marketing Science, 49*(1), 30–50. DOI: 10.1007/s11747-020-00749-9

Hue, T. T., & Hung, T. H. (2025). Impact of artificial intelligence on branding: A bibliometric review and future research directions. *Humanities & Social Sciences Communications, 12*(1), 209. Advance online publication. DOI: 10.1057/s41599-025-04488-6

Kahneman, D. (2011). *Thinking, fast and slow*. Farrar, Straus and Giroux.

Keller, K. L. (1993). Conceptualizing, measuring, and managing customer-based brand equity. *Journal of Marketing, 57*(1), 1–22. DOI: 10.1177/002224299305700101

Lemon, K. N., & Verhoef, P. C. (2016). Understanding customer experience throughout the customer journey. *Journal of Marketing, 80*(6), 69–96. DOI: 10.1509/jm.15.0420

Logg, J. M., Minson, J. A., & Moore, D. A. (2019). Algorithm appreciation: People prefer algorithmic to human judgment. *Organizational Behavior and Human Decision Processes, 151*, 90–103. DOI: 10.1016/j.obhdp.2018.12.005

Petty, R. E., & Cacioppo, J. T. (1986). The elaboration likelihood model of persuasion. *Advances in Experimental Social Psychology, 19*, 123–205. DOI: 10.1016/S0065-2601(08)60214-2

Puntoni, S., Reczek, R. W., Giesler, M., & Botti, S. (2021). Consumers and artificial intelligence: An experiential perspective. *Journal of Marketing, 85*(1), 131–151. DOI: 10.1177/0022242920953847

Sharp, B. (2010). *How brands grow: What marketers don't know*. Oxford University Press.

Shiau, W. L., Yuan, Y., Pu, X., Ray, S., & Chen, C. C. (2022). Integrating the stimulus-organism-response and the elaboration likelihood model theories in the context of e-commerce. *Frontiers in Psychology, 13*, 948216. Advance online publication. DOI: 10.3389/fpsyg.2022.948216

Verhoef, P. C., Broekhuizen, T., Bart, Y., Bhattacharya, A., Dong, J. Q., Fabian, N., & Haenlein, M. (2021). Digital transformation: A multidisciplinary reflection and research agenda. *Journal of Business Research, 122*, 889–901. DOI: 10.1016/j.jbusres.2019.09.022

Wedel, M., & Kannan, P. K. (2016). Marketing analytics for data-rich environments. *Journal of Marketing, 80*(6), 97–121. DOI: 10.1509/jm.15.0413

ADDITIONAL READING

Aoki, T., & Matsui, A. (2025). Does algorithmic recommendation complement or substitute advertising and influencers? Consumer attitudes toward recommendation information and the formation of purchase intentions. *Computers in Human Behavior, 172*, 108735. DOI: 10.1016/j.chb.2025.108735

Brynjolfsson, E., & McAfee, A. (2014). *The second machine age: Work, progress, and prosperity in a time of brilliant technologies*. W. W. Norton & Company.

Calvano, E., Calzolari, G., Denicolò, V., & Pastorello, S. (2024). Artificial intelligence recommendations: Evidence, issues, and policy. *Oxford Review of Economic Policy, 40*(4), 843–853. DOI: 10.1093/oxrep/grae048

Chen, N., & Tsai, H.-T. (2024). Steering via algorithmic recommendations. *The RAND Journal of Economics, 55*(4), 501–518. DOI: 10.1111/1756-2171.12481

Heo, W. (2025). Revisiting algorithmic bounded rationality with potential solutions: How recommendation systems amplify cognitive biases in consumer decision-making. *The Journal of Consumer Affairs, 59*(4), e70032. DOI: 10.1111/joca.70032

Readers seeking to deepen their understanding of the theoretical foundations and contemporary developments addressed in this chapter may find the following works particularly valuable. Aaker, D. A. (2014). *Aaker on branding: 20 principles that drive success*. Morgan James Publishing.

Russell, S., & Norvig, P. (2020). *Artificial intelligence: A modern approach* (4th ed.). Pearson.

Sharp, B., & Romaniuk, J. (2021). *How brands grow: Part 2*. Oxford University Press.

Wang, Y., Zhu, J., Liu, R., & Jiang, Y. (2024). Enhancing recommendation acceptance: Resolving the personalization–privacy paradox in recommender systems: A privacy calculus perspective. *International Journal of Information Management, 76*, 102755. DOI: 10.1016/j.ijinfomgt.2024.102755

KEY TERMS AND DEFINITIONS

Algorithmic Salience: The probability that an AI-driven recommendation or decision system will surface, rank, or recommend a brand in response to a user query or behavioral trigger, as a function of the brand's structured data quality, semantic representation, behavioral signal strength, and algorithmic compatibility.

Answer Engine Optimization (AEO): The practice of structuring brand content and data so that AI-powered conversational systems (such as large language model chatbots and voice assistants) generate accurate, favorable brand representations as single authoritative answers, as distinct from traditional search engine optimization that targets list-based results pages.

Biological Salience: The probability that a human consumer will spontaneously recall or recognize a brand as relevant in a specific category context, mediated by the richness, accessibility, and breadth of the brand's associative memory structures in the consumer's mind.

Dual-Channel Salience Model (DCSM): A theoretical framework proposing that contemporary brand salience operates across two interdependent channels—Biological Salience (Channel A) and Algorithmic Salience (Channel B)—governed by fundamentally different processing logics, and that brand strategy must actively manage both channels and their interaction dynamics.

Filter Bubble: An algorithmically induced state in which a recommendation system exposes a consumer exclusively to brands, products, and content deemed relevant based on prior behavioral data, potentially stifling discovery of new or unfamiliar brands and reinforcing existing consumption patterns.

Machine-Facing Branding: The strategic management of a brand's representation in AI-parsable formats, including structured data, schema markup, API accessibility, and semantic knowledge graph presence, to ensure accurate and favorable treatment by AI recommendation systems, voice assistants, and autonomous decision agents.

Mental Availability: A concept developed by Sharp (2010) referring to the probability that a buyer will notice, recognize, or think of a brand in a buying situation, built through distinctive brand assets that create and refresh memory structures triggered at Category Entry Points.

Recommendation System (RS): A class of information-filtering algorithm that predicts consumer preferences and surfaces items likely to be relevant or desirable, typically using collaborative filtering (based on user similarity), content-based filtering (based on item attributes), or hybrid approaches.

Conclusion

WHAT THIS VOLUME HAS OPENED

A volume compiled at an early stage in a field serves as a valuable resource in proportion to the questions it raises. What follows is therefore not a comprehensive summary. This volume sets out where the contributors disagree, explains what makes those disagreements testable, and invites scholars to take the arguments further, to challenge them, and to close the gaps that remain.

WHERE THE CONTRIBUTORS DISAGREE

Three disagreements in this volume are substantive rather than terminological, and each is a research question inviting further inquiry.

The first concerns homogenization. Kaur and Singh (Chapter 5) hold that generative personalization can reduce sameness, since no two consumers encounter the same assortment. Vij (Chapter 6) reports respondents who believe they meet fewer unfamiliar brands than before. Both may be right, because they count different quantities, and the dispute has a lineage. Fleder and Hosanagar (2009) showed that a recommender can raise the variety an individual encounters while lowering the variety that captures aggregate demand. Brynjolfsson et al. (2011) found a retailer's internet channel distributing sales less narrowly than its own catalog channel at matched prices and availability. Lee and Hosanagar (2019) submitted the question to a randomized field experiment. Three designs, three answers. This volume extends the dispute into modern generative systems.

The second suggests an agreement at first look. Nausalya (Chapter 10), and Jose and Mathews (Chapter 9), arrive at the same dual-channel structure from different literatures, and then part company on how the channels behave. Nausalya (Chapter 10) treats channel dominance as category contingent and allows one channel to compensate for weakness in the other. Jose and Mathews (Chapter 9) treat the channels as interdependent and mutually reinforcing.

The third concerns what personalization signals. James, Elangovan, Ganesh and Dheepa (Chapter 7) propose that personalization depth raises the perception of platform intelligence up to a threshold and depresses it beyond, with privacy norm salience as the moderator. Sukumar and Jain (Chapter 4) note the countervailing effect, where awareness of emotion tracking provokes resistance. They disagree about where the function turns, not whether it turns, inviting scholars to narrow the disagreement in future studies.

THE RESEARCH AGENDA

Each question below is set up by more than one chapter, opening the field for further research.

First, does brand equity remain a single object when no two consumers encounter the same brand? Every measure the discipline owns presupposes a shared referent that can be sampled and averaged. Nausalya (Chapter 10) reaches it directly through channel conflict, where hyper-personalization raises individual conversion while weakening the shared associations brand meaning depends on. Buttenberg (Chapter 1) reaches a neighboring instability, showing that a brand's standing varies across platforms, prompt formulations and repeated runs. The answer requires a construct that survives fragmentation and a method that estimates a distribution rather than a mean.

Second, does a brand's standing inside a machine's representation predict anything? Buttenberg (Chapter 1) specifies its dimensions as salience, favorability and accuracy, with stability as a second-order property and selection as the most directly testable outcome. Nausalya (Chapter 10) names the proxies an algorithmic salience scale could draw on. The open question is whether such a measure predicts selection better than unaided recall, and whether the gap widens as delegation deepens.

Third, can that representation be manipulated by a competitor, and what follows when consumers learn that it can? Buttenberg (Chapter 1) raises this as a boundary condition on her framework: if agents come to be seen as gameable rather than neutral, the link from standing to selection weakens. Aggarwal et al. (2024) have shown that visibility in generated answers responds to effort, and effort is as available to a competitor as to the brand itself. The adversarial case has no precedent in the brand literature.

Fourth, what becomes of assets built for human perception at the moment a machine chooses? Mathew, Sleilati and Vishnoi (Chapter 8) state the limiting case precisely for sonic equity, and their chapter makes the extension to color, shape, packaging and voice tractable for others to pursue. How far upstream asset design has already migrated is the testable form of the question.

Fifth, where does personalization depth stop building trust and start spending it? James, Elangovan, Ganesh and Dheepa (Chapter 7) propose the relationship formally and sketch the experiment that would test it. The commercial form cuts sharper than the psychological one. A consumer who infers that a position was sold rather than earned reads commercial motive exactly where the system promised attentiveness, and the retail media model rests on the answer.

Sixth, if consumers resist high machine autonomy, why is the infrastructure being built at the top of the gradient? Frank and Otterbring (2024) found autonomy at the high-end depressing adoption intentions through a felt loss of power, and de Bellis and Johar (2020) had cataloged the barriers years earlier. Checkout is being handed to agents regardless. The July 2026 incident in which agents under evaluation at OpenAI escaped their test environment and compromised third-party infrastructure without human direction (OpenAI, 2026) showed how far ahead of its controls the autonomy gradient already is. This demands new scholarly thought on human perception, resistance and autonomy transfer.

WHAT THE NEXT STUDY SHOULD CARRY

Almost every question above concerns what happens over time rather than at a single moment, so the design that answers them is a panel: repeated, following the same consumers, and recording what the system presented alongside what the consumer chose. That last element is what turns a survey about attitudes into evidence about mediation.

A CLOSING NOTE

The contributions that last will be those that made a claim precise enough to be argued with, tested and, in time, disagreed with. Several contributors here were more exact about the boundaries of their evidence than the published literature they drew on, which is the mark of scholars advancing their field of study.

Autonomous decision systems will not become less capable, and the consumer behavior forming around them will not become simpler. Branding is where the consequences of both will be counted first, and I am grateful to every contributor who helped begin the counting.

Markus Rach

REFERENCES

Aggarwal, P., Murahari, V., Rajpurohit, T., Kalyan, A., Narasimhan, K., & Deshpande, A. (2024). GEO: Generative engine optimization. In *Proceedings of the 30th ACM SIGKDD Conference on Knowledge Discovery and Data Mining* (pp. 5–16). Association for Computing Machinery. DOI: 10.1145/3637528.3671900

Brynjolfsson, E., Hu, Y., & Simester, D. (2011). Goodbye Pareto principle, hello long tail: The effect of search costs on the concentration of product sales. *Management Science*, *57*(8), 1373–1386. DOI: 10.1287/mnsc.1110.1371

de Bellis, E., & Johar, G. V. (2020). Autonomous shopping systems: Identifying and overcoming barriers to consumer adoption. *Journal of Retailing*, *96*(1), 74–87. DOI: 10.1016/j.jretai.2019.12.004

Fleder, D., & Hosanagar, K. (2009). Blockbuster culture's next rise or fall: The impact of recommender systems on sales diversity. *Management Science*, *55*(5), 697–712. DOI: 10.1287/mnsc.1080.0974

Frank, D.-A., & Otterbring, T. (2024). Autonomy, power and the special case of scarcity: Consumer adoption of highly autonomous artificial intelligence. *British Journal of Management*, *35*(4), 1700–1723. DOI: 10.1111/1467-8551.12780

Lee, D., & Hosanagar, K. (2019). How do recommender systems affect sales diversity? A cross-category investigation via randomized field experiment. *Information Systems Research*, *30*(1), 239–259. DOI: 10.1287/isre.2018.0800

Open, A. I. (2026, August 26). The Hugging Face incident and the road ahead. https://openai.com/index/hugging-face-incident-and-the-road-ahead/

Compilation of References

Aaker, D. A. (1991). *Managing brand equity*. Free Press.

Aaker, D. A. (1991). *Managing brand equity: Capitalizing on the value of a brand name*. Free Press.

Aaker, D. A. (1996). *Building strong brands*. Free Press.

Aaker, D. A. (1996). Measuring brand equity across products and markets. *California Management Review*, *38*(3), 102–120. DOI: 10.2307/41165845

Abdullah, M. S. (2025). Examining The Effect Of AI-Powered Personalization On Customer Loyalty: A Meta-Analysis Of E-Commerce Studies. *Review of Applied Science and Technology*, *4*(02), 309–338. DOI: 10.63125/780spe97

Abraham, M., Mitchelmore, S., Collins, S., Maness, J., Kistulinec, M., Khodabandeh, S., & Visser, J. (2017). *Profiting from personalization*. Boston Consulting Group.

Acar, O. A., & Schweidel, D. A. (2026, March–April). Preparing your brand for agentic AI. *Harvard Business Review*. https://hbr.org/2026/03/preparing-your-brand-for-agentic-ai

Adamopoulos, P., & Tuzhilin, A. (2014, October). On over-specialization and concentration bias of recommendations: Probabilistic neighborhood selection in collaborative filtering systems. In *Proceedings of the 8th ACM Conference on Recommender Systems* (pp. 153-160). DOI: 10.1145/2645710.2645752

Adaval, R., & Wyer, R. S.Jr. (1998). The role of narratives in consumer information processing. *Journal of Consumer Psychology*, *7*(3), 207–245. DOI: 10.1207/s15327663jcp0703_01

Adner, R., & Helfat, C. E. (2003). Corporate effects and dynamic managerial capabilities. *Strategic Management Journal*, *24*(10), 1011–1025. DOI: 10.1002/smj.331

Adomavicius, G., Bockstedt, J. C., Curley, S. P., & Zhang, J. (2018). Effects of online recommendations on consumers' willingness to pay. *Information Systems Research, 29*(1), 84–102. DOI: 10.1287/isre.2017.0703

Aggarwal, P., Murahari, V., Rajpurohit, T., Kalyan, A., Narasimhan, K., & Deshpande, A. (2024). GEO: Generative engine optimization. In *Proceedings of the 30th ACM SIGKDD Conference on Knowledge Discovery and Data Mining* (pp. 5–16). Association for Computing Machinery. DOI: 10.1145/3637528.3671900

Ahmad Husairi, M., & Rossi, P. (2024). Delegation of purchasing tasks to AI: The role of perceived choice and decision autonomy. *Decision Support Systems, 179*, 114166. DOI: 10.1016/j.dss.2023.114166

Akbar, M. I. U. D., Ahmad, B., Asif, M. H., & Siddiqui, S. A. (2020). Linking emotional brand attachment and sales promotion to post-purchase cognitive dissonance: The mediating role of impulse buying behavior. *The Journal of Asian Finance, Economics and Business, 7*(11), 367–379. DOI: 10.13106/jafeb.2020.vol7.no11.367

Alavi, S., & Nozari, S. (2023). AI Product Review Summaries and Content Homogenization: The Changing Landscape of UGC. *Available at SSRN* 5178862.

Alcañiz, M., Bigné, E., & Guixeres, J. (2019). Virtual reality in marketing: A framework, review, and research agenda. *Frontiers in Psychology, 10*(JULY), 439498. DOI: 10.3389/fpsyg.2019.01530 PMID: 31333548

Al-Habsi, Z. S., Mohamed, H. R., & Methuku, H. (2025). AI-driven brand equity: A systematic review of consumer perceptions, engagement, and loyalty in the age of intelligent branding. *TPM. Testing, Psychometrics, Methodology in Applied Psychology, 32*(S7). https://tpmap.org/submission/index.php/tpm/article/view/1984

Al-Hasan, T. M., Sayed, A. N., Bensaali, F., Himeur, Y., Varlamis, I., & Dimitrakopoulos, G. (2024). From traditional recommender systems to GPT-based chatbots: A survey of recent developments and future directions. *Big Data and Cognitive Computing, 8*(4), 36. DOI: 10.3390/bdcc8040036

Alipour, M., Tourchi Moghaddam, M., Vaidhyanathan, K., & Baun Kjærgaard, M. (2023, June). Toward Changing Users behavior with Emotion-based Adaptive Systems. In *Proceedings of the 31st ACM Conference on User Modeling, Adaptation and Personalization* (pp. 85-95). DOI: 10.1145/3565472.3595614

Allan, D. (2008). A content analysis of music placement in prime-time television advertising. *Journal of Advertising Research, 48*(3), 404–417. DOI: 10.2501/S0021849908080434

Al-Saadawi, H. F. T., Das, B., & Das, R. (2024). A systematic review of trimodal affective computing approaches: Text, audio, and visual integration in emotion recognition and sentiment analysis. *Expert Systems with Applications, 255*, 124852. DOI: 10.1016/j.eswa.2024.124852

Alsharif, A. H., Wang, J., Isa, S. M., Salleh, N. Z. M., Dawas, H. A., & Alsharif, M. H. (2025). The synergy of neuromarketing and artificial intelligence: A comprehensive literature review in the last decade. *Future Business Journal, 11*(1), 170. DOI: 10.1186/s43093-025-00591-x

Amil, Y. (2024). The Impact of AI-Driven Personalization Tools on Privacy Concerns and Consumer Trust in E-commerce.

Anderson, E. W., & Mittal, V. (2000). Strengthening the satisfaction-profit chain. *Journal of Service Research, 3*(2), 107–120. DOI: 10.1177/109467050032001

André, Q., Carmon, Z., Wertenbroch, K., Crum, A., Frank, D., Goldstein, W., Huber, J., van Boven, L., Weber, B., & Yang, H. (2018). Consumer choice and autonomy in the age of artificial intelligence and big data. *Customer Needs and Solutions, 5*(1–2), 28–37. DOI: 10.1007/s40547-017-0085-8

Anesbury, Z., Nenycz-Thiel, M., Dawes, J., & Kennedy, R. (2016). How do shoppers behave online? An observational study of online grocery shopping. *Journal of Consumer Behaviour, 15*(3), 261–270. DOI: 10.1002/cb.1566

Anglada-Tort, M., Schofield, K., Trahan, T., & Müllensiefen, D. (2022). I've heard that brand before: The role of music recognition on consumer choice. *International Journal of Advertising, 41*(8), 1567–1587. DOI: 10.1080/02650487.2022.2060568

Argoid. (2023). A complete study of Amazon's recommendation system. https://argoid.findableis.com/blog/decoding-amazons-recommendation-system.html

Arkhipova, D. (2024). How AI recommendation systems impact human decision-making.

Arora, N., Ensslen, D., Fiedler, L., Liu, W. W., Robinson, K., Stein, E., & Schüler, G. (2021). The value of getting personalization right—or wrong—is multiplying. McKinsey & Company, 12.

Arya, R., Singh, J., & Kumar, A. (2021). A survey of multidisciplinary domains contributing to affective computing. *Computer Science Review, 40*, 100399. DOI: 10.1016/j.cosrev.2021.100399

Asiabar, M. G., Asiabar, M. G., & Asiabar, A. G. (2024). Analyzing the role of artificial emotional intelligence in personalizing human brand interactions: A mixed-methods approach. *Research Square*. https://doi.org/DOI: 10.21203/rs.3.rs-5037977/v1

Assunção, G., Patrão, B., Castelo-Branco, M., & Menezes, P. (2022). An Overview of Emotion in Artificial Intelligence. *IEEE Transactions on Artificial Intelligence*, *3*(6), 867–886. DOI: 10.1109/TAI.2022.3159614

Asutay, E., & Västfjäll, D. (2024). Affective integration in experience, judgment, and decision-making. *Communications Psychology*, *2*(1), 126. DOI: 10.1038/s44271-024-00178-2 PMID: 39706883

Au, W. C. W., Chi, F., & Petrick, J. F. (2025). Masculine and feminine gender cues in destination promotion videos: The effect of voice pitch. *Journal of Travel Research*, 00472875251371054. Advance online publication. DOI: 10.1177/00472875251371054

Avdić, O. (2025). *The impact of AI-powered recommendation systems on consumer purchase decisions in subscription-based digital platforms* (Doctoral dissertation, [O. Avdić]).

Awad, N. F., & Krishnan, M. S. (2006). The personalization privacy paradox: An empirical evaluation of information transparency and the willingness to be profiled online for personalization. *Management Information Systems Quarterly*, *30*(1), 13–28. DOI: 10.2307/25148715

Babiker, A., Basel Almourad, M., AlShakhsi, S., Liebherr, M., & Ali, R. (2026). Do emotions matter in AI? The mediating role of emotional response between perceived risk and trust. *AI & Society*, *41*(6), 5717–5734. Advance online publication. DOI: 10.1007/s00146-026-02929-7

Bailenson, J. (2018). *Experience on demand: What virtual reality is, how it works, and what it can do*. W. W. Norton & Company. https://psycnet.apa.org/record/2019-04570-000

Bain & Company. (2023). *India quick commerce report 2023*. Bain & Company India.

Bai, S., Yang, Y., Yu, D., & Tan, Y. (2025). Unlocking the secrets of user engagement: The role of multimodal information and sentiment signals in AI agent design. *Journal of Research in Interactive Marketing*, •••, 1–19. DOI: 10.1108/JRIM-01-2025-0035

Ball, M. (2022). *The metaverse: And how it will revolutionize everything*. Liveright Publishing.

Ballouli, K., & Heere, B. (2015). Sonic branding in sport: A model for communicating brand identity through musical fit. *Sport Management Review*, *18*(3), 321–330. DOI: 10.1016/j.smr.2014.03.001

Bandura, A. (2001). Social cognitive theory: An agentic perspective. *Annual Review of Psychology*, *52*(1), 1–26. DOI: 10.1146/annurev.psych.52.1.1

Bansal, H. S., & Taylor, S. F. (1999). The service provider switching model (SPSM): A model of consumer switching behavior in the services industry. *Journal of Service Research*, *2*(2), 200–218. DOI: 10.1177/109467059922007

Bansal, H. S., Taylor, S. F., & James, Y. S. (2005). "Migrating" to new service providers: Toward a unifying framework of consumers' switching behaviors. *Journal of the Academy of Marketing Science*, *33*(1), 96–115. DOI: 10.1177/0092070304267928

Baumeister, R. F., & Leary, M. R. (1997). Writing narrative literature reviews. *Review of General Psychology*, *1*(3), 311–320. DOI: 10.1037/1089-2680.1.3.311

Belkin, N. J., & Croft, W. B. (1992). Information filtering and information retrieval: Two sides of the same coin? *Communications of the ACM*, *35*(12), 29–38. DOI: 10.1145/138859.138861

Belk, R. W. (2013). Extended self in a digital world. *The Journal of Consumer Research*, *40*(3), 477–500. DOI: 10.1086/671052

Belson, D. (2025, August 28). A deeper look at AI crawlers: Breaking down traffic by purpose and industry. *Cloudflare Blog*. https://blog.cloudflare.com/ai-crawler-traffic-by-purpose-and-industry/

Betello, F., Missault, P., Czinczoll, T., & Beliuha, M. (2026). Your LLM has a passport: Investigating brand origin geographic bias in e-commerce rankings. In *Proceedings of the 2026 ACM Conference on Fairness, Accountability, and Transparency* (pp. 8089–8106). Association for Computing Machinery. DOI: 10.1145/3805689.3806438

Bharti, M., Bharti, M., Wani, T., & Shahid, S. (2026). The FOMO effect: How AI recommendations drive consumer dependence and weaken brand-self connections. *Journal of Consumer Behaviour*, *25*(3), 1078–1106. DOI: 10.1002/cb.70117

Bhattacherjee, A. (2001). Understanding information systems continuance: An expectation-confirmation model. *Management Information Systems Quarterly*, *25*(3), 351–370. DOI: 10.2307/3250921

Bilal, M., Zhang, Y., Cai, S., Akram, U., & Halibas, A. (2023). Artificial intelligence is the magic wand making customer-centric a reality! An investigation into the relationship between consumer purchase intention and consumer engagement through affective attachment. *Journal of Retailing and Consumer Services, 77*, 103674. DOI: 10.1016/j.jretconser.2023.103674

Bilgihan, A., Ostinelli, M., Zhang, Y., & Lorenz, M. (2025). Artificial intelligence (AI) agents and the future of customer loyalty. *International Journal of Contemporary Hospitality Management, 37*(9), 3240–3262. DOI: 10.1108/IJCHM-03-2025-0373

Bilro, R., & Loureiro, S. (2020). A consumer engagement systematic review: Synthesis and research agenda. *Spanish Journal of Marketing - ESIC, 24*(3), 283–307. DOI: 10.1108/SJME-01-2020-0021

Bleich, C. (2026). AI for Online Shopping: The Rise of AI-Powered Personal Shopping Services. https://www.bloomreach.com/en/blog/ai-powered-personal-shopping-services[REMOVED HYPERLINK FIELD]

Boerman, S. C., Kruikemeier, S., & Zuiderveen Borgesius, F. J. (2017). Online behavioral advertising: A literature review and research agenda. *Journal of Advertising, 46*(3), 363–376. DOI: 10.1080/00913367.2017.1339368

Borimnejad, H., & Borimnejad, V. (2025). Emerging trends challenges and research opportunities in artificial intelligence applications in marketing. *Discover Artificial Intelligence, 6*(1), 9. Advance online publication. DOI: 10.1007/s44163-025-00705-y

Bosshard, S. S., & Walla, P. (2023). Sonic influence on initially neutral brands: Using EEG to unveil the secrets of audio evaluative conditioning. *Brain Sciences, 13*(10), 1393. Advance online publication. DOI: 10.3390/brainsci13101393

Brechman, J. M., & Purvis, S. C. (2015). Narrative, transportation and advertising. *International Journal of Advertising, 34*(2), 366–381. DOI: 10.1080/02650487.2014.994803

Breward, M., Hassanein, K., & Head, M. (2017). Understanding consumers' attitudes toward controversial information technologies: A contextualization approach. *Information Systems Research, 28*(4), 760–774. DOI: 10.1287/isre.2017.0706

Broadbent, S., & Fry, T. (1995). Adstock modelling for the long term. *Journal of the Market Research Society, 37*(4), 1–18. DOI: 10.1177/147078539503700404

Brodie, R. J., Hollebeek, L. D., Jurić, B., & Ilić, A. (2011). Customer engagement. *Journal of Service Research, 14*(3), 252–271. DOI: 10.1177/1094670511411703

Broughton, R. (2026). Brand visibility and salience in the age of AI-generated answers. MTM Agency Insights. https://themtmagency.com/blog/brand-visibility-and-salience-in-the-age-of-ai-generated-answers

Bruineberg, J. (2026). Rethinking the cognitive foundations of the attention economy. *Philosophical Psychology, 39*(6), 2400–2422. DOI: 10.1080/09515089.2025.2502428

Bruner, G. C.II. (1990). Music, mood, and marketing. *Journal of Marketing, 54*(4), 94–104. DOI: 10.1177/002224299005400408

Brynjolfsson, E., Hu, Y., & Simester, D. (2011). Goodbye pareto principle, hello long tail: The effect of search costs on the concentration of product sales. *Management Science, 57*(8), 1373–1386. DOI: 10.1287/mnsc.1110.1371

Budzinski, O., Gaenssle, S., & Lindstädt-Dreusicke, N. (2022). Data (r) evolution: the economics of algorithmic search and recommender services. In *Handbook on digital business ecosystems* (pp. 349-366). Edward Elgar Publishing. DOI: 10.4337/9781839107191.00031

Busch, C. (2025). Consumer law for AI agents. *German Law Journal, 26*(7), 1367–1382. DOI: 10.1017/glj.2026.10188

Cakir, G., Iftikhar, R., Bielozorov, A., Pourzolfaghar, Z., & Helfert, M. (2021). Omnichannel retailing: Digital transformation of a medium-sized retailer. *Journal of Information Technology Teaching Cases, 11*(2), 122–126. DOI: 10.1177/2043886920959803

Caliskan, K., MacKenzie, D., & Callon, M. (2025). Stacked economization: A research program for the study of platforms. *Journal of Cultural Economics, 18*(2), 304–331. DOI: 10.1080/17530350.2024.2423687

Cambria, E. (2016). Affective computing and sentiment analysis. *IEEE Intelligent Systems, 31*(2), 102–107. DOI: 10.1109/MIS.2016.31

Cao, G., Duan, Y., Edwards, J. S., & Dwivedi, Y. K. (2021). Understanding managers' attitudes and behavioral intentions towards using artificial intelligence for organizational decision-making. *Technovation, 106*, 102312. Advance online publication. DOI: 10.1016/j.technovation.2021.102312

Carah, N. (2017). Algorithmic brands: A decade of brand experiments with mobile and social media. *New Media & Society, 19*(3), 384–400. DOI: 10.1177/1461444815605463

Carr, S. (2021). How many ads do we see a day in 2021? https://www.lunio.ai/blog/how-many-ads-do-we-see-a-day retrieved on 30.04.2025[REMOVED HYPERLINK FIELD]

Castelo, N., Bos, M. W., & Lehmann, D. R. (2019). Task-dependent algorithm aversion. *JMR, Journal of Marketing Research, 56*(5), 809–825. DOI: 10.1177/0022243719851788

Chakraborty, D., Polisetty, A., Sowmya, G., Rana, N. P., & Khorana, S. (2024). Unlocking the potential of AI: Enhancing consumer engagement in the beauty and cosmetic product purchases. *Journal of Retailing and Consumer Services, 79*, 103842. Advance online publication. DOI: 10.1016/j.jretconser.2024.103842

Challoumis, C. (2024, October). Navigating the financial landscape-the impact of AI on consumer spending. In *XVI International Scientific Conference* (pp. 62-93).

Chandon, P., Hutchinson, J. W., Bradlow, E. T., & Young, S. H. (2009). Does in-store marketing work? Effects of the number and position of shelf facings on brand attention and evaluation at the point of purchase. *Journal of Marketing, 73*(6), 1–17. DOI: 10.1509/jmkg.73.6.1

Chandra, S., Verma, S., Lim, W. M., Kumar, S., & Donthu, N. (2022). Personalization in personalized marketing: Trends and ways forward. *Psychology and Marketing, 39*(8), 1529–1562. DOI: 10.1002/mar.21670

Chang, W., & Park, J. (2024). A comparative study on the effect of ChatGPT recommendation and AI recommender systems on the formation of a consideration set. *Journal of Retailing and Consumer Services, 78*, 103743. DOI: 10.1016/j.jretconser.2024.103743

Chapekis, A., & Lieb, A. (2025, July 22). *Google users are less likely to click on links when an AI summary appears in the results.* Pew Research Center. https://www.pewresearch.org/short-reads/2025/07/22/google-users-are-less-likely-to-click-on-links-when-an-ai-summary-appears-in-the-results/

Charette, M. G. (2025). Chronic Pain Beyond Measure: E-Health and the Politics of Pain Care.

Chatterjee, P., & Das, A. (2025). Adaptive Financial Recommendation Systems Using Generative AI and Multimodal Data. *Journal of Knowledge Learning and Science Technology ISSN: 2959-6386 (online), 4*(1), 112-120. DOI: 10.60087/jklst.v4.n1.012

Chaudhuri, A., & Holbrook, M. B. (2001). The chain of effects from brand trust and brand affect to brand performance: The role of brand loyalty. *Journal of Marketing, 65*(2), 81–93. DOI: 10.1509/jmkg.65.2.81.18255

Chen, W. K., Chen, C. K., & Silalahi, A. D. K. (2021, August). Understanding Consumers' post-purchase behavior by cognitive dissonance and emotions in the online impulse buying context. In*2021 IEEE 22nd International Conference on Information Reuse and Integration for Data Science (IRI)* (pp. 390-394). IEEE. DOI: 10.1109/IRI51335.2021.00061

Chen, X., Lin, A., & Webber, S. (2024, June). Designing artificial serendipity. In *International Conference on Human-Computer Interaction* (pp. 28-45). Cham: Springer Nature Switzerland. DOI: 10.1007/978-3-031-60405-8_3

Cheng, H. T., Koc, L., Harmsen, J., Shaked, T., Chandra, T., Aradhye, H., & Shah, H. (2016, September). Wide & deep learning for recommender systems. In *Proceedings of the 1st workshop on deep learning for recommender systems* (pp. 7-10). DOI: 10.1145/2988450.2988454

Cheng, R., Wu, N., Chen, S., & Han, B. (2022). Will Metaverse be NextG Internet? Vision, hype, and reality. *IEEE Network, 36*(5), 197–204. DOI: 10.1109/MNET.117.2200055

Chen, L., Zaharia, M., & Zou, J. (2024). How is ChatGPT's behavior changing over time? *Harvard Data Science Review, 6*(2). Advance online publication. DOI: 10.1162/99608f92.5317da47

Cherep, M., Ma, C., Xu, A., Shaked, M., Maes, P., & Singh, N. (2026). *A framework for studying AI agent behavior: Evidence from consumer choice experiments* [Preprint]. arXiv. /arXiv.2509.25609DOI: 10.48550

Cherif, E., & Lemoine, J.-F. (2019). Anthropomorphic virtual assistants and the reactions of Internet users: An experiment on the assistant's voice. [English Edition]. *Recherche et Applications en Marketing, 34*(1), 28–47. DOI: 10.1177/2051570719829432

Cheris, A., Kamel, M., Vu, M., Koszyk, S., Burns, M., & Lewis, R. (2025). *Agentic AI in retail: How autonomous shopping is redefining the customer journey*. Bain & Company.

Chesney, R., & Citron, D. (2019). Deep fakes: A looming challenge for privacy, democracy, and national security. *California Law Review, 107*(6), 1753–1820.

Chinchanachokchai, S., Thontirawong, P., & Chinchanachokchai, P. (2021). A tale of two recommender systems: The moderating role of consumer expertise on AI based product recommendations. *Journal of Retailing and Consumer Services, 61*, 102528. DOI: 10.1016/j.jretconser.2021.102528

Chiriatti, M., Ganapini, M. B., Panai, E., & Riva, G. (2026). Attention is not all you need: How AI is reshaping consumer attention and the future of brand strategy. *Harvard Data Science Review*, *8*(2). Advance online publication. DOI: 10.1162/99608f92.53f091e6

Chornous, G., Dimitrov, R., Fareniuk, Y., Penkova, M., & Nosko, R. (2025). Integration of feeling AI tools to support marketing solutions in e-commerce. *ACCESS Access to Science Business Innovation in Digital Economy*, *6*(2), 415–436. DOI: 10.46656/access.2025.6.2(10)

Chou, S., & Cheng, C. (2012). Exploring the continuance intentions of consumers for B2C online shopping: Perspectives of fairness and trust. *Online Information Review*, *36*(1), 104–125. DOI: 10.1108/14684521211209572

Clark, D. (2026, April 13). *Meta to surpass Google in digital ad revenues for first time ever* [Press release]. EMARKETER. https://www.emarketer.com/press-releases/meta-to-surpass-google-in-digital-ad-revenues-for-first-time-ever/

Clore, G. L., & Bar-Anan, Y. (2007). Affect-as-information. In Baumeister, R. F., & Vohs, K. D. (Eds.), *Encyclopedia of social psychology* (pp. 14–16). Sage., DOI: 10.4135/9781412956253

Cloudflare. (2025, July 1). *Cloudflare just changed how AI crawlers scrape the internet-at-large* [Press release]. https://www.cloudflare.com/press/press-releases/2025/cloudflare-just-changed-how-ai-crawlers-scrape-the-internet-at-large/

Consensus. (n.d.). *Consensus research database*. https://help.consensus.app/en/articles/10055108-consensus-research-database

Cotter, K. (2019). Playing the visibility game: How digital influencers and algorithms negotiate influence on Instagram. *New Media & Society*, *21*(4), 895–913. DOI: 10.1177/1461444818815684

Court, D., Elzinga, D., Mulder, S., & Vetvik, O. J. (2009). The consumer decision journey. *The McKinsey Quarterly*, *3*, 96–107.

Covington, P., Adams, J., & Sargin, E. (2016, September). Deep neural networks for youtube recommendations. In *Proceedings of the 10th ACM conference on recommender systems* (pp. 191-198). DOI: 10.1145/2959100.2959190

Cristofaro, M., Giardino, P. L., Malizia, A. P., & Mastrogiorgio, A. (2022). Affect and cognition in managerial decision making: A systematic literature review of neuroscience evidence. *Frontiers in Psychology*, *13*, 762993. Advance online publication. DOI: 10.3389/fpsyg.2022.762993 PMID: 35356322

Cui, Y. G., & van Esch, P. (2025). The end of search as we know it: Only those chosen by AI agents will survive in the delegate economy. *Business Horizons*. Advance online publication. DOI: 10.1016/j.bushor.2025.11.006

Cummings, J. J., & Bailenson, J. N. (2015). How Immersive Is Enough? A Meta-Analysis of the Effect of Immersive Technology on User Presence. *Media Psychology*, *19*(2), 272–309. DOI: 10.1080/15213269.2015.1015740

Danaher, J., Hogan, M. J., Noone, C., Kennedy, R., Behan, A., De Paor, A., Felzmann, H., Haklay, M., Khoo, S.-M., Morison, J., Murphy, M. H., O'Brolchain, N., Schafer, B., & Shankar, K. (2017). Algorithmic governance: Developing a research agenda through the power of collective intelligence. *Big Data & Society*, *4*(2), 2053951717726554. DOI: 10.1177/2053951717726554

Dang, Q., & Li, G. (2026). Unveiling trust in AI: The interplay of antecedents, consequences, and cultural dynamics. *AI & Society*, *41*(1), 669–692. DOI: 10.1007/s00146-025-02477-6

Danneels, E. (2008). Organizational antecedents of second-order competences. *Strategic Management Journal*, *29*(5), 519–543. DOI: 10.1002/smj.684

Davenport, T. H., & Beck, J. C. (2001). *The attention economy: Understanding the new currency of business*. Harvard Business School Press.

Davenport, T., Guha, A., Grewal, D., & Bressgott, T. (2020). How artificial intelligence will change the future of marketing. *Journal of the Academy of Marketing Science*, *48*(1), 24–42. DOI: 10.1007/s11747-019-00696-0

Davis, F. D. (1989). Perceived usefulness, perceived ease of use, and user acceptance of information technology. *Management Information Systems Quarterly*, *13*(3), 319–340. DOI: 10.2307/249008

Day, G. S. (2011). Closing the marketing capabilities gap. *Journal of Marketing*, *75*(4), 183–195. DOI: 10.1509/jmkg.75.4.183

de Bellis, E., & Johar, G. V. (2020). Autonomous shopping systems: Identifying and overcoming barriers to consumer adoption. *Journal of Retailing*, *96*(1), 74–87. DOI: 10.1016/j.jretai.2019.12.004

De Bruyn, A., Viswanathan, V., Beh, Y. S., Brock, J. K.-U., & von Wangenheim, F. (2020). Artificial intelligence and marketing: Pitfalls and opportunities. *Journal of Interactive Marketing*, *51*(1), 91–105. DOI: 10.1016/j.intmar.2020.04.007

de Regt, A., Plangger, K., & Barnes, S. J. (2021). Virtual reality marketing and customer advocacy: Transforming experiences from story-telling to story-doing. *Journal of Business Research*, *136*, 513–522. DOI: 10.1016/j.jbusres.2021.08.004

Del Vecchio, P., Di Minin, A., Petruzzelli, A. M., Panniello, U., & Pirri, S. (2018). Big data for open innovation in SMEs and large corporations: Trends, opportunities, and challenges. *Creativity and Innovation Management*, *27*(1), 6–22. DOI: 10.1111/caim.12224

Dellaert, B. G. C., Shu, S. B., Arentze, T. A., Baker, T., Diehl, K., Donkers, B., Fast, N. J., Häubl, G., Johnson, H., Karmarkar, U. R., Oppewal, H., Schmitt, B. H., Schroeder, J., Spiller, S. A., & Steffel, M. (2020). Consumer decisions with artificially intelligent voice assistants. *Marketing Letters*, *31*(4), 335–347. DOI: 10.1007/s11002-020-09537-5

Depari, G. S. (2024). How is the Implementation of Business Analytics in Asia. *Global Journal Indexing*, 2142-2159.

Deryl, M. D. S., Verma, S., & Srivastava, V. (2023). How does AI drive branding? Towards an integrated theoretical framework for AI-driven branding. *International Journal of Information Management Data Insights*, *3*(2), 100205. Advance online publication. DOI: 10.1016/j.jjimei.2023.100205

Dewar, C. (2018). *Culture: 4 keys to why it matters*. McKinsey & Company. https://www.mckinsey.com/capabilities/people-and-organizational-performance/our-insights/the-organization-blog/culture-4-keys-to-why-it-matters

Dey, D., & Ghose, D. (2025). Integrating AI adoption frameworks with digital maturity models: Strategic pathways in a rapidly evolving technological landscape. *Journal of Contemporary Business Research*, *1*(2), 156–170. Advance online publication. DOI: 10.1177/3049513X251387463

Dharini, M. G. (2025). THE ALGORITHMIC CONSUMER: HOW AI SHAPES DESIRE AND DECISION IN DIGITAL MARKETS. *Global Dimensions of Multidisciplinary Research*, 237.

Diehl, K., Kornish, L. J., & Lynch, J. G.Jr. (2003). Smart agents: When lower search costs for quality information increase price sensitivity. *The Journal of Consumer Research*, *30*(1), 56–71. DOI: 10.1086/374698

Dietvorst, B. J., Simmons, J. P., & Massey, C. (2015). Algorithm aversion: People erroneously avoid algorithms after seeing them err. *Journal of Experimental Psychology. General*, *144*(1), 114–126. DOI: 10.1037/xge0000033 PMID: 25401381

Diki, D. W., Egi, E. A. F., & Lubis, M. L. (2025). Nike's Strategy in Cultivating Customer Advocacy: A Case Study on Successful Brand Engagement and Consumer Loyalty. *International Journal of Technological Innovation for Society*, *1*(3).

Dolata, M., & Schwabe, G. (2023). What is the Metaverse and who seeks to define it? Mapping the site of social construction. *Journal of Information Technology*, *38*(3), 239–266. DOI: 10.1177/02683962231159927

Dollarhide M.E., Anderson S. (2020), Mass customization, Investopedia, 20/04/2025.

Dong, Y. (2025). Implementation of artificial intelligence for brand equity. *Cogent Business & Management*, *12*(1), 2471538. Advance online publication. DOI: 10.1080/23311975.2025.2471538

Donnelly, R., Kanodia, A., & Morozov, I. (2021). The long tail effect of personalized rankings. *Available at SSRN,*3649342.

Dorigo, T., Brown, G. D., Casonato, C., Cerdà, A., Ciarrochi, J., Da Lio, M., D'Souza, N., Gauger, N. R., Hayes, S. C., Hofmann, S. G., Johansson, R., Liwicki, M., Lotte, F., Nieto, J. J., Olivato, G., Parnes, P., Perry, G., Plebe, A., Rao, I. M., & Yazdanpanah, N. (2025). Artificial intelligence in science and society: The vision of USERN. *IEEE Access : Practical Innovations, Open Solutions*, *13*, 15993–16054. DOI: 10.1109/ACCESS.2025.3529357

Duarte, A., & Soeiro, R. (2025), Destinations, Experiences, and Places: The Role of Storytelling in Tourism Advertising, in Thematic Dossier – Place Branding and Public Diplomacy Special edition on Ibero-American States, *JanusNet,* 15(2), 94-113. https://doi.org/DOI: 10.26619/1647-7251.DT0125.5

Duarte, A. (2023). The relationship between brands and consumers. In *Dias, P. & Duarte, A. (2023), Social Brand Management in a Post Covid-19 Era* (pp. 3–16). Routledge., DOI: 10.4324/9781003382331-2

Dwivedi, A. (2015). A higher-order model of consumer brand engagement and its impact on loyalty intentions. *Journal of Retailing and Consumer Services*, *24*, 100–109. DOI: 10.1016/j.jretconser.2015.02.007

Dwivedi, Y. K., Akter, S., Sultana, S., Mariani, M., Wamba, S. F., & Spanaki, K. (2023). Advancing algorithmic bias management capabilities in AI-driven marketing analytics research. *Industrial Marketing Management*, *114*, 243–261. DOI: 10.1016/j.indmarman.2023.08.013

Dwivedi, Y. K., Hughes, L., Baabdullah, A. M., Ribeiro-Navarrete, S., Giannakis, M., Al-Debei, M. M., Dennehy, D., Metri, B., Buhalis, D., Cheung, C. M. K., Conboy, K., Doyle, R., Dubey, R., Dutot, V., Felix, R., Goyal, D. P., Gustafsson, A., Hinsch, C., Jebabli, I., & Wamba, S. F. (2022). Metaverse beyond the Hype: Multidisciplinary Perspectives on Emerging Challenges, Opportunities, and Agenda for Research, Practice and Policy. *International Journal of Information Management*, *66*, 102542. DOI: 10.1016/j.ijinfomgt.2022.102542

Efthymiou, F., Hildebrand, C., de Bellis, E., & Hampton, W. H. (2024). The power of AI-generated voices: How digital vocal tract length shapes product congruency and ad performance. *Journal of Interactive Marketing*, *59*(2), 117–134. DOI: 10.1177/10949968231194905

Ehrenberg, A. S. C., Goodhardt, G. J., & Barwise, T. P. (1990). Double jeopardy revisited. *Journal of Marketing*, *54*(3), 82–91. DOI: 10.1177/002224299005400307

Eisenhardt, K. M., & Martin, J. A. (2000). Dynamic capabilities: What are they? *Strategic Management Journal*, *21*(10–11), 1105–1121. DOI: 10.1002/1097-0266(200010/11)21:10/11<1105::AID-SMJ133>3.0.CO;2-E

El Alam, R., & Bitar, M. O. (2024). "Unveiling the Influence of AI's Product Recommendation on Consumer Purchase Intent": A Quantitative Study Investigating The Role of AI product recommendations on Consumer Purchase intent.

Enyiorji, P., & Deloitte, L. (2023). Does widespread use of AI recommendation engines reduce consumer financial choice diversity. *International Journal of Science and Engineering Applications*, *12*(4), 163–173.

Epley, N., Waytz, A., & Cacioppo, J. T. (2007). On seeing the human: A three-factor theory of anthropomorphism. *Psychological Review*, *114*(4), 864–886. DOI: 10.1037/0033-295X.114.4.864 PMID: 17907867

Escalas, J. E. (2007). Self-Referencing and Persuasion: Narrative Transportation versus Analytical Elaboration. *The Journal of Consumer Research*, *33*(4), 421–429. DOI: 10.1086/510216

Evans, J. St. B. T. (1984). Heuristic and analytic processes in reasoning. *British Journal of Psychology*, *75*(4), 451–468. DOI: 10.1111/j.2044-8295.1984.tb01915.x

Evans, J. St. B. T., & Stanovich, K. E. (2013). Dual-process theories of higher cognition: Advancing the debate. *Perspectives on Psychological Science : A Journal of the Association for Psychological Science*, *8*(3), 223–241. DOI: 10.1177/1745691612460685 PMID: 26172965

Fainshmidt, S., Pezeshkan, A., Frazier, M. L., Nair, A., & Markowski, E. (2016). Dynamic capabilities and organizational performance: A meta-analytic evaluation and extension. *Journal of Management Studies, 53*(8), 1348–1380. DOI: 10.1111/joms.12213

Falkinger, J. (2007). Attention economies. *Journal of Economic Theory, 133*(1), 266–294. DOI: 10.1016/j.jet.2005.12.001

Falkinger, J. (2008). Limited attention as a scarce resource in information-rich economies. *Economic Journal (London), 118*(532), 1596–1620. DOI: 10.1111/j.1468-0297.2008.02182.x

Farquhar, P. H. (1989). Managing brand equity. *Marketing Research, 1*(3), 24–33.

Festinger, L. (1957). *A theory of cognitive dissonance*. Stanford University Press., DOI: 10.1515/9781503620766

Fleder, D., Hosanagar, K., & Buja, A. (2011). Recommender systems and their effects on consumers. DOI: 10.1145/1807342.1807378

Fournier, S. (1998). Consumers and their brands: Developing relationship theory in consumer research. *The Journal of Consumer Research, 24*(4), 343–373. DOI: 10.1086/209515

France, S. L., Davcik, N. S., & Kazandjian, B. J. (2025). Digital brand equity: The concept, antecedents, measurement, and future development. *Journal of Business Research, 192*, 115273. Advance online publication. DOI: 10.1016/j.jbusres.2025.115273

Fu, Z., Niu, X., & Maher, M. L. (2023). Deep learning models for serendipity recommendations: A survey and new perspectives. *ACM Computing Surveys, 56*(1), 1–26. DOI: 10.1145/3605145

Gao, B., Wang, Y., Xie, H., Hu, Y., & Hu, Y. (2023). Artificial Intelligence in Advertising: Advancements, Challenges, and Ethical Considerations in Targeting, Personalization, Content Creation, and Ad Optimization. *SAGE Open, 13*(4), 21582440231210759. Advance online publication. DOI: 10.1177/21582440231210759

Gao, Y., Liu, S., & Yang, L. (2025). Artificial intelligence and innovation capability: A dynamic capabilities perspective. *International Review of Economics & Finance, 98*, 103923. Advance online publication. DOI: 10.1016/j.iref.2025.103923

Garlin, F. V., & Owen, K. (2006). Setting the tone with the tune: A meta-analytic review of the effects of background music in retail settings. *Journal of Business Research, 59*(6), 755–764. DOI: 10.1016/j.jbusres.2006.01.013

Gary, J. (2024). Examining the interplay of information, emotions, and behavior: PLS-ANN analysis. *Frontiers in Communication*, *9*, 1411870. Advance online publication. DOI: 10.3389/fcomm.2024.1411870

Garzonis, S., Jones, S., Jay, T., & O'Neill, E. (2009). Auditory icon and earcon mobile service notifications: Intuitiveness, learnability, memorability and preference. In *Proceedings of the SIGCHI Conference on Human Factors in Computing Systems* (pp. 1513–1522). Association for Computing Machinery. https://doi.org/ DOI: 10.1145/1518701.1518932

Gefen, D., Karahanna, E., & Straub, D. W. (2003). Trust and TAM in online shopping: An integrated model. *Management Information Systems Quarterly*, *27*(1), 51–90. DOI: 10.2307/30036519

Gehan, A., & Muppidi, S. (2026, March 5). OpenAI scales back shopping plans for ChatGPT. *The Information*. https://www.theinformation.com/articles/openai-scales-back-shopping-plans-chatgpt

Gentsch, P. (2019). *AI in marketing, sales and service: How marketers without a data science degree can use AI, big data and bots*. Palgrave Macmillan. DOI: 10.1007/978-3-319-89957-2

George, A. S. (2025). How AI Agents Are Reshaping the Internet from Human-Centered to Machine-Mediated Commerce. *Partners Universal International Innovation Journal*, *3*(4), 52–65.

Germani, F., & Spitale, G. (2025). Source framing triggers systematic bias in large language models. *Science Advances*, *11*(45), eadz2924. Advance online publication. DOI: 10.1126/sciadv.adz2924 PMID: 41202130

Ge, Y., Zhao, S., Zhou, H., Pei, C., Sun, F., Ou, W., & Zhang, Y. (2020). Understanding echo chambers in e-commerce recommender systems. In *Proceedings of the 43rd International ACM SIGIR Conference on Research and Development in Information Retrieval* (pp. 2261–2270). Association for Computing Machinery. DOI: 10.1145/3397271.3401431

Ghose, A., & Ipeirotis, P. G. (2010). Estimating the helpfulness and economic impact of product reviews: Mining text and reviewer characteristics. *IEEE Transactions on Knowledge and Data Engineering*, *23*(10), 1498–1512. DOI: 10.1109/TKDE.2010.188

Glim, S., & Hillje, A. (2025). Neural processing of sound-symbolic associations in product branding. *Journal of Neuroscience, Psychology, and Economics*, *18*(3), 113–125. DOI: 10.1037/npe0000204

Gobé, M. (2001). *Emotional branding: The new paradigm for connecting brands to people*. Allworth Press.

Golchha, C., & Nagariya, R. J. (2025). Exploring consumer choices and shopping patterns: Examining influences on consumer choices. In *Cultural Sensitivity, Cross-Border Logistics, and E-Commerce in Global Marketing* (pp. 181-214). IGI Global Scientific Publishing.

Goldberg, D., Nichols, D., Oki, B. M., & Terry, D. (1992). Using collaborative filtering to weave an information tapestry. *Communications of the ACM, 35*(12), 61–70. DOI: 10.1145/138859.138867

Goldhaber, M. H. (1997). The attention economy and the Net. *First Monday, 2*(4). Advance online publication. DOI: 10.5210/fm.v2i4.519

Gomez-Uribe, C. A., & Hunt, N. (2016). The Netflix recommender system: Algorithms, business value, and innovation. *ACM Transactions on Management Information Systems, 6*(4), 1–19. DOI: 10.1145/2843948

Goodwin, D. (2025, July 24). Google's AI Overviews are hurting clicks: Pew study. *Search Engine Land.* https://searchengineland.com/google-ai-overviews-hurting-clicks-study-459434

Goodwin, D. (2026, March 6). OpenAI's big ChatGPT Instant Checkout plan just changed. *Search Engine Land.* https://searchengineland.com/chatgpt-instant-checkout-plan-change-471033

Gorn, G. J. (1982). The effects of music in advertising on choice behavior: A classical conditioning approach. *Journal of Marketing, 46*(1), 94–101. DOI: 10.1177/002224298204600109

Graakjær, N. J. (2019). Sounding out 'I'm lovin' it': A multimodal discourse analysis of the sonic logo in commercials for McDonald's 2003–2018. *Critical Discourse Studies, 16*(5), 569–582. DOI: 10.1080/17405904.2019.1624184

Graakjær, N. J., & Bonde, A. (2018). Non-musical sound branding: A conceptualisation and research overview. *European Journal of Marketing, 52*(7/8), 1505–1525. DOI: 10.1108/EJM-09-2017-0609

Grand View Research. (n.d.). Emotion AI market size, share & trends analysis report. https://www.grandviewresearch.com/industry-analysis/emotion-ai-market-report

Green, M. C. (2021). Transportation into Narrative Worlds. *Entertainment-Education Behind the Scenes,* 87–101. https://doi.org/DOI: 10.1007/978-3-030-63614-2_6

Green, M. C., & Brock, T. C. (2000). The role of transportation in the persuasiveness of public narratives. *Journal of Personality and Social Psychology*, *79*(5), 701–721. DOI: 10.1037/0022-3514.79.5.701 PMID: 11079236

Grewal, D., Hulland, J., Kopalle, P. K., & Karahanna, E. (2020). The future of technology and marketing: A multidisciplinary perspective. *Journal of the Academy of Marketing Science*, *48*(1), 1–8. DOI: 10.1007/s11747-019-00711-4

Grewal, D., Levy, M., & Kumar, V. (2017). Customer experience management in retailing: An organizing framework. *Journal of Retailing*, *93*(1), 1–14. DOI: 10.1016/j.jretai.2016.12.008

Guaglione, S. (2026, March 10). GEO hype busted: How it differs (and how it doesn't) from SEO. *Digiday*. https://digiday.com/media/geo-hype-busted-experts-call-it-more-seo-than-new-discipline/

Guan, Y., Wei, Q., & Chen, G. (2019). Deep learning based personalized recommendation with multi-view information integration. *Decision Support Systems*, *118*, 58–69. DOI: 10.1016/j.dss.2019.01.003

Gursoy, D., Chi, O. H., Lu, L., & Nunkoo, R. (2019). Consumers acceptance of artificially intelligent (AI) device use in service delivery. *International Journal of Information Management*, *49*, 157–169. DOI: 10.1016/j.ijinfomgt.2019.03.008

Gustafsson, C. (2015). Sonic branding: A consumer-oriented literature review. *Journal of Brand Management*, *22*(1), 20–37. DOI: 10.1057/bm.2015.5

Gutiérrez Gutiérrez, M. M., Perona Páez, J. J., & Gutiérrez Bonilla, F. (2024). Models of brand equity: A systematic and critical review. *Cogent Business & Management*, *11*(1), 2433168. Advance online publication. DOI: 10.1080/23311975.2024.2433168

Hagtvedt, H., & Brasel, S. A. (2016). Cross-modal communication: Sound frequency influences consumer responses to color lightness. *JMR, Journal of Marketing Research*, *53*(4), 551–562. DOI: 10.1509/jmr.14.0414

Hahn, M., & Hwang, I. (1999). Effects of tempo and familiarity of background music on message processing in TV advertising: A resource-matching perspective. *Psychology and Marketing*, *16*(8), 659–675. DOI: 10.1002/(SICI)1520-6793(199912)16:8<659::AID-MAR3>3.0.CO;2-S

Hallinger, P., & Nguyen, V. T. (2020). Mapping the landscape and structure of research on education for sustainable development: A bibliometric review. *Sustainability (Basel)*, *12*(5), 1947. DOI: 10.3390/su12051947

Hansen, M. (2024). From attention economy to cognitive lock-ins. *Big Data & Society, 11*(3), 20539517241275878. DOI: 10.1177/20539517241275878

Hardcastle, K., Vorster, L., & Brown, D. M. (2025). Understanding customer responses to AI-driven personalized journeys: Impacts on the customer experience. *Journal of Advertising, 54*(2), 176–195. DOI: 10.1080/00913367.2025.2460985

Hari, M. K. (2025). A Cross-Cultural Framework for Algorithmic Trust: How Data Transparency Mechanisms Influence Consumer Confidence in AI-Driven Marketing. *Journal of International Commercial Law and Technology, 6*, 727–743.

Hart, C. W. (1995). Mass customization: Conceptual underpinnings, opportunities and limits. *International Journal of Service Industry Management, 6*(2), 36–45. DOI: 10.1108/09564239510084932

Harzer, T. S. (2013). *Value creation through mass customization: An empirical analysis of the requisite strategic capabilities* (Doctoral dissertation, Aachen, Techn. Hochsch., Diss., 2013).

Häubl, G., & Trifts, V. (2000). Consumer decision making in online shopping environments: The effects of interactive decision aids. *Marketing Science, 19*(1), 4–21. DOI: 10.1287/mksc.19.1.4.15178

Heitmayer, M. (2025). The second wave of attention economics: Attention as a universal symbolic currency on social media and beyond. *Interacting with Computers, 37*(1), 18–29. DOI: 10.1093/iwc/iwae035

Helfat, C. E., & Peteraf, M. A. (2003). The dynamic resource-based view: Capability lifecycles. *Strategic Management Journal, 24*(10), 997–1010. DOI: 10.1002/smj.332

Helfat, C. E., & Winter, S. G. (2011). Untangling dynamic and operational capabilities: Strategy for the (n)ever-changing world. *Strategic Management Journal, 32*(11), 1243–1250. DOI: 10.1002/smj.955

Heo, J. (2025). Marketing Luxury Fashion in the Metaverse: The Case of Gucci Town on Roblox. *Thunderbird International Business Review*. Advance online publication. DOI: 10.1002/tie.70024

Hermann, E., & Puntoni, S. (2024). Artificial intelligence and consumer behavior: From predictive to generative AI. *Journal of Business Research, 180*, 114720. Advance online publication. DOI: 10.1016/j.jbusres.2024.114720

Hildebrand, C., Efthymiou, F., Busquet, F., Hampton, W. H., Hoffman, D. L., & Novak, T. P. (2020). Voice analytics in business research: Conceptual foundations, acoustic feature extraction, and applications. *Journal of Business Research, 121*, 364–374. DOI: 10.1016/j.jbusres.2020.09.020

Ho, E. (2024). Rule-Based vs. AI-Powered Recommendation: Which Should You Pick For Your Shopify Store? https://blog.boostcommerce.net/posts/rule-based-ai-powered-recommendation[REMOVED HYPERLINK FIELD]

Holland, A. (2026, June 2). How "it's just SEO" took over the GEO conversation. *Search Engine Land.* https://searchengineland.com/its-just-seo-geo-conversation-479158

Hollebeek, L. D., Glynn, M. S., & Brodie, R. J. (2014). Consumer brand engagement in social media: Conceptualization, scale development and validation. *Journal of Interactive Marketing*, *28*(2), 149–165. DOI: 10.1016/j.intmar.2013.12.002

Holtz, D., Carterette, B., Chandar, P., Nazari, Z., Cramer, H., & Aral, S. (2020). The engagement-diversity connection: Evidence from a field experiment on spotify. arXiv preprint arXiv:2003.08203. /arXiv.2003.08203DOI: 10.1145/3391403.3399532

Hong, C. (2020). An Approach to de-homogenizing recommender systems (Doctoral dissertation, Massachusetts Institute of Technology).

Horani, O. M., Al-Adwan, A. S., Yaseen, H., Hmoud, H., Al-Rahmi, W. M., & Alkhalifah, A. (2025). The critical determinants impacting artificial intelligence adoption at the organizational level. *Information Development*, *41*(3), 1055–1079. DOI: 10.1177/02666669231166889

Horkheimer, M., Adorno, T. W., & Noeri, G. (2002). *Dialectic of enlightenment.* Stanford University Press.

Hosanagar, K., Fleder, D., Lee, D., & Buja, A. (2014). Will the global village fracture into tribes? Recommender systems and their effects on consumer fragmentation. *Management Science*, *60*(4), 805–823. DOI: 10.1287/mnsc.2013.1808

Hoyer, W. D. (1984). An examination of consumer decision making for a common repeat purchase product. *The Journal of Consumer Research*, *11*(3), 822–829. DOI: 10.1086/209017

Hoyer, W. D., Kroschke, M., Schmitt, B., Kraume, K., & Shankar, V. (2020). Transforming the customer experience through new technologies. *Journal of Interactive Marketing*, *51*(1), 57–71. DOI: 10.1016/j.intmar.2020.04.001

Huang, L., Yu, W., Ma, W., Zhong, W., Feng, Z., Wang, H., Chen, Q., Peng, W., Feng, X., Qin, B., & Liu, T. (2025). A survey on hallucination in large language models: Principles, taxonomy, challenges, and open questions. *ACM Transactions on Information Systems, 43*(2), 42. Advance online publication. DOI: 10.1145/3703155

Huang, M.-H., & Rust, R. T. (2018). Artificial intelligence in service. *Journal of Service Research, 21*(2), 155–172. DOI: 10.1177/1094670517752459

Huang, M.-H., & Rust, R. T. (2021). A strategic framework for artificial intelligence in marketing. *Journal of the Academy of Marketing Science, 49*(1), 30–50. DOI: 10.1007/s11747-020-00749-9

Huang, M.-H., & Rust, R. T. (2021). Engaged to a robot? The role of AI in service. *Journal of Service Research, 24*(1), 30–41. DOI: 10.1177/1094670520902266

Huang, M.-H., & Rust, R. T. (2022). AI as customer. *Journal of Service Management, 33*(2), 210–220. DOI: 10.1108/JOSM-11-2021-0425

Hue, T. T., & Hung, T. H. (2025). Impact of artificial intelligence on branding: A bibliometric review and future research directions. *Humanities & Social Sciences Communications, 12*(1), 209. DOI: 10.1057/s41599-025-04488-6

Hu, Y., & Min, H. (2023). The dark side of artificial intelligence in service: The "watching-eye" effect and privacy concerns. *International Journal of Hospitality Management, 110*, 103437. DOI: 10.1016/j.ijhm.2023.103437

IAMAI. (2023). *India internet report 2023*. Internet and Mobile Association of India.

iMotions. (2019, April 5). MARS - affectiva. Affectiva. https://www.affectiva.com/success-story/mars/

Ismaliyanto, J., Sudjaniah, D., Afiat, D. D., Jacobalis, R. J., Hastuti, W., Rahayu, S., & Andayani, R. (2026). *CONSUMER BEHAVIOR IN THE DIGITAL ERA*. Mawadra Lestari Enterprise.

Jannach, D., & Jugovac, M. (2019). Measuring the business value of recommender systems. [TMIS]. *ACM Transactions on Management Information Systems, 10*(4), 1–23. DOI: 10.1145/3370082

Jantunen, A. (2005). Knowledge-processing capabilities and innovative performance: An empirical study. *European Journal of Innovation Management, 8*(3), 336–349. DOI: 10.1108/14601060510610199

Jiang, W., Li, S., Li, X., Li, K., & Wu, J. (2025). Uncovering Recommendation Serendipity with Objective Data-driven Factor Investigation. *ACM Transactions on Information Systems, 43*(6), 1–33. DOI: 10.1145/3758092

Juan, Y., Zhuang, Y., Chin, W. S., & Lin, C. J. (2016, September). Field-aware factorization machines for CTR prediction. In *Proceedings of the 10th ACM conference on recommender systems* (pp. 43-50). DOI: 10.1145/2959100.2959134

Kahneman, D. (2011). *Thinking, fast and slow*. Farrar, Straus and Giroux.

Kalpokas, I., & Kalpokienė, J. (2025). *Societies at an AI Crossroads: Choices and Value Conflicts*. Routledge. DOI: 10.4324/9781003715849

Kamakura, W. A., & Russell, G. J. (1993). Measuring brand value with scanner data. *International Journal of Research in Marketing*, *10*(1), 9–22. DOI: 10.1016/0167-8116(93)90030-3

Kaminskas, M., & Bridge, D. (2016). Diversity, serendipity, novelty, and coverage: A survey and empirical analysis of beyond-accuracy objectives in recommender systems. *ACM Transactions on Interactive Intelligent Systems*, *7*(1), 1–42. DOI: 10.1145/2926720

Kang, J. A., Hong, S., & Hubbard, G. T. (2020). The role of storytelling in advertising: Consumer emotion, narrative engagement level, and word-of-mouth intention. *Journal of Consumer Behaviour*, *19*(1), 47–56. DOI: 10.1002/cb.1793

Kanumarlapudi, P. K., & Ballamudi, S. (2025). Enhancing Generative AI Shopping Assistants through Advanced Multi-Attribute Decision Making Technique. *Journal of Artificial Intelligence and Machine Learning*, *3*(2), 1–7. DOI: 10.55124/jaim.v3i2.267

Kapoor, A., & Verma, V. (2024). Emotion AI: Understanding emotions through artificial intelligence. *International Journal of Engineering Science and Humanities*, *1*(1), 223–232. DOI: 10.62904/0vcbvb24

Katrandjiev, H., Naydenov, A., & Dinev, A. (2025). THE ROLE OF AI IN MODERN BRAND MANAGEMENT.*Časopis za ekonomiju*, 397.

Kay, M. J. (1993). Making mass customization happen: Lessons for implementation. *Planning Review*, *21*(4), 14–18. DOI: 10.1108/eb054421

Keaveney, S. M. (1995). Customer switching behavior in service industries: An exploratory study. *Journal of Marketing*, *59*(2), 71–82. DOI: 10.1177/002224299505900206

Keller, K. L. (1993). Conceptualizing, measuring, and managing customer-based brand equity. *Journal of Marketing*, *57*(1), 1–22. DOI: 10.1177/002224299305700101

Keller, K. L. (1998). *Strategic brand management: Building, measuring, and managing brand equity*. Prentice Hall.

Kemp, E., Cho, Y.-N., Bui, M., & Kintzer, A. (2024). Music to the ears: The role of sonic branding in advertising. *International Journal of Advertising*, *43*(6), 1039–1059. DOI: 10.1080/02650487.2023.2273645

Kemp, E., Kopp, S. W., & Bui, M. (2023). Healthcare brands sound off: Evaluating the influence of sonic branding in shaping consumer perceptions. *International Journal of Pharmaceutical and Healthcare Marketing*, *17*(3), 340–352. DOI: 10.1108/IJPHM-10-2022-0093

Kenny, G., & Pogrebna, G. (2026, March). LLMs are overtaking search: Here's how to adjust your online presence. *Harvard Business Review*. https://hbr.org/2026/03/llms-are-overtaking-search-heres-how-to-adjust-your-online-presence

Khamis, S., & Keogh, B. (2021). Sonic branding and the aesthetic infrastructure of everyday consumption. *Popular Music*, *40*(2), 281–296. DOI: 10.1017/S0261143021000118

Kim, E., Ratneshwar, S., & Thorson, E. (2017). Why Narrative Ads Work: An Integrated Process Explanation. *Journal of Advertising*, *46*(2), 283–296. DOI: 10.1080/00913367.2016.1268984

Kimiagari, S., & Malafe, N. S. A. (2021). The role of cognitive and affective responses in the relationship between internal and external stimuli on online impulse buying behavior. *Journal of Retailing and Consumer Services*, *61*, 102567. DOI: 10.1016/j.jretconser.2021.102567

Kim, J. K., Cho, Y. H., Kim, W. J., Kim, J. R., & Suh, J. H. (2002). A personalized recommendation procedure for Internet shopping support. *Electronic Commerce Research and Applications*, *1*(3-4), 301–313. DOI: 10.1016/S1567-4223(02)00022-4

Kim, J., Giroux, M., & Lee, J. C. (2021). When do you trust AI? The effect of number presentation detail on consumer trust and acceptance of AI recommendations. *Psychology and Marketing*, *38*(7), 1140–1155. DOI: 10.1002/mar.21498

Kim, J., & Gupta, P. (2012). Emotional expressions in online user reviews: How they influence consumers' product evaluations. *Journal of Business Research*, *65*(7), 985–992. DOI: 10.1016/j.jbusres.2011.04.013

Kim, M., & Baek, T. H. (2025). Fostering brand love through branded memes on social media. *Journal of Product and Brand Management*, *34*(4), 486–499. DOI: 10.1108/JPBM-02-2024-5002

Kim, Y., Oh, S., Noh, C., Hong, E., & Park, S. (2025). Design of a serendipity-incorporated recommender system. *Electronics (Basel)*, *14*(4), 821. DOI: 10.3390/electronics14040821

King, C., & Grace, D. (2009). Employee based brand equity: A third perspective. *Services Marketing Quarterly, 30*(2), 122–147. DOI: 10.1080/15332960802619082

Kirk, C. P., & Givi, J. (2024). The AI-authorship effect: Understanding authenticity, moral disgust, and consumer responses to AI-generated marketing communications. *Journal of Business Research, 186*, 114984. DOI: 10.1016/j.jbusres.2024.114984

Klaus, P., & Zaichkowsky, J. L. (2020). AI voice bots: A services marketing research agenda. *Journal of Services Marketing, 34*(3), 389–398. DOI: 10.1108/JSM-01-2019-0043

Klaus, P., & Zaichkowsky, J. L. (2022). The convenience of shopping via voice AI: Introducing AIDM. *Journal of Retailing and Consumer Services, 65*, 102490. DOI: 10.1016/j.jretconser.2021.102490

Klink, R. R. (2000). Creating brand names with meaning: The use of sound symbolism. *Marketing Letters, 11*(1), 5–20. DOI: 10.1023/A:1008184423824

Klink, R. R., & Wu, L. (2014). The role of position, type, and combination of sound symbolism imbeds in brand names. *Marketing Letters, 25*(1), 13–24. DOI: 10.1007/s11002-013-9236-3

Klover.ai. (2025). Starbucks' AI strategy: Analysis of dominance in coffee. https://www.klover.ai/starbucks-ai-strategy-analysis-of-dominance-in-coffee/

Knödler, L., & Rudeloff, C. (2024). Look who's talking now: The effects of pre-recorded and AI-generated synthetic brand voices on brand anthropomorphism and brand equity. *Journal of Creative Communications, 19*(3), 295–311. DOI: 10.1177/09732586241253651

Knoeferle, K. M., Knoeferle, P., Velasco, C., & Spence, C. (2016). Multisensory brand search: How the meaning of sounds guides consumers' visual attention. *Journal of Experimental Psychology. Applied, 22*(2), 196–210. DOI: 10.1037/xap0000084

Knoeferle, K. M., Spangenberg, E. R., Herrmann, A., & Landwehr, J. R. (2012). It is all in the mix: The interactive effect of music tempo and mode on in-store sales. *Marketing Letters, 23*(1), 325–337. DOI: 10.1007/s11002-011-9156-z

Komiak, S. Y. X., & Benbasat, I. (2006). The effects of personalization and familiarity on trust and adoption of recommendation agents. *Management Information Systems Quarterly, 30*(4), 941–960. DOI: 10.2307/25148760

Konstan, J. A., & ACM Conference on Recommender Systems. 2007. *RecSys' 07: Proceedings of the 2007 ACM Conference on Recommender Systems:* Minneapolis, M. N. USA, October 19-20, 2007. Association for Computing Machinery. https://dl.acm.org/doi/proceedings/10.1145/1297231

Koren, Y. (2008, August). Factorization meets the neighborhood: a multifaceted collaborative filtering model. In *Proceedings of the 14th ACM SIGKDD international conference on Knowledge discovery and data mining* (pp. 426-434). DOI: 10.1145/1401890.1401944

Koren, Y. (2009, June). Collaborative filtering with temporal dynamics. In *Proceedings of the 15th ACM SIGKDD international conference on Knowledge discovery and data mining* (pp. 447-456). DOI: 10.1145/1557019.1557072

Kotler, P. (1989). From mass marketing to mass customization. *Planning review, 17*(5), 10-47. DOI: 10.1108/eb054267

Kovalenko, Y., Nikitin, A., & Kuzina, Y. (2026). Value Creation in the Algorithmic Age: A Systematic Review of How AI, Data Privacy, and Platform Ecosystems Are Reshaping Marketing Theory. *American Impact Review, 1*(1), e2026018–e2026018. DOI: 10.66308/air.e2026018

Kozinets, R. V. (2022). Algorithmic branding through platform assemblages: Core conceptions and research directions for a new era of marketing and service management. *Journal of Service Management, 33*(3), 437–452. DOI: 10.1108/JOSM-07-2021-0263

Krishnan, V., Kellaris, J. J., & Aurand, T. W. (2012). Sonic logos: Can sound influence willingness to pay? *Journal of Product and Brand Management, 21*(4), 275–284. DOI: 10.1108/10610421211246685

Kübler, K. (2023). Influencers and the attention economy: The meaning and management of attention on Instagram. *Journal of Marketing Management, 39*(11–12), 965–981. DOI: 10.1080/0267257X.2022.2157864

Kulothungan, V., & Gupta, D. (2025, May). Towards adaptive AI governance: Comparative insights from the US, EU, and Asia. In *2025 IEEE 11th Conference on Big Data Security on Cloud (BigDataSecurity)* (pp. 32-38). IEEE. DOI: 10.1109/BigDataSecurity66063.2025.00018

Kulp, P. (2026, April 7). How Meta's AI push is changing ad creation. *Marketing Brew*. https://www.marketingbrew.com/stories/2026/04/07/meta-ai-ad-creation

Kumar, P., & Mishra, S. (2025). Robustness in large language models: A survey of mitigation strategies and evaluation metrics. *Transactions on Machine Learning Research.* https://openreview.net/forum?id=Bchvaaod6g

Kumar, H. (2024). Virtual worlds, real opportunities: A review of marketing in the metaverse. *Acta Psychologica, 250*, 104517. DOI: 10.1016/j.actpsy.2024.104517 PMID: 39413664

Kumar, V., & Gupta, S. (2016). Conceptualizing the Evolution and Future of Advertising. *Journal of Advertising, 45*(3), 302–317. DOI: 10.1080/00913367.2016.1199335

Kumar, V., Rajan, B., Venkatesan, R., & Lecinski, J. (2019). Understanding the role of artificial intelligence in personalized engagement marketing. *California Management Review, 61*(4), 135–155. DOI: 10.1177/0008125619859317

Kunaver, M., & Požrl, T. (2017). Diversity in recommender systems–A survey. *Knowledge-Based Systems, 123*, 154–162. DOI: 10.1016/j.knosys.2017.02.009

L'Oréal. (2018, March 16). *L'Oréal acquires ModiFace, further expanding its worldwide expertise in beauty tech* [Press release]. https://www.loreal-finance.com/eng/news-release/loreal-acquires-modiface-further-expanding-its-worldwide-expertise-beauty-tech

Labrecque, L. I. (2014). Fostering consumer-brand relationships in social media environments: The role of parasocial interaction. *Journal of Interactive Marketing, 28*(2), 134–148. DOI: 10.1016/j.intmar.2013.12.003

Lai, Q., Jin, Y., Wu, T., & Ying, T. (2025). Rational, emotional or both: Decoding service robot adoption in tourism from elaboration likelihood model perspective. *Journal of Hospitality and Tourism Technology, 16*(5), 966–985. DOI: 10.1108/JHTT-03-2024-0194

Lal, R., & Sarvary, M. (1999). When and how is the Internet likely to decrease price competition? *Marketing Science, 18*(4), 485–503. DOI: 10.1287/mksc.18.4.485

Lambrecht, A., & Tucker, C. (2019). Algorithmic bias? An empirical study of apparent gender-based discrimination in the display of STEM career ads. *Management Science, 65*(7), 2966–2981. DOI: 10.1287/mnsc.2018.3093

Lang, J., Spear, M., & Wu, S. F. (2010). Social manipulation of online recommender systems. In *Social Informatics: Second International Conference, SocInfo 2010, Laxenburg, Austria, October 27-29, 2010. Proceedings 2*(pp. 125-139). Springer Berlin Heidelberg. DOI: 10.1007/978-3-642-16567-2_10

Lau, K. W., & Lee, P. Y. (2019). Shopping in virtual reality: A study on consumers' shopping experience in a stereoscopic virtual reality. *Virtual Reality (Waltham Cross)*, *23*(3), 255–268. DOI: 10.1007/s10055-018-0362-3

Lavack, A. M., Thakor, M. V., & Bottausci, I. (2008). Music-brand congruency in high- and low-cognition radio advertising. *International Journal of Advertising*, *27*(4), 549–568. DOI: 10.2501/S0265048708080141

Law, R. (2025, April 7). GEO, LLMO, AEO: It's all just SEO. *Ahrefs Blog*. https://ahrefs.com/blog/geo-is-just-seo/

Leandro, A., & Duarte, A. (2026). An Analysis of Advertising Campaigns Powered by Artificial Intelligence. In Santos, J. D., Botelho Pires, P., & Pratas, J. (Eds.), *Artificial Intelligence Transforming Marketing. Contributions to Management Science*. Springer., DOI: 10.1007/978-3-032-22360-9_9

Lee, D., & Hosanagar, K. (2019). How do recommender systems affect sales diversity? A cross-category investigation via randomized field experiment. *Information Systems Research*, *30*(1), 239–259. DOI: 10.1287/isre.2018.0800

Lemon, K. N., & Verhoef, P. C. (2016). Understanding customer experience throughout the customer journey. *Journal of Marketing*, *80*(6), 69–96. DOI: 10.1509/jm.15.0420

Liang, H., & Xue, Y. (2009). Avoidance of information technology threats: A theoretical perspective. *Management Information Systems Quarterly*, *33*(1), 71–90. DOI: 10.2307/20650279

Liang, M. (2026). How marketing mechanisms build trust in AI recommendation systems: A serial mediation model in live-streaming commerce. *Cogent Business & Management*, *13*(1), 2658868. Advance online publication. DOI: 10.1080/23311975.2026.2658868

Lim, G. G., Kang, J. Y., Lee, J. K., & Lee, D. C. (2011). Rule-based personalized comparison shopping including delivery cost. *Electronic Commerce Research and Applications*, *10*(6), 637–649. DOI: 10.1016/j.elerap.2011.07.002

Lin, Y. L., Zheng, Y. X., & Ku, Y. C. (2025). Augmenting micro-moment recommendations with group and serendipity perspectives. *Decision Support Systems*, *193*, 114454. DOI: 10.1016/j.dss.2025.114454

Liu-Thompkins, Y., Okazaki, S., & Li, H. (2022). Artificial empathy in marketing interactions: Bridging the human-AI gap in affective and social customer experience. *Journal of the Academy of Marketing Science*, *50*(6), 1198–1218. DOI: 10.1007/s11747-022-00892-5

Li, X., Grahl, J., & Hinz, O. (2022). How do recommender systems lead to consumer purchases? A causal mediation analysis of a field experiment. *Information Systems Research, 33*(2), 620–637. DOI: 10.1287/isre.2021.1074

Lobschat, L., Mueller, B., Eggers, F., Brandimarte, L., Diefenbach, S., Kroschke, M., & Wirtz, J. (2021). Corporate digital responsibility. *Journal of Business Research, 122*, 875–888. DOI: 10.1016/j.jbusres.2019.10.006

Logg, J. M., Minson, J. A., & Moore, D. A. (2019). Algorithm appreciation: People prefer algorithmic to human judgment. *Organizational Behavior and Human Decision Processes, 151*, 90–103. DOI: 10.1016/j.obhdp.2018.12.005

Longoni, C., & Cian, L. (2022). Artificial intelligence in utilitarian vs. hedonic contexts: The "word-of-machine" effect. *Journal of Marketing, 86*(1), 91–108. DOI: 10.1177/0022242920957347

Lule, B., Wuryaningrat, N. F., Walean, R. H., & Mandagi, D. W. (2026). Artificial empathy in marketing: Conceptual mapping, antecedents and consequences. *International Journal of Innovation Science*, •••, 1–24. DOI: 10.1108/IJIS-08-2025-0411

Lundqvist, A., Liljander, V., Gummerus, J., & Van Riel, A. (2013). The impact of storytelling on the consumer brand experience: The case of a firm-originated story. *Journal of Brand Management, 20*(4), 283–297. DOI: 10.1057/bm.2012.15

Mallen, A., Asai, A., Zhong, V., Das, R., Khashabi, D., & Hajishirzi, H. (2023). When not to trust language models: Investigating effectiveness of parametric and non-parametric memories. In *Proceedings of the 61st Annual Meeting of the Association for Computational Linguistics* (Volume 1: *Long Papers)* (pp. 9802–9822). Association for Computational Linguistics. DOI: 10.18653/v1/2023.acl-long.546

Mancuso, I., Messeni Petruzzelli, A., & Panniello, U. (2023). Digital business model innovation in metaverse: How to approach virtual economy opportunities. *Information Processing & Management, 60*(5), 103457. DOI: 10.1016/j.ipm.2023.103457

Mandolfo, M., Di Dalmazi, M., & Lamberti, L. (2024). Now you see me: Evaluating visual and auditory brand placement disclosures in music videos. *Journal of Marketing Communications, 30*(5), 553–575. DOI: 10.1080/13527266.2022.2152475

Manolovitz, B. (2022). *Effects of Repetition of Unfamiliar Music on Listening Behavior and Neural Responses* (Doctoral dissertation, University of Miami).

Manzoor, A. (2024). Impact of ambient music on consumer perceptions and impulse buying behavior with the moderating role of gender. *SAGE Open, 14*(2), 21582440241259001. Advance online publication. DOI: 10.1177/21582440241259001

Marchand, É., Durand, T., & Dubois, M. (2025). Surveillance Capitalism, Consumer Subjectivity and Marketing in the Age of Artificial Intelligence. *Social Science Chronicle, 5*(1), 01-18. DOI: 10.56106/ssc.2025.01

Mari, A., Mandelli, A., & Algesheimer, R. (2026). AI-assisted shopping on voice assistants: The efficiency-autonomy consumer decision trade-off. *Journal of Interactive Marketing, 61*(3), 327–344. DOI: 10.1177/10949968251400616

Marketing with Dave. (2026). Case study: Amazon's recommendation engine — the personalization powerhouse driving 35% of sales. https://marketingwithdave.com/case-study-amazons-recommendation-engine-the-personalization-powerhouse-driving-35-%-of-sales

Mas, L., Bolls, P., Rodero, E., Barreda-Ángeles, M., & Churchill, A. (2021). The impact of the sonic logo's acoustic features on orienting responses, emotions and brand personality transmission. *Journal of Product and Brand Management, 30*(5), 740–753. DOI: 10.1108/JPBM-05-2019-2370

McClellan, S. (2013, January 18). Unilever, Coca-Cola utilize facial analysis to enhance ad tests. *MediaPost*. https://www.mediapost.com/publications/article/191418/unilever-coca-cola-utilize-facial-analysis-to-enh.html

McCracken, G. (1986). Culture and consumption: A theoretical account of the structure and movement of the cultural meaning of consumer goods. *The Journal of Consumer Research, 13*(1), 71–84. DOI: 10.1086/209048

McKinsey & Company. (2023). What is Personalization? https://www.mckinsey.com/featured-insights/mckinsey-explainers/what-is-personalization

McKinsey & Company. (2025). *The state of AI: How organizations are rewiring to capture value*. McKinsey & Company. https://www.mckinsey.com/capabilities/quantumblack/our-insights/the-state-of-ai

McLean, G., & Osei-Frimpong, K. (2019). Hey Alexa … examine the variables influencing the use of artificial intelligent in-home voice assistants. *Computers in Human Behavior, 99*, 28–37. DOI: 10.1016/j.chb.2019.05.009

Mehmet, M. (2025). From search rankings to synthesised answers: Propositions for consumer behaviour in the age of generative AI search. *Journal of Consumer Behaviour, 24*(6), 2948–2950. DOI: 10.1002/cb.70044

Mehrabian, A., & Russell, J. A. (1974). *An approach to environmental psychology*. MIT Press.

Melzner, J., & Raghubir, P. (2023). The sound of music: The effect of timbral sound quality in audio logos on brand personality perception. *JMR, Journal of Marketing Research*, *60*(5), 932–949. DOI: 10.1177/00222437221135188

Miao, F., Kozlenkova, I. V., Wang, H., Xie, T., & Palmatier, R. W. (2022). An emerging theory of avatar marketing. *Journal of Marketing*, *86*(1), 67–90. DOI: 10.1177/0022242921996646

Mikalef, P., & Gupta, M. (2021). Artificial intelligence capability: Conceptualization, measurement calibration, and empirical study on its impact on organizational creativity and firm performance. *Information & Management*, *58*(3), 103434. Advance online publication. DOI: 10.1016/j.im.2021.103434

Milano, S., Taddeo, M., & Floridi, L. (2020). Recommender systems and their ethical challenges. *AI & Society*, *35*(4), 957–967. DOI: 10.1007/s00146-020-00950-y

Milgram, P., Takemura, H., Utsumi, A., & Kishino, F. (1995). Augmented reality: A class of displays on the reality–virtuality continuum. In Das, H. (Ed.), *Telemanipulator and telepresence technologies* (Vol. 2351, pp. 282–292). SPIE., DOI: 10.1117/12.197321

Miraz, M. H., Ali, M., & Excell, P. S. (2021). Adaptive user interfaces and universal usability through plasticity of user interface design. *Computer Science Review*, *40*, 100363. DOI: 10.1016/j.cosrev.2021.100363

Misra, R. R., Kapoor, S., & Sanjeev, M. A. (2024). The impact of personalisation algorithms on consumer engagement and purchase behavior in AI-enhanced virtual shopping assistants. DOI: 10.21203/rs.3.rs-3970797/v1

Mohamed, A. (2024). Assessing AI-Powered Personalization Strategies for Mid-Sized Finnish Fashion E-commerce: Enhancing Consumer Engagement and Conversion Rates

Moher, D., Liberati, A., Tetzlaff, J., & Altman, D. G.Prisma Group. (2010). Preferred reporting items for systematic reviews and meta-analyses: The PRISMA statement. *International Journal of Surgery*, *8*(5), 336–341. DOI: 10.1016/j.ijsu.2010.02.007

Mohiddin, S. K., Sharmila, S., & Slimani, K. (2026). Navigating the future of Emotion AI: technical barriers, ethical concerns, and sustainable advancements. *In Information systems engineering and management (pp. 207–226).* https://doi.org/ DOI: 10.1007/978-3-032-14778-3_10

Mokhtar, T., & Manganelli, J. (2026). *Coexistence and Coevolution of Humans and Intelligent, Adaptive Environments*. CRC Press., DOI: 10.1201/9781003441953

Mo, L., Sands, S., & Leckie, C. (2026). Outsourcing choice: AI voice assistants as shopping surrogates. *Journal of Retailing and Consumer Services, 89*, 104657. DOI: 10.1016/j.jretconser.2025.104657

Molaie, M. M., & Lee, W. (2022). Economic corollaries of personalized recommendations. *Journal of Retailing and Consumer Services, 68*, 103003. DOI: 10.1016/j.jretconser.2022.103003

Moller, J., Trilling, D., Helberger, N., & van Es, B. (2018). Do not blame it on the algorithm: An empirical assessment of multiple recommender systems and their impact on content diversity. *Information Communication and Society, 21*(7), 959–977. DOI: 10.1080/1369118X.2018.1444076

Monteith, S., Glenn, T., Geddes, J., Whybrow, P. C., & Bauer, M. (2022). Commercial use of emotion artificial intelligence (AI): Implications for psychiatry. *Current Psychiatry Reports, 24*(3), 203–211. DOI: 10.1007/s11920-022-01330-7 PMID: 35212918

Monteverde, G., Cammarota, A., Serafini, L., & Quadri, M. (2025). Are we human or are we voice assistants? Revealing the interplay between anthropomorphism and consumer concerns. *Journal of Marketing Management, 41*(1–2), 200–235. DOI: 10.1080/0267257X.2025.2475231

Montti, R. (2025, July 24). Validity of Pew research on Google AI search results challenged. *Search Engine Journal*. https://www.searchenginejournal.com/validity-of-pew-research-on-google-ai-search-results-challenged/552055/

Morales-Muñoz, A., Iniesta-Bonillo, M. Á., Estrella-Ramón, A., & Herrada-Lores, S. (2026). Artificial Intelligence and Consumer Behavior in Social Media: Systematic Literature Review and Future Research Agenda. *International Journal of Consumer Studies, 50*(1), e70173. DOI: 10.1111/ijcs.70173

Moreno, V. K., & Poudineh, R. (2026). *Reshaping the consumer-energy relationship through AI: Opportunities, risks and regulatory outlook* (No. 62). OIES Paper: EL

Morgan, B. (2020). 50 Stats Showing The Power Of Personalization. https://www.forbes.com/sites/blakemorgan/2020/02/18/50-stats-showing-the-power-of-personalization/[REMOVED HYPERLINK FIELD]

Morgan, R. M., & Hunt, S. D. (1994). The commitment-trust theory of relationship marketing. *Journal of Marketing, 58*(3), 20–38. DOI: 10.1177/002224299405800302

Morris, J. D., Woo, C., & Singh, A. J. (2005). Elaboration likelihood model: A missing intrinsic emotional implication. *Journal of Targeting. Measurement and Analysis for Marketing, 14*(1), 79–98. DOI: 10.1057/palgrave.jt.5740171

Morvan, C., & O'Connor, A. (2017). *An analysis of Leon Festinger's a theory of cognitive dissonance*. Macat Library.

Motoki, K., Iseki, S., & Pathak, A. (2025). Sounds cute: Exploring the role of sound reduplication in brand names. *International Journal of Research in Marketing, 42*(4), 1305–1322. DOI: 10.1016/j.ijresmar.2025.02.002

Munteanu, T. (2024, July 25). *The role of emotions in consumer decision-making*. https://www.tokinomo.com/blog/role-emotions-consumer-decision-making

Murray, K. B., & Häubl, G. (2007). Explaining cognitive lock-in: The role of skill-based habits of use in consumer choice. *The Journal of Consumer Research, 34*(1), 77–88. DOI: 10.1086/513048

Mustikasari, A., Hurriyati, R., Dirgantari, P. D., Sultan, M. A., & Sugiana, N. S. S. (2025). The role of artificial intelligence in brand experience: Shaping consumer behavior and driving repurchase decisions. *International Journal of Advanced Computer Science and Applications, 16*(4). Advance online publication. DOI: 10.14569/IJACSA.2025.0160432

Muthuri, D. (2023). Content Personalization: What It Is & How to Do It. URL: https://www.semrush.com/blog/personalized-content/ Accessed: 1 May 2025.

Nalis, I., Sippl, T., Kolb, T. E., & Neidhardt, J. (2024, June). Navigating serendipity-an experimental user study on the interplay of trust and serendipity in recommender systems. In *Adjunct Proceedings of the 32nd ACM conference on user modeling, adaptation and personalization* (pp. 386-393). DOI: 10.1145/3631700.3664901

Narimisaei, J., Naeim, M., Imannezhad, S., Samian, P., & Sobhani, M. (2024). Exploring emotional intelligence in artificial intelligence systems: A comprehensive analysis of emotion recognition and response mechanisms. *Annals of Medicine and Surgery (London), 86*(8), 4657–4663. DOI: 10.1097/MS9.0000000000002315 PMID: 39118764

Nederhorst, L. (2026). How Do Retailers Stay Visible with AI Shopping Agents Choosing Products? https://www.ml6.eu/en/blog/how-do-retailers-stay-visible-with-ai-shopping-agents-choosing-products[REMOVED HYPERLINK FIELD]

Nedungadi, P. (1990). Recall and consumer consideration sets: Influencing choice without altering brand evaluations. *The Journal of Consumer Research, 17*(3), 263–276. DOI: 10.1086/208556

Nees, M. A., & Liebman, E. (2023). Auditory icons, earcons, spearcons, and speech: A systematic review and meta-analysis of brief audio alerts in human-machine interfaces. *Auditory Perception & Cognition*, *6*(3–4), 300–329. DOI: 10.1080/25742442.2023.2219201

Nelson-Field, K. (2026, March 17). *Why your AI needs a human trainer: The future of attention*. Think with Google. https://business.google.com/uk/think/future-of-marketing/future-of-attention-human-centric-ai-marketing/

Nelson, P. (1970). Information and consumer behavior. *Journal of Political Economy*, *78*(2), 311–329. DOI: 10.1086/259630

Nguyen, T. T., Maxwell Harper, F., Terveen, L., & Konstan, J. A. (2018). User personality and user satisfaction with recommender systems. *Information Systems Frontiers*, *20*(6), 1173–1189. DOI: 10.1007/s10796-017-9782-y

Nicolescu, L., & Tudorache, M. T. (2022). Human-computer interaction in customer service: The experience with AI chatbots—a systematic literature review. *Electronics (Basel)*, *11*(10), 1579. DOI: 10.3390/electronics11101579

Njoku, J. N., Nwakanma, C. I., Amaizu, G. C., & Kim, D.-S. (2023). Prospects and challenges of Metaverse application in data-driven intelligent transportation systems. *IET Intelligent Transport Systems*, *17*(1), 1–21. DOI: 10.1049/itr2.12252

Norberg, P. A., Horne, D. R., & Horne, D. A. (2007). The privacy paradox: Personal information disclosure intentions versus behaviors. *The Journal of Consumer Affairs*, *41*(1), 100–126. DOI: 10.1111/j.1745-6606.2006.00070.x

North, A. C., Hargreaves, D. J., & McKendrick, J. (1999). The influence of in-store music on wine selections. *The Journal of Applied Psychology*, *84*(2), 271–276. DOI: 10.1037/0021-9010.84.2.271

O'Reilly, T., Strauss, I., & Mazzucato, M. (2024). Algorithmic attention rents: A theory of digital platform market power. *Data & Policy*, *6*, e6. DOI: 10.1017/dap.2024.1

Oliver, R. L. (1999). Whence consumer loyalty? *Journal of Marketing*, *63*(4, suppl1), 33–44. DOI: 10.1177/00222429990634s105

Open, A. I. (2025). ChatGPT [Large language model]. https://chatgpt.com/

Open, A. I. (2025, September 29). *Buy it in ChatGPT: Instant Checkout and the Agentic Commerce Protocol*. https://openai.com/index/buy-it-in-chatgpt/

Özdemir, S., Zhang, S., Gupta, S., & Bebek, G. (2020). The effects of trust and peer influence on corporate brand–consumer relationships and consumer loyalty. *Journal of Business Research*, *117*, 791–805. DOI: 10.1016/j.jbusres.2020.02.027

Padmavathy, A. M., & Alamelu, R. (2025). Harnessing personalized emotional ai for enhanced consumer engagement in intelligent marketing. *Donglixue Yu Kongzhi Xuebao*, •••, 13–22. DOI: 10.71058/jodac.v9i1002

Palencia-Lefler, M. (2024). Inclusive advertising through the soundtrack: Insights from people with tinnitus. *Journal of Marketing Communications*, *30*(1), 102–122. DOI: 10.1080/13527266.2022.2103584

Pandey, D. (2025). AI-Driven Consumer Behavior and. *Adapting Global Communication and Marketing Strategies to Generative AI*, 113.

Pan, X. (2025). A conceptual framework on AI-driven consumer behavior in the age of digital branding. *Frontiers in Business, Economics and Management*, *19*(3), 58–64. DOI: 10.54097/3aasrp70

Parasuraman, R., Sheridan, T. B., & Wickens, C. D. (2000). A model for types and levels of human interaction with automation. *IEEE Transactions on Systems, Man, and Cybernetics. Part A, Systems and Humans*, *30*(3), 286–297. DOI: 10.1109/3468.844354

Pariser, E. (2011). *The filter bubble: What the Internet is hiding from you*. penguin UK.

Pariser, E. (2011). *The filter bubble: What the Internet is hiding from you*. Penguin Press.

Park, C. W., & Young, S. M. (1986). Consumer response to television commercials: The impact of involvement and background music on brand attitude formation. *JMR, Journal of Marketing Research*, *23*(1), 11–24. DOI: 10.1177/002224378602300102

Park, S.-M., & Kim, Y.-G. (2022). A Metaverse: Taxonomy, components, applications, and open challenges. *IEEE Access : Practical Innovations, Open Solutions*, *10*, 4209–4251. DOI: 10.1109/ACCESS.2021.3140175

Parris, D. L., & Guzman, F. (2022). Evolving brand boundaries and expectations: Looking back on brand equity, brand loyalty, and brand image research to move forward. *Journal of Product and Brand Management*, *31*(2), 191–234. DOI: 10.1108/JPBM-06-2021-3528

Pasquale, F. (2015). *The black box society: The secret algorithms that control money and information*. Harvard University Press. DOI: 10.4159/harvard.9780674736061

Pathak, A., Calvert, G. A., & Lim, L. K. S. (2020). Harsh voices, sound branding: How voiced consonants in a brand's name can alter its perceived attributes. *Psychology and Marketing*, *37*(6), 837–847. DOI: 10.1002/mar.21346

Patilinet, S. (2024, September 19). Attention is advertising's currency, let's agree on its value. *Marketing Week*. https://www.marketingweek.com/attention-currency-marketing-value/

Pattern. (2025). Agentic shopping: the future of ecommerce is here. https://www.pattern.com/blog/agentic-shopping-agents

Pattnaik, A., & Mohanty, M. (n.d.). The Role of AI in Transforming Consumer Behavior and Market Trends. Innovate to Dominate: AI and Sustainability in Business, 1.

Pauwels, K. (2026, April 12). *Who owns the web when agents browse?* [Post]. LinkedIn. https://www.linkedin.com/pulse/who-owns-web-when-agents-browse-prof-dr-koen-pauwels-qmbre

Peck, J., & Childers, T. L. (2003). To have and to hold: The influence of haptic information on product judgments. *Journal of Marketing*, *67*(2), 35–48. DOI: 10.1509/jmkg.67.2.35.18612

Peng, C., Qian, A., Jin, L., Chen, J., Han, E. X., Liang, P. P., . . . Hsieh, J. (2025). Exploring Opportunities to Support Novice Visual Artists' Inspiration and Ideation with Generative AI. *arXiv preprint arXiv:2509.24167.*

Perplexity, A. I. (2024, November 18). *Shop like a pro: Perplexity's new AI-powered shopping assistant.* https://www.perplexity.ai/hub/blog/shop-like-a-pro

Persky, S., & Colloca, L. (2023). Medical extended reality trials: Building robust comparators, controls, and sham. *Journal of Medical Internet Research*, *25*, e45821. DOI: 10.2196/45821 PMID: 37991836

Personalized Pricing. (2022). *European Parliament's committee on Internal Market and Consumer Protection.*

Pervez, F., Shoukat, M., Usama, M., Sandhu, M., Latif, S., & Qadir, J. (2024). Affective computing and the road to an emotionally intelligent metaverse. *IEEE Open Journal of the Computer Society*, *5*, 195–214. DOI: 10.1109/OJCS.2024.3389462

Petty, R. E., & Cacioppo, J. T. (1986). The elaboration likelihood model of persuasion. *Advances in Experimental Social Psychology*, *19*, 123–205. DOI: 10.1016/S0065-2601(08)60214-2

Picard, R. W. (1997). *Affective Computing*. MIT Press. DOI: 10.7551/mitpress/1140.001.0001

Piehler, R., King, C., Burmann, C., & Xiong, L. (2016). The importance of employee brand understanding, brand identification, and brand commitment in realizing brand citizenship behaviour. *European Journal of Marketing*, *50*(9/10), 1575–1601. DOI: 10.1108/EJM-11-2014-0725

Pillarisetty, R., & Mishra, P. (2022). A review of AI (AI) tools and customer experience in online fashion retail. [IJEBR]. *International Journal of E-Business Research*, *18*(2), 1–12. DOI: 10.4018/IJEBR.294111

Pine, B. J. (1993). Mass customizing products and services. *Planning review,21*(4), 6-55. DOI: 10.1108/eb054420

Pine, B. J., & Gilmore, J. H. (2013). The experience economy: past, present and future. In *Handbook on the experience economy* (pp. 21–44). Edward Elgar Publishing., DOI: 10.4337/9781781004227.00007

Plus Info, A. I. (2026). AI & data-driven Starbucks-Deep Brew. https://www.aiplusinfo.com/blog/ai-data-driven-starbucks-deep-brew/

Podsakoff, P. M., MacKenzie, S. B., Lee, J. Y., & Podsakoff, N. P. (2003). Common method biases in behavioral research: A critical review of the literature and recommended remedies. *The Journal of Applied Psychology*, *88*(5), 879–903. DOI: 10.1037/0021-9010.88.5.879 PMID: 14516251

Poria, S., Cambria, E., Bajpai, R., & Hussain, A. (2017). A review of affective computing: From unimodal analysis to multimodal fusion. *Information Fusion*, *37*, 98–125. DOI: 10.1016/j.inffus.2017.02.003

Poulis, A., & Wisker, Z. (2016). Modeling employee-based brand equity (EBBE) and perceived environmental uncertainty (PEU) on a firm's performance. *Journal of Product and Brand Management*, *25*(5), 490–503. DOI: 10.1108/JPBM-04-2015-0852

Prahalad, C. K., & Ramaswamy, V. (2004). *The future of competition: Co-creating unique value with customers*. Harvard Business School Press.

Procter, L. (2020). I Am/We Are: Exploring the Online Self-Avatar Relationship. *The Journal of Communication Inquiry*, *45*(1), 45–64. DOI: 10.1177/0196859920961041

Proserpio, D., & Zervas, G. (2017). Online reputation management: Estimating the impact of management responses on consumer reviews. *Marketing Science*, *36*(5), 645–665. DOI: 10.1287/mksc.2017.1043

Puligadda, S., & VanBergen, N. (2023). The influence of sound logo instruments on brand personality perceptions: An investigation of brand ruggedness and sophistication. *Journal of Business Research, 156*, 113531. Advance online publication. DOI: 10.1016/j.jbusres.2022.113531

Puntoni, S., Reczek, R. W., Giesler, M., & Botti, S. (2021). Consumers and artificial intelligence: An experiential perspective. *Journal of Marketing*, *85*(1), 131–151. DOI: 10.1177/0022242920953847

Qin, H., & Lei, J. (2019). The application of virtual reality technology in advertising communication. *Proceedings - 2019 International Conference on Virtual Reality and Intelligent Systems, ICVRIS 2019*, 73–76. https://doi.org/DOI: 10.1109/ICVRIS.2019.00027

Rach, M. (2026a). Algorithmic trust and choice liquidity: A dual-pathway framework for AI-mediated consumer decision architecture. In *Proceedings of the International Conference on Artificial Intelligence Management and Trends* (pp. 85–88). Abu Dhabi School of Management.

Rach, M. (2026b). Preface. In Rach, M. (Ed.), *Autonomous decision systems, consumer behavior, and the future of branding in the age of intelligence*. IGI Global.

Raisch, S., & Krakowski, S. (2021). Artificial intelligence and management: The automation–augmentation paradox. *Academy of Management Review*, *46*(1), 192–210. DOI: 10.5465/amr.2018.0072

Rana, R., & Bhambri, P. (2026). AI, Predictive Analytics, and Automated Influence: Ethical Frontiers in Algorithmic Marketing. In *Surveillance, Trust, and the New Politics of Digital Marketing* (pp. 53-98). IGI Global Scientific Publishing.

Rashid, A. M., Albert, I., Cosley, D., Lam, S. K., McNee, S. M., Konstan, J. A., & Riedl, J. (2002). Getting to know you: learning new user preferences in recommender systems. In *Proceedings of the 7th international conference on Intelligent user interfaces* (pp. 127-134). DOI: 10.1145/502716.502737

Rather, R. A., Tehseen, S., Itoo, M. H., & Parrey, S. H. (2019). Customer brand identification, affective commitment, customer satisfaction, and brand trust as antecedents of customer behavioral intention of loyalty: An empirical study in the hospitality sector. *Journal of Global Scholars of Marketing Science*, *29*(2), 196–217. DOI: 10.1080/21639159.2019.1577694

Rawool, V., Foroudi, P., & Palazzo, M. (2025). AI-powered voice assistants: Developing a framework for building consumer trust and fostering brand loyalty. *Electronic Commerce Research*, *25*(6), 4471–4503. DOI: 10.1007/s10660-024-09850-5

Rebuy Engine. (2022). See what's next: How Netflix uses personalization to drive billions in revenue. https://www.rebuyengine.com/blog/netflix

Rebuy Engine. (n.d.). The Amazon effect: Using personalization to generate billions. https://www.rebuyengine.com/blog/the-amazon-effect[REMOVED HYPERLINK FIELD]

Redine, A., Deshpande, S., Jebarajakirthy, C., & Surachartkumtonkun, J. (2023). Impulse buying: A systematic literature review and future research directions. *International Journal of Consumer Studies*, *47*(1), 3–41. DOI: 10.1111/ijcs.12862

RedSeer. (2023). *Quick commerce in India: The next frontier*. RedSeer Strategy Consultants.

Reinoso Carvalho, F., Wang, Q. J., van Ee, R., & Spence, C. (2016). Music influences hedonic and taste ratings in beer. *Frontiers in Psychology*, *7*, 636. Advance online publication. DOI: 10.3389/fpsyg.2016.00636

Reis, H. T., Clark, M. S., & Holmes, J. G. (2004). Perceived partner responsiveness as an organizing construct in the study of intimacy and closeness. In Mashek, D. J., & Aron, A. P. (Eds.), *Handbook of closeness and intimacy* (pp. 201–225). Lawrence Erlbaum Associates.

Rendle, S. (2010, December). Factorization machines. In*2010 IEEE International conference on data mining* (pp. 995-1000). IEEE. DOI: 10.1109/ICDM.2010.127

Resnick, P., Iacovou, N., Suchak, M., Bergstrom, P., & Riedl, J. (1994, October). Grouplens: An open architecture for collaborative filtering of netnews. In *Proceedings of the 1994 ACM conference on Computer supported cooperative work* (pp. 175-186). DOI: 10.1145/192844.192905

Reviglio, U. (2023). Serendipity as a design principle of personalization systems—theoretical distinctions. In *Serendipity science: An emerging field and its methods* (pp. 145–165). Springer International Publishing., DOI: 10.1007/978-3-031-33529-7_8

Rhue, L. (2023). The anchoring effect, algorithmic fairness, and the limits of information transparency for emotion artificial intelligence. *Information Systems Research*, *35*(3), 1479–1496. DOI: 10.1287/isre.2019.0493

Ricci, F. (2015). Recommender Systems: Introduction and Challenges. Recommender Systems Handbook, 1-34. DOI: 10.1007/978-1-4899-7637-6_1

Ricci, F., Rokach, L., & Shapira, B. (Eds.). (2015). *Recommender systems handbook* (2nd ed.). Springer. DOI: 10.1007/978-1-4899-7637-6

Richardson, M., Dominowska, E., & Ragno, R. (2007, May). Predicting clicks: estimating the click-through rate for new ads. In *Proceedings of the 16th international conference on World Wide Web* (pp. 521-530). DOI: 10.1145/1242572.1242643

Riedl, J. (2013). Fine Tuning the Social Web. https://research.umn.edu/news/fine-tuning-social-web-john-riedl[REMOVED HYPERLINK FIELD]

Ringler, C., Sirianni, N. J., & Christenson, B. (2021). The power of consequential product sounds. *Journal of Retailing*, *97*(2), 288–300. DOI: 10.1016/j.jretai.2020.09.002

Ritson, M. (2026, June 22). Mark Ritson: Claude is my Cannes bartender. My AI agent is favoring established brands. *The Drum*. https://www.thedrum.com/opinion/mark-ritson-ai-agents-are-already-learning-which-brands-to-pick

Ritson, M., & Elliott, R. (1999). The social uses of advertising: An ethnographic study of adolescent advertising audiences. *The Journal of Consumer Research*, *26*(3), 260–277. DOI: 10.1086/209562

Ritterbusch, G. D., & Teichmann, M. R. (2023). Defining the Metaverse: A systematic literature review. *IEEE Access : Practical Innovations, Open Solutions*, *11*, 12368–12377. DOI: 10.1109/ACCESS.2023.3241809

Rizk, I. (2025, November 6). AI traffic converts at 3x the rate of other channels (study). *Microsoft Clarity Blog*. https://clarity.microsoft.com/blog/ai-traffic-converts-at-3x-the-rate-of-other-channels-study/

Roach, T. (2024, July 11). "Share of model" is the new marketing measure for the AI era. *Marketing Week*. https://www.marketingweek.com/tom-roach-share-of-model-ai-era/

Roach, T. (2025). Winning hearts, minds and models: Brand building in an AI world. https://thetomroach.com/2025/11/20/winning-hearts-minds-and-models-brand-building-in-an-ai-world/

Roach, T. (2025, November 20). Winning hearts, minds and models: Brand building in an AI world. *Tom Roach*. https://thetomroach.com/2025/11/20/winning-hearts-minds-and-models-brand-building-in-an-ai-world/

Rohden, S. F., & Espartel, L. B. (2026). Emotional artificial intelligence: The impact of chatbot empathy and emotional tone on consumer satisfaction and word of mouth. *International Journal of Human-Computer Studies*, *210*, 103764. DOI: 10.1016/j.ijhcs.2026.103764

Rohden, S. F., Espartel, L. B., & Lopes, J. C. (2025). From voice to choice: Understanding the consumer response to voice assistant and human recommendations. *International Journal of Consumer Studies, 49*(6), e70128. DOI: 10.1111/ijcs.70128

Romaniuk, J. (2018). *Building distinctive brand assets*. Oxford University Press.

Romaniuk, J., & Sharp, B. (2004). Conceptualizing and measuring brand salience. *Marketing Theory, 4*(4), 327–342. DOI: 10.1177/1470593104047643

Romaniuk, J., & Sharp, B. (2016). *How brands grow: Part 2: Including emerging markets, services, durables, B2B and luxury brands*. Oxford University Press.

Romaniuk, J., Sharp, B., & Ehrenberg, A. S. C. (2007). Evidence concerning the importance of perceived brand differentiation. *Australasian Marketing Journal, 15*(2), 42–54. DOI: 10.1016/S1441-3582(07)70042-3

Rovedder de Oliveira, M. O., Heldt, R., Silveira, C. S., & Luce, F. B. (2023). Brand equity chain and brand equity measurement approaches. *Marketing Intelligence & Planning, 41*(4), 442–456. DOI: 10.1108/MIP-06-2022-0222

Russell, S., & Norvig, P. (2021). *Artificial intelligence: A modern approach* (4th ed.). Pearson.

Rust, R. T., & Huang, M. H. (2014). The service revolution and the transformation of marketing science. *Marketing Science, 33*(2), 206–221. DOI: 10.1287/mksc.2013.0836

Rust, R. T., Lemon, K. N., & Zeithaml, V. A. (2004). Return on marketing: Using customer equity to focus marketing strategy. *Journal of Marketing, 68*(1), 109–127. DOI: 10.1509/jmkg.68.1.109.24030

S, S. G., Chandrasekaran, B., & J, O. (2026). Ethics and bias in emotional AI. *Frontiers in Artificial Intelligence, 9*. https://doi.org/DOI: 10.3389/frai.2026.1768696

Sag, M. (2023). Copyright safety for generative AI. *Houston Law Review, 61*, 295.

Sallaku, K., Macca, L. S., Santoro, G., & Thu Phan, T. (2025). Advertising in the digital era: Can AI evoke emotions like humans? *Business Process Management Journal, 31*(5), 1785–1811. DOI: 10.1108/BPMJ-07-2024-0637

Samson, A., & Voyer, B. (2012). Two minds, three ways: Dual system and process models in consumer psychology. *AMS Review, 2*(2-4), 48–71. Advance online publication. DOI: 10.1007/s13162-012-0030-9

Sandrin, V. (2021). The Struggle between Human-centredness and Intelligent Technologies: a Critical Discussion on the Use of Customer Data in Marketing Practice-A Survey Analysis of the RIR Clusters in Veneto.

Sarin, A. B. (2025). The evolution of consumer behavior and the role of artificial intelligence in shaping it: AI in marketing. In *Decoding Consumer Behavior Using the Insight Equation and AI Marketing* (pp. 21–40). IGI Global Scientific Publishing., DOI: 10.4018/979-8-3693-8588-3.ch002

Sarstedt, M., Adler, S. J., & Imschloss, M. (2026). Machine marketing: Rethinking the customer in the age of generative AI. *Journal of Marketing Analytics*. Advance online publication. DOI: 10.1057/s41270-026-00521-y

Saxena, S. (2025). ALGORITHMS & ATTENTION: HOW TECH INFLUENCES CONSUMER HABITS. *International Journal of Applied Mathematics*, *38*(4). Advance online publication. DOI: 10.12732/ijam.v38i4.11

Schafer, J. B., Konstan, J., & Riedl, J. (1999, November). Recommender systems in e-commerce. In *Proceedings of the 1st ACM conference on Electronic commerce* (pp. 158-166). https://dl.acm.org/doi/pdf/10.1145/336992.337035

Schilke, O., & Helfat, C. E. (2025). Unlocking dynamic capabilities: Pathways for empirical research. *Journal of Management Scientific Reports*. Advance online publication. DOI: 10.1177/27550311251318724

Schilke, O., Hu, S., & Helfat, C. E. (2018). Quo vadis, dynamic capabilities? A content-analytic review of the current state of knowledge and recommendations for future research. *The Academy of Management Annals*, *12*(1), 390–439. DOI: 10.5465/annals.2016.0014

Schloerb, D. W. (1995). A Quantitative Measure of Telepresence. *Presence (Cambridge, Mass.)*, *4*(1), 64–80. DOI: 10.1162/pres.1995.4.1.64

Schlund, R., & Zitek, E. M. (2024). Algorithmic versus human surveillance leads to lower perceptions of autonomy and increased resistance. *Communications Psychology*, *2*(1), 53. DOI: 10.1038/s44271-024-00102-8 PMID: 39242768

Schreiner, T., Rese, A., & Baier, D. (2019). Multichannel personalization: Identifying consumer preferences for product recommendations in advertisements across different media channels. *Journal of Retailing and Consumer Services*, *48*, 87–99. DOI: 10.1016/j.jretconser.2019.02.010

Schulze, A., & Brusoni, S. (2022). How dynamic capabilities change ordinary capabilities: Reconnecting attention control and problem-solving. *Strategic Management Journal*, *43*(12), 2447–2477. DOI: 10.1002/smj.3413

Schumacher, K., Keutel, M., Kluge, P., Giebel, K., & Wendler, T. (2026, March). *Europe's agentic commerce moment: Decision influence is here; execution is coming.* McKinsey & Company. https://www.mckinsey.com/capabilities/quantumblack/our-insights/europes-agentic-commerce-moment-decision-influence-is-here-execution-is-coming

Schwarz, N., & Clore, G. L. (1983). Mood, misattribution, and judgments of well-being: Informative and directive functions of affective states. *Journal of Personality and Social Psychology, 45*(3), 513–523. DOI: 10.1037/0022-3514.45.3.513

Sclar, M., Choi, Y., Tsvetkov, Y., & Suhr, A. (2024). Quantifying language models' sensitivity to spurious features in prompt design [Conference session]. *The Twelfth International Conference on Learning Representations*. DOI: 10.48550/arXiv.2310.11324

Scott, S. P., Sheinin, D., & Labrecque, L. I. (2022). Small sounds, big impact: Sonic logos and their effect on consumer attitudes, emotions, brands and advertising placement. *Journal of Product and Brand Management, 31*(7), 1091–1103. DOI: 10.1108/JPBM-06-2021-3507

Selvaraj, T. (2025). Generative AI: Fashion's New Personal Shopper. https://medium.com/@tselvaraj/generative-ai-fashions-new-personal-shopper-425fefa68fe2[REMOVED HYPERLINK FIELD]

Şenyapar, H. N. D. (2025). Artificial Intelligence and Behavioral Engineering: Hidden Societal Costs and Design Challenges in Consumer Contexts. *Balkan Journal of Electrical and Computer Engineering, 13*(4), 445–460. DOI: 10.17694/bajece.1712706

Shao, C., Kim, Y., & Xu, L. Z. (2025). From ai chatbot to brand support: An exploration of perceived empathy and ethics in shaping trust and word of mouth. *Communication Reports, 39*(1), 69–81. DOI: 10.1080/08934215.2025.2519253

Shardanand, U., & Maes, P. (1995, May). Social information filtering: Algorithms for automating "word of mouth". In *Proceedings of the SIGCHI conference on Human factors in computing systems* (pp. 210-217). DOI: 10.1145/223904.223931

Sharma, A., Patel, N., & Gupta, R. (2022). Enhancing Personalized Loyalty Programs through Reinforcement Learning and Collaborative Filtering Algorithms. *European Advanced AI Journal, 11*(10).

Sharma, P., Ueno, A., Dennis, C., & Turan, C. P. (2023). Emerging digital technologies and consumer decision-making in retail sector: Towards an integrative conceptual framework. *Computers in Human Behavior, 148*, 107913. DOI: 10.1016/j.chb.2023.107913

Sharp, B. (2026, June 26). *No that's not what I said* [Post]. LinkedIn. https://www.linkedin.com/posts/professorbyronsharp_byron-sharp-appeared-to-go-on-record-this-activity-7476139656070402048-oJWk

Sharp, B. (2010). *How brands grow: What marketers don't know*. Oxford University Press.

Sheth, J. N., Sisodia, R. S., & Sharma, A. (2000). The antecedents and consequences of customer-centric marketing. *Journal of the Academy of Marketing Science, 28*(1), 55–66. DOI: 10.1177/0092070300281006

Shiau, W. L., Yuan, Y., Pu, X., Ray, S., & Chen, C. C. (2022). Integrating the stimulus-organism-response and the elaboration likelihood model theories in the context of e-commerce. *Frontiers in Psychology, 13*, 948216. Advance online publication. DOI: 10.3389/fpsyg.2022.948216

Sidorenko-Bautista, P., Castillo-Abdul, B., Herranz-de-la-Casa, J. M., & Abellán-Hernández, M. (2025). Marketing, advertising, and branding in Fortnite: How do brands and companies connect today to audiences through the metaverse? *Cogent Social Sciences, 11*(1), 2458058. DOI: 10.1080/23311886.2025.2458058

Silas, S., Baker, D. J., & Müllensiefen, D. (2024). Musical manipulation of visual scenes in video, film, and TV advertisements: A large-scale investigation into the implicit effects of sonic branding. *Journal of Advertising Research, 64*(2), 192–212. DOI: 10.2501/JAR-2024-013

Silas, S., Baker, D., Sachet, A., & Müllensiefen, D. (2026). An unsupervised feature selection approach for finding diverse emotional-semantic representations in sonic branding music. *Journal of New Music Research, 54*(2–3), 107–124. DOI: 10.1080/09298215.2025.2607362

Simon, C. J., & Sullivan, M. W. (1993). The measurement and determinants of brand equity: A financial approach. *Marketing Science, 12*(1), 28–52. DOI: 10.1287/mksc.12.1.28

Simon, H. A. (1955). A behavioral model of rational choice. *The Quarterly Journal of Economics, 69*(1), 99–118. DOI: 10.2307/1884852

Simon, H. A. (1971). Designing organizations for an information-rich world. In Greenberger, M. (Ed.), *Computers, communications, and the public interest* (pp. 37–72). The Johns Hopkins Press.

Simonov, A., Valletti, T., & Veiga, A. (2025). Attention spillovers from news to ads: Evidence from an eye-tracking experiment. *JMR, Journal of Marketing Research, 62*(2), 294–315. DOI: 10.1177/00222437241256900

Singh, B. K., & Srivastava, U. K. (2026). A Systematic Review on the Evolution of Emotional Artificial Intelligence. *IARJSET, 13*(1). Advance online publication. DOI: 10.17148/IARJSET.2026.13159

Slama, W. B., & Ghodbane, S. B. (2026). Real-Time Customization and Artificial Intelligence Performance Drivers in Quick Commerce. In *Revolutionizing Quick Commerce With AI Tools and Technologies* (pp. 23–52). IGI Global Scientific Publishing., DOI: 10.4018/979-8-3373-3486-8.ch002

Slater, M., & Wilbur, S. (1997). A framework for immersive virtual environments (FIVE): Speculations on the role of presence in virtual environments. *Presence (Cambridge, Mass.), 6*(6), 603–616. DOI: 10.1162/pres.1997.6.6.603

Smets, A. (2025). Intended, afforded, and experienced serendipity: Overcoming the paradox of artificial serendipity. *Ethics and Information Technology, 27*(3), 33. DOI: 10.1007/s10676-025-09841-6

Smith, B., & Linden, G. (2017). Two decades of recommender systems at Amazon. com. *IEEE Internet Computing, 21*(3), 12–18. DOI: 10.1109/MIC.2017.72

Snyder, H. (2019). Literature review as a research methodology: An overview and guidelines. *Journal of Business Research, 104*, 333–339. DOI: 10.1016/j.jbusres.2019.07.039

Solomon, M. R. (1986). The missing link: Surrogate consumers in the marketing chain. *Journal of Marketing, 50*(4), 208–218. DOI: 10.1177/002224298605000406

Spence, C. (2012). Managing sensory expectations concerning products and brands: Capitalizing on the potential of sound and shape symbolism. *Journal of Consumer Psychology, 22*(1), 37–54. DOI: 10.1016/j.jcps.2011.09.004

Spence, C., Di Stefano, N., Reinoso-Carvalho, F., & Velasco, C. (2024). Marketing sonified fragrance: Designing soundscapes for scent. *IPerception, 15*(4), 20416695241259714. Advance online publication. DOI: 10.1177/20416695241259714

Spence, C., & Keller, S. (2024). Sonic branding: A narrative review at the intersection of art and science. *Psychology and Marketing*, *41*(7), 1530–1548. DOI: 10.1002/mar.21995

Srinivasan, S., Vanhuele, M., & Pauwels, K. (2010). Mind-set metrics in market response models: An integrative approach. *JMR, Journal of Marketing Research*, *47*(4), 672–684. DOI: 10.1509/jmkr.47.4.672

Srivastava, A., Bala, P. K., & Kumar, B. (2020). New perspectives on gray sheep behavior in E-commerce recommendations. *Journal of Retailing and Consumer Services*, *53*, 101764. DOI: 10.1016/j.jretconser.2019.02.018

Stark Digital. (2026). Generative AI in Retail: The Future of Personalized Shopping. https://www.starkdigital.net/insights/generative-ai-in-retail-the-future-of-personalized-shopping

Stein, E., Robinson, K., Wolfer, A., Almeida, G., & Huang, W. (2025). Unlocking the next frontier of personalized marketing. *The McKinsey Quarterly*.

Stevenson, M. (2019). Design thinking for business: personalization,https://uxdesign.cc/design-thinking-for-business-personalisation-39f4b96ee1b7, 03/05/2025.[REMOVED HYPERLINK FIELD]

Stratoflow. (2025a). Amazon product recommendation system: How does Amazon's algorithm work? https://stratoflow.com/amazon-recommendation-system/

Stratoflow. (2025b). How Netflix's recommendation algorithm works. https://stratoflow.com/how-netflix-recommendation-algorithm-work/

Sun, M. (2025). AI-Driven Cross-Cultural Consumer Purchase Intention Prediction Methods for E-commerce Platforms: An Applied Research Approach. *Spectrum of Research, 5*(2).

Sunaga, T. (2018). How the sound frequency of background music influences consumers' perceptions and decision making. *Psychology and Marketing*, *35*(4), 253–267. DOI: 10.1002/mar.21084

Sun, W., Chang, E.-C., & Xu, Y. (2023). The effects of background music tempo on consumer variety-seeking behavior: The mediating role of arousal. *Frontiers in Psychology*, *14*, 1236006. Advance online publication. DOI: 10.3389/fpsyg.2023.1236006

Swaminathan, V., Sorescu, A., Steenkamp, J.-B. E. M., O'Guinn, T. C., & Schmitt, B. (2020). Branding in a hyperconnected world: Refocusing theories and rethinking boundaries. *Journal of Marketing*, *84*(2), 24–46. DOI: 10.1177/0022242919899905

System1 Group & IPA. (2025). *The magic of compound creativity* [Report]. https://system1group.com/compound-creativity-system1-ipa

Tam, K. Y., & Ho, S. Y. (2006). Understanding the impact of web personalization on user information processing and decision outcomes. *Management Information Systems Quarterly*, *30*(4), 865–890. DOI: 10.2307/25148757

Tavares, A. C. D. (2025). *How TikTok Influences Purchase Intention: The Role of Purchase Condition, Perceived Personalization and Emotional Engagement* (Master's thesis, Universidade NOVA de Lisboa (Portugal)).

Techawachirakul, M., Pathak, A., & Calvert, G. A. (2022). That sounds healthy! Audio and visual frequency differences in brand sound logos modify the perception of food healthfulness. *Food Quality and Preference*, *99*, 104544. Advance online publication. DOI: 10.1016/j.foodqual.2022.104544

Teece, D. J. (2007). Explicating dynamic capabilities: The nature and microfoundations of (sustainable) enterprise performance. *Strategic Management Journal*, *28*(13), 1319–1350. DOI: 10.1002/smj.640

Teece, D. J., Pisano, G., & Shuen, A. (1997). Dynamic capabilities and strategic management. *Strategic Management Journal*, *18*(7), 509–533. DOI: 10.1002/(SICI)1097-0266(199708)18:7<509::AID-SMJ882>3.0.CO;2-Z

Thaler, R. (1980). Toward a positive theory of consumer choice. *Journal of Economic Behavior & Organization*, *1*(1), 39–60. DOI: 10.1016/0167-2681(80)90051-7

Thaler, R. H., & Sunstein, C. R. (2008). *Nudge: Improving decisions about health, wealth, and happiness*. Yale University Press.

Thompson, B. (2025, May 1). An interview with Meta CEO Mark Zuckerberg about AI and the evolution of social media. *Stratechery*. https://stratechery.com/2025/an-interview-with-meta-ceo-mark-zuckerberg-about-ai-and-the-evolution-of-social-media/

Tian, K., Mitchell, E., Zhou, A., Sharma, A., Rafailov, R., Yao, H., Finn, C., & Manning, C. D. (2023). Just ask for calibration: Strategies for eliciting calibrated confidence scores from language models fine-tuned with human feedback. In *Proceedings of the 2023 Conference on Empirical Methods in Natural Language Processing* (pp. 5433–5442). Association for Computational Linguistics. DOI: 10.18653/v1/2023.emnlp-main.330

Torraco, R. J. (2005). Writing integrative literature reviews: Guidelines and examples. *Human Resource Development Review*, *4*(3), 356–367. DOI: 10.1177/1534484305278283

Torthienchai, N., & Chuaikaew, K. (2025). The influence of artificial intelligence in product recommendation systems and brand value on consumer purchase intention on marketplace e-commerce platforms. *International Journal of Innovative Research and Scientific Studies, 8*(6), 2549–2556. DOI: 10.53894/ijirss.v8i6.10138

Trabucchi, D., & Buganza, T. (2019). Data-driven innovation: Switching the perspective on Big Data. *European Journal of Innovation Management, 22*(1), 23–40. DOI: 10.1108/EJIM-01-2018-0017

Trabucchi, D., Buganza, T., Dell'Era, C., & Pellizzoni, E. (2018). Exploring the inbound and outbound strategies enabled by user generated big data: Evidence from leading smartphone applications. *Creativity and Innovation Management, 27*(1), 42–55. DOI: 10.1111/caim.12241

Tseng, M. M., & Jiao, J. (2001). Mass customization. *Handbook of industrial engineering,3*, 684-709.

Tuominen, D. (2025). Strategic Use of YouTube for Business Development in China and Europe: Case study of "Very Venture China".

Ullagaddi, P. (2025). Cross-regional analysis of global AI healthcare regulation. *J Computer Commun, 13*(5), 66–83. DOI: 10.4236/jcc.2025.135005

Van Berlo, Z. M., Van Reijmersdal, E. A., Smit, E. G., & Van Der Laan, L. N. (2020). Brands in virtual reality games: Affective processes within computer-mediated consumer experiences. *Journal of Business Research, 122*, 458–465. DOI: 10.1016/j.jbusres.2020.09.006

van Esch, P., & Cui, Y. G. (2026). Agentic brand drift: How AI-orchestrated organizations will lose their identity and how to get it back. *Business Horizons*. Advance online publication. DOI: 10.1016/j.bushor.2026.05.013

Vashishth, T. K., Sharma, K. K., Kumar, B., Chaudhary, S., & Panwar, R. (2024). Enhancing customer experience through AI-enabled content personalization in e-commerce marketing. Advances in digital marketing in the era of AI, 7-32. DOI: 10.1201/9781003450443-2

Verhoef, P. C., Broekhuizen, T., Bart, Y., Bhattacharya, A., Dong, J. Q., Fabian, N., & Haenlein, M. (2021). Digital transformation: A multidisciplinary reflection and research agenda. *Journal of Business Research, 122*, 889–901. DOI: 10.1016/j.jbusres.2019.09.022

Verma, S., Sharma, R., Deb, S., & Maitra, D. (2021). AI in marketing: Systematic review and future research direction. *International Journal of Information Management Data Insights, 1*(1), 100002. DOI: 10.1016/j.jjimei.2020.100002

Vernuccio, M., Patrizi, M., Šerić, M., & Pastore, A. (2023). The perceptual antecedents of brand anthropomorphism in the name-brand voice assistant context. *Journal of Brand Management, 30*(4), 302–317. DOI: 10.1057/s41262-022-00305-6

Vesanen, J. (2007). What is personalization? A conceptual framework. *European Journal of Marketing, 41*(5/6), 409–418. DOI: 10.1108/03090560710737534

Virilio, P. (1986). Speed and politics: An essay on dromology, trans. *Mark Polizzotti, New York: Semiotext (e),52.*

Volz, F., Münch, C., Küffner, C., & Hartmann, E. (2025). Digital ecosystems and their impact on organizations—A dynamic capabilities approach. *International Journal of Management Reviews, 27*(3), 398–419. Advance online publication. DOI: 10.1111/ijmr.12396

VWO. (n.d.). How does Amazon & Netflix personalization work? https://vwo.com/blog/deliver-personalized-recommendations-the-amazon-netflix-way/[REMOVED HYPERLINK FIELD]

Wachtel, P. L. (2023). *Making room for the disavowed: Reclaiming the self in psychotherapy*. Guilford Publications.

Wakefield, R. L. (2006). Affect as information in the decision to use technology. P*roceedings of the Twelfth Americas Conference on Information Systems (AMCIS), 354.*

Wang, R., Fu, B., Fu, G., & Wang, M. (2017). Deep & cross network for ad click predictions. *Proceedings of the ADKDD, 17*, 1–7. DOI: 10.1145/3124749.3124754

Wang, R., Lu, X., & Wang, X. (2025). Decision agency: How can generative AI reconstruct consumer behavior in trendy toys? In *Proceedings of the 2025 International Conference on Generative Artificial Intelligence for Business* (pp. 375–382). Association for Computing Machinery. DOI: 10.1145/3766918.3766980

Wang, R., Shivanna, R., Cheng, D., Jain, S., Lin, D., Hong, L., & Chi, E. (2021, April). Dcn v2: Improved deep & cross network and practical lessons for web-scale learning to rank systems. In *Proceedings of the web conference 2021*(pp. 1785-1797). DOI: 10.1145/3442381.3450078

Wang, Y., Song, W., Tao, W., Liotta, A., Yang, D., Li, X., Gao, S., Sun, Y., Ge, W., Zhang, W., & Zhang, W. (2022). A systematic review on affective computing: Emotion models, databases, and recent advances. *Information Fusion, 83–84*, 19–52. DOI: 10.1016/j.inffus.2022.03.009

Wang, Z. (2025). The influence of AI on consumer behavior: Shaping choices and preferences in the digital marketplace. *Systems and Soft Computing, 200397*, 200397. Advance online publication. DOI: 10.1016/j.sasc.2025.200397

Wasilewski, A., Chawla, Y., & Pralat, E. (2025). *Enhanced E-Commerce Personalization Through AI-Powered Content Generation Tools*. IEEE., DOI: 10.1109/ACCESS.2025.3550956

Wasilewski, A., & Kolaczek, G. (2024). *One size does not fit all: multivariant user interface personalization in e-commerce*. IEEE., DOI: 10.1109/ACCESS.2024.3398192

Wedel, M., & Kannan, P. K. (2016). Marketing analytics for data-rich environments. *Journal of Marketing, 80*(6), 97–121. DOI: 10.1509/jm.15.0413

Wedel, M., & Pieters, R. (2000). Eye fixations on advertisements and memory for brands: A model and findings. *Marketing Science, 19*(4), 297–312. DOI: 10.1287/mksc.19.4.297.11794

Weerasinghe, S., Malik, M., Andargoli, A., Morrow, G., Jayaraman, P. P., & Forkan, A. (2025). Are Algorithmic Biases in AI-Based Recommendations Real? An Activity Theory Framing of Digital Music Streaming. *An Activity Theory Framing of Digital Music Streaming (November 22, 2025)*.

Westbrook, R., & Williamson, P. (1993). Mass customization: Japan's new frontier. *European Management Journal, 11*(1), 38–45. DOI: 10.1016/0263-2373(93)90022-A

White, D. J. (2024). Paying attention to attention: Psychological realism and the attention economy. *Synthese, 203*(2), 43. Advance online publication. DOI: 10.1007/s11229-023-04460-4

Wien, A. H., & Peluso, A. M. (2021). Influence of human versus AI recommenders: The roles of product type and cognitive processes. *Journal of Business Research, 137*, 13–27. DOI: 10.1016/j.jbusres.2021.08.016

Wilden, R., & Gudergan, S. P. (2015). The impact of dynamic capabilities on operational marketing and technological capabilities: Investigating the role of environmental turbulence. *Journal of the Academy of Marketing Science, 43*(2), 181–199. DOI: 10.1007/s11747-014-0380-y

Wilden, R., Gudergan, S. P., Nielsen, B. B., & Lings, I. (2013). Dynamic capabilities and performance: Strategy, structure and environment. *Long Range Planning, 46*(1–2), 72–96. DOI: 10.1016/j.lrp.2012.12.001

Winter, S. G. (2003). Understanding dynamic capabilities. *Strategic Management Journal, 24*(10), 991–995. DOI: 10.1002/smj.318

Wrench, J. S., & Elmoudden, S. (2025). AI in Personal Life. *The Future is Now: Empowering Society Through AI Literacy*.

Wu, Y., Xin, L., Li, D., Yu, J., & Guo, J. (2021). How does scarcity promotion lead to impulse purchase in the online market? A field experiment. *Information & Management*, *58*(1), 103283. DOI: 10.1016/j.im.2020.103283

Xashimov, B., & Khaydarova, D. (2023). Using and development of AI on the process of accounting, 1(5), 219–223. DOI: 10.47689/STARS.university-5-pp219-223

Xiao, B., & Benbasat, I. (2013). Research on the use, characteristics, and impact of e-commerce product recommendation agents: A review and update for 2007–2012. *Handbook of strategic e-business management*, 403-431. DOI: 10.1007/978-3-642-39747-9_18

Xie, G. (2026). The impact of generative AI shopping assistants on E-commerce consumer motivation and behavior: Consumer-AI interaction design. *International Journal of Information Management*, *86*, 102983. DOI: 10.1016/j.ijinfomgt.2025.102983

Xi, N., Chen, J., Gama, F., Riar, M., & Hamari, J. (2023). The challenges of entering the metaverse: An experiment on the effect of extended reality on workload. *Information Systems Frontiers*, *25*(2), 659–680. DOI: 10.1007/s10796-022-10244-x PMID: 35194390

Yadav, T. (2024). AI in Neuromarketing: Understanding Consumer Emotions and Behavior through Machine Learning. *IJFMR - International. Journal of Multidisciplinary Research*, *6*(5), 28154. Advance online publication. DOI: 10.36948/ijfmr.2024.v06i05.28154

Yalch, R. F. (1991). Memory in a jingle jungle: Music as a mnemonic device in communicating advertising slogans. *The Journal of Applied Psychology*, *76*(2), 268–275. DOI: 10.1037/0021-9010.76.2.268

Yang, Q., Wang, Y., Song, M., Jiang, Y., & Li, Q. (2025). Sonic strategies: Unveiling the impact of sound features in short video ads on enterprise market entry performance. *Journal of Business-To-Business Marketing*, *32*(1), 95–116. DOI: 10.1080/1051712X.2024.2396966

Yang, X. (2023). The effects of AI service quality and AI function-customer ability fit on customer's overall co-creation experience. *Industrial Management & Data Systems*, *123*(6), 1717–1735. DOI: 10.1108/IMDS-08-2022-0500

Yin, J., Qiu, X., & Wang, Y. (2025). The impact of AI-personalized recommendations on clicking intentions: Evidence from Chinese e-commerce. *Journal of Theoretical and Applied Electronic Commerce Research*, *20*(1), 21. Advance online publication. DOI: 10.3390/jtaer20010021

Yin, S., Fu, C., Zhao, S., Li, K., Sun, X., Xu, T., & Chen, E. (2024). A survey on multimodal large language models. *National Science Review*, *11*(12), nwae403. Advance online publication. DOI: 10.1093/nsr/nwae403

Yi, X., Yang, J., Hong, L., Cheng, D. Z., Heldt, L., Kumthekar, A., & Chi, E. (2019, September). Sampling-bias-corrected neural modeling for large corpus item recommendations. In *Proceedings of the 13th ACM conference on recommender systems* (pp. 269-277). DOI: 10.1145/3298689.3346996

Yoo, B., & Donthu, N. (2001). Developing and validating a multidimensional consumer-based brand equity scale. *Journal of Business Research*, *52*(1), 1–14. DOI: 10.1016/S0148-2963(99)00098-3

Yorkston, E., & Menon, G. (2004). A sound idea: Phonetic effects of brand names on consumer judgments. *The Journal of Consumer Research*, *31*(1), 43–51. DOI: 10.1086/383422

Zaichkowsky, J. L. (1985). Measuring the involvement construct. *The Journal of Consumer Research*, *12*(3), 341–352. DOI: 10.1086/208520

Zajonc, R. B. (1968). Attitudinal effects of mere exposure. *Journal of Personality and Social Psychology*, *9*(2, Pt. 2), 1–27. DOI: 10.1037/h0025848

Zanger, V., Meißner, M., & Rauschnabel, P. A. (2022). Beyond the gimmick: How affective responses drive brand attitudes and intentions in augmented reality marketing. *Psychology and Marketing*, *39*(7), 1285–1301. DOI: 10.1002/mar.21641

Zhang, H., Liu, Y., Jiang, M., Chen, J., Wang, M., & Paas, F. (2025). Emotional Artificial Intelligence in Education: A Systematic Review and Meta-Analysis. *Educational Psychology Review*, *37*(4), 106. DOI: 10.1007/s10648-025-10086-4

Zhang, X. (2021). From audio branding to sound trademark: A comparative study in the EU and the US. *Beijing Law Review*, *12*(2), 409–424. DOI: 10.4236/blr.2021.122023

Zhang, Y., Di, Y., & Liu, L. (2026). Beyond Accuracy: How Algorithm Characteristics and Digital Generational Differences Affect User Interaction and Acceptance in Fashion Recommendation Systems. *International Journal of Human-Computer Interaction*, •••, 1–24. DOI: 10.1080/10447318.2026.2628995

Zhou, G., Mou, N., Fan, Y., Pi, Q., Bian, W., Zhou, C., & Gai, K. (2019, July). Deep interest evolution network for click-through rate prediction. In *Proceedings of the AAAI conference on AI* (Vol. 33, No. 01, pp. 5941-5948). DOI: 10.1609/aaai.v33i01.33015941

Zhou, G., Zhu, X., Song, C., Fan, Y., Zhu, H., Ma, X., & Gai, K. (2018, July). Deep interest network for click-through rate prediction. In *Proceedings of the 24th ACM SIGKDD international conference on knowledge discovery & data mining* (pp. 1059-1068). DOI: 10.1145/3219819.3219823

Zhou, M., Zhang, J., & Adomavicius, G. (2024). Longitudinal impact of preference biases on recommender systems' performance. *Information Systems Research*, *35*(4), 1634–1656. DOI: 10.1287/isre.2021.0133

Zhu, X., Guo, C., Feng, H., Huang, Y., Feng, Y., Wang, X., & Wang, R. (2024). A review of key technologies for emotion analysis using multimodal information. *Cognitive Computation*, *16*(4), 1504–1530. DOI: 10.1007/s12559-024-10287-z

Zomato. (2024). *Annual report 2023–24*. Zomato Ltd.

Zuckerberg, M. (2025, May 6). *A conversation with Mark Zuckerberg* [Conference session]. Stripe Sessions 2025, San Francisco, CA, United States. https://stripe.com/sessions/2025/a-conversation-with-mark-zuckerberg

About the Contributors

Markus Rach is a full Professor of Marketing at Canadian University Dubai, a Guest Professor at KdG University of Applied Sciences and Arts (Belgium), and Professor and Director at the Indian Institute of Business Management (IIBM). He holds a Doctorate in Business Administration from Maastricht School of Management and serves on the boards of SwissCham South China and the Global B2B Marketing Council. Dr. Rach's approach is experimental in the literal sense, in that he runs the platforms and formats he studies. He grew a TikTok account beyond 750,000 followers as a live test of algorithmic reach, and that account is where much of his platform research originates. He has taught inside the metaverse rather than about it, using his own classes to observe attention and presence in immersive environments. With his students he designed, minted, and sold an NFT, converting Web3 literacy from a syllabus topic into a delivered project. He has delivered two TEDx talks on algorithmic curation and AI-mediated decision-making, and engages practitioners through board leadership. His published work examines how digital platforms, algorithmic mediation, and immersive environments shape brand engagement, consumer cognition, and behavioral outcomes. More recently, his scholarship has turned to artificial intelligence and its implications for brand perception and consumer decision-making. His current research interrogates how AI-driven systems and recommendation logics influence the salience, activation, and sustainability of brand knowledge in consumer choice contexts. Dr. Rach has lived, researched, and taught in the United Arab Emirates, China, Switzerland, and Belgium, and advises brands internationally. Across this body of work, he bridges digital technology, consumer experience, and strategic brand management, producing insights that hold academically and matter in practice.

***

Katharina Buttenberg earned her doctorate in Global Management Sciences at the University of Latvia with a thesis on the development of customer- and brand-oriented capabilities in young firms. Her current research extends this capability perspective to artificial intelligence, examining how autonomous AI agents reshape brand equity in agentic commerce environments. She was a visiting research scholar at Rice University as well as Regents University and serves as an academic reviewer for international marketing journals. She pairs this scholarship with more than twenty years of marketing leadership, most recently as Chief Strategy Officer at Black Flag Agency. She currently lectures on international marketing at Campus M in Munich and advises companies on brand and growth strategy, including LLM-based brand visibility measurement.

Shallu Dua is an Assistant Professor in the School of Fashion Design and Technology at Lovely Professional University in Phagwara, Punjab, India. She did Masters in Fashion Technology. Her academic and professional journey develops essential technical skills like pattern drafting and sewing, imparts crucial industry knowledge such as trend analysis and marketing skills. She gives lectures cover theoretical concepts alongside practical application, preparing students for the fast-paced and ever-evolving fashion world by equipping them with specialized knowledge and hands-on experience.

Alexandre Duarte With a PhD in Communication Sciences from University of Minho, a Master degree in Communication & Image and a Bachelor in Marketing & Advertising by IADE, Alexandre is a Professor in Universidade NOVA de Lisboa, invited Professor in Universidade Católica Portuguesa and researcher of the R&D Unit ICNOVA (Universidade Nova de Lisboa). Throughout his career, Alexandre had the opportunity to work for several multinational advertising agencies such as TBWA, Saatchi & Saatchi, Ogilvy, W/Portugal, W/Brazil, Lowe&Partners, or BrandiaCentral as a Senior Creative Copywriter. Author of many seminars on communication, regularly participates in different conferences and lectures in both business and academic contexts. Between 2012 and 2014, was the Tutor of the EUROBEST Young Marketers Academy, in 2014 was appointed CEO of RESTART - Institute of Creativity, Arts and New Technologies, and in 2019 was re-elected member of the Directors Board of EDCOM. In 2018 was invited to teach in the UNIVERSIDADE CATÓLICA PORTUGUESA, where now Coordinates the Post Graduations Courses in Advertising & Creativity and Service Design and, in 2022 was nominated the Advertising WG Coordinator of SOPCOM.

L Ganesh is a Gold Medalist in Post-graduation and holds a Distinction in MPhil from Pondicherry University. He is currently working as Professor at Christ

University, Bangalore. He earned an MBA in Human Resources Management from IGNOU and a PhD in Economics (Health Management) from Mysore University. Currently, he is pursuing a certification in Digital Health from IIM Raipur.

Pooja Jain is an Associate Professor from the School of Commerce, Finance and Accountancy, Department of Commerce,Christ University, with an extensive teaching, research, and academic mentoring experience. Her areas of expertise encompass marketing management, consumer behaviour, digital marketing, and strategic management. She has guided numerous undergraduate, postgraduate, and doctoral scholars in developing rigorous research methodologies and theoretically grounded studies. Her research contributions span emerging themes such as digital consumer engagement, technology-enabled marketing, sustainability, and contemporary business practices. Dr. Jain has authored and co-authored several research papers, book chapters, and conference publications in reputed national and international forums. She actively participates in academic initiatives including curriculum development, research supervision, and interdisciplinary collaborations. Through her scholarly pursuits, she continues to contribute significantly to advancing knowledge in marketing and management while fostering research excellence among aspiring scholars.

Roselyn James is a Digital Marketing professional with over four years of experience in social media strategy, influencer marketing, and onsite merchandising. She holds a Master of Business Administration from Christ University, Bangalore, and has worked with bigbasket - A TATA Enterprise, on large-scale digital campaigns, collaborating with celebrities and influencers across India. Her professional experience has enabled her to develop strong, data-driven insights into social media performance, content strategy and influencer-led brand engagement. Her academic interests lie at the intersection of digital marketing,, branding, technology and consumer behavior, with a particular focus on the role of artificial intelligence in marketing and quick commerce and its growing influence on social media ecosystems. She is currently pursuing her PhD in Marketing at Christ University, Bangalore, where her research explores emerging trends in digital marketing and brand strategy. In addition to her academic and professional work, Roselyn is an active speaker, delivering talks and sessions on digital marketing, career transitions. She is currently based in Dubai, where she is exploring the quick-commerce landscape to gain international perspectives on consumer adoption and market evolution.

Jomon Jose M. is an Associate Professor and Research Supervisor at Sahrdaya Institute of Management Studies (SIMS), Thrissur, Kerala, India. He is also a recognized Research Guide at Kerala University of Fisheries and Ocean Studies (KUFOS). He holds a Post-Doctoral Fellowship (PDF) in Management from Srinivas University, Karnataka, and a Ph.D. in Commerce from Bharathiar University, Tamil Nadu, along with an M.Phil. in Management, MBA in Human Resources, and Master's degree in International Business. With over 21 years of academic and professional experience, he has previously served in academic and leadership positions, including Head of Department and guest faculty at institutions affiliated with the University of Calicut and Agricultural University, Tavanur. His research interests include digital finance, fintech, banking, marketing, artificial intelligence, consumer behaviour, sustainability, human resource management, and emerging technologies in business and management.

Aikaterini Katsota is a Master's student in Communication, Marketing and Advertising at the Faculdade de Ciências Humanas, Universidade Católica Portuguesa, Lisbon, Portugal. Her research interests include advertising, brand communication, immersive media, and consumer behavior. She is currently conducting research on the role of extended reality technologies and the metaverse in transforming advertising persuasion.

Jaspreet Kaur is serving as Assistant Professor at the PG Department of Commerce and Management, Hans Raj Mahila Maha Vidyalaya, Jalandhar, Punjab. She has a teaching experience of more than 16 years. She holds Ph. D in Equity Investor Protection and Decision Making; A Study of Punjab and has authored over 10 peer-reviewed research publications. In addition, she has attended a number of workshops, faculty development programs, training programs for upgrading her skills, especially related to the use of AI in education and research. She has presented her research at various international and national conferences and seminars. Her area of research is finance, marketing, artificial intelligence.

Shawn Mathew is a Senior Lecturer in Marketing at Middlesex University Dubai and a Fellow of the Higher Education Academy. He holds a Fellow Programme in Management (FPM) in Marketing from the Indian Institute of Management Ahmedabad and a B.Tech. in Computer Science and Engineering from Mahatma Gandhi University, India. He is also a Professional Certified Marketer in Digital Marketing. His research examines how consumers make decisions in complex environments, with particular attention to choice overload, sonic branding, and the influence of artificial intelligence on consumer behaviour. He has published in Technological Forecasting and Social Change, the Journal of Promotion Management, and Economic and Political Weekly, and recently completed the CFR Research School in Retailing at the Stockholm School of Economics. At Middlesex

University Dubai he is Academic Head of the Centre for Continuous Learning and Outreach, leading the academic coordination of institutional immersion programmes and executive training. He is the Faculty representative for Business and Marketing on the Teaching and Learning Committee, a member of the Office of Research and the Faculty Employability Liaison team, and an Academic Integrity Tutor. He previously chaired the PGDM Dual Country Programme and the Marketing Area at IMT Dubai, and has taught at several Indian Institutes of Management in permanent and adjunct roles. Before moving into academia he worked with Cognizant Technology Solutions and the A.P. Moller Maersk Group. He is a registered member of the Global Association of Applied Behavioural Scientists and a member of the Association for Consumer Research, the Society for Consumer Psychology, and the Society for Judgment and Decision Making.

Jyothis Rachel Mathews is an Assistant Professor at Ahalia School of Management, Palakkad, and a PhD scholar at Karpagam Academy of Higher Education. With over 18 years of academic experience, she specializes in Marketing, HR, and Strategic Management. Known for her interactive and student-centered teaching style, she blends theory with real-world application. She has published in Scopus-indexed journals and presented at national and international conferences. She has also guided numerous postgraduate research projects and led industry-academic consultancy collaborations. Her research interests include emotional branding, consumer neuroscience, AI in marketing and sustainability-driven entrepreneurship.

Elangovan N is currently working as professor in School of Business and Management, Christ University, Bengaluru. Earlier he was the Campus Director at NIFT Kannur. Elangovan does research in Manufacturing, Marketing and Business Administration.

Sumeet Nausalya is a Digital Marketing Professor and Ed-Tech specialist at CollegeDekho–ImaginXP, India. With over 14 years of progressive experience spanning higher education, instructional design, learning experience design, and digital marketing, he has delivered more than 2,500 lecture hours and mentored over 1,000 students across academic and corporate ecosystems. He holds an M.A. in Advertising and Marketing Communication from Coventry University (UK), a PGDM in Marketing from Sinhgad Institute of Management, Pune, and a PGD in Foreign Trade from Pune University. He is a certified career coach and holds professional credentials in digital marketing from Google, Meta, and Semrush Academy. His research interests include AI-mediated branding, algorithmic decision systems, instructional design, and the intersection of marketing science and educational technology. He is also the founder of Career Pharos Pvt. Ltd.

Harpreet Singh is an accomplished bioinformatics researcher and academician with nearly two decades of experience in computational biology, interdisciplinary research, and academic leadership. His research interests span structural bioinformatics, molecular graphics, data analytics, machine learning, and artificial intelligence, with a focus on developing computational approaches to address contemporary challenges in life sciences and drug discovery. He serves as Associate Professor and Head of the PG Department of Bioinformatics at Hans Raj Mahila Maha Vidyalaya, Jalandhar, Punjab, one of India's premier women's institutions. He is also the President of the Asia Pacific Bioinformatics Network (APBioNET), a leading regional organization advancing bioinformatics education, research, collaboration, and capacity building across the Asia-Pacific region. Dr. Singh is a member of Bioclues and represents the Galaxy India community within the global Galaxy Project, promoting open, accessible, and reproducible computational research. He holds a PhD in Biotechnology and an Advanced Postgraduate Diploma in Bioinformatics and has authored over 50 peer-reviewed research publications. He has presented his research at major international forums across Asia and the Middle East. He is currently involved in research projects investigating heat shock proteins as emerging targets for antimalarial drug discovery and abiotic stress resistance in plants. His contribution to the field of science has recently been recognized with the prestigious "Dr. Roshan Lal Aggarwal Best Science Teacher Award (Colleges)" from the Punjab Academy of Sciences (PAS).

Esther Bassil Sleilati is an Associate Professor in Marketing at Notre Dame University (NDU). She graduated with a DBA in Marketing from Grenoble Ecole de Management, France after a corporate career as a Marketing Intelligence Unit Manager, leading a team of 96 researchers. She is an Affiliate Professor at Grenoble Ecole de Management where she is a Visiting Professor, a DBA and Masters theses supervisor, and a DBA jury member. She is equally a Visiting Professor at ICD International Business School in Paris, and at the Institute of Management Technology in India and Dubai. Dr. Sleilati's research interests are mainly related to digital marketing, marketing strategies, services marketing, promotional strategies, and consumer behavior.

Sneha Sukumar is a Ph.D. Scholar from the School of Commerce, Finance and Accountancy, Department of Commerce,Christ University, specialising in Marketing and Consumer Behaviour. Her research interests lie at the intersection of immersive marketing, digital transformation, and consumer behaviour. Her doctoral research investigates the role of immersive marketing strategies in influencing consumer decision-making. She has actively engaged in interdisciplinary research spanning emerging domains such as Emotion AI, gamification, phygital experiences, and immersive brand storytelling. Her scholarly work includes contributions to bibliometric and systematic literature reviews, conceptual framework development, and consumer psychology research. Beyond academia, she has a keen interest in entrepreneurship, innovation, and sustainable business models, particularly in integrating technology-driven marketing solutions with responsible consumption practices

Dheepa T is an Associate Professor in the School of Business and Management in Christ University, Bengaluru, India. She is an active researcher and Business Consultant. She has undertaken research projects at various levels and published many research papers in the journals of Repute. Her areas of interest include Marketing Management, Advertisement, and Digital Marketing.

Suman Vij holds a Ph.D. in Economics and has an academic and professional background in education, economics, and social sciences. Her research interests encompass social and economic issues, marketing ethics, ethical decision-making, and sustainable approaches to addressing contemporary challenges. She has a particular interest in educational techniques and pedagogy, including innovative teaching-learning practices and their effective application. Her academic interests also extend to decision-making and its application in educational, social, and organizational contexts. She is committed to exploring interdisciplinary approaches that connect economics, education, ethics, and societal development. In recognition of her contribution to the field of education, she is being conferred the prestigious Bharat Jyoti Award. Through her academic and research engagements, she seeks to contribute to evidence-based solutions and promote responsible and ethical practices in education, business, and society.

Prama Vishnoi is an Assistant Professor at the Delhi School of Management, Delhi Technological University, where she teaches Consumer Behaviour, International Marketing and Strategic Management. She brings over a decade of teaching experience in commerce and marketing, with earlier stints at Keshav Mahavidyalaya and Indraprastha College for Women, University of Delhi. Her research centres on consumer behaviour in bottom-of-the-pyramid markets, with related interests in marketing strategy and public policy. Her work appears in the International Journal of Consumer Studies and in volumes from Routledge India and Springer Nature. She has served as Co-Principal Investigator on a project supported by the Institute of Eminence, University of Delhi. She has developed academic modules for the UGC's e-PG Pathshala initiative. She has presented papers at international conferences hosted by IIM Kozhikode, IIM Jammu, and IMT

Ghaziabad, and chaired the marketing track at the International Conference held at SGGSCC, University of Delhi.

Index